Conventional and Unconventional War

Conventional and Unconventional War

A History of Conflict in the Modern World

Thomas R. Mockaitis

BLOOMSBURY ACADEMIC
NEW YORK • LONDON • OXFORD • NEW DELHI • SYDNEY

BLOOMSBURY ACADEMIC
Bloomsbury Publishing Inc
1385 Broadway, New York, NY 10018, USA
50 Bedford Square, London, WC1B 3DP, UK
29 Earlsfort Terrace, Dublin 2, Ireland

BLOOMSBURY, BLOOMSBURY ACADEMIC and the Diana logo
are trademarks of Bloomsbury Publishing Plc

First published in the United States of America by ABC-CLIO 2017
Paperback edition published by Bloomsbury Academic 2024

Copyright © Bloomsbury Publishing Inc, 2024

Jacket design by Silverander Communications
Cover photos: North America at war. (halbergman/iStockphoto);
Abstract explosion-like reflections on a metal plate. (magneticstorm/iStockphoto);
Napoleonic Wars, Napoleon meeting with Czar Alexander. (Don Troiani/Corbis);
Cadets watch data on a computer at the United States Military Academy in West Point, New York,
April 9, 2014. (AP Photo/Mel Evans)

All rights reserved. No part of this publication may be reproduced or
transmitted in any form or by any means, electronic or mechanical,
including photocopying, recording, or any information storage or retrieval
system, without prior permission in writing from the publishers.

Bloomsbury Publishing Inc does not have any control over, or responsibility for,
any third-party websites referred to or in this book. All internet addresses given
in this book were correct at the time of going to press. The author and publisher
regret any inconvenience caused if addresses have changed or sites have
ceased to exist, but can accept no responsibility for any such changes.

Library of Congress Cataloging-in-Publication Data
Names: Mockaitis, Thomas R., 1955-author.
Title: Conventional and unconventional war: a history of conflict in the
modern world / Thomas R. Mockaitis.
Other titles: History of conflict in the modern world
Description: Santa Barbara, California: Praeger, an imprint of ABC-CLIO, LLC, [2017] |
Includes bibliographical references and index.
Identifiers: LCCN 2016039728 (print) | LCCN 2016043443 (ebook) |
ISBN 9781440828331 (alk. paper) | ISBN 9781440828348 (ebook)
Subjects: LCSH: Military history, Modern. | War—History. | Asymmetric
warfare—History. | Military art and science—History.
Classification: LCC D214 .M625 2017 (print) |
LCC D214 (ebook) | DDC 355.0209—dc23
LC record available at https://lccn.loc.gov/2016039728

ISBN: HB: 978-1-4408-2833-1
PB: 979-8-7651-1983-9
ePDF: 978-1-4408-2834-8
eBook: 979-8-2160-6610-1

To find out more about our authors and books visit www.bloomsbury.com
and sign up for our newsletters.

In memoriam:
Wayne MacDonald ("Mac") Ross
Rochelle Diane Merzon Robkin

Contents

Introduction		1
Chapter 1	The Military Transformation of Early Modern Europe	13
Chapter 2	An Era of Limited War	31
Chapter 3	The Era of Revolutionary Wars: North America	57
Chapter 4	French Revolution and Napoleonic Wars	83
Chapter 5	Industrialization and the American Civil War	105
Chapter 6	Prussian Military Reforms and the Wars of German Unification	127
Chapter 7	The Long Peace	141
Chapter 8	World War I	159
Chapter 9	The Interwar Period	183
Chapter 10	World War II in Europe	199
Chapter 11	World War II in Asia	225
Chapter 12	The Cold War: A New Era of Limited Conflicted?	239
Chapter 13	Conflict in the Post–Cold War World	269

Conclusion: The New Security Environment and the Future of Warfare 293

Notes 307
Bibliography 339
Index 357

Introduction

"Only the dead have seen the end of war," quipped the philosopher George Santayana.[1] Sadly, history in this case confirms the wisdom of philosophy. The 5,000 years since human civilization began have been plagued by almost incessant conflict. Humanity has been at peace for only 268 of the last 3,400 years.[2] This unpleasant historical fact raises a troubling philosophical, or perhaps biological, question: Are humans innately violent? Many anthropologists have concluded that aggression gave humans a competitive edge in the struggle to survive. Our ancestors, they insist, no sooner made tools than they used them to kill each other. Richard Leakey challenges this view, arguing that cooperation rather than conflict characterized prehistoric hunter-gatherer societies. Human populations were too small and too vulnerable to afford the luxury of fratricide. Organized warfare, he concludes, began with the advent of material culture at the time of the agricultural revolution, some 10,000 years ago. Only when humans had something worth fighting over (land, crops, flocks, etc.) did they go to war.[3]

Whether the fault lies in our stars or in ourselves, most people throughout the world consider war an evil to be avoided. As the bloody record of human civilization reveals, however, they have seldom succeeded in doing so. The Romans had their own formula for preventing conflict. "If you want peace, prepare for war," an old Latin proverb proclaimed. This approach works so long as potential belligerents maintain enough military power to deter others from aggression. Sooner or later, however, one side or the other believes it has enough of an advantage to pursue its objective by force. Preparing for war did not bring lasting peace to the Romans, nor has it worked terribly well for anyone else. This realization led the British military theorist Sir Basil Liddell Hart to modify the Roman adage: "If you wish for peace, understand war."[4]

This book takes the wisdom of Liddell Hart as its point of departure, seeking to promote a better understanding of organized human conflict. Unlike many military histories, however, it forgoes detailed examination of every war and battle, opting instead for a thematic approach that traces the evolution of warfare within the broader context of history. By situating war in the mainstream of events, the book seeks to correct a problem noted by Julian Jackson: conventional historical studies pay little attention to war, while military histories often fail to consider the larger world in which wars take place, to the detriment of both.[5] This study does of course discuss wars and battles, but only to the degree that they illustrate specific ideas at the core of its argument. That argument rests on three broad premises. First, armed forces reflect the societies that create them. Second, contemporary attitudes toward war and peace shape the use of those armed forces. Third, technology affects the nature of wars. From these premises comes an important deduction: ideologically motivated conflicts have been more destructive than wars fought for more pragmatic reasons. The combination of improved weaponry and emerging nationalism made conflict increasingly more deadly, until the total war waged from 1939 to 1945 made clear that the process could go no further if humans wished to survive.

This book also differs from traditional military histories in one other important respect. It combines study of conventional and unconventional war in an integrated history of armed conflict. Unconventional war has been sorely neglected in most military histories. If they cover guerrillas, partisans, and insurgents at all, these studies treat them as ancillary to the conventional operations. The few really good historical surveys of unconventional war, such as Robert Asprey's *War in the Shadows* or Max Boot's *Invisible Armies* (2013), suffer from an analogous weakness. They treat unconventional conflict as a distinct phenomenon that is at best peripheral to and at worst entirely separate from conventional conflicts. This false dichotomy has led to much pointless discussion of whether or not wars such as the American Revolution were conventional or unconventional. It has also clouded contemporary debates over force structure and national strategy.

Conventional and unconventional operations usually formed different parts of the same conflict. Most wars since 1648 have been hybrid affairs involving both activities. Many wars were predominantly conventional, but none was exclusively so. During the second half of the 20th century the pattern changed. Unconventional conflicts became more prevalent than conventional ones. This shift emerged from the nuclear stalemate that made large-scale conventional war far too risky. However, the new

Introduction

unconventional wars were also hybrid affairs, in which conventional operations occurred, albeit in smaller proportion to activities as a whole. The study of war must, therefore, be based on this reality

Writing a truly comprehensive world history challenges those who study war just as much as it does any other type of historian. The danger of Eurocentrism, the tendency to see things from the perspective of the West, looms large before those who tackle any form of global history. In the study of modern warfare, however, the flow of events themselves dictates a Western focus, at least until the 20th century. Once cheap, reliable gunpowder weapons became widely available in the 16th century, the states and principalities of Europe began an arms race that continues to the present. Driven by a continual series of wars among themselves, their quest for more and more lethal weapons enabled the European powers to dominate much of the globe.[6] Throughout the modern era non-Western nations have been imitators rather than innovators in the art and science of conventional war. In the arena of unconventional conflict, however, the East has led the West. Insurgents defeated the government of China and overthrew colonial regimes throughout Asia and Africa. They continue to challenge conventional forces in the Middle East. Their activities thus deserve a prominent place in the story of modern conflict.

For most of human history wars have been won or lost on land, so this work focuses on land warfare. During the modern era naval power contributed indirectly to victory. By imposing a blockade and preying on maritime commerce, navies could erode an enemy's economic ability to wage war. In the case of Great Britain, its fleets protected the island nation from invasion. Navies also allowed European powers to build global empires, primarily by transporting and supplying conquering troops. During the 17th and 18th centuries naval engagements among the Dutch, French, and British determined control of colonies and trade routes. However, World War II (1939–1945) in the Pacific was perhaps the only predominantly naval war. Even then, victories at sea had to be followed up with land operations by soldiers and marines to secure air bases and ultimately occupy Japan itself.

Airplanes made their military debut during World War I (1914–1918), but they had little impact on the conflict. The primitive bi- and triplanes were too small to carry large bomb loads and too slow and vulnerable to ground fire to be effective at strafing. They had some reconnaissance value, but even that could be foiled by night marches and other ruses. Airpower was, however, the wave of the future. The Spanish Civil War (1936–1939) hinted at its devastating potential, which became more fully manifest with the invasion of Poland in 1939 and the advent of blitzkrieg against France and the Low Countries, but airpower demonstrated its ultimate destructive power in a mushroom cloud over Hiroshima. Despite its lethality, though, airpower alone has not won wars, although as a deterrent during the Cold War it may have prevented them. It must be considered as part of the combined-arms approach that has characterized warfare since 1939.

A history of conflict that examines only its technical aspects would be incomplete. War is a profoundly human experience and needs to be considered as such. "What was it like to be there?" is probably the most interesting but also the most difficult question to answer. For most of history and even much of the modern period, the mass of humanity was illiterate. Officers could write, but their experiences differed to a considerable extent from those of the rank and file who did most of the killing and dying. We can thus learn about the experiences of ordinary soldiers only indirectly, when others wrote about them. By the middle of the 19th century free, compulsory public education began to change this situation in Western Europe and the United States. Large numbers of literate soldiers filled the ranks of the Union and Confederate armies during the American Civil War (1861–1865) and left accounts of their experiences. The mass of humanity had found its voice. That voice is included in this book.

This study also considers prevailing attitudes toward and ideas about the use of force. The mayhem of the Thirty Years' War (1618–1648) encouraged the idea that nation-states should engage in conflicts only for valid reasons and should wage them according to rules that protected non-combatants and guaranteed fair treatment of enemy soldiers. Since the 17th century a growing body of literature, customary practice, and formal agreements, which came to be called the "laws of land warfare," has sought to mitigate the worst effects of armed conflict. From the mid- to late 18th century onward, however, nationalism and "scientific racism" worked against this ethical regime to make wars more lethal and destructive.

The organization of this book derives from and supports its objectives. Chapters provide a chronological survey of warfare from the 17th century to the present. Each chapter contains an overview of the period it covers and a summary of major conflicts within it. Each chapter then examines the nature of warfare based on the three themes of technology, society, and attitudes toward violence. It analyzes representative battles or campaigns to reveal larger themes and considers the relationship between conventional and unconventional war. Finally, each chapter considers the experience of battle from the perspective of ordinary soldiers.

Since this work is intended for the general educated reader as well as the soldier and the academic, it begins with an overview of the nature and organization of armies and a broad, theoretical explanation of how

Introduction

wars are conducted. While most people have a sense of what the terms "strategy" and "tactics" mean, they probably do not understand their precise use by professional soldiers. "Operations," a relatively new concept, is even more confusing, while "logistics" is fairly straightforward. The terms "conventional" and "unconventional" applied to warfare also need precise definition.

The Organization of Armies

While the size and composition of units has changed over time, the division of armies into broad functional categories has remained relatively constant. Since antiquity armies have consisted of infantry, cavalry, and artillery. The term "armor" traditionally applied to protection worn by mounted troops and, sometimes, foot soldiers. In the 20th century "armor" designated a new category of warriors who rode into battle in motorized vehicles protected by a thick metal shell and armed with various crew-serviced weapons. Each of these categories requires further discussion before delving into the history of warfare.

Infantry refers to foot soldiers armed during the modern era with some type of individual projectile weapon. By the end of the 17th century that weapon was the single-shot, smoothbore flintlock musket tipped with a socket bayonet for protection against cavalry and use against enemy infantry during an attack. This basic armament would not change until the middle of the 19th century, when the smoothbore gave way first to the rifled musket and then to the breech-loading rifle. Muskets are loaded from the bore (front barrel) of the weapon, breechloaders from the back of the barrel. Rifling (grooves rotated 360 degrees along the interior length of the barrel) cause the projectile to spin, much like the tight spiral of a football thrown by a quarterback, increasing its range and penetrating power. After the breechloader became standard issue, manufacturers improved upon its basic design, adding a multiple round magazine and thus increasing rate of fire from single-shot, to semiautomatic, to fully automatic. The machine gun is an extension of the automatic rifle.

Infantry has long been dubbed "the queen of battle," a reference to the game of chess, in which the queen is the most powerful and maneuverable piece on the board. Counterintuitive though it may seem, men on foot have an advantage over men on horseback, provided they operate in a disciplined body. An individual foot soldier stands little chance against a mounted warrior, but infantry massed in ranks can withstand any number of cavalry. Having more sense than its rider, a horse will not willingly impale itself on a spear, a pike, or a bayonet.

Raising an army of foot soldiers, however, costs a great deal. Infantrymen must be recruited, clothed, fed, housed, and trained. Only through constant drill can they be kept in a state of readiness to maneuver and fight in the formations that make them effective. Only strong states with reliable systems of taxation and finance could afford such an expense. Before the rise of royal armies in the 17th century, the Romans had been the last European civilization to deploy large bodies of trained infantry as the backbone of their army. The medieval knight in shining armor was not a testament to the superiority of cavalry, but a concession to the weakness of feudal kingdoms. Once large bodies of infantry reappeared on the battlefields of Europe, cavalry shrank proportionally, to at most one-third of royal army strength, and never again rose above that level.[7]

Cavalry may have lost its preeminence in the early modern era, but it remained an important combat arm until World War I. Mounted warriors enjoyed an advantage in speed, mobility, and shock power. Infantry formations were vulnerable to cavalry attacks against their flanks and rear. Horsemen armed with sabers, lances, or pistols could be devastating in pursuit and destruction of infantry whose formations had been broken by artillery and/or concentrated musket fire. Cavalry also proved its worth in scouting and in interdiction of enemy supply lines.

When the rifle replaced the smoothbore musket in the 19th century, increasing the lethal range of infantry weapons exponentially, cavalry charges all but disappeared. Horses still played an important role on the battlefield, however. Lancers and hussars (cavalrymen armed with sabers) converted to mounted infantry. Armed with carbines (short-barreled rifles), they used their horses to deploy rapidly to key positions and then dismounted to fight on foot. A brigade of cavalry armed with Spencer repeating rifles and light horse artillery held off a much larger Confederate force on the first day of the battle of Gettysburg, giving the Union infantry an opportunity to occupy the high ground east of the town.

Die-hard cavalrymen resisted giving up the lance and the saber once these weapons became obsolete. They clung to the cavalry charge long after concentrated rifle fire demonstrated its futility. In the last futile gasp of the age of chivalry, Polish lancers charged into battle in 1939. German machine guns mowed them down like grass. The day of the mounted warrior had long since passed. Thenceforward "cavalry" troopers would ride into battle on motorized vehicles and later fly in helicopters.

Artillery refers to large, crew-serviced projectile weapons. Generally speaking, whatever moves on wheels is a cannon. Early cannon fell into two broad categories: field guns small enough to be easily transported and deployed against infantry and cavalry on a battlefield and siege guns, larger cannon capable of battering down the stone walls of castles and forts. Field guns and the earliest siege cannon fired shells on a flat trajectory. Simply put, they shot straight at their target. Such weapons did little damage to trenches or the new fortifications with sloped walls and earthworks designed to counter the effects of bombardment. Two modifications addressed these challenges. Mortars are short-barreled cannon that lob shells at low velocity on an arced trajectory at short range. They can thus drop a shell into a trench or over a wall. Howitzers operate on the same principle as mortars, but they have a longer barrel, enabling them to fire over a greater distance. Within each broad category cannon were classified first by the weight of shot they fired and later by the diameter of their bore measured in caliber (inches) or millimeters.

Artillery projectiles also evolved. The earliest cannon fired spherical stone balls, but these shells were soon replaced by smaller, denser iron balls that could be fired by lighter (and thus more mobile) guns. In addition to solid balls, cannon fired grape and canister shot for use against infantry on land or sailors on ships. Grape shot consisted of small bullets or other individual projectiles such as nails and pieces of broken glass. Canister or case shells were containers of lead bullets that opened over the target, spewing the lethal pellets over infantry formations. Armor-piercing shells (most useful against ships) and exploding balls (named for their creator, Henry Shrapnel) that would spread pieces of sharp metal amid a mass of infantrymen made their debut during the 19th century.

Cannon, like muskets, were originally smoothbore weapons. Rifled artillery became feasible at about the same time as rifled muskets, in the middle of the 19th century. Shells fired from rifled cannon had far greater range and penetrating power than those launched from smoothbore guns. In the later 20th century, however, the increased size of tank gun bores made rifling impractical, as the barrel would have to be unmanageably long to accommodate the rifling. Designers discovered that they could achieve the same effect produced by rifling with fins attached to artillery shells. These fins caused the shells to spiral through the air in the same manner as shells fired from rifled guns.

The Conduct of War

In addition to familiarity with the organization of armies, studying military history requires understanding how wars are conducted. Warfare involves three broad activities: strategy, tactics, and logistics. In an actual conflict, the three interact synergistically. A flaw in one area can result in defeat, but strength in one area can also overcome deficits in the others. For purposes of discussion, however, they need to be considered separately.

Strategy refers to the plans a nation develops to use its military power to achieve its political objectives. Those objectives might be as narrow as capturing a fortress along a vital trade route or as broad as defeating and occupying an enemy country. Because states have rarely used purely military means to achieve objectives during the modern era, military thinkers coined the term *grand strategy* to define plans for using all the resources of a state to achieve a desired objective. During the 18th century, for example, Great Britain wished to check French ambitions on the continent of Europe. It devised a grand strategy that employed diplomatic, economic, and military means. Britain forged alliances to isolate France, used its wealth to finance war, deployed its army to participate in campaigns, and used its navy to disrupt French commerce and capture French colonies.

Tactics refers to the precise manner in which military forces are employed on the battlefield. The arrangement of infantry, cavalry, and artillery; maneuvering of troops; and use of specific weapons individually and collectively all fall under the heading of tactics. If strategy has to do with plans for achieving a result, tactics involve the means for implementing those plans. A simple analogy using American football (arguably the quintessential martial sport) illustrates the differences between strategy and tactics and reveals how the two interact in war. When two teams take the field, they both aim to win the game. They may, however, have two different strategies for victory. If team "A" has good runners but average receivers, it will design a game strategy that relies on its running game. If team "B" has an excellent quarterback and good receivers but only average runners, its strategy will rely on the passing game. The tactics both teams employ will be pretty much the same. Blocking, running pass patterns, pass-rushing, and covering receivers require the same skills no matter what strategy the team employs. To extend this analogy a bit further, the steps management takes in the off-season to produce a winning team (drafting players, making trades, hiring coaches) represent the franchise's grand strategy for success.

Contemporary militaries have devised a third category of activity between strategy and tactics. *Operations* are events designed to accomplish a specific objective in pursuit of a broader strategic goal. For example, the raid to kill Osama bin Laden was an operation conducted as part of a broader strategy targeting al-Qaeda leadership. To return to the football analogy, a specific running play would be an operation within the coach's broader game strategy.

Logistics refers to the tasks involved in equipping and supplying an army during peace and war. Logistics has long been considered the least military aspect of armed conflict, so much so that early modern armies hired contractors to provide supply services, a practice revived by the U.S. military in the post–Cold War era. Even when logistics became a regular function of armies, promotion to the highest ranks went to those serving in combat arms. Despite its second-class status, however, logistics is vital to success in modern warfare. The Germans recognized the primacy of supply when they coined the term *Materialschlacht* (battle of supply). They lost both world wars, not because they were outfought, but because they faced an alliance that produced an exponentially greater amount of war material. Admiral Isoroku Yamamoto, the architect of the attack on Pearl Harbor, understood the importance of supply. He knew that Japan could not win a long war with the United States. Having lived in the United States before the war, he understood its great resources and manufacturing capability.

Conventional and Unconventional War

Wars differ markedly depending on the circumstances under which they are fought, but armed conflicts fall into two broad categories: conventional and unconventional. Unconventional war has been the more problematic of the two to define, primarily because it has become a catchall term for a broad range of activities loosely related to one another. The tendency to group unconventional operations conducted during conventional wars with largely unconventional conflicts further confuses the issue. Like most complex phenomena, unconventional war is more easily described than precisely defined. A study that takes a comprehensive approach to war must, however, make some effort to cut through the confusion and obfuscation to make sense of the various types of conflict it proposes to consider.

Conventional war refers to conflict between the regular armed forces of states, operating in uniform along more or less clear lines of battle. Uniforms allow belligerents to identify one another on the battlefield, and they distinguish soldiers from civilians. Until smokeless powder improved visibility during combat and thus put a premium on camouflage, uniforms were brightly colored. When rules governing the conduct and treatment of soldiers began to develop in the 17th century, they applied only to regular armies. As the conduct of war became the prerogative of disciplined armies, military activities by anyone not in uniform lacked legitimacy. In fact, engaging in military operations out of uniform made a person subject to summary execution if caught. The tendency of conventional soldiers to view unconventional ones as illegitimate persists to the present.

Unconventional war describes a variety of military activities other than conventional war. Contemporary analysts coined the term "asymmetric warfare" because unconventional war has so often been employed by non-state actors against states whose armed forces they could never hope to defeat by conventional means. Three of these activities stand out as most important to the history of conflict: guerrilla warfare, insurgency, and terrorism. These distinct but related phenomena have often been conflated in the popular imagination. In the post-9/11 world, the media and even some military writers have treated them as synonyms. Because they differ in key respects, however, they must be clearly defined before they can be discussed.

Guerrilla warfare entered the military lexicon during the Napoleonic war in Spain (1808–1815), although the practice of guerrilla warfare had been around since long before then. Spanish for "small war," *guerrilla* referred to the unconventional forces that harassed French troops in Spain. These ordinary Spanish peasants ambushed supply columns and small military units. They often wore no uniforms and melted back into the general population when confronted by superior conventional forces. Frustrated by their inability to identify, let alone come to grips with, these irregulars, French troops punished entire Spanish communities, thus establishing a pattern of attack and reprisal that has characterized unconventional warfare to the present day.

Guerrilla warfare can be employed by different actors for different purposes. Those who operate in support of conventional forces or to resist foreign occupation are usually called "partisans" or "resistance" fighters. Resistance groups sprang up all over occupied Europe during World War II, although they varied greatly in competence and effectiveness. Partisans gathered intelligence for Allied forces, assassinated German officers and local collaborators, and attacked supply lines. They also paid a terrible price for engaging in these activities. The Germans adopted a policy of *Schrecklichkeit* (terror), holding entire communities responsible for attacks carried out by partisans. They summarily executed 100 French citizens for every German soldier killed by the Resistance. In retaliation for the assassination of SS general Reinhardt Heydrich, the Nazis leveled the Czech village of Lidice. How much attacks by resistance groups contributed to the war effort remains a subject of debate.

Insurgency is sophisticated political movement to gain control of a country from within, in much the same way that a virus gains control of healthy cells. Insurgents develop a comprehensive strategy employing an information campaign to win support for their cause, guerrilla warfare to attack the police and military, and terror to frighten government supporters and to keep their own adherents in line.[8] Because it requires a degree of education and political sophistication among the ordinary people, insurgency is a modern phenomenon. A spate of successful insurgencies took place during the period of decolonization following World War II. More recently, the United States and its allies have faced insurgencies in Iraq and Afghanistan.

Terrorism generally refers to a movement by nonstate actors (an organization or network) to effect political or social change through the use of terror. A clear distinction must be made between "terror" and "terrorism." "Terror" is a weapon or tactic employed by a variety of actors to achieve a result through frightening people. States have used terror for centuries, primarily to keep their own subjects peaceful and compliant. Pontius Pilate did not have Jesus strangled in the basement of the Antonia fortress; he nailed him to a cross on a hill outside Jerusalem to die an agonizing death in public view as a warning to any who would defy Rome. Criminal organizations also use terror, killing their enemies in gruesome ways to send a message to their members and rivals. Insurgents employ terror in a similar fashion, frightening those who work for or support the established government. The term "terrorism" should be reserved for a campaign of violence that uses terror but has not risen to the level of insurgency. Some analysts would argue that such activity belongs in the realm of criminality rather than warfare. However, like insurgents, terrorists are motivated by ideology. Criminals are motivated by desire for profit.

CHAPTER ONE

The Military Transformation of Early Modern Europe

Anyone wishing to understand the intimate relationship between warfare and society would do well to consider the transformation of Europe that took place between 1300 and 1700. At the beginning of this period numerous small principalities dotted the map of the continent. The German-speaking lands alone consisted of over 300 independent political entities. Even the larger kingdoms such as France and England contained numerous fiefdoms whose lords could and frequently did defy the crown. A mass of peasant farmers known as serfs or villains comprised 80 percent or more of the population and supported a small warrior elite. Towns had been growing, but most people still lived on the land. With some notable exceptions, the bulk of trade and commerce took place locally and regionally. The entire continent lagged behind China and the Muslim world in science and technology.

By 1700 Europe had changed dramatically. Powerful, unified kingdoms had replaced the fragmented landscape of feudalism. Serfdom had disappeared in Western Europe, cities had grown larger and more numerous, and European merchants engaged in trade around the world. Spain, France, England, and the Netherlands had planted colonies in North and South America, Africa, and Asia. The scientific revolution had taken place, soon to be followed by the Enlightenment and the Industrial Revolution.

Europe had pulled ahead of the Ottoman Empire, China, and India, all with ancient civilizations that had once eclipsed it. In the next two centuries European states would dominate the globe while gradually expanding prosperity and representative democracy at home.

This transformation owed much to changes in the nature of warfare. The rise of larger professional armies equipped with gunpowder weapons, coupled with new fortress systems guarding major towns and defending frontiers, both encouraged and necessitated the growth of strong, centralized states. With few exceptions, only the wealthiest kingdoms could afford both a ring of fortresses capable of withstanding artillery bombardment to protect their territory and a large standing army. In 1300 heavily armored mounted knights armed with swords and lances formed the backbone of feudal armies, with infantry forces operating in support. With the exception of small bodies of household troops protecting the king, most of these warriors were part-time soldiers who spent most of their time managing their estates. They lived in fortified manor houses or castles with their own retinues of soldiers. Armies as such had to be assembled for a campaign.

By 1700 the monarchs of Europe possessed standing armies of full-time professional soldiers trained, equipped, clothed, and housed by the state. Infantry armed with smooth-bore muskets tipped with socket bayonets comprised the bulk of these royal armies. Cavalry had been reduced to a supporting arm in battle, seldom comprising more than one-third of total army strength. Historians who see the bulk of changes that brought about this transformation as occurring within a century or so speak of a revolution in warfare, while others believe the transformation occurred more gradually as part of an evolution in the nature of conflict. Neither group disputes the importance of the change.

Technological Change

The Longbow

Beginning in the 14th century, a series of inventions led to changes in tactics and the composition of armies, both of which led to changes in strategy. The first technological change gave infantry a more effective projectile weapon. Although bows of various types had existed since antiquity, the English showed up on the battlefields of the Hundred Years' War with a new more powerful bow that unceremoniously knocked the knight in shining armor off his high horse. The longbow first appears in the historical record during the last quarter of the 12th century. The chronicler Gerald of Wales described a powerful new weapon encountered by English forces in Wales:

> William de Braose also testifies that one of his soldiers, in a conflict with the Welsh, was wounded by an arrow, which passed through his thigh and the armour with which it was cased on both sides, and, through that part of the saddle which is called the alva [seat], [and] mortally wounded the horse.[1]

Made from a single piece of cured yew wood, the longbow stood the height of the archer, who drew its string across his entire body and back to his ear. The size of the bow and its greater draw length gave it a much greater draw weight (the amount of weight the archer pulls as he draws it measured in foot pounds) and thus increased its range and penetrating power. The common English term "bow length" (taken to be 400 yards) suggests the range of the weapon, although it was probably only accurate to about 250 yards.[2] In the hands of a skilled archer the longbow was a deadly weapon capable of penetrating chain mail and, at close range, even plate armor. A skilled archer could fire 10 arrows per minute.[3] So important to English arms had the longbow become that King Edward I issued a statute requiring yeoman archers to practice their craft for a certain number of hours each month. The military value of archers lay not in their individual prowess, however, but in their ability en masse to fire a large, steady volume of arrows into enemy troops. This they did with devastating effect at the battles of Crecy (1346), Poitiers (1348), and Agincourt (1415).

Agincourt in particular illustrates the importance of the new weapon and the tactics developed to employ it. On October 25, 1415, an English army of 6,000 men headed for Calais found its way blocked by a French force of 24,000 near the town of Agincourt.[4] The composition of the forces mattered as much as their total numbers. The English had 5,000 archers and 1,000 men at arms (armored warriors); the French had 10,000 men at arms, 10,000 attendants who could also fight on foot (one attendant for each man at arms), and 4,000 archers and crossbowmen.[5] Crossbows could penetrate armor but lacked the range of longbows and took much longer to load. The English had grasped the importance of the foot soldier armed with a projectile weapon, while the French had not. The English archers outnumbered the men at arms five to one. The French still relied on men at arms, mounted or fighting on foot, with archers and crossbowmen in support.

The wisdom of relying on archers would be born out. The battlefield of Agincourt occupied a narrow strip of land between two woods, so the English had to defend a line only about 750 yards long. The confined space nullified the numerical advantage of the French and rendered their battle plan unworkable. They had intended to place their archers and crossbowmen in front of a mass of dismounted men at arms in the center of their formation, with mounted knights on both flanks.[6] After the archers had fired the armored foot soldiers were to have engaged the enemy, while the mounted warriors would outflank the smaller English army on both sides.[7] The French had no compelling reason to accept battle on terrain so favorable to the English king, Henry V. Their numerically superior forces stood between Calais and an English army made up of tired, hungry, and sick soldiers. The French could simply have waited until desperation forced the English to attack them on more favorable ground. They probably decided to attack because they were supremely confident in the ability of their armored warriors to win an easy victory no matter the terrain.

The decision to fight at Agincourt need not have doomed the French to defeat, however. They still could have deployed their archers to the fore as the English did. Instead they placed them in the rear, where they saw no action during the battle. This decision stemmed not from terrain but from an outmoded approach to war that relied on the shock power of a charge by mounted knights followed by victory in the melee, a battle of individual combats. The French considered archers and crossbowmen superfluous.[8] The ensuing battle would prove them disastrously wrong. The French men-at-arms mounted and on foot slogged across the field turned to mud by the previous night's rain. A hail of longbow arrows, fired by archers ranged behind pairs of crossed, sharpened stakes set up to halt cavalry, felled many of the attackers. The exhausted few who made it to the English front line stood little chance against Henry's knights, fighting on foot alongside the yeoman. The French withdrew from the field. English foot soldiers armed with knives and poleaxes finished off many of the dismounted knights. Estimates place French casualties at 7,000 to 10,000, with 1,500 captured. The English lost just over 100 killed and wounded.[9]

At the hands of William Shakespeare and in the British imagination, Agincourt assumed mythic proportions. Though tactically decisive, the battle had little strategic impact. Henry's weakened army lacked the strength to exploit the victory and returned to Calais. The French went on to win the Hundred Years' War. To the military historian, however, the value of Agincourt lies in the lessons it taught. It confirmed a change Cliff Rogers has dubbed the "infantry revolution," a process by which, during the 14th and 15th centuries, infantrymen armed with pikes (long poles tipped with metal points), halberds (pikes with combined spear point and an axe head), or bows were supplanting mounted knights as the backbone of armies.[10]

Agincourt also illustrates an important principle that would be reiterated throughout the history of warfare: a technological innovation has little value unless tactical/strategic thinking makes proper use of it. The French bows and crossbows may have been inferior to the English longbows, but not decisively so. Had they chosen to fight on ground more suitable to the army they had and deployed their shooters to greater advantage, the French might still have won. Lack of imagination, not lack of archers, cost the French the battle.

Gunpowder

Despite its effectiveness, the longbow had no future in warfare. Even as the English archers loosed their arrows at Agincourt, a new invention was already making its presence felt on the battlefield. Eventually it would provide infantry with a new projectile weapon. Long before that happened, however, the innovation was transforming siege warfare. Gunpowder is an explosive mixture of charcoal, potassium nitrate (commonly known as "saltpeter"), and sulfur. The proportion of potassium nitrate in the mixture determines the reaction when it is lit. A mixture of 60 percent saltpeter produces a bright flash and a weak explosion suitable for fireworks and rockets. Increasing the amount of saltpeter produces a mixture suitable for bombs and primitive guns with weak barrels incapable of containing a more violent explosion. The ideal combination for projectile weapons is a mixture of 75 percent saltpeter, 15 percent charcoal, and 10 percent sulfur.[11] The earliest guns could not, however, use the most explosive mixture, because gun makers could not forge barrels strong enough to contain the explosion. Designers faced an additional problem. In a loose mixture, gunpowder is insufficiently concentrated to produce a forceful explosion; compacted, all but the surface of the mix lacks the oxygen necessary to explode. Mixing the components wet and allowing the mixture to dry as granules, a process known as "corning," solved this problem by creating a greater surface area for combustion, thus enhancing the explosive power of the powder.

Although it would transform warfare in a manner that would allow the West to dominate the world, gunpowder was not invented in Europe. A Chinese manuscript from the mid-11th century contains the first known recipe for the explosive mixture.[12] The Chinese used it in bombs, rockets, incendiary devices, and projectile weapons. From China gunpowder moved westward, helping the Mughals to conquer northern India and the Ottoman Turks to build an empire in the Middle East, Africa, and the Balkans. Roger Bacon wrote of Chinese firecrackers as early as the 1260s, but the first European document to deal with the substance in depth, *Liber Ignium ad Comburendos Hostes* (Book of fires for the burning of enemies), appeared around 1300.[13] By the middle of the century gunpowder weapons began to appear on the battlefield, and by 1420 "corning" was widely used in Western Europe.[14] From then on an arms race commenced to produce more effective cannon and handheld firearms.

Gunpowder changed siege warfare long before it affected infantry battles. Medieval castles and town fortifications, with their perpendicular curtain walls, were particularly vulnerable to bombardment by cannon. Cannon were large tubes of bronze or iron open at one end (the bore), with small touchholes at the closed back of the gun. The gunners loaded powder and shot down the muzzle (although some early cannon had a detachable breech for loading at the rear), put additional powder on the touchhole, and ignited it to set off the main charge and propel the projectile out the barrel. The earliest cannonballs were spherical stones fired from guns made of wrought iron or bronze rods welded together with hoops. Later cast bronze cannon fired cast iron balls whose density allowed smaller projectiles to have the same impact as much larger stone balls. Smaller guns mounted on wheeled carriages could thus have the same impact as much larger ones that had to be placed on sleds drawn by oxen or manufactured at the site of a siege.

Although a single large gun might suffice to batter down the walls of a medieval fortress, cannon proved most effective en masse. In April 1453 the Ottoman Turkish sultan Mehmet II forged a gun 26 feet long capable of hurling a stone weighing several hundred pounds at the ancient walls of Constantinople. The city, which had held out for centuries, fell in a one-month siege.[15] The Turkish gun had to be forged in nearby Adrianople and dragged by oxen to the siege. A large number of small, more mobile guns would, however, soon prove more effective than a few large ones. The combined armies of Aragon and Castile maintained a siege train of 180 cannon, which allowed them to reduce in less than a month Moorish fortresses that would previously have taken a year each to capture.[16]

Handheld firearms took much longer to make their presence felt on the battlefield. The earliest weapons lacked the range, accuracy, and rate of fire of bows. They did, however, have one enormous advantage: they did not require the skill and training demanded of archers. The decline of archery as a skill rather than the inferiority of the bow as a weapon led to its replacement by the gun.[17] Perhaps too, Renaissance military thinkers sensed that gunpowder represented the future. Before infantry could be equipped with firearms, however, some technical problems had to be solved. Like its larger cousin, the cannon, the individual firearm consisted of a metal tube with an open muzzle for loading and firing and a touchhole for igniting the powder that would propel the projectile out the barrel. To make the weapon easier to hold, gunsmiths attached a wooden stock. Some early guns were braced against the chest of the infantryman, but designers soon adopted the shoulder stock still in use today, perhaps inspired by the crossbow constructed the same way. Early guns fell into two categories, the lighter harquebus and the longer, heavier musket firing a larger ball capable of piercing plate armor at close range. The earliest models were so heavy that they required a forked stand attached to the stock. Until armies adopted a lighter, simpler musket during the last quarter of the 17th century, the two weapons were employed together.

The firing mechanism presented the greatest challenge in producing reliable handheld firearms. At first soldiers had to apply a lit cord to the touchhole of the gun, but this approach proved unreliable and dangerous, since the match might be extinguished by wind or rain or ignite the infantryman's store of gunpowder. Gunsmiths then developed the slow match and a firing mechanism for employing it. Slow match was a tightly wound rope dipped in quicklime and sulfur. When lit, it would smolder rather than burn, making it much safer to use than a flame. Wind would not easily blow it out, but rain still presented a problem. The matchlock employed an "s"-shaped hook attached to the side of the stock and connected to a trigger underneath it. The infantryman would cut a small length of slow match and attach it to the top of the hook. Once he had loaded and primed the gun, he would pull the trigger, bringing the top of the hook down and the slow match into contact with the touchhole to ignite the powder.

Matchlocks worked reasonably well for infantrymen, provided it did not rain during a battle, but they proved less satisfactory for pistols used by cavalry troopers. The wheel lock offered a more reliable firing mechanism for the smaller guns. Using a small crank, the soldier wound a spring connected to a metal wheel. The trigger released a hammer containing a piece of iron pyrites, which contacted the spinning wheel to produce a spark that would ignite the gunpowder. Although the wheel lock eliminated the need for a match, it had two disadvantages: it cost much more to make, and if it broke, only a gunsmith in a workshop could repair it.

In the early 17th century a French gunsmith hit upon the cheapest, most reliable firing mechanism until the invention of the percussion cap in the 19th century. The mechanism employed a hammer with a piece of flint connected to a trigger. When the infantryman pulled the trigger the flint would strike a metal plate, creating a spark that would ignite the gunpowder. By 1700 the smoothbore musket had assumed the standard form it would retain until the Minié rifle replaced it in the mid-19th century.

The trigger connected to a hammer and to a lid over the priming pan. The soldier would take a paper cartridge filled with powder and shot, bite off the end nearest the powder, pour a small amount of powder in the priming pan, close the pan, and pour the rest of the powder and shot down the muzzle. He would then insert the paper as wadding and tamp it down the barrel using a ramrod. When he pulled the trigger, the firing mechanism opened the priming pan just as the flint was contacting the metal plate. The resultant spark would ignite the priming powder, which in turn set off the main charge and propelled the musket ball. Sometimes the soldier would forget to pull the hammer all the way back, so that the flint did not strike the firing plate with enough force to create a spark (hence the expression, "going off half-cocked"). On other occasions the priming powder would explode without igniting the main charge, creating a "flash in the pan."

From Pike to Bayonet

To be effective, musketeers operated in large formations capable of delivering a steady volume of fire. The musketeers had to be protected from cavalry as they reloaded their guns, a process requiring more than 70 individual steps and taking as much as three minutes. Initially armies solved this problem by creating mixed formations of musketeers and pike men. The pike was a ten-foot-long pole tipped with a metal point. Heavily armored and positioned on the flanks of a firing line, the pike men would step forward and crisscross their pikes to form a wall of steel spikes that horses could not penetrate.

Having two different types of infantry, however, proved inefficient. The bayonet solved this problem. Attaching a long knife to the end of a musket allowed the weapon to be used both as firearm and pike. Plug bayonets inserted into the barrel of the gun came into use in the 1670s. Because it prevented the gun from being fired with the bayonet in place, however, the plug bayonet gave way to the socket or sleeve bayonet, which became standard issue in European armies by the end of the century. The socket was a hollow tube that fit over the barrel and attached to a bayonet raised above the bore so as not to obstruct firing the gun. The gun and bayonet combination has persisted as a standard infantry weapon down to the present.

Fortifications

The cannon did not render fortifications obsolete, but it changed profoundly how they were built. The perpendicular curtain wall of medieval castles and towns was especially vulnerable to bombardment because of the "dead spots" (places that could not be covered by defending fire) at its base and because cannonballs could easily destroy it. By firing repeatedly at the base of a flat, perpendicular stretch of wall, a besieging army could breech it quite easily. Military engineers addressed these weaknesses by developing a new type of fortification dubbed the *trace Italienne* because Italians developed it in the mid-15th century. They began by lowering the curtain wall and angling it outward to deflect cannonballs. They then surrounded the wall with a moat, in front of which they erected an angled ramp of stone or brick covered with earth to absorb shells. They also changed the outline or "trace" of the fortification from a square or rectangle to a polygon (often described as a "star") with pointed bastions at the corners. This arrangement guaranteed that every foot of wall could be covered by defensive fire.

During the 16th and 17th centuries "star" forts popped up all over Europe. Fortification developed into an art form under the direction of the brilliant French engineer Sebastian le Pestre de Vauban (1633–1707). Vauban built a series of forts along the French frontier, each uniquely adapted to the geography of its location. Detached bastions (small forts themselves) supported the main installations. Forts thus became systems of fortification with numerous small, independent, but mutually supporting positions defending the central one. Together these systems protected the frontiers of France. A similar development took place in the United Provinces (the Netherlands), where the Dutch constructed a series of star forts to reinforce the natural barriers provided by the country's rivers. These defensive works in combination with its reformed field army and navy helped the United Provinces win independence from Spain during the Eighty Years' War (1568–1648).

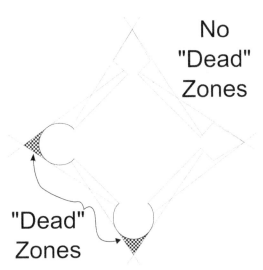

Line-of-fire shown for star forts and nonstar forts, indicating the "dead" zones created by the latter. Inspired by figure in John A. Lynn, "The *trace italienne* and the Growth of Armies: The French Case," in *The Military Revolution Debate* (1995). (Courtesy of Foxhunt King).

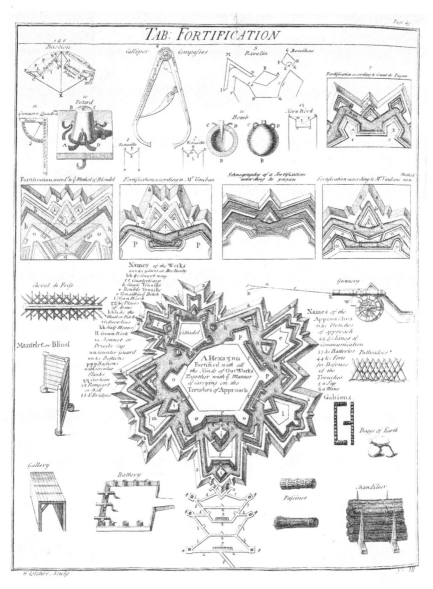

The "Table of Fortification" from Abraham Rees's *Cyclopaedia*. *Source:* Abraham Rees, *The Cyclopaedia*, vol. I (London: Longman, Hurst, Rees, Orme and Brown, 1819).

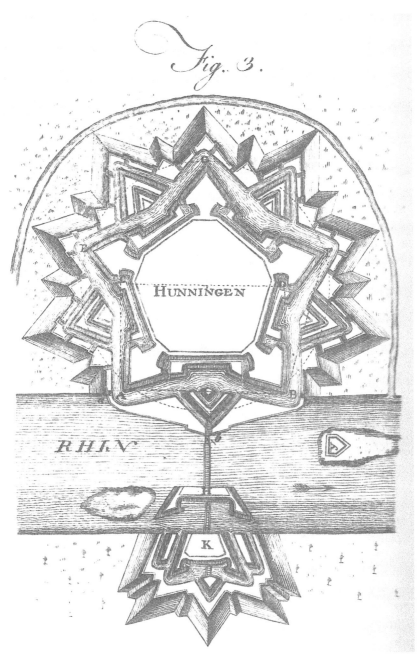

The intricate defenses designed by the French military engineer Vauban, during the reign of Louis XIV, to defend Huningue (Hüningen) on the Rhine. *Source:* Sébastien Le Prestre de Vauban, ed., *Encyclopædia Britannica*, 1st ed. (1768–1826), vol. 2, plate LXXXV.

Naval Warfare

The technological changes that transformed armies also revolutionized navies. The broad-beamed, deep-draught vessels designed to ply the rough waters of the North Sea and the Bay of Biscay proved ideal platforms for the new artillery.[18] At first sailors deployed small cannon to "castles" at the bow and stern of the ship. In those positions they could be used to fire on enemy sailors but had little chance of sinking ships. Once gunsmiths mastered the art of casting smaller, sturdier bronze guns firing iron balls, ships' cannon moved from the castle to the deck, firing through gun ports in the side. Designers increased the length to breadth ratio of ships, removed the cumbersome castles, and improved the arrangements of sails and rigging to make the ships faster and more maneuverable. The English designed a four-wheeled gun carriage known as a "truck" that allowed the cannon to be run out to fire and then hauled back using pulleys to be reloaded. The most significant changes in naval architecture and gunnery occurred during the 16th century.[19]

Tactics

The new gunpowder weapons necessitated a change in tactics. The basic goal of battle remained what it had been at Agincourt: to break up enemy formations with projectile weapons so that a charge by cavalry and/or infantry could finish off the disorganized foot soldiers and drive the enemy from the field. Firearms, however, made accomplishing this goal more complicated. Musketeers had to be protected during the slow process of reloading their guns. Pikes provided the necessary weapon but did not dictate the best formation for providing the optimal mix of shot (provided by musketeers) and shock (provided by charging pike men and cavalry). Ideally, the musketeers should be deployed in the longest line that could be protected by pike men.

During the Italian wars of the late 15th and early 16th centuries the Spanish Hapsburgs developed a formation known as the *tercio*. This formation, varying in size from 1,500 to 3,000 infantry, consisted of a square of pike men with four squares of arquebuses deployed at each of its corners, a layout that looked much like a castle. A line of musketeers stood in front of the pike square. Each component of the formation could act independently and in support of the others. Although the Spanish *tercio* dominated the battlefields of the 16th century, it had serious disadvantages. The tightly packed formation moved slowly and had limited flexibility. The arquebus squares did not maximize the frontage its soldiers could cover.

Maurice of Nassau, the Prince of Orange and leader of the Dutch revolt, improved upon the *tercio*, introducing volley firing by rank. In this system the first rank of musketeers would fire their weapons, then fall back to reload. The second rank would step forward, fire, and fall back. This process would continue until the first rank had reloaded and stepped forward to fire again. Pike men deployed between the companies of musketeers prepared to step forward and shield them from cavalry attack. The number of ranks depended on the speed of loading. By the end of the 17th century the standard infantry formation consisted of battalions of foot soldiers armed with flintlock muskets tipped with socket bayonets, ranged three to five ranks deep and capable of delivering a nearly continuous volume of fire.

Commanders had to adapt cavalry and artillery to the new infantry tactics. They deployed cavalry units on the wings of the infantry, where it could outflank the opposing line, protect its own infantry from a similar move by enemy cavalry, and charge once fire broke up the enemy formation. Cavalrymen added wheel lock pistols to their traditional armaments, sword and lance. Lighter, more mobile cannon could be deployed as field artillery. Placed in front of the infantry at points along the line, the guns could tear holes in the enemy formation with solid balls or rake it with canister shot, containers of lead balls. The Swedish army of Gustavus Adolphus developed a highly mobile cast bronze gun capable of firing a two-pound shot.

In the new gunpowder armies, drill replaced marksmanship. Archers firing over several hundred yards had to aim at their targets. Musketeers firing at a densely packed enemy line fewer than 100 yards away had merely to point their guns in the right direction. Volley firing in formation, not marksmanship, won battles. Success depended on the speed with which a solider could reload and his ability to maneuver in sync with other members of his unit. Soldiers spent hours learning to march, countermarch, and deploy from column to line formations. They practiced the 30 steps it took (reduced from over 70 by the end of the 17th century) to load a musket. They did not need to waste valuable powder and shot on target practice, as hitting a long line of men some 50 yards away did not require accuracy.

Sieges also changed in response to the technological transformation of warfare. Reducing a castle or city before the invention of heavy cannon usually required starving it into submission. Medieval siege engines rarely damaged fortifications faster than the defenders could repair them. Living in unsanitary camps, the besiegers might succumb to disease sooner than the inhabitants of a town ran out of food. As previously noted, cannon proved highly successful at breeching medieval walls in short order.

The *trace Italienne*, however, restored some balance between besieger and defender. Capturing fortresses, like constructing them, became a science. It should come as no surprise that the man who knew most about building star forts demonstrated equal skill at reducing them.

Vauban's 1669 *Manual of Siegecraft and Fortification* describes in great detail the process of besieging a fortified place.[20] The attackers first encircled the town or fortress with fieldworks to prevent the garrison being resupplied. They then began the laborious process of advancing a system of trenches connected by saps (trenches dug perpendicular to those encircling the fort) ever closer to the walls. The trenches allowed attackers to move their artillery forward to a point where it could breach the walls. At the same time that they tightened the noose on the fortress, the besieging army also had to defend against any relief operation mounted by the enemy's field army. So methodical had this process become that Vauban could determine the length of a siege within an acceptable margin of error before operations had even begun.[21]

Dynastic Armies and Early Modern Society

The technological advances in warfare and the changes they wrought in strategy, tactics, and the organization of armies helped transform Europe from a continent of feudal principalities to one of emerging nation-states and empires. New weapons and fortifications cost a great deal of money, as did fleets of ships armed with cannon. Because monarchs had to garrison the new forts as well as maintain field forces, armies grew larger and became part of a permanent establishment instead of units raised for a single campaign and dismissed at its conclusion. Soldiers had to be housed, clothed, fed, and paid year-round at state expense. The new dynastic or royal armies required barracks, hospitals, workshops to manufacture guns and uniforms, and a host of other costly provisions that only the wealthiest states could afford. These expenses necessitated increased revenue and improved systems of taxation for collecting it. Changes in warfare thus encouraged the growth of the modern bureaucratic state and allowed it to exert greater control over its territory.

Whether these changes constitute a "revolution," as first proposed by Michael Roberts and later supported (with modification) by Geoffrey Parker, or "punctuated evolution," as argued by Clifford Rogers, remains the subject of considerable debate.[22] No one doubts, however, that a series of changes between the 14th and the 17th centuries brought about by gunpowder and heavily concentrated in the 16th century profoundly changed the nature of armies and navies and the conduct of war. The term "transformation" thus seems the most accurate way of describing these changes. Two armies in particular illustrate the magnitude of the change: the Swedish army of Gustavus Adolphus and the French army of Louis XIV.

During the 16th and the first half of the 17th centuries rulers made war with ad hoc forces. Unwilling or unable to bear the cost of a standing army, they augmented a small number of regular units with mercenaries known as "free companies" hired for the duration of a campaign. Through their captains, soldiers received pay only for the campaigning season (usually late spring to late fall). They augmented their meager wages with plunder and, during long wars, lived off the land between campaigns. This approach saved rulers from the financial burden of maintaining a standing army but at enormous social cost. During the Thirty Years' War (1618–1648) free companies devastated the German lands as they engaged in rapine and pillaging for fun and profit. By the end of this disastrous conflict, virtually all European rulers saw the necessity and the wisdom of maintaining disciplined standing armies.

Gustavus Adolphus (1594–1632) created Europe's first dynastic army, a standing force with a core of national soldiers complemented by mercenaries kept on full pay during peacetime. Such an army required reliable systems for recruiting soldiers and financing war. The Swedish king established both. Like all monarchs of his day, he needed to recruit fit men without seriously reducing the number of his most economically productive, tax-paying subjects. The Swedish system required all able-bodied men between 15 and 60 who had no home of their own to be registered. From this group one-tenth of those between 18 and 35 were chosen by drawing lots.[23] Conscription thus fell heaviest on men whom the Swedish economy could most afford to lose: wage laborers and the unemployed. To pay for his army, Gustavus Adolphus relied on income from land. During peacetime the crown granted farms to officers and billeted soldiers with peasant farmers. Gustavus Adolphus also taxed homesteads, imposed tolls, received voluntary contributions from wealthy subjects, and compelled foreigners to pay subsidies.[24]

The quintessential dynastic army of the early modern era, however, belonged not to Gustavus Adolphus but to Louis XIV (1638–1715). Between 1661 and 1700 the "Sun King" transformed the French army from a loose collection of units into the most formidable fighting force in Europe. The key to implementing this change lay not in the army but in the state it served. Unlike the Swedish king, Louis did not play a direct role in reform, but he enabled his ministers to undertake it. When Cardinal Mazarin died in 1661, the king did not appoint a new chief minister. This decision afforded other ministers greater latitude to undertake reforms and gave them direct access to the king. Contrary to what many historians have claimed, Louis did not create a rigidly centralized state. The government of 17th-century France balanced central authority with devolution, a system described as a "patrimonial bureaucracy."[25] Royal offices became institutionalized, while the right to hold them belonged to specific families. The crown gave everyone from the minister of war to the lowliest captain greater security over the office he held, including the right to pass it along to his son or sell it, provided he paid an annual fee and did his job well. This "venalization" of office coupled with better oversight thus made all institutions of government more effective, especially the military.[26]

The French army consisted of companies, regiments, and battalions. Regiments functioned as administrative units capable of raising a number of combat or garrison battalions depending on need. Companies formed the basic tactical unit of battle. The number of companies per battalion varied, as did the size of companies until 1684, when the ministry of war fixed company strength at 35–50 men.[27] Colonels, who commanded regiments, and captains, who led companies, purchased their commissions and paid an annual fee to keep them. They got much more than a rank for their money. They had, in fact, bought a sinecure, an office from which they could expect to profit, provided they invested in it and performed their duties adequately. They might have to supplement government subsidies from their own funds at various times during their careers, while at other times they would come out ahead. They bought equipment in bulk at a discount and sold it to their soldiers at a profit. When they retired, they could pass their commission on to a son or sell it for a handsome profit.

To diminish the inevitable abuses inherent in such a system, the French created an elaborate government oversight mechanism. In 1667 Minister of War François-Michel le Tellier, Marquis de Louvois, created the office of Inspector General of Infantry to make certain that regiments were adequately prepared for combat. *Intendants d'armée* supervised supply and payment of troops (and other matters). *Commissaires de guerre* aided in recruitment, and *contrôleurs de guerre* kept accurate records of men serving in the army. These overseers reported to the Ministry of War in Paris, subdivided into five departments to handle specific aspects of military administration.[28] The French war machine thus combined elements of an ancient patronage system and a modern bureaucracy. Over time bureaucracy edged out patronage as the state took over more and more functions once performed by regimental officers. Only in the 1760s, though, did the French Ministry of War assume responsibility for recruitment.

With all of their imperfections, these reforms allowed the French to maintain an army of over 400,000 (on paper) with an actual fighting strength of 255,000 to 340,000 in 1707, several times larger than armies of the previous century and the largest in Europe at the time.[29] The army drew upon two elements of society: the officer corps came from the aristocracy, and the lowest class, whose members had few other options in life, provided the rank and file. Aristocrats, many of them younger sons of nobles or members of the lesser gentry, comprised 80 percent of the French officer corps, with the remainder coming from the ranks of well-to-do commoners such as merchants.[30] Those nobles with substantial holdings could recruit men from their own estates. Other officers paid enlistment bounties and/or duped gullible recruits into believing enlistments would be short. Vagrants, criminals, and orphans also found themselves pressed into service. Local militias mandated by the state provided a further source of recruits. The crown wished to fill the rank and file of its army with the least economically productive elements of society. Mercenaries continued to have a place in dynastic armies. These included foreign troops recruited into French regiments and entire units of auxiliaries employed for a campaign. In 1690 German Protestants serving in French units made up 10 percent of Louis's army at a time when the Sun King was persecuting the Protestant Huguenots.[31]

As the French army expanded and became more effective, the Ministry of War instituted other reforms. Gradually during the first decades of the 18th century, drill, weapons, and uniforms were standardized. From 1727 on the government supplied each soldier with a musket without charging him or the colonel of his regiment for it.[32] The state constructed barracks, magazines, and military hospitals. It regularized pay and even built a retirement home for soldiers, les Invalides.[33] Engineers also became a specialized unit within the army.

Similar reforms occurred throughout Europe. By the middle of the 18th century most states had standing armies, albeit of different quality and with local variations in organization. Virtually all relied on aristocratic officers and recruits from the lowest orders of society, although recruitment methods varied. The Russians conscripted serfs, as did the Prussians. The British employed press gangs to sweep up drunks and vagrants. Everyone relied to some degree on volunteers and employed mercenaries. Equipped with smoothbore muskets tipped with socket bayonets, these soldiers filled the ranks of the armies that would fight Europe's wars for most of the 18th century.

Europe Pulls Ahead

The military transformation of the early modern era not only encouraged the creation of powerful nation-states, it also propelled Europe toward world domination. From the 16th to the 20th centuries Europeans conquered much of North and South America, most of Africa, and vast areas of Asia. Since gunpowder technology developed in China and spread first to Islamic lands, this dominance requires considerable explanation. Why did Europe, which in so many areas had lagged so far behind the Chinese, Ottoman, and Mughal empires during the 15th century, pull so far ahead by the 19th century?

The simple answer is that Europe fought more wars over a longer period of time during a crucial era in human history. The desire to gain an advantage in battle encouraged technological and tactical innovation. Such innovation had occurred in China from about 850 to 1360 CE, a period characterized by continuous warfare, but a subsequent period of peace lasting until the 1830s provided no incentive for further developments.[34] During this long period of Chinese peace, Europe engaged in nearly continuous warfare. Conflict provided a powerful incentive to improve weapons, tactics, and military administration.[35]

This explanation begs a larger question: Why was the early modern period in Europe so violent? In *The Rise and Fall of the Great Powers*, Paul Kennedy suggests that the answer lies in geography. Unlike China, South Asia, or the Ottoman lands, Europe contains too many internal divisions for any power to impose hegemony over it. Rivers and mountains divide the continent into a patchwork quilt of smaller territories, which developed into unified nation-states. Barring a dramatic technological advantage, no one state could dominate the others, especially when all pursued a balance of power policy to prevent a hegemon from emerging. Several centuries of internecine warfare produced a military transformation that allowed Europe to dominate the world.[36] Superior military technology does not mean superior culture, but the empire builders would of course interpret it that way.

CHAPTER TWO

An Era of Limited War

The period 1648 to 1789 has been characterized as an era of limited war. Compared to those fought in the century and a half of conflict ending with the Thirty Years' War (1618–1648) that preceded it and the wars of the French Revolution and Napoleon (1792–1815) that followed, conflicts during this period were generally less bloody and less destructive. The nature of armies combined with pragmatic and ethical considerations to produce this limitation. Restraint also stemmed from the gradual disappearance of a major factor that had made the wars of the 16th and early 17th centuries so destructive: religion. Statecraft, the pragmatic consideration of costs and benefits based on national interest, took its place. Ideologically motivated wars often lead to demonization of the enemy, which in turn increases the lethality of conflict. A soldier who considers enemy soldiers and even civilians of a different religion as infidels doomed to perdition may behave more brutally toward them than one who does not. The Thirty Years' War took the lives of seven to eight million people out of a population of approximately twenty million in the Holy Roman Empire and caused widespread destruction, which reduced the economic capacity of entire areas for years to come. To take a single example, economic production in the Basse-Meuse district on the Franco-Belgian border decreased by an average of 15 percent per year between 1620 and 1750 due to war, and in some years declined to 25 percent of normal.[1]

The crowned heads of Europe determined to avoid repetition of this wasteful approach to armed conflict. Standing armies composed of professional soldiers trained, equipped, housed, and paid by the state and kept in line by brutal discipline were far less likely to rape, pillage, and plunder. Generals did forage for food and supplies when they needed to do so, and they razed towns and villages for strategic reasons (e.g., to force an enemy to fight), but they did not allow hordes of undisciplined soldiers to wreak havoc at will. In addition to deliberate restraint exercised by generals fighting on behalf of kings, emerging rules of "civilized" warfare may also have reduced the lethality and destructiveness of conflicts, at least between Christian armies in Western Europe. In the Balkans and Eastern Europe, where Orthodox Slavs and Catholic Austrians fought Muslim Turks, however, wars remained as bloody as ever.

By the beginning of the 18th century royal or dynastic armies assumed the more or less standardized form they would keep for the next century and a half. The monarchs of Europe raised permanent professional bodies of troops trained, equipped, clothed, housed, and fed at state expense. The rank and file came from the least economically productive elements of society (vagrants, criminals, social misfits, the unemployed) pressed into long-term service. Aristocrats, whose raison d'être for centuries had been the profession of arms, filled the officer corps. Officers often had to purchase their commissions and in some cases to raise their own regiments. Trained soldiers thus represented a substantial investment in time and money that monarchs did not wish to squander in an ill-conceived engagement. "It is better to put off the attack for several days," declared the French Field Marshal Maurice de Saxe, "than to expose oneself to losing rashly a single grenadier: he has been twenty years in the making."[2]

Technological Change

While the organization and supply of armies changed dramatically from the previous century, their equipment did not. Weapons improved little during the 18th and early 19th centuries. The smoothbore flintlock musket tipped with a socket bayonet remained the standard infantry weapon throughout the period. Pike men disappeared from armies as did grenadiers, although the term remained and came to designate elite infantry units. Cavalry armed with lances, swords, pistols, carbines, or a combination of these weapons formed a smaller percentage of armies (usually no more than a third of the total) than previously. Field artillery capable of providing close infantry support had increased in importance throughout the 17th century and remained essential to warfare.

An Era of Limited War   33

Technological change during this era of dynastic armies consisted primarily of refinements of existing weapons. The Prussians developed an iron ramrod less prone to breaking than its wooden predecessor. An elevation screw located under the breech made cannon easier to aim. The French General Jean Baptiste Vaquette de Gribeauval developed a process for drilling rather than casting gun barrels, which allowed them to be thinner, sturdier, and lighter. This change and the lighter gun carriages he designed made artillery more mobile.

Technology also affected naval warfare. Ships became larger, more maneuverable, and more heavily armed. From the middle of the 17th century until the middle of the 19th, the two premier maritime powers, France and Britain, built their navies around "ships of the line." Ships of the line were three-masted, wooden sailing vessels, 100 to 120 feet long and 30 to 60 feet wide, mounting 40 to 130 guns on two to three decks with crews of approximately 400, at least half of whom were necessary to man the guns. Ships became narrower and more maneuverable and by the middle of the 18th century carried, on average, one hundred guns.[3] Launched in 1765, HMS *Victory* was the premier warship in the British navy and a prime example of the ship of the line. Built from 2,000 oak trees, the ship carried four acres of sail controlled by 27 miles of cordage. It was 220 feet long and 50 feet 6 inches wide at the beam and had a crew of 821 sailors and marines. *Victory* mounted 104 guns on three decks: 32 pounders on the lowest deck, 24 pounders on the middle deck, and 12 pounders on the top deck.[4]

The advent of the ship of the line changed naval warfare from a melee of battles between sailors and marines on ships grappled to one another to gun duels between massed ships of the line.[5] Large fleets battled one another to establish naval supremacy, while smaller warships such as frigates (faster but mounting fewer guns) patrolled the sea lanes, escorted convoys, and raided enemy ports. Success in battle depended on the skill of admirals maneuvering fleets, captains skillfully handling individual ships, and sailors firing and reloading guns with the greatest speed. Naval supremacy allowed the dominant maritime power (the Dutch in the late 17th century and the British thereafter) to expand its empire at the expense of rival states.

Land Warfare

Since weapons determine how troops deploy and operate in battle, tactics also changed relatively little during the 18th and early 19th centuries. Infantry units consisted of 10 to 12 "platoons" (the equivalent of a modern company) of approximately 100 men each, usually formed into lines of three to five ranks. Gaps between each company could be filled with artillery and provided an avenue for reinforcements to move forward. Cavalry deployed at the ends of the infantry line from where it could attack the flanks of an enemy formation or protect its own troops from flank attack by enemy cavalry. Once musket and artillery fire broke the enemy infantry line, cavalry would sweep in to pursue the fleeing soldiers.

The short range and limited accuracy of the smoothbore musket made firing individual aimed shots ineffective for massed infantry. Success on the battlefield depended on delivering a large volume of continuous fire. The speed with which soldiers could discharge and reload their weapons determined the depth of the infantry formation. Firing could be done by caracole, with each soldier moving to the end of the file to reload after firing or with the next soldier behind him moving forward after the first had discharged his musket. Firing could also be done by ranks, with two to three ranks firing and then reloading in place. Caracole allowed soldiers to fire while advancing or retreating, but firing by ranks delivered a greater volume of shot. Firing by ranks required the first rank to kneel, the second to crouch, and the third to stand. The second and third ranks would both be able to stand if they staggered themselves. The Dutch and British developed a modified version of firing by ranks known as "platoon firing." Commanders divided the line into four "firings," groups of alternating platoons that discharged their muskets simultaneously. Staggering the men in each rank created enough room for them to pivot their muskets slightly to the right or left and thus provide oblique fire into the enemy line.[6] No matter the method, firing usually occurred at less than 50 yards, and often much closer.

Success in battle depended heavily on the skill and discipline of the rank and file. Maneuvering and volley firing in tight formations required extensive training. Recruits spent hours on parade ground drill and on loading their muskets according to a strict manual of arms. Target practice would have been a waste of valuable powder and shot. Hitting a formation of infantry standing shoulder to shoulder three ranks deep in a line hundreds of yards wide and less than one hundred yards away required little skill. The command prior to firing was not "aim," but "level your muskets" or "present." Speed of reloading and the resultant volume of fire, not marksmanship, determined success in battle.

In the 18th century as in the 21st, noncommissioned officers (NCOs) formed the backbone of the army. "Your job is to show the men how to die," the Duke of Wellington allegedly told his junior officers. "The sergeants will do the rest." Noncommissioned officers trained recruits, maintained discipline among the men, led them in battle, and saw to their needs in camp. Junior officers deployed at the rear and on the flanks of platoons to direct fire, maintain order, and prevent men fleeing. "Showing the men how to die" referred to the noblesse oblige notion that aristocrats must lead by example. Senior officers stayed to the rear, where they could oversee the battle.

Wars

European states fought one another almost incessantly from 1689 to 1789. Most of their people, however, had no direct experience of war. Even in long conflicts battles occurred infrequently and in confined areas. Trade and commerce continued even between belligerents, as did travel. The vast majority of Europeans thus enjoyed a century of relative peace. The state taxed them to pay for its wars and recruited (or pressed into service) their sons to fight them, but unless they lived in the path of armies, ordinary men and women encountered little military violence themselves.

Wars during this period fell roughly into two broad categories. In the first, the Russians and Austrians expanded their frontiers, primarily against the Turks. The Austrians fought three wars with the Ottoman Empire (1716–1718, 1737–1739, 1768–1774), advancing down the Danube and into the Balkans. The Russians engaged the Turks in two wars (1735–1739, 1768–1774), driving south to the Black Sea and southeast toward Istanbul, an axis of expansion they would pursue up to World War I. Russia also fought two wars with Sweden for control of the Baltic littoral, two with Finland (1701–1721, 1741–1743), and one with Persia (1722–1723) in an effort to expand into the Southern Caucasus and the northern Caspian regions. Because the eastern border lands contained fewer fortresses than did the states of central and Western Europe, these wars contained a higher proportion of battles to sieges. On the open steppes of southern Russia and on the Hungarian plain, cavalry played a larger role than it did in Western Europe.

In Western and Central Europe states also sought to gain advantage against one another, which usually meant conquering territory. These wars between nation-states, however, conformed to a different pattern. Monarchs generally sought to preserve a balance of power among the major states. If they could not dominate the continent themselves, they made sure no one else could. The series of conflicts between France and Britain, dubbed "the Second Hundred Years' War (1689–1815)," reveal this tendency most clearly. As the preeminent land power in Western Europe, France sought to expand into the Low Countries (modern-day Belgium,

Luxembourg, and the Netherlands), dominate the small German states on its eastern border, and weaken the Holy Roman (Austrian) Empire. Britain realized that if France succeeded, it would be able to devote more resources to its navy and so challenge Britain for maritime supremacy.[7] To counter this threat London developed a deep-water strategy: it financed and contributed troops to anti-French alliances on the Continent while attacking French commerce and colonies outside Europe.[8]

The first Anglo-French conflict in this long struggle began in 1688. In the War of the League of Augsburg (1688–1697), also known as the "Nine Years' War," France fought the Grand Alliance of England, Scotland, the Dutch Republic, the Holy Roman Empire, Piedmont Savoy, Spain, and Sweden (until 1691). Louis XIV sought to gain control of the Rhineland, Savoy, and the Spanish Netherlands (parts of France, Luxembourg, and Belgium). The French king also backed efforts to restore King James II to the English throne via rebellion in Ireland. The war ended with a negotiated peace that secured Alsace for France but denied Louis his other goals.

The War of the Spanish Succession (1701–1713) continued this struggle against French hegemony. Louis XIV sought to put his grandson Philip on the Spanish throne, which would have significantly enhanced French power. To prevent this expansion of the house of Bourbon, England (Great Britain after 1707), the Holy Roman Empire, Savoy, the Dutch Republic, Portugal, and those Spaniards opposed to Philip fought France, Bavaria (which left the alliance in 1704), and Philip's Spanish supporters. After more than 20 years of fighting, a series of treaties signed in 1713–1714 in Utrecht brought the war to a close. Louis achieved his original goal of securing the Spanish throne for his grandson with the condition that the two kingdoms never unite, but in doing so he lost territory in Europe and North America to the British and in Europe to the Austrians.

For 27 years after the Peace of Utrecht (1713), Britain remained at peace with a weakened France. Then in 1740 the War of the Austrian Succession broke out when France and Prussia claimed that as a woman, Maria Theresa could not inherit the crown of the Holy Roman Empire. Unwilling to see Austria defeated, Britain supported Maria Theresa, who held onto her throne. France supported Prussia, and so Britain and its ally the Dutch went to war with their old enemy and Prussia's ambitious king Frederick the Great. The war ended in a strategic draw. The empress of Austria kept her throne, but at the price of ceding Silesia to Prussia. Frederick thus gained the most, but he knew Austria would move to retake Silesia as soon as it had the strength to do so.

The Seven Years' War and the Rise of Prussia

The War of the Austrian Succession had introduced a new player into the game of European power politics. Since the end of the Thirty Years' War, the electorate of Brandenburg-Prussia, which became the kingdom of Prussia in 1701, had expanded its territory in north-central Europe. By the middle of the 18th century it included much of northern Germany and parts of Poland, Lithuania, and Denmark. Since the Treaty of Aixe la Chappelle (dubbed a "peace of exhaustion") ending the War of the Austrian Succession left no one but Prussia content with the status quo, Frederick faced the prospect of renewed war, as did Britain, whose struggle with France over North America remained unresolved. Britain allied with Prussia to protect Hanover, whose elector was also the British king. Frederick began the war with a preemptive strike, invading Saxony. Although initially successful, he was checked by the Austrians at Kolin in June 1757. Only subsequent victories at Rosbach and Leuthen (his greatest victory) later in the year saved him from defeat. He spent the rest of the war surviving the combined efforts of Austria and Russia to defeat him, until Empress Elizabeth died and her pro-Prussian son Peter III switched sides. The Treaty of Paris (1763), which brought the war to a close, required the Prussians to return Saxony to Austria and confirm the Hapsburg succession but left Frederick in possession of Silesia.

The British fared even better. In addition to bankrolling Frederick, they had successfully defended Hanover. They expanded their holdings in India and the Caribbean. Their greatest success, however, occurred in North America. Following the victory of General James Wolf over the Marquis de Montcalm on the Plains of Abraham outside Quebec in September 1759, Britain retained control of Canada. It also gained possession of Florida. Perhaps most important, the war established British naval supremacy, which would last until World War II.

Students of war have pored over Frederick the Great's writings and analyzed his battles down to the finest detail. Of far greater importance in the development of warfare, however, were the organization of the Prussian state and the army it fielded. Such a relatively small country should never have been able to face a mighty empire like Austria or Russia, never mind survive a war against both. A unique approach to recruitment, however, enabled Prussia to put a significantly larger percentage of its male population in uniform and by so doing compete with more populous states. In 1733 Frederick I (father of Frederick the Great) created the "canton system," which divided Prussia into recruitment districts assigned to specific army regiments. All able-bodied men were eligible to be drafted for long service in the regular army. Contrary to the practice in other European establishments, however, recruits completed a year's training and then served for only a few months each year. Because these Prussian soldiers continued to be productive, tax-paying subjects as well as soldiers, the crown could draft more of them. Reserve units (*Überkomplette*) of 9,000 men per regiment trained at local garrisons. Given the relative brevity of campaigns, Prussia could thus rapidly increase the size of its army in time of war without adversely affecting its economy.[9] In addition to drafting a much larger percentage of its able-bodied men, Prussia spent 80 percent of its budget on the military.[10]

Although the canton system was the first modern European draft, supplying 75 percent of Prussia's manpower needs,[11] it would be a mistake to describe these men as citizen soldiers. They may have been loyal to their king and had some sense of belonging to a larger community, but it is not clear that patriotism motivated them to fight. Prussian military discipline was notoriously brutal, and Frederick's army suffered the same high desertion rates that plagued all dynastic armies. Informed of low morale in the army, Frederick quipped, "the cat [whip] will be employed until morale improves." It would take the American and French Revolutions to give ordinary men a sense of belonging to a nation worth defending and make possible a draft of citizen soldiers. The canton system was, however, a step in that direction.

If the army of Frederick the Great had characteristics from the era of dynastic wars in which it fought and the era of national conflicts to follow, the Prussian king was himself also something of a transitional figure. In *General Principles of War* Frederick provided his officers instruction on all aspects of leading an army in camp, on the march, and in battle. He had a very modern grasp of strategy, seeking not merely limited gain but decisive victories to achieve his political objectives as rapidly as possible. "Our wars should be short and sharp," he concluded. "A long war destroys the admirable discipline [of our army], depletes the population of our country, and exhausts our resources."[12] This conclusion foreshadows the after-action report drafted by the Germans after World War I. It also anticipated Napoleon's predilection for battles of annihilation, which not only produced rapid victories, but also dissuaded his enemies from regrouping too quickly to attack him again.

Prussian militarism drew criticism in its own day, however, and since World War II historians have scrutinized it in an effort to understand the antecedents of the Third Reich. A famous quote, usually attributed to the French statesman Mirabeau, declared that while other states had armies, Prussia was an army that had a state. Like all such hyperbole, this quip is off the mark, but it does contain a kernel of truth. The influence of 18th-century Prussian militarism on subsequent German history continues to be hotly debated. The *Sonderweg* (exceptionalist) thesis, which argues that Prussia's and later Germany's unique position in central Europe necessitated a strong military and an authoritarian state, still has wide currency but has also been challenged.

The Nature of Battle

Of the numerous battles fought between the beginning of the War of the League of Augsburg (1688) and the end of the Seven Years' War (1763), the era of dynastic armies, none can truly be said to be typical. Each engagement was unique, and trying to analyze even the major ones would take several volumes. The key to understanding 18th-century warfare lies not in reviewing every battle, but in examining a representative engagement, whose conduct reveals the elements of tactics and generalship as dynastic armies practiced them throughout the period. For that purpose a straightforward encounter between two relatively small armies might serve as a more instructive example than a complex engagement between much larger forces. The Battle of Blenheim, fought on August 13, 1704, serves this didactic purpose quite well.

Blenheim (German, Blindheim) was the culmination of a major campaign in the War of the Spanish Succession, the conflict in which Great Britain, the Netherlands, the Austrian Empire, and their smaller allies fought to prevent Louis XIV expanding French power. In the spring of 1704 Louis sent a French army under the command of Marshal Camille de Tallard across the Rhine to link up with his Bavarian allies, march on Vienna, and knock Austria out of the war. To counter this move the British commander in the Low Countries, Captain General John Churchill, the Duke of Marlborough, moved his army of British, Hessian, and Dutch troops into Bavaria to link up with the imperial forces commanded by Prince Eugene of Savoy to engage the French and Bavarian forces threatening the Austrian capital.

Marlborough affected his union with Eugene before the French and Bavarians joined forces. He thus saw an opportunity to defeat the enemy in detail. The duke dispatched Eugene to cover the French advance, while he despoiled Bavaria, burning villages and destroying crops. Unlike what had occurred during the Thirty Years' War, this deliberate destruction of property was a means to an end, not an end in itself. Marlborough wished to draw the Bavarian army, led by Elector Maximilian and the French commander assigned to assist him, Marshal Ferdinand Comte de Marsin, into battle or force them to surrender before the French army arrived. The two, however, refused to take the bait and linked up with Tallard in early August. If they wished to save Vienna, Marlborough and Eugene had no choice but to bring the joint Franco-Bavarian force to battle. Knowing that the allies would have to attack them gave Tallard and Maximilian a strategic advantage.

The two armies collided on the River Danube in Southern Bavaria on August 12. The French and Bavarians encamped at the village of Blenheim, and the allied forces bivouacked along the river five miles to the northeast. Tallard had chosen a strong position. His and Maximilian's forces occupied a four-mile stretch of land from Blenheim on the Danube in the east to the village of Lutzingen adjacent to forested hills in the west. Midway between these villages laid a third hamlet, Oberglau, in front of which the Nebel River ran through swampy ground until it joined the Danube. Anchoring their line on the three villages, the French and Bavarians could not be outflanked on either side and held a strong fortified position in their center. To attack them the allied forces would have to cross a river under fire and advance uphill. The Franco-Bavarian forces also had a significant numerical advantage in troops and artillery: 56,000 men and 90 cannon to the ally's 52,000 men and 66 guns.[13]

Under such favorable circumstances, Tallard might have expected the allied forces to withdraw. Eighteenth-century wars involved maneuver and positioning as much as combat. By the rules of its "chessboard warfare," Marlborough and Eugene might have decided that facing a superior enemy in a strong position, they had already been beaten and must withdraw.[14] Indeed, when he first received word early on the morning of the battle that Marlborough had decamped, Tallard wrote to Versailles that he believed the allies were withdrawing. Once he realized they intended to attack, he had every reason to be confident in the outcome based on the advantages he enjoyed.

Almost from the moment the smoke had cleared on the battlefield, analysts and historians have been highly critical of Tallard's troop dispositions at Blenheim. Had he won, which he might well have done, they would be praising his genius. Eighteenth-century commanders typically deployed lines of infantry battalions with cavalry squadrons on the flanks and artillery interspersed with the infantry units. The French and Bavarians deviated from this practice. Tallard deployed 16 infantry battalions into Blenheim village supported by 12 squadrons of cavalry. Another 25,000 Bavarian and French troops were stationed in the villages of Lutzingen and Oberglau and in the open space between them. In the gap between Oberglau and Blenheim, Tallard deployed just nine infantry battalions and the

An Era of Limited War

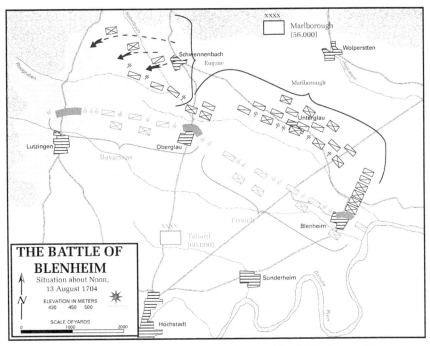

Battle of Blenheim, situation around noon, August 13, 1704. *Source:* Department of History, United States Military Academy.

bulk of the French cavalry, some 64 squadrons. Some historians consider these troop dispositions a failure of generalship, while others attribute them to poor French-Bavarian cooperation.

Because Marlborough won the battle by breaking through the French center, Tallard has been roundly criticized for failing to see the weakness at this point in his line. It is hard to imagine, however, such a veteran commander overlooking so obvious a vulnerability. The marshal probably acted deliberately, setting a trap for the British. He wanted Marlborough to cross the Nebel and engage the French center. Tallard quite reasonably expected his heavy cavalry charging downhill to annihilate infantry and cavalry units trying to form up after crossing a river under fire. Allied troops would also be exposed to flanking fire and perhaps even attack from French forces in Oberglau and Blenheim. This stratagem explains Tallard's other controversial decision, not to use the Nebel River as a natural line of defense by digging in on its west bank. Were it not for superior allied fire discipline and Marlborough's skill, however, Tallard's plan might have succeeded. Tallard probably thought that if it failed, he could rely on his reserves deployed behind Blenheim, strategically located to reinforce either the French right or center as needed. He could not have known that a fatal error by his commander in the village would deprive him of these troops at a critical moment.

Marlborough counted on just such a mistake. He had seen the weakness in the French center and devised a plan to exploit it. Eugene's imperial troops would engage the Bavarians while British, Dutch, and Hessian forces attacked Blenheim and Oberglau to secure the flanks of his attack on the French center and with the additional objective of tying down any reserves that might otherwise have reinforced the line between the two villages. The plan worked. Neither Lutzigen on the Bavarian left nor Oberglau and Blenheim on the French flanks fell to the initial allied assaults, but the attacks served their purpose. Maximilian had to devote his energy to holding Lutzigen.[15] More important, in the face of the determined attack, Lieutenant-General the Marquis de Clérembaut, the commander charged with holding Blenheim, ordered the French reserves into the town without asking Tallard.[16] Sixteen allied infantry battalions were now holding down twenty-seven French infantry battalions and twelve dismounted squadrons of cavalry, the Franco-Bavarian numerical advantage had been canceled out, and Tallard had virtually no reserves with which to bolster his center if an attack threatened to break through there.[17]

The next phase of his plan required Marlborough to push his cavalry and infantry across the Nebel to attack the French center. His engineers had spent most of the morning repairing the bridge at Unterglau and constructing five pontoon bridges between Unterglau and Blenheim. Tallard's squadrons charged the British first line of cavalry almost as soon as it crossed the river, driving it back in disarray. The second line and the infantry, however, drove off the French cavalry and together advanced on the French infantry. Superior fire discipline probably helped the allies in this crucial engagement. The French were still using an outdated system of volley firing along the entire line of a formation five ranks deep, while the British army relied on the more effective system of platoon firing, which allowed more than one of its three ranks to fire at once and enabled platoons to support each other with oblique fire.[18]

Despite the initial British success, however, had Tallard been able to deploy his reserves to bolster his center, he might have saved the day, but Clérembaut had squandered those troops by crowding them into Blenheim. Marlborough's troops broke through the French line and wheeled right and left. Sensing defeat, the Bavarians disengaged and withdrew from the field. The encircled troops inside Blenheim fought on as long as they could, but surrendered to avoid being massacred. The allies took

An Era of Limited War

14,000 prisoners, which on top of the 20,000 French and Bavarian troops killed or wounded amounted to a stunning loss. The victory, however, was not cheap: 4,500 allied soldiers lost their lives, and nearly 8,000 were wounded. No matter how limited dynastic warfare was as a whole, individual battles were brutal. Allied troops had begun to march at 2:00 a.m.; the engagement began around 9:00 a.m. and did not end until 9:00 p.m. Soldiers on both sides endured hours of artillery bombardment and then engaged one another at close quarters. They fought to the limits of human endurance and would not have had the energy to pursue the fleeing Bavarians even if they had been inclined to do so.[19]

Blenheim reveals a great deal about how 18th-century battles were fought and won. Most engagements occurred between armies of comparable size and equipment. Commanders preferred to have a numerical advantage before they attacked, but as Blenheim illustrates, the side with the larger force did not always win. At Leuthen (1757), a Prussian army of 36,000 defeated an Austrian force more than twice its size. In both battles generalship proved to be crucial. A commander could influence the outcome of a campaign in three ways: by making sure his men

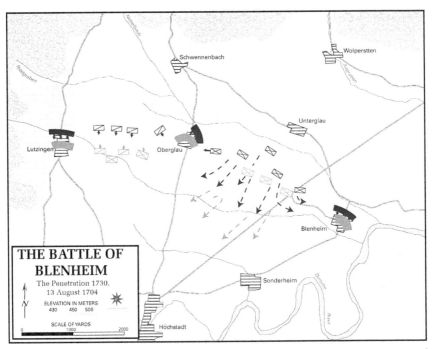

Battle of Blenheim, the penetration, August 13, 1704. *Source:* Department of History, United States Military Academy.

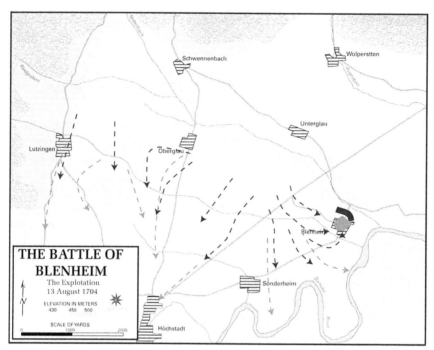

Battle of Blenheim, exploitation, August 13, 1704. *Source:* Department of History, United States Military Academy.

were thoroughly prepared and trusted in him, by effectively planning the engagement, and by acting decisively at key points during the battle. Marlborough excelled at all three. He had thoroughly trained his soldiers and took such good care of them that they nicknamed him "Corporal Jack," a reference to the NCO, who saw to the welfare of an army's smallest tactical unit. He devised a brilliant stratagem for dislodging a larger force from a very strong defensive position and intervened decisively when the assault on Oberglau faltered and the Franco-Bavarian forces threatened to split the two wings of the allied line and perhaps win the battle.[20]

Unconventional Warfare

The term "dynastic warfare" conjures up images of soldiers in brightly colored uniforms advancing in close formation to the sound of fife and drum to blaze away at one another at point-blank range. As Blenheim illustrates, such chess-piece battles were indeed the mainstay of ancien régime warfare, but they do not constitute its totality. A variety of unconventional activities carried out by special units in regular armies or irregular groups acting independently but in support of regular operations took place in most 18th-century wars. These activities differed qualitatively from conventional battle, although those who conducted them did so in support of conventional military activities.

Anyone who has studied unconventional war will not be surprised that defining and describing this type of conflict proved as challenging for writers in the 18th century as it does for those in the 21st. Contemporary practitioners used a variety of terms to describe unconventional operations. The most common was "small war" (French, *petite guerre*; German, *klein Krieg*), but both the French and the English used the term "partisan." Germans also used the terms *Parteigängerkrieg* (literally "war between followers of a party") and *Postenkrieg* (war between outposts or small detachments). Eighteenth-century partisan warfare differed in one important respect from partisan warfare after the French Revolution. Modern military writers use the term "partisan" to apply to irregular forces trying to drive out a foreign army occupying their country. The partisan forces that arose in the aftermath of the German invasions of Yugoslavia and the Soviet Union during World War II provide the best examples of modern partisans. Eighteenth-century partisans were not, however, motivated by nationalist or any other ideology.[21]

Although irregular forces had been employed by armies since antiquity, their formal inclusion in 18th-century establishments originated on the fringes of Europe's empires. As the Austrians pushed the Turks out of Hungary and Croatia, they increased the length of their military frontier. They also faced rebellion by the Hungarians, whom they had liberated from the Ottoman yoke and who now wanted independence. To defend their borders against the Turks the Austrians employed locally raised bands of Croat irregulars known as "Pandurs," infamous for their ferocity. In Hungary the Austrians faced an irregular campaign waged by "Hussars," light cavalry that engaged in unconventional warfare. Once they had subdued these revolts, the Hapsburgs employed this light cavalry in their own army.[22] The Russian tsars had a similar relationship with the Cossacks in Ukraine, alternately subduing and employing them.

While the Hapsburgs intended such irregular forces for service on the frontier, necessity flung them into the center of European warfare. When Frederick the Great invaded Silesia in 1740, Marie Theresa found herself at war with a coalition that included Prussia, France, Spain, and Bavaria. Hard pressed to raise enough troops to defend her crown, the empress deployed irregulars from the borderlands to fight the invaders.[23] The troops, especially the Croat Pandurs, had a reputation for brutality, which included, according to the Austrian prince Johann Joseph Khevenhüller-Metsch, "setting fire to houses, pillaging churches, cutting off ears and eyes, murdering citizens and raping women."[24]

Despite their reprehensible behavior, irregulars in the Hapsburg army proved very effective at harassing enemy troops. They attacked outposts, supply convoys, and patrols. They sprung ambushes and nipped at the heels of retreating armies. M. de Grandmaison, an officer in the French army and author of a famous 18th-century treatise on *petite guerre*, commented on the effectiveness of irregulars against French forces who lacked such troops.[25] Most European armies soon formed units of irregulars. While they recognized the utility of such forces, however, monarchs did not wish to see a return to the savagery that had characterized the Thirty Years' War. To address this problem they placed irregular units under the command of regular officers, who imposed military discipline on them. The irregulars wore uniforms, often distinctively different from those of regular line infantry, and were housed, fed, and paid like regular troops.

"Partisans" thus became light infantry performing tasks that today would be called "out of area operations" or, in some cases, "special operations" in support of conventional armies.[26] In a 1759 treatise Captain de Jeney, one of Grandmaison's contemporaries, listed the various tasks of light troops operating at some distance from the main army:

> To protect [regular forces] on the march and in camp; to reconnoiter the country and the enemy forces; to remove their outposts, convoys, and escorts; to set ambushes; and to make use of every appropriate ruse to surprise or disquiet them.[27]

Eleven years after Jeney published his treatise, the British officer Roger Stevenson wrote his own book on irregular warfare. His description of the function of light troops reads like a carbon copy of Jeney's:

> This corps [of partisans] is a light party from one hundred to two thousand men, separated from the army, to secure the camp or a march; to reconnoitre the enemy or the country; to seize their posts, convoys, and escorts; to plant ambuscades, and put in practice every stratagem for surprising or disturbing the enemy: which is called carrying on the Petite Guerre.[28]

Light units fought small bodies of regulars or protected their own troops from enemy light forces. Indeed, generals relied on their own light troops to protect formations, convoys, and baggage trains from attack by the enemy's. Grandmaison concluded that "an army with a large number of light troops has a distinct advantage over an army that does not"; without such forces a commander had to assign regular troops to protect his flanks, supplies, and so forth.[29] For this reason, irregular forces made up about 20 percent of European armies by the 1770s.[30]

Andres Emmerich, who held a commission in the Prussian army and served with the British army during the American Revolution, described a similar set of tasks and noted the importance of unconventional forces. "In war, no army can act without light troops," he concluded. "Its operations, and even existence depends upon them."[31] Emmerich's assessment highlights the key difference between unconventional warfare in the age of dynastic wars and its practice in subsequent eras. Light troops were an integral part of regular armies that operated in support of conventional operations. Some of these light units were quite specialized, such as the Tyrolean *Jagers* in the Austrian army or the French *Chasseurs*, literally "hunters." Soldiers in these units carried rifles rather than smoothbore muskets, which allowed them to hit individual targets at a distance. As previously noted, 18th-century rifles took too long to load to be standard weapons for regular infantry, but they were still very effective when used by sharpshooters firing from concealed positions. Whatever their composition and armament, however, light troops supported regular ones.

Frontier Warfare

While the vast majority of irregular warfare during the ancien régime consisted of out-of-area operations conducted by light troops in support of regular forces, in at least one arena unconventional forces operated independently, engaging in what today would clearly be recognized as guerrilla warfare. British and French colonists in North America fought intermittently with the Indian populations they displaced and with one another as part of a series of Anglo-French conflicts that occurred over much of the 18th century. To garrison a vast, sparsely populated, but expanding wilderness frontier, the mother countries could spare few troops, who were in any case ill equipped or trained to fight in such terrain. Left to their own devices, colonial governors developed what John Grenier has dubbed "the first American way of war."[32] Faced with Indian raids on isolated farms and villages, settlers waged what he describes as a blend of unlimited and irregular warfare: "unlimited in its ends and irregular in its means."[33] This form of frontier warfare consisted of three elements: extirpative war (wholesale destruction of Indian crops and villages and the murder of men, women, and children), the taking of scalps for bounty, and the use of special military units known as "rangers."[34]

Rangers differed considerably from units employed in Europe. They did not operate merely in support of conventional armies, but were the main military force on the frontier. They saw their most extensive service in New England, where they faced not only Indians but Indians supported by the French in Canada, who paid them to attack British settlements. Colonial governors commissioned captains to raise small companies of 50 or fewer men skilled in hunting and living in the forest. They set ambushes and attacked Indian villages, burning crops and massacring the native population regardless of age or gender. They were generally mercenaries paid a bounty for each scalp they took.[35]

Robert Rogers, the most famous American ranger, explained how his own background prepared him to be a ranger:

> Between the years 1743 and 1755 my manner of life was such as led me to a general acquaintance both with the British and the French settlements in North America and especially within the uncultivated wilderness, the mountains, valleys, rivers, lakes, and several passes that lay between and contiguous to the said settlements. Nor did I content myself with the accounts I received from Indians or the information of hunters but traveled over large tracts of the country myself, which tended not more to gratify my curiosity than to inure me to hardships and, without vanity I may say, to qualify me for the very service I have since been employed in.[36]

Rogers enlisted in a ranger company in 1745 at the age of 14 after Abenaki Indians employed by the French attacked his family's homestead in New Hampshire.[37]

The French and Indian War (Seven Years' War in Europe) saw the British combine conventional war with the American ranger tradition. American historians have sometimes argued that the British were woefully unprepared for wilderness warfare, a weakness the colonists would exploit during the American Revolution. They cite as compelling evidence General Edward Braddock's resounding defeat by French and Indian forces near Fort Duquesne (present-day Pittsburgh) in July 1755. "Braddock's defeat on the Monongahela clearly indicates the disregard of even the most rudimentary tactics and techniques of petite guerre in mid-eighteenth-century British military culture," John Grenier concluded.[38] Other historians have, however, disputed this view. Robert Russell maintains that Braddock had conducted a skillful march through the Pennsylvania wilderness and only suffered defeat because of a lapse in attentiveness on the day of the battle.[39] The effective use to which the British put American rangers and Indian allies throughout the French and Indian War supports the conclusion that

An Era of Limited War

Braddock's defeat was an aberration, not an iconic example of disregard for irregular warfare.

Robert Rogers not only excelled as a ranger; he kept a journal detailing his activities, which provides historians with an invaluable account of unconventional operations in the war that drove the French from Canada and the Ohio valley. In March 1756 Rogers received a commission from William Shirley, governor of Massachusetts and commander in chief of British forces in North America. The commission directed Rogers to form "an independent company of rangers," comprised of 60 privates, 3 sergeants, an ensign, and a lieutenant.[40] Shirley instructed Rogers:

> from time to time, to use my best efforts to distress the French and their allies by sacking, burning, and destroying their houses, barns, barracks, canoes, bateaux [flat bottomed boats] & c. [sic] and by killing their cattle of every kind; and at all times to endeavor to waylay, attack, and destroy their convoys of provisions by land and water, in any part of the country where I could find them.[41]

American rangers were prepared to be more destructive than most of their European counterparts. Croat irregulars had behaved with such cruelty during the War of the Austrian Succession that European armies had taken steps to rein in such behavior. The treatises on *petite guerre*, *klein Krieg*, or small wars do not list wholesale destruction of property as a core task. Its inclusion in Rogers's orders is particularly noteworthy because his commission stated that his rangers were to be subject to "military discipline and the articles of war."[42] Ranger operations blended American extirpative warfare with European *petite guerre*. Because both the French and British made extensive use of their Indian allies, they may have decided that brutal tactics reserved for war against native populations might also be appropriate for enemy settlers.

Whether such brutality actually contributed anything to the British victory in North America is debatable. Rogers's journals suggest that intelligence gathering by rangers, not raiding villages, proved most helpful to British commanders. Rangers did force the French to detach valuable troops to protect convoys and outposts. Interdiction of supplies no doubt proved troubling but did not decisively affect the outcome of any battle, never mind the war. The British won the Seven Years' War in North America through a series of conventional victories, most notably the Battle of the Plains of Abraham (1759), which resulted in the conquest of Quebec. As in Europe, irregular forces played a supporting role, whose precise value to the overall campaign is difficult to determine.

Attitudes toward War

The tendency of European officers to describe the behavior of Croat irregulars as savage or barbaric suggests that attitudes toward war had changed since the religious conflicts of the 15th and 16th centuries. Few monarchs or generals questioned the utility of war as an instrument of statecraft, but they did try to wage it in a more controlled manner. The desire to avoid the carnage of the Thirty Years' War encouraged sovereigns to regulate the behavior of their troops, but the intellectual climate of the age also encouraged restraint. The scientific revolution of the 17th century and the Enlightenment of the 18th taught that natural law regulated all things, including human society. These intellectual movements dampened the religious fervor that had made previous wars so bloody, but they also encouraged a revival of just-war doctrine and the beginnings of international law, which insisted that war, like everything else, must be subject to rules.

Western just-war doctrine (or just-war theory) has its origins in the writings of the fourth-century theologian Augustine of Hippo and has been reiterated and modified at various times down to the present. No matter what its specific content, just-war thinking has always rested on two broad principles, expressed in the Latin phrase *Jus ad bellum, jus in bello*. Simply put, war had to be fought for a just cause, and it had to be conducted using just means. Both of these precepts were, however, subject to diverse interpretations.

The most influential just-war theorist of the 17th and 18th centuries was the Dutchman Hugo Grotius. Writing in response to the violence of the wars of religion, Grotius articulated what may be the first modern expression of just-war theory. In 1625, during the Thirty Years' War, Grotius published his multivolume *De jure belli ac pacis* (*On the Laws of War and Peace*). Grotius acknowledged that war was both necessary and in some cases desirable:

> For both the End of War (being the Preservation of Life or Limbs, and either the securing or getting Things useful to Life) is very agreeable to those first Motions of Nature; and to make use of Force, in case of Necessity, is in no wise disagreeable thereunto; since Nature has given to every Animal Strength to defend and help itself.[43]

Grotius believed war had to be declared by legitimate civil authority and recognized three valid reasons for waging it: "defence, the recovery of what's our own, and punishment."[44] He also specified when wars were unjust. A state should not make war to weaken another state that shows no sign of preparing to attack it, and it should not make war to seize territory from another state or to subjugate people, although he did allow for conquest of inhabited if "uncivilized" lands.[45] Grotius also opposed revolution: "Nor is the taking up Arms upon the Account of Liberty, justifiable in particular Persons, or a whole Community; as if to be in such a State, or a State of Independence, was naturally, and at all Times, every one's Right."[46]

In keeping with the just-war tradition, Grotius considered not only when but how wars should be fought. His version of *jus in bello* had less to do with absolute prohibition of certain acts than with moderation in all things. "It be not properly my Design to enquire, what it is advantageous to do or not to do," he asserted, "but to reduce the extravagant Licence [sic] of War to what natural Equity allows."[47] Killing and destruction of property should be kept to a minimum and only be done to bring the war to a successful conclusion. The monarchs of the ancien régime took this advice to heart even if they had never read Grotius.

While Hugo Grotius wrote as an ethicist, basing his argument on classical texts and Christian theology, the Swiss Emmerich de Vattel approached war as a philosopher and diplomat steeped in the Enlightenment faith in reason and natural law. Like Grotius, de Vattel insisted that only states had the authority to make war. He also shared the 18th-century abhorrence of unrestrained warfare born of the sad experience of religious conflict. He argued that war should be the last resort, not the preferred option, in international affairs. Only states had the right to make war, and then only for a limited set of reasons: "The right of employing force, or making war, belongs to nations no farther than is necessary for their own defense, and for the maintenance of their rights."[48] For de Vattel, wars stemmed from injury or the threat of injury to a nation. A state could wage preemptive war, but only if a threat were clear and imminent. A war waged "merely from motives of advantage" was unjust.[49]

In addition to specifying just reasons for making war, de Vattel detailed what actions could lawfully be taken during war. He insisted that enemy soldiers who surrendered must be given quarter and treated humanely, with one exception: a commander who continued to defend a position after it was certain to fall might be executed. Noncombatants should be spared, especially women, children, and the aged. In all respects, de Vattel concluded, war should be waged as humanely as possible:

> Let us never forget that our enemies are men. Though reduced to the disagreeable necessity of prosecuting our necessity by force of arms, let us

not divest ourselves of that charity which connects us with all mankind. Thus we will defend our countries' rights without violating those of human nature. Let our valor preserve itself from every stain of cruelty and the luster of victory will not be tarnished by brutal and inhuman actions.[50]

De Vattel and Grotius drew very similar conclusions about when wars were just and how they should be justly waged. They based their conclusions, however, on different foundations. Grotius reasoned from Christian theology and classical (Greco-Roman) texts. Like other Enlightenment thinkers, de Vattel appealed to natural law. He also referenced what he saw as emerging custom among civilized nations. Custom would eventually evolve into the laws and usages of land warfare, which have governed the behavior of Western armies, at least in principle, since the 18th century.

Determining the precise impact (if any) of thinkers like Grotius and de Vattel upon those who made war is of course impossible. The relationship between theorists and people acting in the real world has always been complex and difficult to map. Thinkers articulate prevailing attitudes at least as often as they create new ones. Just-war theory is no exception. Even a cursory examination of ancien régime wars reveals that monarchs paid little attention to *jus ad bellum*. While they always tried to maintain the moral high ground by finding a valid pretext for war, they fought primarily to gain that advantage over other states that de Vattel found most objectionable. As de Vattel's near contemporary Karl von Clausewitz later observed, they used warfare as an instrument of statecraft.

However much they ignored *jus ad bellum*, however, the kings and queens of Europe did adhere much more to *jus in bello*. In general, 18th-century rulers waged war more humanely than had their predecessors. Whether they did so out of moral compunction or expediency is another question. The disappearance of religion as a motive for conflict made it harder for opposing sides to demonize one another. Pragmatism probably guided the policy of giving quarter and treating prisoners humanely. Treating captured soldiers well encouraged the enemy to treat one's own soldiers with the same regard. Abuse of prisoners, rape, pillage, and plunder of civilians perpetrated by one side would invite reciprocal treatment by the other. The resultant loss of life and destruction of property served no one's interests. Armies did sometimes destroy livestock and even villages, but they usually did so to induce an opponent to fight or to deny an invading army supplies. Pragmatism certainly played a role in mitigating the worst effects of war, but so did an emerging sense of how civilized nations ought to behave, at least toward one another. With some

An Era of Limited War

notable exceptions, wars (or at least those between Western nations) would continue to be fought by rules until World War II swept away most of these restraints.

The Experience of War

Military historians too often neglect the human element of war. Technical descriptions of weapons, strategy, tactics, and battles often reduce the lives and deaths of countless human beings to mere statistics. Discussion of warfare during the ancien régime would therefore be incomplete without some consideration of the ordinary men (and in some cases women) who filled the ranks of European armies. What did these soldiers think and feel about their experiences? Some officers have left accounts of their endeavors, but the mass of illiterate peasant soldiers remained silent. They wrote no accounts of their own, and their social betters either ignored them or spoke of them as rabble to be developed into fighting automatons through training and harsh discipline.

Enough evidence does exist, however, to allow for some tentative conclusions about 18th-century military life. Warfare was, of course, brutal. A lead ball fired at close range from a low-velocity weapon usually stayed in the body it hit, causing serious damage and promoting infection. Wounds to the chest or abdomen were usually fatal. Arms and legs hit by musket or cannonballs often had to be amputated. Although Louis XIV established *l'Hôpital des Invalides* (literally, "hospital for invalids") as a home for aged, ill, and injured soldiers in 1670, most states made little or no provision for soldiers maimed by war and/or too old to continue serving in the army. In addition to suffering wounds in battle, soldiers endured diseases such as dysentery, which until World War I killed more men than bullets, shells, and bayonets combined.

Fortunately, battles were few and far between. A rank-and-file soldier spent most of his 20 years of service living in barracks, engaging in drills, and doing chores. The state issued him clothing, provided him with adequate food, put a roof over his head, paid him a meager salary, and even offered him advancement. Most of his civilian counterparts could not take these necessities of life for granted. Hunger and malnutrition were common in the ancien régime, and famine still occurred, though less frequently than it had in medieval Europe. Since monarchs recruited the rank and file from the lowest tier of society, ordinary soldiers left behind a civilian world that afforded them few opportunities. Ordinary people in the 18th century lived lives circumscribed by the accident of birth. This limitation probably kept their expectations very limited. A person cannot regret making choices he never had or forgoing opportunities that never existed. Barracks life was probably no worse than what soldiers experienced in their home villages and might have been somewhat better. On the other hand, the need to press men into the ranks, the iron discipline employed to keep them in line, and the high desertion rates in all European armies, despite severe penalties for running away, suggest that a significant number of ordinary soldiers desperately wanted to escape military service.

A rare eyewitness account of life in a dynastic army has survived. In September 1806, 23-year-old Nadezhda Durova disguised herself as a boy, left her husband and child, and joined the Russian army. Translated and published in English as *The Cavalry Maiden*, Durova's journal contains invaluable information on military life in the Russian army, which for its peasant soldiers had changed little if at all over the previous century.[51] While most accounts by male officers of the 18th and early 19th centuries chronicle their activities on campaign, Durova reveals what she thought and felt about her experiences. Anyone reading this book for elaborate descriptions of battle will be disappointed. Durova spent most of her time on campaign marching, setting up and breaking camp, and foraging for food and fodder. Always tired, frequently wet and cold, and often hungry, she faced French bullets far less often than she struggled with exhaustion and want. Her description of one retreat illustrates the suffering soldiers endured:

> I was dropping from lack of sleep and fatigue. My clothing was soaked. For two days I had neither slept nor eaten, I had been constantly on the march, and, even when we stopped, I was on horseback with only my uniform to wear, exposed without protection to the cold, wind and rain.[52]

Durova insisted that she experienced a certain exhilaration from battle and felt no fear, though she may have been expressing what was expected of an aristocratic cavalry officer rather than what she actually felt. She did distinguish between officers, who chose to serve, and peasant conscripts, who were compelled to fight:

> I have already seen a great many killed and severely wounded. It is pitiful to watch the latter crawling over the so-called field of honor. What can mitigate the horror of a position like that of a common soldier? A recruit? For an educated man it is a completely different matter: the lofty feeling of honor, heroism, devotion to the emperor, and sacred duty to his native land compel him to face death fearlessly, endure suffering courageously, and part with life calmly.[53]

Whether officers really did face suffering and death with such stoic equanimity is debatable, but Durova's description of what common soldiers endured rings true. Even she, however, had to speculate about what these illiterate men really felt. Nonetheless, her account has a certain timeless quality to it. The particulars of pain, suffering, and death might have changed as war developed over the succeeding centuries, but the experience of it would not.

CHAPTER THREE

The Era of Revolutionary Wars: North America

Historians have long divided time into meaningful epochs based on significant events. Useful though this academic convention may be, it creates the misleading impression that people living at the time of those events actually understood themselves to be on the cusp of a new era. Beginning in the mid-20th century, social and cultural historians fundamentally altered the way the profession thinks about the past by demonstrating that beneath the surface of turbulent change lie currents of continuity, flowing across the boundaries of seemingly different historical periods. This realization serves as a reminder that the divisions of time into epochs can be done only in retrospect and even then has serious limitations.

The period 1776 to 1815 did witness significant political change in Europe and North America, but that change did not alter the way the vast majority of people lived their lives day to day. If a person baked bread under Louis XVI, his son baked it under Napoleon, and his grandson baked it under Louis XVIII. An American merchant or farmer who took up arms against George III fought so that he and his children would be allowed to conduct their affairs without interference from London, as his father had been allowed to do because of the British policy of salutary neglect. Both the American and French Revolutions did, however, create conditions that over time would change profoundly how the grandchildren and great-grandchildren of the baker, the merchant, and the farmer would live. They could not, however, have foreseen such momentous change nor understood how their actions contributed to it.

This same combination of continuity and change characterized warfare in the age of revolutions. The basic organization and equipment of armies remained much as they had been in the age of limited war. The smooth-bore musket tipped with a socket bayonet was still the standard infantry weapon, although iron ramrods, which were less likely to break, replaced wooden ones. Lighter gun carriages and cast barrels made artillery more mobile and somewhat more powerful, but these refinements produced no major change in tactics. The standard battle formation still consisted of infantry supported by artillery interspersed along a line with cavalry on both wings. Battalions lined up in three ranks, the optimal depth given the speed of reloading, and advanced to within 50 paces before firing. Cavalry still sought to sweep around an exposed flank and to mop up broken infantry formations. If the Duke of Marlborough, Marshal Saxe, or Frederick the Great had appeared on a battlefield of the Napoleonic Wars, he would have felt at home, although the increased size of armies and the ferocity with which they pursued a retreating enemy might have surprised him.

What did change, at least in some armies, was the reason for which states went to war and why individual soldiers fought. Balance of power and territorial expansion still mattered, but the American and French Revolutions reintroduced ideology into warfare. Instead of the religious fervor of the 16th century, a new, far more virulent faith emerged to motivate soldiers: nationalism. This new "religion" would take half a century to develop, but it was born in the struggles of 1776 and 1789. It began with the idea that ordinary people, or at least men of property, could rule themselves. Along with that idea, however, grew the popular notion that the country for which one fought and died was superior to all others. Inculcated by free, compulsory public education and combined with Social Darwinism and "scientific racism," nationalism would be a principal cause of most wars within Europe during the 19th century and the justification for building European empires in Asia and Africa. Such thinking would eventually lead Europe to the gates of the Nazi death camp at Auschwitz. Along with rapid technological change brought about by the Industrial Revolution, the reintroduction of ideology began a process by which warfare became increasingly total, a process that reached its horrific climax in mushroom clouds over the Japanese cities of Hiroshima and Nagasaki. No one at the time, however, comprehended the implications of the powerful forces unleashed by the revolutions of the

18th century. The wars of this era must, therefore, be examined within the context of their own times but also situated within the evolution of modern warfare.

The American Revolution

Myths and Reality

The first war of the age of revolutions occurred not in Europe but in North America. In July 1776 the 13 British colonies along the Atlantic seaboard declared their independence from Great Britain and then fought a protracted war over the next seven years to secure it. Much of the war consisted of a cat-and-mouse game in which British armies pursued American forces over an area the size of Western Europe. The British could occupy cities so long as they garrisoned them, but found it impossible to hold the surrounding countryside. They inflicted defeats on the fledgling Continental army but were never able to destroy it. French intervention proved crucial to the colonists' victory, but ultimately the mother country recognized that it could not subdue the rebels at anything close to an acceptable cost in blood and treasure. At the end of the day, the wisest policy seemed a negotiated settlement.

Like most revolutionary conflicts, the American War of Independence has been tightly scripted into the national mythology of the country it created. This mythology not only romanticizes the cause for which the colonists fought but also warps perceptions of how the war was actually conducted. Popular portrayals feature colonial Minutemen using guerrilla warfare learned from Indians to defeat British regulars incapable of adapting their rigid tactics to the American wilderness. Henry Wadsworth Longfellow's famous 1860 poem, "Paul Revere's Ride," epitomizes this view:

> You know the rest. In the books you have read,
> How the British Regulars fired and fled,—
> How the farmers gave them ball for ball,
> From behind each fence and farmyard-wall,
> Chasing the red-coats down the lane,
> Then crossing the fields to emerge again
> Under the trees at the turn of the road,
> And only pausing to fire and load.[1]

More recently the feature film *The Patriot* (2000) extolled the superiority of American guerrilla tactics against British regulars. Longfellow was describing only the British return from Concord, during which the colonists did employ ambush tactics, and *The Patriot* dealt with irregular warfare in the Carolinas. The depictions in these works, however, reflect generalized perceptions of the war as a whole.

Any discussion of the American Revolution thus ought to begin by demythologizing it. To begin with, the conflict was not the popular rising it has often been portrayed as. Following a long period of salutary neglect, London increased taxation, in part to pay for the French and Indian War it had just fought on the colonists' behalf. The resultant cry of "no taxation without representation" hid an underlying difference of opinion about what representation actually meant. The British held to their notion of virtual representation, according to which all members of parliament represented the empire as a whole. While Boston had no representative of its own in Westminster, neither did Manchester, Birmingham, or a host of other British towns. Fewer than one Englishman in 20 could vote. The colonists preferred a more direct form of representation, electing representatives to colonial assemblies, although only free white men with property could vote, and perhaps 20 percent of the entire population consisted of African American slaves with no rights at all.

While many American colonists no doubt opposed taxation, not all of those who did wished to sever ties with Britain. The best estimate based on limited data suggests that 19.8 percent (roughly one person in five) of a free white population of around 2.5 million in 1783 remained loyal to the British crown.[2] The remainder of the population varied considerably in their attitudes toward the war. Estimates of those who supported the revolution range from 40 percent to just over 50 percent of the free population.[3] The level of support among this group no doubt varied with time and circumstances, and that left a full 30 percent of the free population hedging their bet, trimming their sails to the prevailing wind, hoping to come out on the right side no matter who won. The presence of so many fence-sitters, however, meant that both sides sought to gain and retain popular support. Small wonder that John Adams would later write: "The Revolution was in the hearts and minds of the people."[4]

That popular support mattered in this struggle for independence does not mean that the American Revolution was a guerrilla insurgency. Neither, however, was it a traditional 18th-century conflict. It was a hybrid war involving regular armies, citizen militias, and irregular forces. The most important engagements were conventional battles. Only three of these engagements were of great strategic significance. Bunker Hill (1775), although a tactical defeat, inflicted such high casualties on the British that it persuaded them the rebellion could not be easily or quickly crushed.

The defeat of General Burgoyne's army at Saratoga on the Hudson River (1777) weakened British military strength in North America and convinced France to enter the war on the side of the fledgling republic. The successful siege of Yorktown (1781) by American and French forces supported by a French fleet effectively ended the war. These conventional battles would not have been successful, however, without the unconventional operations that supported them.

The American Revolution was what today would be called an asymmetric conflict. The colonists fought a total war for their very existence; the British fought a limited engagement to retain one corner of a global empire. Once the French allied with the infant United States, Britain had to defend its interests in Europe, Canada, India, and the Caribbean, real estate at least as valuable as the 13 North American colonies. As often occurs in such an uneven contest, a time came when the side with the limited investment decided to cut its losses. Subduing the rebellion was not worth the cost in blood and treasure. The economic reality of the situation perhaps made it easier for the British to quit. Under classic mercantilism colonies served three purposes: they supplied the mother country with raw materials, they provided a protected market for its goods, and they offered an outlet for surplus population. In the short term at least, Britain retained all these advantages. Language and culture tied the two nations together. The United States needed British manufactured goods and was happy to trade resources to get them. The new country would continue to welcome immigrants from the British Isles. The only thing London lost in the short run was the cost of administering and defending its troublesome colonies.

Opposing Forces

A cursory examination of the disproportionate population, resources, and military power of Great Britain and its 13 American colonies suggests that the rebels stood little chance of winning. Great Britain (England, Scotland, and Wales) and Ireland had a combined population of approximately 11 million in 1781.[5] The colonies had a population of around 3 million, 20 percent of whom were slaves. Britain had already begun to industrialize as early as 1750, and its wealth and resources far exceeded those of the Americans. National wealth does not, however, always or easily translate into military strength. Great Britain is an island nation and a maritime power whose first line of defense from the 18th through the 20th centuries was its navy. It had colonies to defend around the world and enemies in Europe, especially France. The king could not levy taxes without consent of Parliament, which represented landed aristocrats and wealthy merchants eager to keep government expenditures low.

As a result of these limitations Britain had a formidable navy but, by European standards, a modest army. At the outbreak of the war the regular establishment numbered 48,647 of all ranks, but by the end of the conflict its strength had reached 110,000.[6] Only a fraction of these forces were available for service against the rebels. In 1775 the British had deployed only some 8,000 regular troops in all of North America.[7] By 1781 the number of British regulars in North America and the West Indies had risen to 56,000.[8] While most of these were employed against the rebels, French entry into the war in 1778 necessitated defense of Canada and colonies in the Caribbean. Throughout the war the British found themselves seriously short of troops to secure a vast territory, two of whose colonies (Pennsylvania and Virginia) had a greater combined area than all of Great Britain. To augment its forces the government in London resorted to three expedients: hiring German mercenaries (mostly Hessian), forming loyalist militias, and employing Native Americans to harry settlers on the frontier. All three measures would have disastrous consequences for the British cause.

The American forces raised to defend independence fell into three categories. At the outbreak of hostilities every colony had its own militia establishment. Raised for local defense and staffed by men from across the social spectrum, militia units were the forerunners of the modern National Guard. Their part-time citizen soldiers stood on the village greens at Lexington and Concord and fought the British at Bunker Hill. It soon became clear, however, that local forces with short-term enlistments and loyalty to their own states would not be sufficient to secure American independence. During the summer of 1775 the Continental Congress created a regular army under the command of George Washington. The Continental army reached its peak strength of 35,000 in 1778.[9] In addition to the militias and the regulars, the rebels deployed bands of partisans to support conventional operations.

The nature and quality of the British and American forces that fought in the Revolutionary War varied widely. Although the Continental army improved considerably as the war progressed, it was never the equal of the British in a classic battle. The genius of General Washington lay in refusing to be drawn into such an engagement. The British Regulars and German mercenaries were long-service, professional soldiers comprised of rank and file drawn from the lower orders of society, led by aristocratic officers, highly disciplined and often with extensive combat experience. Ironically, the Continental army adopted a similar recruitment pattern. Once it became clear that preserving independence would require a long war, the patriotic enthusiasm of 1775 waned. Men were still willing to serve for short periods in their local militias provided that they did not journey far from the borders of their state, but they did not flock to the colors of the regular army. The Continental Congress paid enlistment bounties just as the British did, and states drafted the least economically productive men into the regiments they raised. South Carolina, for example, required "all idle, lewd, disorderly men" with no fixed abode or regular employment, "all sturdy beggars and all strolling or straggling persons . . . to serve in one of the Continental Regiments of this state."[10] Recruits became skilled professional soldiers through a combination of drill and discipline similar to that employed in Europe.

Colonial militias fired the first shots in defense of independence and continued to play a vital role in the war. Popular culture has promulgated the image of a farmer at a moment's notice grabbing his musket from the rack over the mantelpiece, racing to the village green, and forming up with his fellows to face the advancing British. Colonial militias were indeed called "minutemen," but they were much more than an ad hoc gathering of armed locals. Beginning in 1774, as trouble with Britain loomed, the New England colonies expanded their militias. The other colonies followed suit. Commanded by competent officers and funded by their states, militia units trained to the point that they could be considered "a semiprofessional military institution and not just a loosely controlled rabble of local militiamen."[11] While these soldiers could not by themselves face a European army in a set-piece battle, they could fight very effectively from entrenched positions, in wooded or broken terrain, and as skirmishers. Many in the Continental Congress and the country at large hoped to fight the war solely with these troops alone, fearing a standing army would become an instrument of tyranny. The limitations of militias, however, persuaded them to create a regular force. Short-term enlistments and reluctance to journey far from their own states hampered the ability of militias to function as a national army. The Continental army did not, however, eliminate the militias, which remained a vital part of revolutionary forces throughout the war. Their numbers swelled to 44,000 at the height of the conflict.[12]

A host of irregular and specialized troops supported the Continental army and colonial militias. These forces ranged from light troops to partisan bands. Irregulars hindered British foraging parties, ambushed small units, and scouted on behalf of the Continental army. They intimidated loyalists, both real and suspected. The key to the American victory lay in the skill with which its commanders combined these three elements of colonial military power to fight the British at times and places of the rebels' choosing.

Strategies and Campaigns

The British and Americans each had a clear, simple objective. The colonists wished to preserve their independence, and the British sought to suppress what they understood as a rebellion against legally constituted authority. The British had the more difficult task. They had to reassert control throughout the colonies, while the colonists had to continue the struggle until the British tired of the effort. This situation helps explain why for the first two years of the war the American approach was reactive rather than proactive, as the colonials sought to check British moves to restore rule from London.

Although the British had an unambiguous objective, they never developed a clear, consistent strategy for achieving it. Throughout the war they clung to the dubious assumption that the majority of American colonists were loyal subjects cowed by radicals. Given half a chance these loyalists would come out in support of the Crown. They also assumed that there was a geographic center of gravity for both the revolt and the loyalist opposition to it. British commanders and the government in London, however, disagreed as to what these key areas were. Initially they focused on New England as the source of rebellion. They then focused on controlling the middle colonies and, later on Virginia, as essential to winning the war. From these assumptions developed a series of operations.

Initially, London adopted a policy of firmness combined with leniency. The British Parliament had responded to the Boston Tea Party with measures dubbed by the colonists "the Intolerable Acts," one of which closed Boston harbor. These acts led the New England colonies to expand their militias. In April 1775 Governor Thomas Gage ordered a detachment from the Boston garrison to seize militia arms at Concord in hopes that such decisive action would deter further rebel moves. The operation enraged the colonists, especially after British regulars killed Americans at Lexington and Concord. Minutemen came out in droves to harry the Redcoats back to Boston. The losses they inflicted on the British emboldened the colonists. Militias from Massachusetts and neighboring colonies converged on Boston. They fortified Breeds and Bunker Hills, threatening the city. Governor Thomas Gage offered a pardon for all but the top leaders of the rebellion, at the same time that he prepared to break the siege. Having little respect for militia soldiers, British forces stormed the positions. The Minutemen may not have been adept at volley firing in formation, but they

The Era of Revolutionary Wars: North America 65

Principle battles and campaigns of the American Revolution.

proved highly effective at firing aimed shots downhill from behind well-constructed earthworks. They repelled two assaults and only withdrew when they ran out of ammunition. The siege of Boston remained until the rebels captured Fort Ticonderoga in upstate New York and transported its cannon to Dorchester heights above the harbor. The British position in Boston became untenable.

The British gained two things from the siege of Boston: a greater respect for colonial militias and the realization that the rebellion would not be quickly or easily suppressed. The newly appointed commander of British forces in North America, General William Howe, and his brother Lord Richard Howe, commander of naval forces in American waters, wanted a negotiated settlement that would end the rebellion with minimal loss of life and no legacy of bitterness.[13] As a result they sought to draw American forces into a decisive battle while asserting control over territory in order to encourage loyalists to come out in support of the crown. They very nearly succeeded in August 1776, when Washington unwisely accepted battle on Long Island. The British outflanked him and might have destroyed his army were it not for Howe's reluctance to repeat the bloodshed of Bunker Hill and a well-executed American withdrawal across the East River.

Up until the battle of Long Island and the retreat into New Jersey, American strategy had been largely reactive, as the Continental army and state militias tried to counter British moves. Other than a failed effort to take Quebec in 1775, rebel forces remained largely on the defensive. By late 1776, however, a proactive American strategy began to emerge. This strategy hinged on the symbiotic relationship George Washington had developed with state militias. He used the Continentals as a mobile force, a national army operating across the colonies, leaving the militias responsible for local defense and calling upon them to augment regular strength for a campaign or battle.[14] Washington also understood the importance of preserving the Continental army at all costs. After the Long Island debacle, he accepted battle only under the most favorable circumstances. This approach frustrated Howe as he tried repeatedly to draw Washington into a classical engagement, in which his Redcoats and German mercenaries would have the advantage. Since the revolution had no geographic center of gravity, no city the rebels had to defend to preserve their cause, Howe and his successor, the general Charles Lord Cornwallis, could move from New York to Philadelphia to Charleston but could not force the colonials into a decisive battle. General Sir Henry Clinton argued this very point when he tried to dissuade Howe from taking Philadelphia in order to force Washington to fight. "The rebels are too wise to offer such a battle, and we are powerless to force," he argued. Clinton also understood the futility of trying to seize territory in hope of encouraging loyalist support. Howe's army would be "tied down, holding on to this territory," he warned, adding that "the territory could not be held by any quickly raised body of loyalists."[15] By forcing the British into a cat and mouse game, the rebels hoped to wear down their forces and their resolve until London gave up and/or the colonists received help from Britain's enemy, France.

The need to preserve his small army did not, however, prevent Washington and his generals from fighting at opportune times and places. Indeed, his genius as a commander lay in his ability to discern when decisive action would have the greatest effect as well as in his skill at handling the complex politics of the Continental Congress that had appointed him and the 13 state assemblies, which controlled the militias with whom he needed to work. The surprise attacks on Trenton and Princeton, New Jersey, illustrate this skill. With enlistments due to expire at the end of the year and the rank and file demoralized by the defeat at New York, Washington badly needed a victory. The December 26 attack on the Hessian garrison in Trenton, followed a week later by another on Princeton (January 3), provided just the morale boost the army needed.

As the Revolution entered its third year, some British commanders realized that occupying cities and trying to force a battle was not working. They decided on a different strategy. General John ("Gentleman Johnny") Burgoyne would advance down from Canada via Lake Champlain and the Hudson River, while another British force moved up the Hudson from New York to meet it at Albany. A third force, led by Colonel Barry St. Leger, would advance east from Fort Oswego on Lake Ontario, and a fourth loyalist force would advance from the southeast. If successful, this campaign would separate New England from the other colonies and leave the British in control of much of the fertile farmland that fed the rebel-held areas. The plan had a reasonable chance of success, but it required close cooperation between Howe in New York and Burgoyne in Canada. It also carried an enormous risk. Burgoyne would have to advance hundreds of miles from his base of supply at Quebec through wilderness country ideally suited to the kind of warfare at which rebel militias and partisans excelled.

Burgoyne's advance up Lake Champlain went well enough. He captured Fort Ticonderoga, "the Gibraltar of North America," in early July. Unfortunately, unbeknownst to him, General Howe had embarked for Philadelphia the same month and thus would not be advancing to meet him at Albany. Howe still hoped for decisive victory over the Continental army, which he almost achieved when political pressure forced Washington to fight outside Philadelphia. Washington suffered a serious defeat at Brandywine in September, but once again his troops disengaged before Howe could destroy or capture them. Meanwhile Burgoyne's advance slowed. Encumbered with too many heavy cannon and too much personal baggage of Burgoyne and his officers, the British and German troops had to cut roads through the woods to advance toward Albany. American rangers and militia dogged them every step of the way, cutting down trees to block roads, attacking foraging parties, and using sharpshooters to pick off soldiers on the line of march.

Thanks to reinforcements he had received along the way, when Burgoyne crossed to the west bank of the Hudson his original force of 7,863 men (including 250 loyalist militiamen and 400 Indians) had only been reduced to 7,700.[16] However, he had to detach 1,800 men to guard his boats, and illness or wounds had incapacitated another 1,400, leaving an effective fighting strength of just 4,500.[17] Even these troops were tired, hungry, and short of supplies. Quebec lay 250 miles to their rear, and an American army comprised of Continental regulars, militiamen, and rangers barred the way to Albany. By this time Burgoyne had received word that Howe had embarked for Pennsylvania and would not be coming to his aid. He also learned that St. Leger's force had been halted by Americans at Fort Stanwix and another supporting loyalist force defeated at Flockey.

When he finally encountered the American main body north of Albany, Burgoyne found that the Continentals, led by General Horatio Gates, were holding fortified positions on high ground. Their line stretched from the Hudson River west to heavily forested hills. Burgoyne could either retreat or try to break through to Albany. He chose the latter option. On September 19 he attacked a gap on the far left of the American line. General Benedict Arnold, who would later betray the rebel cause, and Colonel Daniel Morgan with his elite rifle corps, forestalled the British attack at Freeman's farm. The day ended with the British in possession of the farm but no closer to a breakthrough. For the next two and a half weeks each side fortified its positions. Burgoyne could not, however, remain on the defensive. Gates's position improved by the day as reinforcements continued to arrive, while shortage of food and supplies as well as desertion plagued the British. On October 7 Burgoyne again tried to break through on the American left. Gates had, however, extended his line to fill the gap that had been there on September 19. The Americans drove back the British and German regulars, along with their loyalist allies, overran Burgoyne's line, and forced him to retreat toward Saratoga. Ten days later, with his camp just north of the town surrounded, Burgoyne surrendered.

Gates claimed credit for the victory. A cautious, conventional commander, he did well in choosing Bemis Heights as a defensive position. Left to his own devices, however, he would have remained behind his earthworks. By persuading him to let the patriot left wing advance to engage the British at Freeman's farm, his subordinates checked a flank attack that might otherwise have broken through a gap Gates had failed to fortify. Hard fighting by Arnold and Morgan saved the day. The duo also led the fight at Bemis Heights 12 days later, even though Arnold had been relieved of command, while Gates remained at his headquarters. General Philip Schuyler, whom the Continental Congress had replaced with Gates for largely political reasons shortly before battle, deserves much credit for impeding the British advance and for his tireless efforts to keep the army supplied even after he had been removed from command. Gates would, however, share none of the credit. This unwillingness to acknowledge the contributions of others angered his officers, and his disinclination to lead from the front made him less than popular with the troops. His limitations as a battlefield commander would become clear at Camden, South Carolina, three years later when he faced a British army without the support of skilled subordinates.

Few battles have truly been decisive, but Saratoga should be numbered among them. At a single stroke American forces had reduced British strength in North America by as much as 20 percent. Burgoyne surrendered 5,791 officers and men at Saratoga, another 1,800 had been captured in battles leading up to that surrender, and hundreds more lay in shallow graves along the route from Canada.[18] In addition to seriously depleting British forces and boosting rebel morale, the victory at Saratoga encouraged France to recognize the infant United States and enter the war against Britain in 1778 and support its ally with money, arms, and troops. The French alliance had several important ramifications. The British would have to defend their possessions in the Caribbean and India against French encroachment, they would need to keep more of their navy in home waters and so could not take naval supremacy in American waters for granted, and they faced the prospect of French troops operating in cooperation with the Continental army

The patriots had further reasons to be optimistic than the victory at Saratoga and the French alliance. Washington's army spent the infamous winter at Valley Forge, but the general put the time to good use. Friedrich Wilhelm von Steuben, a Prussian officer who had immigrated to America and was appointed a major general, developed a manual of arms for the Continental army and trained its soldiers. General Henry Knox reorganized and expanded the artillery. On June 28, 1778, that revitalized army of 12,600 pursued a British force of about the same number under the command of General Clinton, who had replaced Howe in command of British troops in North America.[19] Washington ordered General Charles Lee to attack Clinton's rear guard at Monmouth, New Jersey. The attack faltered due to Lee's incompetent handling of troops, but Washington arrived to recoup the situation, relieving Lee and taking personal command. The Continentals reformed and repelled a British assault. At the end of the day, the British continued their march toward New York, leaving the Americans in possession of the field.

The Battle of Monmouth was a tactical draw with little military strategic significance, but like Trenton, it gave the Americans renewed confidence in the fighting quality of their soldiers. Washington claimed it as a victory because his troops held the field. Clinton insisted that he had defeated an attack on his rear guard. The British suffered 358 killed or wounded, the Americans 356.[20] The real significance of Monmouth, however, lay in what it revealed about the Continental army. No longer avoiding battle, Washington had actually sought an engagement. His troops had gone muzzle to muzzle with British regulars. When their initial attack failed they retreated in good order, formed a new defensive line, and drove the enemy back. The raw recruits of 1776 had become battle-hardened veterans with good drill and fire discipline.

After Clinton reached New York, the British shifted their strategy again. While small engagements and sporadic fighting continued, Monmouth was the last major battle in the north. Having failed to achieve a decisive result in New England or the middle colonies, the British focused on the south. They planned to take Charleston and use it as a base to clear the backcountry of the Carolinas and Georgia of patriot resistance and then expand out of this secured area to reassert control of the other colonies. Once again, British politicians and military commanders presumed the presence of a large body of loyalists who would rise in support of their king once the Redcoats arrived.

The southern strategy began well. In May 1780 Clinton captured Charleston along with its garrison of just over 3,300. He then returned to New York to deal with Washington and French troops, which had landed in Rhode Island in July under command of the Marquis de Rochambeau. Clinton left Charles Lord Cornwallis in charge of operations in the southern theater. In August Cornwallis faced Gates at Camden, South Carolina. With just over a third as many troops (2,100 to 3,700), Cornwallis routed the American forces. Without officers like Morgan or Arnold to provide better counsel, Gates engaged in a set-piece battle in which superior British training and discipline, to say nothing of far better generalship, prevailed.

Camden, however, was the last significant British victory of the war. Beginning in October 1780 the British southern strategy began to unravel. The patriots defeated loyalist forces at King's Mountain on October 7, and a week later Washington replaced Gates with the far more competent Nathanael Greene as commander of American forces in the southern theater. Cornwallis could control Charleston, but the hinterland was slipping away from him. Reasoning that he could not control the South Carolina backcountry without subduing North Carolina, he sent 1,100 men under Banastre Tarleton north. Daniel Morgan met them at Cowpens on January 17, 1781, and destroyed the British force. Just over a month later Greene engaged Cornwallis at Guilford Courthouse, retreating after severely weakening the British force. Greene then harassed Cornwallis to such an extent that he had to fall back to the coast, where he could be supported by the British fleet. Unfortunately for him, the French admiral François de Grasse had gained control of Chesapeake Bay. Seeing a chance to trap Cornwallis, Washington and Rochambeau moved their forces south in August and laid siege to the British camp at Yorktown. With French men-o-war controlling the sea and the Franco-American force tightening the noose, Cornwallis surrendered on October 19. The war dragged on for another 18 months, but after Yorktown its outcome was certain.

Unconventional Warfare

While popular culture often views the entire revolution as a guerrilla war, academic histories of the conflict sometimes go to the other extreme, playing down the role of unconventional operations. Even those who recognize the importance of irregular forces often make a sharp if unnatural distinction between conventional and unconventional warfare during the struggle for independence. The otherwise excellent two-volume work by Robert Doughty, Ira Gruber, and others illustrates this point. The authors treat Saratoga as a conventional interlude and describe Yorktown as a "conventional end to an unconventional war."[21] Only by focusing very narrowly on the fighting at Freeman's farm and Beamis Heights can Saratoga be considered a conventional campaign. Given the role played by Morgan's Rifles and other such units, though, even that conclusion could be challenged. Washington and Rochambeau did defeat Cornwallis with a conventional siege at Yorktown, but only after months of warfare that skillfully blended conventional and unconventional operations. The American Revolution was thus, from beginning to end, a hybrid war.

Recognizing that victory in the war stemmed from an effective blend of regular and irregular operations does not, however, mean deeming all unconventional activity as strategically necessary. A great deal of opportunism, revenge, criminality, and gratuitous violence occurred throughout the war. Much of the needless slaughter and mayhem came from what one historian has called the "civil war within the war against the British."[22] This internecine conflict pitted those supporting independence (dubbed "patriots" or "Whigs") against those favoring continued British rule ("loyalists" or "Tories"). Since both sides made use of militias, these forces clashed with one another. In such engagements they often gave little quarter, and their rage frequently led to attacks on civilians. Such violence did little to bring the war to a swift conclusion but contributed much to its legacy of bitterness. The only strategic importance of fratricide lay in the fact that it discouraged loyalists from coming out in support of the British crown.

The other area of conflict marginal to the war itself occurred on the colonial frontiers. In the Ohio valley, the old southwest, and upstate New York the British incited Native American tribes to attack colonial settlements. Other than occasionally diverting Continental troops, these raids had no positive effect on the British campaign. They did, however, persuade many frontier people to support the Revolution. Rangers and militiamen continued the American tradition of extirpative war: they burned villages; destroyed crops; and murdered men, women and children, collecting their scalps for bounties.[23] British employment of Indian raiders encouraged many on the frontier to support the Revolution no matter what political views they might have held. Not surprisingly, some of the worst violence occurred when loyalist militias combined with loyal Indians to fight patriot frontiersmen. The Seneca and loyalists devastated settlements in Western New York from 1778 to 1781, and American rangers, militia, and Continental troops responded in kind. This activity contributed little to the strategy of either side, but it laid waste to an entire region of the country.[24]

While much irregular warfare fell outside strategic necessity, considerable unconventional activity contributed to rational plans, particularly those of the rebels. Militia units proved particularly adept at attacking foraging parties and preventing loyalists from supplying them. Indeed, the dependence on local supplies made the British vulnerable to guerrilla attacks.[25] Following his surprise victories over the British at Trenton and Princeton, Washington pursued a deliberate strategy of irregular warfare. Unwilling to risk fledgling Continental soldiers in open battle against Redcoats and German mercenaries, he used them as light troops supported by New Jersey, Pennsylvania, and New York militias to attack outposts, foraging parties, and supply depots.[26] The Americans developed clever ruses to ambush the foragers. They would disguise soldiers as farmers and have them drive cattle near the enemy line to draw the British into a carefully laid ambush.[27] The British soon found they could sally forth only with larger detachments and, even then, with an uncertain outcome.

In addition to depriving British garrisons of desperately needed supplies, unconventional operations also supported conventional forces in the field. The Saratoga campaign saw effective use of irregulars to harass Burgoyne's forces. Far from his base of support in Canada, Gentleman

Johnny tried to live off the countryside as he advanced from Fort Ticonderoga toward Albany. General Philip Schuyler dogged him every step of the way. He deprived British foraging parties of food by burning crops and moving cattle into swamps and other safe areas. The Massachusetts militia felled trees and dug trenches to divert streams and swamp water into Burgoyne's path.[28] Sharpshooters hidden in the woods sniped at soldiers as they marched. Even large foraging expeditions were not safe from attack, as a force of German mercenaries and loyalists discovered in August when they marched to Bennington, Vermont, to procure horses and supplies. Vermont militia cut off and surrounded the force, killing or capturing 900 men and so eliminating one-sixth of Burgoyne's army at a single stroke.[29]

Unconventional war was not confined to organized units operating under a definite chain of command. British, German, and loyalist foraging parties found that in addition to facing attack by partisans, they encountered spontaneous resistance at every American farmstead they tried to raid. More than a century of fighting Indians and French irregulars had taught settlers to look after themselves. Every household had at least one musket or rifle, and most if not all of its family members knew how to use it. Houses were designed with at least some thought to their defensibility. Soldiers used to marching into undefended villages in Europe and taking what they wanted found themselves in for a rude awakening when they tried the same tactic in North America.[30] Since Burgoyne employed undisciplined loyalist militias and Indian allies for his foraging and raiding policies, what came to be known as the "Wilderness War" of 1777 was particularly vicious. Neither side gave or expected much quarter. Despite Burgoyne's express instructions to spare women and children, his Iroquois allies often ignored that caveat, knowing they would be paid for every scalp and not caring much from whom it came.[31] Use of Native American and Canadian loyalist militias against American settlers content to be left alone inflamed passions and turned many a neutral and even a lukewarm loyalist into an ardent revolutionary, at least for the duration of this one campaign.

Unconventional warfare did not end when the conventional Battle of Saratoga began. Irregular forces played a crucial role in the American victory. Foremost among these troops was an elite corps of approximately 500 under the command of Colonel Daniel Morgan. While all European armies of the day maintained regiments of sharpshooters, "Morgan's Rifles" were a breed apart. Handpicked woodsmen from the frontiers of Pennsylvania, New Jersey, and Virginia, each man carried a Kentucky long rifle, a tomahawk, and a scalping knife. He wore a hunting shirt made of linen or wool, buckskin leggings or breeches, moccasins, and a soft hat.[32] The Kentucky long rifle (actually invented in Pennsylvania) was a single-shot muzzle loader with a rifled barrel and a flintlock firing mechanism. It had an effective range of 200–250 yards, which far exceeded the range of the Brown Bess musket (80–100 yards), standard issue in both conventional armies, and was superior to European rifles of the time. At Freeman's farm, Morgan's men took cover in buildings and woods and even climbed trees. Their camouflaged clothing and the range of their guns made them hard to spot and even harder to hit. The riflemen not only inflicted heavy casualties on the British; they concentrated on officers, with great effect. Morgan's success at Freeman's farm and a few weeks later at Bemis Heights depended heavily on close cooperation between his forces and Major Henry Dearborn's New Hampshire light infantry. Despite its greater range and accuracy, the long rifle was slower to load than the musket and had no bayonet. Riflemen thus needed the protection of conventional troops in open battle. "My riflemen would have been of little service if they had not always had line of Musquet and Bayonette men to support us [sic]," Morgan later observed. "It is that gives them confidence. They know, if the enemy charges them they have a place to retreat to and are not beat clear off."[33]

Ironically, Morgan's Rifles were disbanded the following year. In 1775 Washington and the Continental Congress had hoped to make riflemen the core of the Continental army. This idea soon encountered a host of problems. Gunsmiths produced long rifles one at a time as hunting weapons without a bayonet mount. Each rifleman had to prepare his own ammunition instead of drawing from standard issue cartridges, as men armed with muskets could do. Rifles fouled more easily and so required finer grain powder. The riflemen themselves did not respond well to the discipline necessary to fight in a linear formation. They did not fit well into the European-style army von Steuben was training to use the musket and bayonet in linear tactics. Riflemen continued to play a vital role in the war, but not as regular units in the Continental army.[34]

While partisans played an important role in every theater of the war, they achieved their greatest notoriety in Georgia and the Carolinas during 1780 and 1781. Clinton's capture of Charleston and Cornwallis's subsequent victory at Camden unleashed a vicious civil war between loyalist and patriot militias and partisan groups. The British began the struggle by unleashing a loyalist reign of terror in the South Carolina backcountry. Far from intimidating the rebels and cowing the neutrals, brutal tactics strengthened the resolve of the already committed and drove the fence-sitters into the patriot camp. Two of the wars' three greatest partisan leaders took up arms at least in part because of British atrocities. Thomas Sumpter had retired from the Continental army in 1778, but rejoined the cause when British forces pillaged and burned his house in 1780, and Andrew Pickens (a Presbyterian elder) took great offense at the burning of Presbyterian churches by loyalists who considered them sources of sedition.[35] The third great leader, Francis Marion, the famous "Swamp Fox," had been in uniform since 1776. Guerrilla bands sometimes numbering several hundred partisans roamed the backcountry, attacking British outposts, ambushing foraging parties, and intimidating loyalists. Armed with rifles or muskets and equipped with horses, the partisans became adept at hit-and-run tactics, striking at vulnerable targets and then disappearing into swamp or forest when pursued by a superior enemy force.

British efforts to counter American partisans further alienated the general population. The British developed irregular forces of their own: Simcoe's Rangers, Hessian *Jägers*, and the Tory Legion (a mixed force of cavalry and infantry) commanded by Lieutenant Colonel Banastre Tarleton. Not surprisingly, such units committed excesses. The most infamous event occurred shortly after the fall of Charleston, when 230 members of the Legion (130 cavalry, 100 mounted infantry) supported by 40 regular dragoons encountered a force of 350–400 Continental soldiers under the command of Colonel Abraham Buford near the town of Waxhaws just south of the Virginia–North Carolina border.[36] The British defeated the Americans handily, but as the Continentals tried to surrender, the loyalist forces continued to kill them. Despite British efforts to deny it, the high number of American casualties (113 killed, 150 wounded) for the loss of only 5 loyalists killed and 14 wounded suggests that a deliberate massacre had occurred.[37] Whether or not Tarleton ordered the killing or simply failed to prevent it (intentionally or not), he earned himself the nickname "Bloody Tarleton," and the Waxhaws massacre inspired a new slogan for revolutionary propagandists. As patriot militiamen closed in on the loyalist unit they had trapped at King's Mountain in October 1780, they shouted "Tarleton's Quarter" to let their enemy know that they did not intend to take prisoners.

Waxhaws had no real military significance but enormous social and psychological importance. Writing in 1785, David Ramsay concluded: "This barbarous massacre gave a more sanguinary turn to the war. Tarleton's quarters became proverbial, and in the subsequent battles a spirit of revenge gave a keener edge to military resentments."[38] Prior to the massacre, the people of Waxhaws had been sympathetic to the revolutionary cause but unenthusiastic about fighting for it.[39] The massacre by itself may not have been enough to push very many of them off the fence, but continued British excesses encouraged them to join the patriot cause. In early June Lord Rawdon, commander of Cornwallis's advance guard, negotiated an agreement with the local inhabitants that would have kept them neutral and even supplying the British with food, but Cornwallis rejected the agreement, demanding that the settlers take up arms in support of the king, surrender their weapons and horses, or be executed.[40] Such intimidation, combined with loyalist attacks on their churches and property and the Waxhaws massacre, encouraged neutrals to support the revolution.

Both sides waged unconventional warfare throughout the conflict. Much of this fighting centered on foraging, and in certain areas it degenerated into a vicious civil war between patriots and loyalists. Even in conventional battles, however, irregular forces played an important role. The American Revolution was not, however, a modern insurgency. Unconventional operations alone could not have secured independence. "The salvation of this country does not depend upon little strokes," Nathanael Greene told Thomas Sumpter. "You may strike a hundred strokes and reap little benefit unless you have a good army to take advantage of your success."[41] Greene would prove to be the consummate practitioner of hybrid war, combining conventional and unconventional tactics.

The Nature of Battle

Among the scores of battles and hundreds of skirmishes fought during the American Revolution, none stands out as typical or even representative of combat in that conflict. One campaign does, however, represent the best example of the synergy achieved when a skilled commander employed partisan guerrillas, state militias, and Continental regulars. From early December 1780, when he assumed command of the southern army, through September 1781, General Nathanael Greene made optimal use of all three elements of patriot power. He did so while navigating the turbulent waters of southern colonial politics. Unlike Gates, Greene willingly took advice and shared the credit for success. This quality enabled him to form a very effective partnership with his subordinate, Colonel Morgan, a brilliant tactician and inspired leader of soldiers. The strategic acumen of Greene combined with the tactical skill of Morgan would regain the Carolinas and drive Cornwallis to his dénouement at Yorktown.[42]

Greene began with a clear understanding of the task before him. Washington had taught him that he must avoid at all costs the destruction of his army. The Continentals had improved significantly since 1776, but they still fared poorly in traditional battles with British regulars. The losses at Charleston and Camden had left Greene a small force of just over 2,300 with a core of 949 regulars from Delaware and Maryland.[43] These troops would be supplemented by units from Virginia and supported by local militias. Greene would use his small army as a mobile strike force, compelling Cornwallis to dissipate his strength in pursuit and accepting battle only on favorable terms. Rather than keep the militiamen with the army, Greene called them up just before a battle and so eliminated the logistical problem of supplying a larger force, which would in any event have slowed him down.[44] As he rebuilt the southern army, partisan units would continue to deny the British control of the country beyond Charleston and a few coastal towns.

The situation in the backcountry improved even before Greene had taken over from Gates. On October 7 a rebel flying column of 900 to 1,000 men surrounded Major Patrick Ferguson's loyalist force of 1,125 at King's Mountain just south of the North Carolina border.[45] Although he held the high ground, Ferguson had failed to fortify his position. Taking advantage of wooded slopes, which provided ample cover, the patriots overran the British camp. They killed 200 loyalists along with their commander and captured 700.[46] Patriots yelling "Tarleton's quarter" cut down some men as they tried to surrender. Defeat at King's Mountain, combined with raids by Sumpter and Marion, convinced Cornwallis that he needed to destroy Greene's army if he were to control the south. He believed he could hold South Carolina with small detachments while he took the bulk of his army north in pursuit of the illusive enemy and away from his own base of supply.

Greene devised a bold strategy to counter Cornwallis. He would divide his army in two, stationing the bulk of the regulars in a strong position on the Pee Dee River to deny the British easy access to loyalist support in the Carolina highlands and make it difficult for Cornwallis to attack him without leaving his outposts in western South Carolina vulnerable. Greene formed the remainder of his force into a flying column under the command of Morgan. As Greene explained, dividing troops

> makes the most of my inferior force, for it compels my adversary to divide his, and holds him in doubt as to his own line of conduct. He cannot leave Morgan behind him to come at me, or his posts at Ninety-six and Augusta [in western South Carolina] would be exposed. And he cannot chase Morgan far, or prosecute his views in Virginia, while I am her with the whole country before me. I am as near to Charleston as he is, and also as near to Hillsborough as I was at Charlotte; so that I am in no danger of being cut off from my reinforcements, while an uncertainty as to my designs has made it necessary to leave a large detachment of the enemy in Charleston.[47]

Cornwallis behaved as Greene had anticipated. He detached Tarleton and the Tory Legion to pursue Morgan and moved his own army north toward the patriot camp on the Pee Dee.

Tarleton caught up with Morgan at a cattle waystation known as Cowpens. Tarleton's force consisted of 400 British regular infantry, 550 troops of the Legion, 50 regular mounted dragoons, some artillerymen manning two light field guns, and various other rank and file, totaling almost 1,100 men.[48] Morgan had 280 Continental regulars from Delaware and Maryland; 200 former Continentals from Virginia; 80 Continental dragoons; and approximately 440 militiamen from the Carolinas, Georgia, and Virginia.[49] Because Tarleton was eager to destroy him, Morgan got to choose his ground and establish a strong defensive position. Cowpens was a field some 300 yards wide sloping gently downhill, with one rise 400 yards from a tree line at the top of the hill and another 150 yards further down. The field was well suited to a conventional 18th-century battle, but Morgan had no intention of giving Tarleton such an engagement, in which his regulars would probably have triumphed. Instead he devised an innovative plan that made effective use of his mixed force.

Perhaps no revolutionary commander understood the unique capabilities of partisans, militia, and Continental regulars better than Daniel Morgan. Few officers enjoyed the confidence and loyalty that he inspired in his soldiers. A backwoodsman himself, Morgan shared the experience and hardships of his men.[50] Before the battle he even inspired some militiamen to stay and fight even though their enlistments were up, appealing to their sense of gallantry and patriotism.[51] Much as he understood the militia, Morgan had no illusions about their limitations. He would not make the mistake Gates had at Camden, expecting militiamen to stand up to the disciplined volley fire of British regulars. He crafted a battle plan that made use of the unique qualities of each type of soldier in his army.

Morgan arrayed his troops in three lines, with Lieutenant-Colonel William Washington's Continental dragoons behind the formation. The third, main line consisted of the Continental infantry and the Virginia militiamen recently retired from the Continental army, positioned on the rise 400 yards downhill from the tree line and commanded by Lieutenant Colonel John Eager Howard. Morgan formed a second line of militiamen under the able command of Pickens on the second rise 150 yards in front of Howard. In front of Howard, Morgan stationed a skirmish line of approximately 120 handpicked riflemen.[52] The skirmishers were to fire a couple of rounds each and then join ranks with Pickens's militiamen, who would then fire a volley at the advancing British before filing off to the left and behind Howard's line. By this stratagem Morgan hoped to entice Tarleton into a precipitous attack on what he would presume to be fleeing militiamen and by so doing, draw him onto the line of regulars.

With a few glitches that the experienced battlefield commander quickly fixed, the plan worked brilliantly. Tarleton sent his men out of the woods early on the morning of the battle. He then ordered forward his dragoons to scatter the American skirmish line, only to have the patriot marksmen shoot 15 of them off their horses and send the rest reeling back. Tarleton then proceeded to form his men in a traditional European battle line: infantry in the center with a cavalry squadron on each flank. Seeing the Continental militia ranged before him, Tarleton may have envisioned another Camden within his grasp. He ordered his infantry to advance. The skirmishers fired off a couple of rounds and fell back to join Pickens. When the British regulars and Tory Legionnaires reached Pickens's militia line, the dour Scots American gave them a solid volley before filing off to the right. This maneuver did not go smoothly, and Tarleton ordered cavalry on his right flank to disrupt it. Recognizing the danger, Morgan ordered Washington's cavalry to counterattack and drive off the British dragoons. The militia thus affected their move to the rear and reformed on the right of the Continental line. Before they could reform, however, Tarleton tried to flank Howard's line on the right. To forestall this move, Howard ordered the units on that side to wheel right to face the advancing British. The troops misunderstood this as an order to fall back. Morgan and Howard assessed the situation and realized that such a retreat would put them in a stronger position to repel the flank attack. Seeing the withdrawal, however, the British broke formation and charged. Howard then ordered his men to turn about and fire point blank at the ragged British line, which broke under the volley. Morgan then executed a well-timed double envelopment, sending the reformed militia against the British right and Washington's cavalry against the left while the Continentals advanced in the center. Under this pressure, Tarleton's force collapsed. Unable to rally his dragoons for a counterattack, Tarleton fled the field, leaving his men to surrender.[53] For the loss of 12 killed and 60 wounded, the patriots destroyed Tarleton's force, killing 110 and capturing 700 along with 2 cannon, 35 wagons, 100 horses, and 800 muskets.[54]

Morgan had won a convincing victory and severely weakened the British force in the Carolinas, but Cowpens did not decide the southern campaign. Cornwallis might have recouped the situation if he had been able to catch and defeat Greene before Morgan's troops could reunite with the main American army. Cornwallis burned his own baggage so that his troops could move more rapidly. The two American commanders, however, eluded the British general, linking up on February 10 at a point from whence they conducted a skillful withdrawal into Virginia, taking advantage of river barriers that slowed Cornwallis's pursuit. In Virginia

Greene rested, regrouped, and resupplied his forces. Ill and worn out from campaigning, Morgan went home to recover. Realizing he would have to return to North Carolina to hearten patriots and prevent a rising of loyalists, Greene headed south on February 22, and Cornwallis moved to intercept him.[55] The two armies met at Guilford Courthouse on March 15. On the advice of Morgan, who wrote to him as he made his way home, Greene arrayed his 4,400 men in the same formation his subordinate had used at Cowpens. The terrain made this plan more difficult, and Greene stationed the lines too far apart to easily effect the maneuver Morgan had used. Nonetheless, he handled his army well enough to inflict serious casualties on the British, after which he prudently withdrew. Because he attacked with a much smaller force of 1,950 and held the field at the end of the day, Cornwallis technically won the battle. In doing so, however, he lost 93 killed and 413 wounded, 50 of whom died from their wounds, to Greene's 79 killed and 84 wounded.[56] Since January, Cornwallis's army had been reduced from approximately 3,300 to 1,400 effectives.[57] Guilford Courthouse had no strategic significance, and Greene's army remained intact. Meanwhile, the Carolina backcountry was slipping from the British grasp. Greene next began pushing British troops in South Carolina into coastal enclaves. Cornwallis arrived in Wilmington, North Carolina, on April 7 with the remnants of his army. From there he departed for the James River and his fateful encounter with Washington and Rochambeau at Yorktown.

Historians have noted that Greene never won a battle during his operations in the Carolinas. That fact does not diminish either the success of his campaign or his skill as a general. Greene made the most effective use of his force to achieve a strategic objective: securing the backcountry of Georgia and the Carolinas while wearing down Cornwallis. Like George Washington who had mentored him, he understood that he must at all costs keep his army from being destroyed. He therefore chose to fight only at times and places of his own choosing. Morgan did achieve an impressive victory at Cowpens, but its importance lay in the contribution it made to Greene's plan. That plan involved the effective use of partisan bands, state militias, and Continentals in waging a hybrid war of regular and irregular operations.

Attitudes toward War

The American Revolution was a hybrid war not only in how it was fought but also in how it was perceived. The British and the Americans had one foot in the 18th century and the other in the 19th. Conventional armies battled one another according to the rules of war observed in

Europe. They gave quarter to those who surrendered, paroled officers, and exchanged prisoners. Some commanders violated these rules, but their behavior was the exception rather than the rule. Prisoners died of malnutrition and disease in prison ships, but usually as a result of neglect and lack of resources rather than malice. In these ways the conflict conformed to the pattern established for limited wars in Europe.

In other ways, however, the American War of Independence was a harbinger of worse conflicts to come. The struggle between loyalist and patriot militias and irregulars did not conform to rules of "civilized" warfare. This conflict was in many ways a war between peoples, rather than a war between states. It stands at the beginning of a process of increasing totality in warfare in which ever more lethal means would be unleashed by ideologically motivated soldiers on a widening segment of the population. Patriot and loyalist militias and especially partisans sometimes refused to give quarter even when the enemy tried to surrender. They destroyed property and sometimes murdered women and children.

As the war progressed, the distinction between combatants and noncombatants became blurred even further. Cornwallis's insistence that the population of the Carolinas not only swear allegiance to the king but actually fight for him treated even neutral noncombatants as enemies. This unwillingness to recognize the neutrality of anyone was a very modern notion of war that would intensify over the next two centuries. Small wonder that the Revolution was, based on per capita casualty rates, the second deadliest war in American history.

The revolutionaries also justified their war on new grounds. Traditional just-war doctrine limits the right to declare war to legitimate authorities. In the 18th century such authority usually resided in established monarchies. Since Christian churches deemed that monarchs held their thrones by divine right, rebellion against kings was immoral as well as illegal. Whether the criterion of legitimate authority, clearly applicable for war between states, applied equally to revolution against such authority is debatable.[58] The revolutionaries built their argument for independence not upon Christian just-war doctrine, but upon Enlightenment concepts of natural law and the social contract theory of government the English had used to depose James II in 1688. As the Declaration of Independence asserted, they were exercising their natural right to abolish a government that threatened their inalienable right to "life, liberty, and the pursuit of happiness."

The elites of colonial society may have embraced these sentiments, but ordinary folk probably had a more basic agenda. They simply wished to be left alone to live their lives with minimal interference from either side. Failure to recognize this desire may have been the biggest mistake the

British made. Many who sympathized with the revolutionary cause but had little desire to fight for it, as well as those who were neutral and perhaps even inclined to be loyalist, became patriots. As historian Charles Royster insightfully concluded, "Americans' wish to be left alone made most of the continent hostile to the British, even when that hostility did not move people to bear arms."[59]

The Experience of War

The conditions of camp life, marching, and battle generally remained as they had been throughout the 18th century, although the different types of units experienced them differently. Both armies faced serious difficulties feeding their soldiers. Neither patriot nor loyalist farmers parted with their produce or livestock without compensation. Requisitioning, commonly attempted by the British, met with armed resistance and pushed many neutrals off the fence and onto the patriot side. Until a massive infusion of French aid, the Continental Congress proved rather stingy about providing money for the army. Continental soldiers thus experienced shortages of shoes and clothing as well as food.

Militiamen probably suffered fewer privations than regular soldiers. They served part time, returning home for plowing and harvesting. They preferred to serve only in their home state, although they might be induced to fight in an adjacent one. They resisted being subject to army discipline and so escaped the lash and the other punishments common in 18th-century armies. Unlike the Continental regulars, militiamen represented a broader cross-section of colonial society. They probably fought out of conviction rather than for financial gain.

Some accounts by members of the Continental army have survived. Jeremiah Greenman, a common soldier, kept a diary from 1775 to 1783. Anyone expecting to find in it vivid accounts of battle, reflections on the hardships of camp life, or diatribes on the cause of liberty will be sorely disappointed. Greenman provides a matter-of-fact record of army life, which consisted primarily of training, marches, and the countless mundane activities of camp. His diary is a sober reminder that no matter what lofty cause motivated political leaders to go to war, ordinary soldiers had to focus on the daily struggle to stay alive.[60] This does not mean that they did not fight for a cause, just that they did not write about it. Many rank-and-file soldiers in the Continental army, like their British counterparts, could not read or write, so what they thought and felt will never be known with certainty.

CHAPTER FOUR

French Revolution and Napoleonic Wars

Few eras of European history have been more politically turbulent than the period from 1789 to 1815. What began as an effort to reform a bankrupt French government rapidly developed into a violent revolution whose leaders executed the king and queen in 1793 and proclaimed a republic. Terrified by the threat radical democracy posed to the established order, the crowned heads of Europe combined to attack France. Supported by mass conscription of citizens motivated to defend their newfound freedom and benefiting from an officer corps open to talent, the French army drove the invaders back. France's defensive struggle, however, soon turned into conquest, particularly after an obscure Corsican officer named Napoleon Bonaparte became dictator (1799) and later emperor (1804).

Within the broad sweep of military history the wars of the French Revolution and Napoleon (usually referred to as the Napoleonic Wars) may be understood within a series of analytical frameworks. As the last of the 18th-century conflicts, they represent the culmination of tactical evolution toward maximizing effective use of troops armed with bayonet-tipped smoothbore muskets. In the history of warfare as a whole, the Napoleonic Wars mark the reintroduction of ideology into European warfare, with a concomitant increase in the lethality of conflicts. From 1789 to 1945 virulent nationalism would make wars increasingly total, until they reached their penultimate escalation in the gas chambers of Auschwitz and the mushroom clouds over Hiroshima and Nagasaki. The Napoleonic Wars also conformed to the balance of political power paradigm, which had operated since the 16th century: European nations sought to maintain a balance of power, preventing any one from dominating the Continent. Members of the coalitions formed to defeat Napoleon feared French military hegemony as much as they did French revolutionary ideology. Finally, the Napoleonic Wars marked the end of what historians have dubbed the "second hundred years' war" between France and Britain. For the ordinary soldiers who fought them, they were the bloody and miserable affairs they had always been, though many soldiers, particularly the French, volunteered to serve in defense of their country.

Changes in Warfare

A general transported from the battlefield of Blenheim, Minden, or Leuthen to that of Marengo, Austerlitz, or Waterloo would have found little, save perhaps the size of armies, to surprise him. From the beginning of the War of the Spanish Succession (1701) to the end of the Napoleonic Wars (1815), no significant technological change in warfare or in the basic structure of armies occurred. The iron ramrod, the artillery elevation screw, and better cannon mounts refined but did not fundamentally change existing weapons. The infantryman armed with a smoothbore musket tipped with a socket bayonet remained the backbone of armies. Cavalry comprising no more than a third of any force operated in support, protecting the infantry's flanks, attacking the enemy's flanks and rear, scouting, and screening the army's movements. Artillery firing solid, grape, or canister shot at relatively close range (usually under 1,000 yards) to kill enemy troops also supported the foot soldiers. Success in battle continued to depend on the rate at which massed infantry could deliver a steady volume of fire, and generalship required skill in maneuvering formations of troops. Both of these activities required extensive drill.

Significant changes in warfare did occur, but they had to do with organization and recruitment, which of course affected operations and tactics. The quarter century before the outbreak of the Revolution saw the French army engage in soul-searching reform because of its poor performance during the Seven Years' War.[1] The army first implemented a major organizational change that would dramatically increase the size of forces that could participate in an operation. Through the middle of the 18th century armies advanced, deployed, and fought as a single entity. Handling such a unified force required not only great skill on the part of commanders but tremendous precision in drill by the rank and file, at which the Prussians excelled, but the French did not.[2] The remedy to this problem lay in dividing the army into manageable units, small enough to maneuver, large enough to defend themselves if attacked, and combinable on the battlefield. The divisional system, introduced by Marshal Victor F. Broglie in 1760, divided the army into infantry and cavalry divisions. Each infantry division consisted of 16 battalions and a battery of 8 guns under command of a lieutenant general.[3] A cavalry division would consist of 24 squadrons and eight guns.[4]

The divisional system addressed the problem of marching and maneuvering large armies in the field, but it had a serious weakness that Napoleon recognized and remedied. Divisions were too small for most independent engagements, and they remained specialized (infantry or cavalry). The solution to that problem lay in creation of the Corps d'Armée, a truly combined-arms formation with its own infantry, cavalry, and artillery. A corps could move with the speed of a division and fight with the capacity of a small army. Corps varied in size as resources and circumstances dictated, but they maintained the two to one infantry to cavalry ratio typical of 18th-century warfare. Napoleon explained the relative advantages of divisions and corps and how they should work together:

> This is a general principle at war. A corps of 25,000 to 30,000 men can be isolated; well led, it can either fight, or avoid battle and maneuver according to circumstances without experiencing any misfortune, because it cannot be forced into battle and finally it should be able to fight for a long time. One division of 9,000 to 12,000 men can be left isolated without running into trouble for one hour. It will contain the enemy, whatever his strength, and will gain time for the army to arrive.[5]

The value of the corps system was vindicated at the twin battles of Jena-Auerstädt in October 1806. On October 13 the emperor encountered a large force, which he mistakenly believed to be the bulk of the Prussian army near the town of Jena. He ordered Marshals Louis-Nicolas Davout and Jean-Baptiste Bernadotte to converge on the town. As Davout advanced, however, he encountered a large enemy force that proved to be the Prussian main body near the town of Auerstädt. With a single corps of 26,000 infantry, 1,622 cavalry, and 46 cannon he defeated an army of nearly twice as many troops (39,550 infantry, 12,250 cavalry, and 163 cannon).[6]

In most battles Napoleon used massed artillery to weaken infantry formations as a prelude to attacks by infantry. This trend had been developing throughout the 18th century but accelerated in the last half due to improved barrel casting techniques and standardized sizes.[7] The French artillery officer Jean Baptiste de Gribeauval standardized French guns and introduced a new elevation screw and sight.[8] Shorter barrels, larger wheels, and better gun carriages made artillery more mobile. Prepackaged rounds of shot and powder increased the rate of fire. Horse artillery, light cannon that could be deployed rapidly to any part of the battlefield, also increased in importance.

The decades immediately preceding the Revolution also saw significant changes in infantry tactics, and again the French led the way. In 1772 Comte Jacques Antoine Hippolyte de Guibert published *Essai général de Tactique* (*General Essay on Tactics*), which despite its title covers strategy and politics as well as tactics. Guibert resolved a debate that had raged since the musket and bayonet became the standard infantry weapon. Maximizing firepower required deploying infantry in long lines two or three ranks deep, the so-called *ordre mince* or "thin order"; maximizing shock power during a bayonet charge necessitated massing troops in deep columns, the *ordre profond* or "deep order." Soldiers could of course learn to fight in both line and column formations, but maneuvering from one to the other under fire in the course of battle could not easily be accomplished. French generals had favored column tactics in large measure because musket fire had limited effect. Guibert argued, however, that greater emphasis on musketry training would make volley firing in linear formation more effective. He also developed a maneuver by which platoons could move from column to line and back rapidly.[9] Finally, Guibert favored an *ordre mixte* (mixed order) of lines interspersed with columns, which enabled a formation to deliver a large volume of musket fire and achieve maximum shock power during an advance with the bayonet.[10]

The corps system and the *ordre mixte* gave the French army greater mobility and tactical flexibility. They did not, however, solve the problem of logistics, which reduced significantly the speed with which an army could move and limited its size. The answer to supply lay in reverting to a practice commonly employed prior to 1648: living off the land. Unencumbered by a long logistics tail, Napoleon's armies could move quickly and strike deep into enemy territory. Requisitioning supplies did of course increase the impact of war on ordinary civilians, who once again suffered the privation of armies foraging for food and fodder.

The Citizen Soldier and His Impact on Warfare

Most of the organizational and tactical innovations Napoleon would combine so brilliantly were thus already in place by 1789. To make them truly effective, however, required the profound social changes the

French Revolution and Napoleonic Wars

Revolution brought about. First and foremost among these was the rise of the citizen soldier motivated by patriotism. Armies of the ancien régime consisted of rank-and-file soldiers drawn from among the lowest, least economically valuable members of society. The French Revolution improved the lot of ordinary people, at least to some degree, made them part of the political process, and thus gave them a country worth defending. The revolutionary Louis Antoine de Saint Just realized the importance of this new sentiment. "You must not expect victory to come only from weight of numbers and discipline," he proclaimed in 1793. "You will secure it only through the progress by the republican spirit within the army."[11] The new government duly set about inculcating that spirit among its troops with a propaganda campaign that succeeded to a significant degree.[12] One battalion commander appealed to his soldiers in terms echoed by countless others in their private letters:

> The homeland summons us, virtuous children obedient to their mother. For this reason, honour will be our guide. . . . We were "serfs." So let us show our former "masters" that the serfs, the *sans-culotttes*, will no longer let the rabbits eat their harvest, nor will they pay the tithe.[13]

The letter contains both a concrete reference to revolutionary reforms (elimination of feudal privileges and an end to church taxes) that benefited ordinary people and an indication that those people were willing to defend their gains. Perhaps the best evidence of this new sentiment comes from Valmy, the battle in fall 1792 that arguably saved the Revolution. General Kellerman rode in front of his victorious troops waving his sword and crying, "*Vive la nation!*" (Long live the nation!), to which they responded with a chorus of "*Vive la nation! Vive la France!*" (Long live the nation! Long live France!).[14]

Patriotic expressions in private letters and journals do not, however, mean that everyone shared these feelings or that revolutionary zeal overcame a natural reluctance to be drafted via the new conscription system known as the *levée en masse*. Factors other than (or in addition to) patriotism motivated men to fight. "Ebullient self-confidence, resting on past success, *esprit de corps* and faith in the general commanding," one historian insists, "normally counted for far more than such background factors as love of country."[15] Valid or not, this assertion serves as a reminder that motives for fighting were mixed, as they have been throughout the history of warfare. Patriotism added a new ingredient to that mix, albeit one intensified by but not beginning with the French Revolution. Guibert envisioned a citizen army before the revolution made it a reality.[16] Armies no doubt fought best when well led, inspired by patriotism, motivated by esprit de corps, and made confident by past success—a combination Napoleon achieved masterfully.

The ability of Napoleon and men like him to rise to the rank of general also resulted from the French Revolution. In their leveling zeal, the revolutionaries opened the officer corps to men of great ability but modest background. Many aristocratic officers fled abroad to escape the guillotine, opening places for others who rose based on merit, not social class. While the Revolution did not produce a completely egalitarian officer corps, it did allow for a more open one. As the military historian Jeremy Black aptly described the change, "the Revolution created an officer-class dominated by talent and connections as opposed to birth and connections."[17] Before the Revolution 85 to 90 percent of officers came from the aristocracy; by 1794 only 3 percent did.[18] Since the new divisional/corps structure required talented leaders capable of taking initiative as well as following orders, this change in officer recruitment was vital.

An army of citizen soldiers fighting for love of country and commanded by officers who earned their rank through merit could employ more flexible tactics, especially the use of light infantry. Irregular units had been employed in warfare throughout the 18th century, but they generally operated as rangers, especially in North America and on the Austrian military frontier with the Ottoman Empire. During the American Revolution light infantry had proved highly effective as skirmishers. Operating in loose formations in front of the regular infantry, skirmishers sniped at and harassed the enemy force, inflicting casualties and causing disruption before it could even engage with their own main body. The success of American forces stirred interest in skirmishers among many European commanders, but the French army of the 1790s employed them in large numbers and to great effect.[19] Increased use of skirmishers by the Continental and revolutionary French armies should come as no surprise. Soldiers operating independently of the main body of an army must be highly motivated to fight, as they could more easily desert than their comrades in tightly packed conventional formations. Given the high desertion rates in virtually all armies of the ancien régime, their commanders were not inclined to make matters worse through extensive use of skirmishers.

Beyond the era of the French Revolution, the advent of patriotism had a lasting, negative effect that would increase dramatically over time. The reintroduction of ideology, which had been largely absent since 1648, made wars increasingly more deadly from 1789 to 1945. Patriotism evolved into aggressive nationalism, which not only celebrates the virtues of a country but elevates it above all others. Belief in the superiority of one's own community leads in wartime to the demonization of the enemy. Intensified by "scientific" racism and disseminated through free, compulsory education, nationalism would make wars increasingly more total, obliterating the distinction between combatant and noncombatant. Increasing lethality of weaponry would contribute to this process, which culminated in the dropping of the atomic bomb.

Navies

Naval warfare did not change dramatically during the 18th century, although ships became larger, more heavily armed, and more numerous. At the time of the French Revolution the backbone of European fleets was the ship of the line (shortened from "ship of the line of battle" and eventually to "battleship"), with three gun decks carrying over 100 cannon. Engagements between naval forces consisted of advancing in line-ahead formation to engage enemy vessels, preferably by crossing their bows or sterns in order to fire a broadside into them. Battles eventually dissolved into individual engagements in which the attacking ship disabled, boarded, and captured its prey. Smaller vessels (frigates, brigs, etc.), mounting fewer cannon, escorted convoys, patrolled the seas, and raided enemy commerce.

France and Britain were the preeminent naval powers of the era. Following Admiral Horatio Nelson's decisive victory over a combined Franco-Spanish fleet at Trafalgar and Napoleon's crushing defeat of Austro-Russian forces at Austerlitz, both in 1805, the Napoleonic Wars became what some described as a battle between the whale and the elephant. The reality of the situation was a bit more subtle. Britain enjoyed naval supremacy from the outset. In 1790 its 195 ships of the line outnumbered its two nearest rivals, France (81) and Spain (72), combined, and by 1815 it had 214 to France's 80 and Spain's 25.[20] Naval supremacy and a string of impressive victories, however, contributed only indirectly to the defeat of Napoleon. The Royal Navy protected the home islands from invasion and supported British commerce. Without the need to pay for both a larger army and navy, Britain could pursue its deepwater strategy, blockading French ports while funding its allies with large land armies.[21] Without those allies, however, naval supremacy would not have been decisive.

Opposing Forces

The Napoleonic Wars witnessed the greatest mobilization of European manpower up to that time. With a population of 28 million, France fielded an army of 600,000 at its peak strength in 1812.[22] The Austrian Empire had a population of 27 million in 1789 and fielded an army with a peak strength of 250,000.[23] From a population of approximately 9 million, Prussia fielded an army of 300,000 in 1813.[24] Only Russia, with a population of 38 million, could match France, with an army of 600,000 at peak strength.[25]

Numbers and resources ultimately tipped the balance against France in the long run, but only after almost 25 years of intermittent warfare. For perhaps 15 of those years, the French army held a decisive qualitative advantage. Its enemies fielded dynastic armies comprised of regiments that were 800–1,000 men strong, "cobbled together on an ad hoc basis."[26] Officers received their commissions based as much if not more on birth than on ability and commanded conscripted peasants controlled through brutal discipline. These forces fared poorly against highly mobile Napoleonic armies deployed using the flexible corps system, led by talented officers, and filled with dedicated rankers. Only when they reorganized themselves along French lines did they do better.[27] Even then they faced a badly overextended French military establishment drawing upon depleted reserves of manpower and fielding troops less well trained than their predecessors.

The Course of Wars

Historians generally distinguish between the Wars of the French Revolution, which lasted from 1792 to 1803, and the Napoleonic Wars, beginning in 1803 and ending in 1815. For the adversaries of France, however, they formed a continuous series of conflicts to prevent French domination and restore the balance of power in Europe. The campaigns have been grouped according to the alliances formed against France: the First Coalition (1792–1797), the Second Coalition (1798–1802), the Third Coalition (1803–1806), the Fourth Coalition (1806–1807), the Fifth Coalition (1809), and the Sixth Coalition (1812–1815). Although they did not all participate in every alliance, Britain, Russia, Prussia, and Austria formed the backbone of the opposition to Napoleon, with smaller nations joining them as time and circumstances dictated.

The European powers squandered their opportunity to strangle the French Revolution in its cradle through lack of effective cooperation, failure to commit sufficient resources to the task, and serious underestimation of how hard the volunteers of 1792 would fight. The First Coalition, consisting of Britain, Austria, and Prussia as well their minor allies, made a paltry effort to defeat France in a war declared, ironically, by Louis XVI as one of his last foreign policy acts as king. One Austrian army moved into the Low Countries, while an Austro-Prussian army of 130,000 led by the Duke of Brunswick invaded France. Weakened by the flight of many officers, the French army fared poorly, and a more concerted effort might have produced greater results. The duke, however, waged a methodical 18th-century campaign, securing his lines of communication with garrisons that depleted his strength. These deployments, along with disease and attrition, reduced his field force to 40,000 by the time it faced the French army in its strong defensive position at Valmy. After an artillery duel and clear indication that the French would not easily give way, Brunswick retreated into Germany.[28] France had gained an invaluable breathing space to rebuild its army into a formidable fighting force.

The key to that rebuilding effort was the *levée en masse*. This proclamation was nothing short of a complete mobilization of the French people in defense of the Revolution:

> From this moment until that in which the enemy shall have been driven from the soil of the Republic, all Frenchmen are in permanent requisition for the service of the armies. The young men shall go to battle; the married men shall forge arms and transport provisions; the women shall make tents and clothing and shall serve in the hospitals; the children shall turn old linen into lint; the aged shall betake themselves to the public places in order to arouse the courage of the warriors and preach the hatred of kings and the unity of the Republic.[29]

This general call to arms had to be worked into a practical system of conscription, but it established the principle that citizenship carried with it the obligation to bear arms in defense of the nation.

Having survived the difficult years of 1792–1793, the French went on the offensive, gaining control of the Netherlands, invading Spain and the Rhineland, and attacking Austria and Piedmont in Italy. The Treaty of Campo Formio, which ended the War of the First Coalition in 1797, recognized French control of Belgium, the Rhineland, part of the Republic of Venice, and other territory in Italy. An army dismissed by the European powers as little more than a rabble had transformed itself and accomplished a great deal in a few years. This period also saw Napoleon so distinguish himself during the siege of Toulon that he was promoted from captain to general and soon took command of French forces in Italy.

The treaty kept France's enemy's at bay for less than a year. Britain had not signed the treaty, but without continental allies, it could do little to hurt France save raid its commerce. Napoleon nonetheless sought to engage the island nation indirectly. His ill-fated effort to seize Egypt in 1798 ended in disaster, but he lost a relatively small force, and the adventure did not damage his reputation, earned in the far more important Italian campaign. He returned to Paris, where he participated in a coup that overthrew the Directory and made him First Consul. Russia and the Hapsburg Empire (Austria) as well as several small states had joined Britain to form the Second Coalition against France in March 1798. Fighting took place in three theaters: the Netherlands, southern Germany and Switzerland, and Italy. The Anglo-Russian force invaded the Netherlands in August 1799, only to withdraw three months later. A French expedition to the Danube (March to December 1799) similarly ended in failure. In Italy, however, Napoleon achieved one of his greatest victories, at Morengo in June 1800, wresting control of northwest Italy from the Austrians. A decisive victory by General Jean Victor Baptiste Moreau over the Austrians and Bavarians at Hohenlinden in December led in February 1801 to the Peace of Luneville, which ended the land war. The British and French continued to fight at sea until the signing of the Peace of Amiens in March 1802.

Like the treaty ending the War of the First Coalition, however, the Peace of Amiens proved to be nothing more than a brief armistice. The issues over which both conflicts had been waged remained unresolved. The balance of power still lay decisively in France's favor, French occupation of the Low Countries threatened British interests, and Napoleon seemed bent upon further conquest. It thus came as no surprise to anyone when Britain declared war on France once again in May 1802, followed by Austria, Russia, Sweden, and the kingdoms of Naples and Sicily in December 1804. Napoleon formed his Grand Army for the invasion of England, which he could only accomplish by achieving naval supremacy or by luring the British fleet far from home waters long enough for troop barges to cross the channel. Neither event occurred. Admiral Horatio Nelson's crushing defeat of a Franco-Spanish fleet at Trafalgar on October 21, 1805, put paid to any invasion plan.

Even before Trafalgar, Napoleon had to turn his attention to the east, where Austrian and Russian forces numbering nearly 400,000 were massing against him.[30] With his superior grasp of strategy and more mobile forces, however, Napoleon moved to defeat his enemies in detail. In October he trapped General Karl von Mack's army in Ulm, forcing 27,000 Austrian troops to surrender.[31] The remaining Austrian and Russian forces retreated, leaving Vienna open to Napoleon. After occupying the capital, he headed east to confront the Austrians and a reinforced Russian army commanded by Tsar Alexander I himself. The two armies collided at Austerlitz on December 2. With 50,000 men, Napoleon routed an enemy force of 88,000, inflicting 27,000 casualties and capturing 13,000 prisoners, for a loss of just 1,305 killed and 6,695 wounded.[32] Austerlitz was arguably Napoleon's greatest victory and is discussed at length later in this chapter.

Although poised to strike should the opportunity arise, Prussia had remained out of the Third Coalition. In July 1806, however, it joined Britain and Russia in yet another anti-French alliance, the Fourth Coalition. Napoleon dealt swiftly with the new threat. He defeated the Prussians decisively at the twin battles of Jena and Auerstädt in October. He then turned to face the Russians, inflicting a limited defeat on Alexander at Eylau in February 1807 and a decisive one at Friedland in June. The Treaty of Tilist in July ended the war, dismembered Prussia, and imposed the Continental System (a boycott of British goods) on Russia. Napoleon was now master of an empire stretching from the Atlantic Ocean to the border of Russia and from the Baltic Sea to the Mediterranean Sea. From this point forward his fortunes would steadily decline.

Napoleon's problems began in Spain and ended in Russia. Resenting French occupation, Spanish peasants rose in revolt and added a new word to the lexicon of war, *guerrilla* (small war). Using classic hit, run, and hide tactics, the rebels supported conventional operations in Portugal and Spain conducted by Arthur Wellesley (later the Duke of Wellington). The Peninsular War, as it came to be called, did not lead directly to the French emperor's downfall, but it did require him to divert troops to a secondary front. Then Tsar Alexander violated the terms of the Treaty of Tilsit by trading with England. This betrayal led Napoleon to invade Russia in 1812. Rather than face him in a decisive battle, however, the Russians traded space for time, retreating deep into their country after scorching the earth in front of the advancing French. This tactic severely hampered an army used to living off the land. Already seriously weakened in the opening battles in western Russia, Napoleon nonetheless marched all the way to Moscow in the vain hope that capturing the city would force the tsar to sue for peace.[33] He won a Pyrrhic victory over the Russians at Borodino just west of Moscow, inflicting approximately 43,000 casualties but at the cost of 28,000 (killed and wound) of 103,000 men engaged, a loss he could not afford.[34] He captured the nearly deserted city, where he remained until mid-October. With winter approaching and no hope of a peace mission coming from the tsar, Napoleon began his long march home. Harsh weather, lack of supplies, and raids by Cossack irregulars further depleted his forces as the Russian army pursued him across the steppes. By the time they crossed the Niemen River into Poland, perhaps as few as 30,000 troops remained of an army of almost 450,000; Napoleon had lost 400,000 men, 200,000 horses, and 1,000 cannon.[35]

The Russian fiasco marked the beginning of the end for Napoleon. In 1813 his Prussian and Austrian allies fell away as the Russians advanced westward. In October he suffered a major defeat at Leipzig ("the battle of the nations"). The road to Paris lay open, and after a few desperate attempts to repel the invaders, Napoleon abdicated on April 6, 1814. He went into exile, only to return in March 1815 to commence the "100 days" that ended at the battle of Waterloo in June.

Victory and Defeat

Napoleon won most of his battles but ultimately lost the war for the same reasons as Louis XIV before him and Hitler after him. France became such a threat to the other states of Europe that they had no choice but to combine against him. Their superior resources eventually overwhelmed Napoleon. Numbers do not, however, tell the entire story of French defeat. Napoleon's adversaries eventually adopted the changes that had given the armies of the French Revolution and Napoleon an initial advantage. Between 1805 and 1809 Duke Charles initiated reforms in the Austrian army, adopting a corps system of organization, removing incompetent officers, and relaxing brutal discipline. These reforms improved the fighting quality of the army and allowed it to win a limited victory over the French at Aspern in 1809.[36] The Russians made limited reforms as well, but these had less effect on defeating Napoleon in 1812 than did cold, hunger, and the ability of General Mikhail Kutuzov to exploit Russia's strategic depth.[37] The British army did not undertake serious reforms, perhaps because it never faced Napoleon in a major battle before Waterloo and it was in any case not Britain's first line of defense. That honor belonged to the Royal Navy. Arthur Wellesley, later the Duke of Wellington, did, however, improve the living conditions of his troops in Spain, which led to better morale and greater confidence in him as a leader.[38]

Of all the forces schooled by Napoleon on the battlefield, the Prussians engaged in the most extensive, effective, and lasting military reforms, perhaps because they had lost the most fighting the French. Success lay in reforming not merely the army but also the society that created it. A reform commission headed by Gerhardt von Scharnhorst proposed eliminating most feudal privileges and making military service an obligation of all citizens. The commission sacked officers who had performed poorly and made ability a condition of promotion. By 1809 only 22 of 142 generals who had been on active duty in 1806 remained; field-grade (major and above) and junior officers suffered an equally extensive purge.[39] The Prussian army adopted a corps system and improved administration. It also developed a new general staff so that "collective intelligence would offset the individual genius of Napoleon."[40] Talented officers studied at the Military Staff College in Berlin and were then assigned to general officers. On campaign, the staff officer would draw up plans that the commander would execute.[41]

None of the reform movements made any of the allied armies by itself a match for the French led by Napoleon. They did, however, make it far more difficult for the emperor to win the battles of annihilation characteristic of his earlier campaigns. A war of attrition replaced one of decisive victories. France (or any single European nation for that matter) could not win such a conflict. Superior resources and weight of numbers ultimately decided the issue in favor of the allies.

The Nature of Battle

The Napoleonic Wars consisted of dozens of major battles and hundreds of minor engagements that took place over more than a decade. While each event was of course unique, one in particular stands out as a good example of Napoleonic warfare. Most analysts view the Battle of Austerlitz, fought on December 2, 1805, between France and a combined Austro-Russian army, as Napoleon's greatest victory. It certainly revealed all the elements of Napoleonic warfare employed in the most effective combination: deception, mobility, boldness, and the destruction of the enemy field army. Following soon after the defeat of a smaller Austrian force at Ulm in late October, the battle proved so decisive that it brought the War of the Third Coalition to an end on terms entirely favorable to Austria.

The campaign that led to Austerlitz resulted from the formidable threat the new alliance posed to France. By April 1805 Britain, Russia, Austria, Sweden, and the kingdoms of Naples and Sicily had not only allied but also devised a bold plan to reverse French gains. While one Austrian force attacked in Italy, a second would block any French advance through Bavaria until Russian forces arrived and the combined army could invade northern France, and a third Russian-British-Swedish force would advance from northern Germany into Holland.[42] Excellent intelligence allowed Napoleon to determine at least the outline of the allied plan and devise a bold strategy to counter it. He would deploy forces to block the allied moves in Italy and the Low Countries and launch the bulk of his forces in a preemptive strike against the Austrians and Russians in central Europe.

In April 1805 the bulk of the French army, some 200,000 frontline troops, were encamped on the Atlantic coast of France waiting for transport to England in the event the French navy defeated the British fleet or at least drew it away from home waters. In light of the new threat from the east, Napoleon renamed his force the Grand Army and began deploying it against the emerging Austro-Russian threat. Relying on speed and mobility, he hoped to defeat the Austrians before the Russians arrived. General Karl Freiherr von Leiberich Mack made this task much easier by advancing into the Black Forest with an army of approximately 72,000 nominally commanded by Archduke Ferdinand. Eager to prevent Napoleon's advance from the west, he marched without waiting for a Russian army under Kutuzov to arrive. Mack failed to consider that Napoleon would advance farther north and then strike southwest across the Danube to cut the Austrian line of communication and supply to Vienna. The French trapped the Austrian general and a sizable portion of his force in the fortified city of Ulm and forced them to surrender on October 15. For the loss of fewer than 200 officers and men, Napoleon captured an entire field army of almost 24,000.[43]

The emperor advanced to Vienna in early November, but capturing the city did not force the Austrians to sue for peace. Napoleon found himself in a perilous situation. The bulk of the Russian army had massed to the northeast and with remaining Austrian forces numbered nearly 90,000; a smaller Austrian force of 33,000 under Archduke Karl was advancing from Italy; and the Prussians, though neutral, were massing nearly 200,000 troops on the Austrian border, awaiting an opportune moment to strike.[44] Napoleon needed to draw the Russians into battle in favorable circumstances before the opposing forces could unite against him. He advanced to Brunn in Moravia, 80 kilometers north of Vienna in what is today the Czech Republic on November 20 and then began a campaign of strategic deception to draw his enemies into an engagement. On the 21st he ordered French forces to occupy the Pratzen Heights and the village of Austerlitz east of Brunn, then had them retreat in feigned disarray as an apparent prelude to withdrawal.[45] He then sent envoys to the Austro-Russian camp, now occupied by both Austrian emperor Francis and Tsar Alexander, requesting to negotiate. Convinced of French weakness, Alexander (who controlled two-thirds of the allied troops) responded with impossibly harsh terms. When Napoleon refused them, the 28-year-old tsar ignored the advice of his experienced commander, General Kutuzov, who advised waiting for reinforcements, and insisted on battle, which took place on December 2, 1805.[46]

Napoleon's plan for conducting the battle proved to be as ingenious as his deception in drawing the allies into it. With approximately 61,000 troops he faced an Austro-Russian army of nearly 86,000. Marshal Davout's corps, numbering 12,000, would arrive on the French right after battle had been joined. Napoleon deployed the French forces in a shallow arc running from the Sazchon Pond (a shallow frozen lake) in the south to an elevated hill on the Omutz Road to the north. He deliberately weakened his right and held two corps in reserve to lure the allies into attacking it. As he had anticipated, the impetuous young tsar took the bait, marching the bulk of his troops across the French front to engage its weakened flank. Dug in behind marshy ground and a stream, the hard-pressed French infantry on the right gave ground but held on until Davout's corps arrived to bolster them.

As five ponderous Austro-Russian columns passed his front, Napoleon committed elements of Marshal Nicolas-Jean de Dieu Soult's corps supported by Marshal Bernadotte to attack the weakened allied center, taking the enemy columns in the flank and rear. At the same time French forces in the north fighting a defensive battle against General Pyotr Bagration's 13,000 Russians went over to the attack to keep those forces from bolstering the weakened allied center. As more French troops appeared on the Pratzen Heights, the now disorganized Austro-Russian columns retreated in disorder toward Austerlitz. The French repelled a determined Russian counterattack and by midafternoon controlled the heights, from which they could fire down upon the fleeing allied troops. The retreat became a rout. With the allied center broken and the bulk of the army enveloped in the south, Bagration had no choice but to retreat toward Olmetz with his remaining forces in the north.

The battle ended in a manner that distinguished it from prerevolutionary engagements. Commanders of the ancien régime would have been content to hold the field and allow the Russians fleeing across the frozen ponds to escape. Napoleon, however, ordered batteries of horse artillery moved up to shell them, killing soldiers and blasting holes in the ice. From this episode grew a myth that thousands drowned in the frozen water. In fact, most either went around or waded through the shallow pond to safety, though many wet, exhausted soldiers fell captive to the French.[47] Napoleon's efforts to kill them as they fled illustrated his maxim that to make omelets, one had to break eggs.

Austerlitz was as decisive a victory as any commander in any age could have desired. Allied losses included 16,000 killed or wounded and 20,000 captured, half of the entire Austro-Russian force deployed.[48] The French casualties amounted to just over 10,600 killed and wounded.[49] The victory also served larger strategic objectives. Following the crushing defeat, Austria sued for peace entirely on Napoleon's terms, bringing the War of the Third Coalition to an abrupt end and consolidating French gains in Italy and the Low Countries.

Unconventional Conflict

Like the Seven Years' War and American Revolution before them, the wars of the French Revolution and Napoleon involved conventional and unconventional operations. Most irregular warfare occurred in response to French invasions, most notably the guerrilla war in Spain. Long before that, however, the fledgling republic faced a threat much closer to home. How the army dealt with this threat foreshadowed its response to the more serious challenge in the Iberian Peninsula 15 years later.

In March 1793 a rebellion broke out in the Atlantic coastal region of France south of the River Loire known as the Vendée. The causes of the outbreak have been the subject of considerable historical debate. Three national issues in particular fueled popular unrest: desire to restore the monarchy; upset over the removal of the Catholic Church from its privileged position; and the new *levée en masse*, which called for the drafting of 300,000 Frenchmen into the army. The rebellion began in 1793 and did not completely end until 1799, although it had been reduced to little more than a nuisance by the end of 1794. During the course of the rebellion 50,000–100,000 people took up arms against the revolutionary government.[50]

The uprising had some characteristics of a traditional peasant revolt and some of a modern insurgency. As the largest of several popular uprisings against republican reforms, the Vendee never by itself posed an existential threat to the new regime, but in combination with the threat of foreign invasion it did cause concern. The rebels dubbed themselves the "Catholic and Royal Army" and adopted a heart with a cross embedded in it above the slogan "God and the King" as their emblem. Most were poorly armed peasants resisting the growing efforts of the central government to exert its authority over them, a process begun by the monarchy and intensified by the republicans.[51] They had grievances and a reactionary agenda but no real strategy. On the other hand, they created an army capable of beating government troops in one engagement. After the French army defeated their conventional forces in December 1793, the rebels conducted guerrilla operations that did not end until 1799, when they wrested concessions from the government in return for laying down arms.

The response of the republican government to the rebellion unfolded in two phases: brutal repression from 1793 to 1795 followed by what might be described as "proto-counterinsurgency" from 1795 to 1799. Most studies have focused on the repression. From the outset of the rebellion, the army showed a determination to be ruthless. General Jean-Baptiste Huché instructed one of his battalion commanders to burn the homes and property of suspected insurgents and to "exterminate without hesitation every individual of whatever age or sex who participated in the war in the Vendee."[52] Ample evidence indicates that troops carried out such orders on a wide scale, though the number who died remains a subject of controversy. One soldier wrote that he witnessed "the horror" of women and girls of suspected rebel families being herded into the street of one village and killed en masse with blows from rifle butts, bayonets, and sabers.[53] General Louis Maire Turreau, who assumed command of French forces in the Vendee in December 1793 carried out the policy of brutal repression to the utmost. Turreau created the infamous *colonnes infernale* (infernal columns), mobile units sent to scour the countryside of rebels. "Every means will be employed to track down the rebels," Turreau instructed his soldiers. "All will be put to the bayonet, and the villages, farms, heath, broom and anything else that can be burned will be consigned to the flames."[54] The extent of the carnage may be inferred by a report General Francois Joseph Westermann wrote in October 1793:

> The Vendee no longer exists. I've just buried it in the marshes and forests of Savenay. Following the orders I have received, I have crushed children beneath the hooves of our horses, and massacred women so that they won't spawn any more brigands. You can't reproach me with having taken any prisoners, the roads are littered with corpses. We haven't stopped shooting the brigands at Savenay.[55]

Casualty figures vary widely owing to lack of sources, but the best estimates put the death toll at from 117,000 to just over 200,000.[56]

The French soon learned, however, what every regime faced with insurgency would discover. Repression alone rarely works, or it works only at an unacceptable cost. By the spring of 1794 the army had broken the back of the revolt, but its brutal tactics failed to eradicate the movement. Having wielded the stick to its maximum effect, the government in Paris decided to offer a carrot. In February 1795 it granted an amnesty to the rebels. Unfortunately not all of them accepted it, emboldened perhaps by an abortive effort by England to provide aid. The army thus had to pursue the remaining guerrillas. In doing so, it decided to change tactics. General Louis Lazar Hoche led the effort. Hoche wrote a brief manual, "Instructions for Those Troops Employed in Fighting the Chouans [Guerrillas]." He stressed the need for aggressive but focused tactics, constant patrolling, security of convoys, and reconnaissance to gather intelligence. He also understood the importance of popular support. "Finally, the Commander in Chief wishes to make clear to officers that they should attempt to live harmoniously with the local inhabitants," Hoche wrote.

His treatment of them should be fair and he should restrict his requests to those permitted in military regulations. On no account must he disturb them on account of their religious principles, the Declaration of Rights makes it clear that they are free to worship as they see fit. He should treat the local population gently and with humanity.[57]

The new approach proved effective, although it would take further concessions, including compensation for losses suffered during the first phase of the war, to bring the revolt to its final conclusion in 1799.[58]

The next major episode of unconventional warfare proved much harder to counter. French forces entered Spain not as invaders but as allies in a war to conquer Portugal. Napoleon soon recognized, however, an opportunity to control the weakened country, so his forces remained in Spain after the Portuguese had been defeated. Their presence stirred unrest, which led to a coup against the unpopular King Charles IV in favor of his son, Ferdinand. Napoleon's failure to recognize the new monarch, coupled with growing resentment of French occupation, led to rebellion in Madrid on May 3, 1808.[59] Brutal suppression of the revolt, including mass executions, by French Marshal Joachim Murat produced widespread anger throughout the country, and revolt spread. In July Spanish troops defeated an entire French army corps at Bailén, inflicting 3,000 casualties and capturing 18,000 out of a total force of 22,000.[60] The French now controlled only the territory between the Pyrenees and the Ebro River. Meanwhile, the British exploited the chaos in Spain by liberating Portugal.

During the summer and fall Napoleon sent in 100,000 reinforcements, many of them veteran troops. From October to December 1808 he defeated the Spanish army in a series of engagements that destroyed its cohesion as a conventional fighting force and opened the way to Madrid. Taking the capital and the major cities did not, however, pacify Spain. The French soon faced a concerted guerrilla warfare campaign on a scale that dwarfed the Vendee uprising. Unlike the French rebels, though, the Spaniards must be classified as partisans in that they fought against an occupying army instead of seeking to overthrow an existing government. Irregular forces ambushed French units on the march, overwhelmed small detachments, pillaged baggage trains, and generally made life difficult for the invaders. Who these guerrillas actually were, what they accomplished, and how the French countered them requires closer examination to find the reality beneath the legend.

Like the Minutemen of the American Revolution, the Spanish guerrillas have been romanticized. Popular accounts cast the partisans as patriotic heroes who rose spontaneously to expel the hated invaders in defense of

French Revolution and Napoleonic Wars

king and country. This simplistic interpretation has been thoroughly discredited.[61] The Spanish guerrillas consisted of various diverse groups with mixed motives, ranging from bands of soldiers to groups of brigands. Far from being patriotic, most peasants viewed the war with indifference, resenting the exactions of the Spanish government as much as they did the privations of the French. Most of the poor who did join guerrilla bands did so for hope of plunder, as one popular phrase indicates: "Long live [King] Ferdinand and let's go robbing!"[62] Bands of former regular soldiers operating in a manner similar to the American rangers had the most success against the French, and even then only when they operated in support of conventional troops. Small independent bodies operating against the enemy "may be extremely useful when these operations are connected and carried on in concert with those of a large body of troops which . . . occupy the whole of the enemy's attention," Wellesley observed.[63] By themselves the guerrillas could not have liberated Spain, but without them Wellesley might not have succeeded, either.

The French did not, of course, sit idly by as the guerrillas made their lives miserable. They employed a number of countermeasures. They constructed lines of blockhouses along some key communication routes. They encouraged the formation of civic guards and created squadrons of gendarmes and other antiguerrilla units. They even hid light cannon mounted on swivels in convoy wagons.[64] Some of these measures proved effective, but they had two negative consequences. They proved costly and thus led to greater exactions from the Spaniards, which in turn encouraged resistance.[65] They also required large numbers of troops, placing further demands on Napoleon's already overextended forces. Indeed, the most valuable contribution of the Spanish guerrillas to the allied war effort may have been tying down large numbers of French troops. At the height of the Peninsular War, Napoleon had to deploy 300,000 men to occupy and defend a country that he had supposed would augment his resources, not deplete them.[66] Following the disaster in Russia, he had no choice but to withdraw his forces from Spain, which soon fell to Wellesley.

The Experience of War

In many respects the conditions in which soldiers lived, fought, and died did not change substantially from what they had been under the ancien régime. Disease continued to kill more men than bullets, and medicine had hardly improved, so that all but superficial wounds often proved fatal. Campaigns consisted more of marching than of actual combat. War remained what it had always been: weeks and months of boredom interspersed infrequently with hours and days of terror. The renewed emphasis on foraging and requisitioning of supplies no doubt increased the misery of soldiers far away from barracks and depots, especially when the defenders scorched the earth in front of an invading army, as happened in Russia. Data for the Russian campaign provide some indication of what soldiers faced. For every 12 soldiers who marched to Moscow 2 survived, 1 was killed in action or succumbed to wounds, 2 were captured, and 7 died of disease or privation (cold and hunger).[67] While far more men died in Russia than in any other single campaign, and cold and hunger contributed disproportionately to the mortality rate, the proportion of men killed by bullets and disease accurately reflects the nature of Napoleonic warfare.

Having soldiers live off the land also increased the suffering of civilians. The wars of the French Revolution and Napoleon reintroduced privations uncommon since the end of the Thirty Years' War. The new emphasis on speed and mobility, coupled with the increased size of armies, made conflict costly for those in the path of invading armies. One French officer described how his soldiers denuded fields of potatoes during the Ulm-Austerlitz campaign. "How many times did we ruin the hopes of villagers," he wrote. "We pillage from them the fruits of an entire year's work."[68] In some cases when an army requisitioned supplies from its own people, civilians received a voucher that entitled them to repayment by the government. More often than not, however, peasants received no compensation for their losses. Although generally unreported, rape and murder no doubt accompanied plunder in at least some instances. Thus began a process that would ultimately obliterate all distinction between combatant and noncombatant. By the outbreak of World War II in 1939, there would be no such thing as an innocent civilian.

In trying to understand how men felt about the wars in which they fought, historians face the same problem that plagues them for earlier wars. Few common soldiers could read and write. Most officers were literate, but they represent a small percentage of those who served, and their views did not necessarily reflect those of the rank and file. Enough written accounts have, however, survived to provide some indication of prevailing attitudes. As previously noted, patriotism motivated many French soldiers from the beginning of the revolutionary and Napoleonic wars and may have spread to other armies by the time these conflicts ended. "I have enrolled at Paris in the Volunteers and I am ready to fight the enemies of the fatherland," one young man wrote to his father in October 1792:

> I was born French and with other Frenchmen I want to share the danger and the glory, and I shall always be careful to respect people and property or to die defending them. My comrades and I, we feel the same. In short, I

am devoting myself, my will and my heart, to the defense of the fatherland, and my motto is, live free or die.[69]

Common though such sentiments may have been, at least at the outset, patriotism alone could not fill the ranks of the French or any other army. Every country had to resort to conscription. France had the *levée en masse*. Russia drafted serfs from their lords' estates. Britain relied on a lottery system, which allowed those who could afford it to hire substitutes. John Harris, a shepherd's son, recorded being "drafted into the 66th Regiment of Foot" despite his father's efforts to get him excused.[70] Others enlisted when a recruiter paid them an enlistment bounty. John Green declined to sign up until he was promised "sixteen guineas for seven years' service."[71] A few found the soldier's life attractive. "Having from my infancy a great predilection for military life," William Surtees wrote, "I embraced the first opportunity that offered, after I became sufficiently grown, to enter the militia of my native county."[72]

Whether drafted or enlisted through motives either noble or base, recruits soon found themselves disabused of any romantic illusions they might have had about the glory of war. "Everything conspired to make me regard a campaign as a pleasant excursion, on which, even if one lost one's head, arms, or legs, one should at least find some diversion," wrote 19-year-old Jean-Baptiste Barrès, a private in the French Imperial Guard:

> I wanted to see the country, the siege of a fortress, a battlefield. I reasoned, in those days, like a child. And at the moment of writing this, the boredom which is consuming me in cantonments (at Schönbrunn [near Vienna]) and four months of marching about, months of fatigue and wretchedness, have proved to me that nothing is more hideous, more miserable than war.[73]

Barrès's disillusionment set in before he had even heard a shot fired in anger. Those who actually experienced battle left vivid accounts of its horrors. British rifleman Harris recalled the Battle of Vimerio in Spain in 1808 in terms that might have applied to any battle of the Revolutionary and Napoleonic Wars. "The battle soon became general," he observed.

> The smoke thickened around, and often I was obliged to stop firing, and dash it aside from my face, and try in vain to get sight of what was going on, whilst groans and shouts and a noise of cannon and musketry appeared almost to shake the very ground. It seemed hell upon earth, I thought.[74]

Men endured such suffering for a variety of reasons. They certainly feared the harsh punishments meted out for infractions, but they also felt a sense of duty to their comrades, loathed being deemed a coward, and felt pride in the accomplishments of their unit. One young lieutenant recorded how in one engagement his unit fought "until we were hardly a regiment" and then concluded with "the worst of the story . . . our colours were taken."[75] Regimental flags, which often had campaign ribbons attached to them, were a source of great pride, and to lose them was a major disgrace. Such altruistic sentiments no doubt blended with the instinct for self-preservation, as they seem to do in any war.

Napoleon and the History of Warfare

No one has effectively challenged Napoleon's place among the great captains of military history. Even those who stress the evolutionary changes in warfare from which he benefited acknowledge that he made the best use of these changes. While the armies of the ancien régime achieved victory through methodical deployment of troops on campaign and their maneuver with parade-ground precision in battle, Napoleon relied on speed, mobility, and flexible tactics. "There are no precise or fixed rules," he wrote.

> Everything depends upon the character that nature has bestowed upon the general, on his qualities and faults, on the character of troops, on the range of arms, on the season, and on a thousand circumstances that are never the same.[76]

This situational awareness led him to decentralize command and control of his armies to a significant degree. He informed his corps commanders of the general plan of campaign and then instructed them to "march to the sound of the guns," in other words, take initiative in converging on the enemy.

If in some respects Napoleonic warfare heralded the beginning of a new era, it also marked the end of an old one. Under Napoleon 18th-century warfare reached its limits. Without a revolution in the means of transporting and supplying them, armies could grow no bigger than the ones he had led. Without a better system of command and control, no single general could lead forces more numerous than those he had handled so adroitly. Without technological change that replaced the smoothbore musket with a better projectile weapon, the lethality of combat would be limited. Within a half century of Napoleon's death, all these changes would take place.

CHAPTER FIVE

Industrialization and the American Civil War

If the period 1648 to 1815 saw only incremental changes in military technology, the century following the battle of Waterloo witnessed an explosion of inventions that fundamentally altered the nature of warfare. The Industrial Revolution transformed war, as it did every other aspect of Western civilization. That transformation involved improvements in weaponry that increased exponentially the lethality of armed forces and profoundly changed the nature of society in ways that encouraged the intensification of ideological feelings first exhibited during the American and French Revolutions.

The Industrial Revolution entailed the application of labor-saving devices to the manufacturing process. It began in Britain in approximately 1750 with the employment of machines to spin raw wool and cotton intro thread and weave thread into cloth, and with the use of steam-driven pumps to remove water from coal mines. These changes led to a self-sustaining chain reaction of inventions and innovations that continues to the present.[1] Machinery created a demand for iron ore, which necessitated an improved process for smelting it. James Watt discovered how to turn the horizontal motion of the earliest steam engines into rotary motion so that they could drive machinery as well as pump water. To go from powering machines to propelling ships and driving trains required a small leap of imagination. Iron eventually gave way to steel, and oil replaced coal for fueling ships and trains. The process of invention spurring further invention continues to this day. By the middle of the 19th century industrialization had spread to Continental Europe and the United States. Over the next century it would gradually extend to the entire world.

Industrialization involved much more than a revolution in the means of production. It transformed human society in a manner unseen since the agricultural revolution 10,000 years before. For all of recorded history up to that point the majority of humans had lived in agricultural communities engaged in primary food production. Industrialization drew people into towns near the mines and factories in which they worked. Improvements in agriculture and the application of machinery to farming made it possible for a decreasing number of people to feed the entire population of a country or, thanks to improved transportation, to import what they could not grow or raise themselves.

Concentration of population in manufacturing centers also helped create the modern class system. The heterogeneous grouping of peoples linked to one another via complex patronage-deference networks in rural communities gave way to homogenous neighborhoods occupied by people related to one another primarily through the work they did.[2] As Karl Marx realized, the new social order led to conflict as people in broad homogenous classes discovered common interests with one another but a diminished connection to the larger society in which they lived. The solution to this tension lay in creating a larger "imagined community," the nation held together by a common language and a shared history, albeit a largely invented one that glorified a particular ethnic group.[3] Nationalism, however, had to be taught. The Italian nationalist Massimo D'Azeglio put his finger on the challenge when he observed after the unification of the Italian states, "We have made Italy, now we have to make Italians." Free compulsory public education, which all European states had instituted by the end of the 19th century, provided the means to instill patriotic fervor in the mass of citizens. Thus, as historian Eugene Weber observed, state-funded schools helped turn "peasants into Frenchmen."[4] Patriotic education made citizens more dedicated soldiers and and wars bloodier.

Advances in Military Technology

The Industrial Revolution impacted three aspects of warfare: transport and supply, communications, and weaponry. The invention that made possible the modern mass army had never been intended for military purposes at all. Initially constructed to transport goods, railroads made it possible to move and supply large numbers of troops over great distances more rapidly than ever before. From 1825 to 1900, European railway mileage increased from 0 to 175,000.[5] Prussia, which would soon become the preeminent military power on the Continent, had laid 3,638 miles of track by 1850.[6] The much larger United States had 8,539 miles of track by 1850 and 30,793 miles in 1860, almost 70 percent of it in territory controlled by northern states, a huge advantage to the North during the American Civil War.[7]

The electric telegraph, which first appeared in the 1830s and developed into a workable system by midcentury, increased strategic communication exponentially. Military headquarters in the capital could now communicate rapidly with army units throughout the country. While telegraphy had significant strategic implications, facilitating mobilization and maneuvering of armies, it had limited operational and tactical significance. Running wires on a fluid battlefield proved impractical, and the lines could in any case be cut by shell fire or deliberate enemy action. Field telephones had been developed by the time of World War I, but only the invention of wireless communication freed commanders from the need for signal flags and couriers.

The technological improvement in weaponry began with a simple solution to the challenge of making the rifle a practical infantry weapon. Although the rifle had been around almost as long as the smoothbore musket, it had been problematic as an infantry weapon because it took so long to load. To ensure that it gripped the grooves inside the barrel, the rifle bullet had to be tamped down forcibly with a ramrod (and with some designs, a hammer). The solution to this problem lay not in changing the design of the gun but in reconfiguring the bullet. In 1848 French Captain Claude Minié improved upon the work of earlier inventors to produce the conical-cylindrical bullet. The new projectile had a cone-shaped tip and drum-shaped base with two to four grooves on its exterior and a curved hollow base. Made slightly smaller than the diameter of the gun bore, the bullet slid smoothly down the barrel just like a spherical musket ball. When the gun was fired, the gases produced by the exploding powder hit the hollow base of the soft lead bullet, causing it to expand and grip the grooves of the barrel, which spun it out the bore with considerably greater force, range, and accuracy than a sphere fired from a smoothbore. Soldiers during the American Civil War referred to the bullet as the "Minié ball," and any rifled musket that fired it was generically described as a "Minié rifle."[8]

The invention of the Minié ball made the rifled musket as easy to load as a smoothbore weapon. A second invention, the percussion cap, increased the speed of loading and made it possible to fire the weapon in inclement weather. The percussion cap was a copper cylinder about the size of a pencil eraser and open at one end. The closed end of the cylinder contained fulminate of mercury, an explosive compound that can be ignited by pressure. Instead of a priming pan, the rifled musket had a hollow nipple over which the percussion cap fit.[9] When the hammer struck the cap, the fulminate of mercury exploded, sending a spark down the hollow nipple to ignite the main charge inside the barrel. The rifle cartridge consisted of a premeasured amount of powder wrapped with the bullet in paper. The soldier bit the powder end of the cartridge, poured the powder and bullet down the barrel, and using the paper as wadding, rammed the round and charge home.

The Minié rifle forced a dramatic change in infantry tactics, though it took armies some time to adjust. With an effective range of 500–800 yards (as opposed to the smoothbore musket's 50–100), the new weapon made the bayonet in its traditional role all but obsolete. The distance between lines of musketeers could be crossed by troops in a bayonet charge in less time than it took an infantryman to reload. With the rifle, the distance was too great for such a dash. Infantry formations also changed. Lines of soldiers advancing shoulder to shoulder proved especially vulnerable to concentrated rifle fire at range, so armies had to adopt more open formations. Finally, because individually aimed shots replaced volley firing in formation, target practice became an important part of training.

By the late 1860s the rifle had replaced the smoothbore as the standard infantry weapon in most Western armies, and it continued to evolve. A bolt-action breech-loading mechanism allowed soldiers to fire and reload from the less-exposed prone position. Inventors then combined bullet, powder, and percussion cap in a single brass cartridge with a copper or lead tip. They then attached multiple-round magazines to the rifle, so that each time the solider opened the bolt, the spent cartridge ejected and a new one popped into place so the bolt could be closed and the gun fired more rapidly. The magazine rifle led in turn to the fully automatic weapon or "machine gun." Artillery went through a similar evolution as rifled cannon replaced smoothbores and breech loading replaced muzzle loading.

The quality and quantity of weaponry also improved through another industrial innovation: mass production using standardized, interchangeable parts. Where previously gunsmiths produced weapons one at a time, factories could now mass produce rifle parts to be assembled later. A defective or broken part could be quickly replaced without putting the entire weapon out of commission until a gunsmith repaired it. Mass production of a simple design with interchangeable parts firing standardized ammunition reduced the cost of equipping the new mass armies of the industrial age.

Revolution in Military Thought

The era of industrialization also saw rapid changes in military theory. Theorists did not, however, focus on how to incorporate technology into warfare, but rather on understanding what the Napoleonic Wars meant for the future of armed conflict and statecraft. The Swiss baron Antoine-Henri Jomini had served as a general in both the French and Russian armies. After his military service he took up residence in Paris and wrote several works on warfare. His most famous work, *Précis de l'Art de la Guerre: Des Principales Combinaisons de la Stratégie, de la Grande Tactique et de la Politique Militaire* (translated into English as *Summary of the Art of War*), published in 1838, provided broad theoretical principles as well practical guidance on military strategy, operations, and tactics. Jomini laid down four maxims for waging war:

1. To throw by strategic movements the mass of an army, successively, upon the decisive points of a theater of war, and also upon the communications of the enemy as much as possible without compromising one's own.
2. To maneuver to engage fractions of the hostile army with the bulk of one's forces.
3. On the battle-field, to throw the mass of the forces upon the decisive point, or upon that portion of the hostile line which it is of the first importance to overthrow.
4. To so arrange that these masses shall not only be thrown upon the decisive point, but that they shall engage at the proper times and with energy.[10]

Because he grasped and clearly articulated the essence of Napoleonic strategy, Jomini was perhaps the most widely read military theorist of the first half of the 19th century.[11]

The American Civil War

Military historians generally regard the American Civil War as the first conflict of the industrial age. The rifled musket was the standard infantry weapon in both armies throughout the war, although a significant number of Union troops had Spencer and Henry repeating rifles by 1865. Most major battles occurred within marching distance of a railhead. Both sides enacted conscription, but volunteers made up the majority of their forces throughout the war. This willingness to serve indicates another modern aspect of the struggle: soldiers in both armies fought for a cause in which they believed, preserving the Union for federal troops and defending their independence for the Confederates. Though it was one underlying cause of the conflict, the desire to abolish or preserve slavery motivated few rank-and-file soldiers. The war pitted an agrarian South against an industrializing North, whose superior resources and manpower arguably decided the issue.

The Balance of Power

The North had enormous human material advantages over the South. To defend a country the size of Western Europe, the 11 states of the Confederacy had a population of approximately 9 million, including 3.5 million slaves who could not be expected to fight. The North, consisting of 25 states (including the border states and newly created West Virginia), had a population of approximately 20 million white citizens, augmented by the influx of 800,000 new immigrants between 1861 and 1865.[12] An even greater disparity in wealth and resources separated the two sides. With its 110,000 manufacturing facilities to the Confederacy's 18,000, the Union produced 94 percent of America's iron, 97 percent of its coal, and 97 percent of its firearms. Three-quarters of the nation's farm acreage lay in northern states, which produced 60 percent of its livestock, 67 percent of its corn, and 81 percent of its wheat. In total, the Union held 75 percent of the national wealth.[13] The North also had 22,000 miles of railroads to the South's 8,500.[14] Most of the U.S. navy's ships and the bulk of its personnel remained loyal to the Union. The Union also had the dockyards and machine shops necessary to build naval vessels rapidly. The South did not.

Such gross disparities in population, resources, and wealth could easily lead anyone to see the outcome of the Civil War as a foregone conclusion. This view overlooks the South's very real chance of victory. The Confederacy could not of course have won the war of attrition that the conflict became. As long as the government in Washington, DC, maintained the will to fight, the North's superior resources would prove decisive in a long war of attrition. The North's advantages could not, however, produce a quick victory. To begin with, lack of industry did not cripple the southern war effort. With the 300,000 rifles and smoothbores (many of which were converted to rifles) its forces possessed at the outset, the 120,000 rifles captured from Union forces, and the 400,000 guns imported from abroad along with a comparable number of cannon, Confederate forces never lacked sufficient weapons and ammunition.[15]

They did, however, suffer serious manpower shortages, but these became critical only as the war dragged on over several years. Food shortages also plagued the Confederate army and were closely related to deficiencies in manpower. Putting men in uniform took them off the farms in an era when agriculture was still very labor intensive. Both problems, however, stemmed more from failure of the government in Richmond to manage its human capital effectively than from an inherent northern advantage in numbers. Throughout the war southern plantation owners stuck to growing cotton in hopes of both immediate and postwar profits and resisted encouragement to shift to food production or to allow their slaves to be used by the army in support roles (as cooks, to repair railroads, etc.).[16] Food shortages in the army and government requisitioning of food from their families back home increased desertion from the army.[17]

Not only were its disadvantages manageable, but the South had a great advantage that might have proven decisive. The Confederacy was fighting a defensive war on its home soil. To win it had merely to survive long enough for the North to tire of the struggle. The North, on the other hand, had to defeat and occupy the South, a strategically far more difficult task. Maintaining the political will to continue the fight proved President Abraham Lincoln's greatest challenge.

Strategy and the Course of War

The governments in Richmond and Washington devised strategies to make the best use of their resources to achieve their respective political goals. The Confederacy planned to fight a defensive war with two broad objectives: (1) to inflict so much suffering on Union forces and perhaps even on the citizens of the North that they would decide that forcing the southern states to stay in the Union against their will was not worth the cost in blood and treasure and (2) to encourage one or more European powers to recognize the Confederacy and perhaps intervene on its behalf. Because the South supplied much of the cotton for the British textile industry, the United Kingdom seemed the most likely European state to support the South. It also had the world's largest navy and could easily have broken the Union blockade of southern ports.

Several factors made British intervention unlikely, however. Although reduction in the supply of American cotton did cause a minor recession in the textile industry, British manufacturers had significant stockpiles of cotton at the time war broke out. They also had alternative sources of supply in India and Egypt. The United Kingdom probably would have preferred two weak states in North America rather than one strong one, especially if it had felt Canada was threatened. The United States had not, however, shown interest in expanding northward since the War of 1812, and both the Maine and Oregon boundary disputes had been settled through negotiations. Even if pragmatic considerations had called for it, Lincoln made intervention morally unacceptable when he issued the Emancipation Proclamation in September 22, 1862. Since Britain had outlawed slavery in its empire and forcibly ended the Atlantic slave trade, it could hardly support a rebellion led by people who owned slaves against a government that sought to free them.

Holding out until war weariness sapped the North's willingness to continue the fight had a much greater chance of success. The Democratic Party adopted a peace platform for the election of 1864, and had General William T. Sherman not won a dramatic victory capturing Atlanta in September, Lincoln might have lost, and the Civil War might have ended in a negotiated settlement. Waging a defensive war did not, however, mean digging in and waiting to be attacked. President Jefferson Davis referred to the Confederate strategy as "offensive-defensive." Confederate forces would block any invasion attempt while attacking northern armies in order to destroy them in a Napoleonic-style battle of annihilation. If possible and/or necessary, the Confederates would make incursions into the North to inflict suffering on its population and so encourage Washington to make peace.

Although the South faced a difficult strategic challenge, the North had an even more daunting one. To win, the Union would have to force the Confederacy to surrender, which could only be accomplished by invading and occupying much of its territory. The sheer size of that territory (roughly equal to the area of Western Europe), combined with its limited number of roads and railroads, made this task more difficult. Nonetheless, commanding general of the U.S. Army Winfield Scott designed a strategy to accomplish it. Named for the snake that strangles its prey, the "Anaconda Plan" called for the navy to blockade Confederate ports while the Union army invaded the South via its rivers. The strategy did ultimately succeed, but it took four bloody years to accomplish.

With the existing federal navy and the ability to build ships rapidly, the Union succeeded in blockading southern ports within a year. In April 1862 Union forces captured New Orleans, giving them control of the lower Mississippi. However, completely sealing off the long southern coastline, with its many rivers, inlets, and small harbors, proved impossible. Recent scholarship has demonstrated that the Union blockade was not very effective at preventing the import of strategic supplies, in particular weapons.[18] Failure to interdict the majority of arms shipments does not, however, mean that the blockade had no impact on the Confederate war effort. Although designed to prevent imports, blockades stopped exports as well. Cotton exports, the South's major source of foreign currency, fell to one-ninth of their prewar level, and the price of what cotton did make it out increased dramatically, making it less competitive with other sources of supply.[19] The blockade also severely hampered interregional trade, especially the transport of cattle from Texas across the Gulf of Mexico, exacerbating already serious food shortages in the Confederate army.[20]

The second element of the Anaconda Plan, invading the South via its river systems, proved to be a more formidable task than blockading its ports. The plan explains the geography of the Civil War. Most major battles took place in three areas: the northern triangle of Virginia (bordered by West Virginia and Maryland), eastern Tennessee, and the lower reaches of the Mississippi. Although Union forces hoped to win a decisive victory in the east, the battle of First Manassas (also known as Bull Run) in July 1861 made it clear that winning the war with a battle of annihilation as Napoleon had so often done would be very difficult, if not impossible. Indeed, the absence of such victories characterized the entire Civil War. Most engagements ended in tactical draws and could be considered strategic victories only in that one side held the field and/or achieved its objective, albeit at horrific cost in blood. Technological changes, which favored the defensive, made it virtually impossible to pursue and destroy a large enemy force following an exhausting battle of attrition. The constricted space in the East made such a decisive engagement event even less likely. Taking advantage of their interior position, the Confederates could concentrate troops to counter Union advances via the Shenandoah valley, up the rivers of eastern Virginia, or directly across the Potomac.

Failure to achieve decisive victories also limited the effectiveness of Confederate strategy. Southern generals could and did inflict major defeats on Union armies, but they never succeeded in destroying them. Both of General Robert E. Lee's invasions of the North ended in disaster. Even the lackluster commander George McClellan managed to stop his first attempt at Antietam in September 1862. A year later, Lee suffered an even worse defeat at Gettysburg in southern Pennsylvania. In both cases, though, he managed to retreat into Virginia with his army intact. The size of armies, their organization into corps and divisions that could defend themselves, and the technological revolution in weapons, which favored the defensive, combined to make victories like Austerlitz virtually impossible. Defeated troops simply fell back and reformed on a new defensive line before they could be destroyed or captured. Capturing the enemy capital proved extremely difficult, since both Washington and Richmond were too well fortified to be taken by storm, and the cities could not be invested with enemy field armies still intact. Richmond fell only after a lengthy siege and within a month of the war's end, after Lee's army had been all but destroyed.

The breakthrough for the Union came, not in the East as originally anticipated, but in the West during the pivotal year 1863. In July Ulysses S. Grant captured Vicksburg, giving the Union control of the entire length of the Mississippi and thus cutting the Confederacy in two. In September Union forces took Chattanooga on the Tennessee River, a hub on the Confederacy's principal east-west rail line and the main invasion route to Atlanta. From then until the end of the war, Grant (who took command of all Union armies in March 1864) kept up constant pressure on Lee's Army of Northern Virginia, inexorably forcing it back on Richmond, while Sherman advanced on and captured Atlanta and from there conducted his famous "march to the sea," cutting a 60-mile wide swathe of destruction through Georgia to Savannah before swinging northward through the Carolinas. The Union thus succeeded because the Civil War became the type of conflict the Confederacy could not hope to win: a long, bloody war of attrition in which superior numbers and resources decided the issue. Had Lincoln not been able to sustain the political will to continue the fight, the war might have ended with a negotiated peace recognizing secession.

The Face of Battle: Gettysburg

No battle of the American Civil War, and few in all of military history, has been as thoroughly studied as the engagement that took place in and around a small town in southern Pennsylvania July 1–3, 1863. The historic site continues to attract more visitors annually than any other Civil War battlefield. Being the place where Lincoln gave his famous address has no doubt increased its attraction. Ironically, though, Gettysburg was in many respects atypical. It was the only major battle to occur outside the South and the border states. It also took place over a smaller area than most major engagements. Civil War battlefields often extended over several miles. The Union line at Gettysburg, however, stretched for slightly less than two miles north to south. Despite its compact size, the three-day engagement proved to be the bloodiest of the entire war. The combined casualties for the two sides totaled 45,438 killed and wounded.[21]

Despite of (or perhaps because of) its atypical nature, Gettysburg has much to commend it as a didactic example of how weapons, strategy, and tactics interacted on a Civil War battlefield. Its very compactness makes it easier to understand than more complex engagements fought over a larger area. Standing on Little Round Top, the hill anchoring the southern end of the Union line, one can take in the entire field in a single sweeping glance. It is easier for even a person with little understanding of warfare to visualize what happened. Gettysburg may also be seen as a microcosm of the war, not because it resembles so many other battles, but because it illustrates so clearly the challenges Civil War commanders faced. All the lessons of the new industrial age warfare are writ large on this one example. So too are the experiences of those who fought and died there.

The campaign that culminated at Gettysburg began with a sobering assessment by the Confederate high command of its situation in the spring of 1863. Despite soundly defeating the Army of the Potomac at Fredericksburg in December 1862 and at Chancellorsville in April 1863, Lee was no closer to victory in the East. In both cases the battered federals had retreated across the Rappahannock River and avoided destruction. In the West, Grant was tightening the noose around Vicksburg, and General William Rosecrans controlled central Tennessee. Once Vicksburg fell, as it seemed certain to do, the North would control the entire length of the Mississippi. The two Union armies would then combine to strike at Chattanooga, thus opening an invasion route to Atlanta and the Deep South. Lee decided that launching a second invasion of the North offered the best chance of recouping the situation. A decisive defeat on their own soil might encourage the people of the North to replace Lincoln with a president willing to make peace. Lee articulated this goal in a letter to his wife. "If successful this year," he wrote, "next fall there will be a great change in public opinion at the North. The Republicans will be destroyed [in the election of 1864] & I think the friends of peace will become so strong that the next administration will go in on that basis."[22]

To achieve such a victory, though, Lee needed to maneuver his Army of Northern Virginia into the open country of Pennsylvania, where he could draw the Army of the Potomac into a decisive battle. This approach, which developed as a response to technological changes, characterized Civil War battles. Victory often went to the side that took the strategic offensive in order to fight on the tactical defensive. Entrenched infantry armed with rifles and supported by artillery could not under most circumstances be dislodged by frontal assault. By placing his force at a strategic point that the enemy could not allow him to keep on a field with protectable flanks, a general could force his opponent to launch just such an attack. Lee calculated that Lincoln could not allow a Confederate army to march through northern territory unchallenged and that Lee could pick the time and place of the engagement. His first assumption proved correct, but not his second.

Beginning on June 3, 1863, Lee began his march northward with a force of approximately 80,000, including 61,500 infantry divided into three corps, commanded by Generals James Longstreet, Richard Ewell, and A. P. Hill.[23] The Confederate Plan called for Ewell and Hill to advance up the Shenandoah valley while Longstreet marched parallel to them east of the Blue Ridge Mountains. General Jeb Stuart's cavalry was to screen the army as it moved north, thus retaining for Lee the element of surprise. Once it learned the Confederates had disembarked, the Army of the Potomac under command of General Joseph Hooker, whom Lincoln would replace with General George Gordon Meade, just 12 days before Gettysburg moved north to intercept Lee, keeping between the Confederates and Washington.

Despite initial success, Lee's plan soon unraveled. Ewell captured Winchester, Virginia, on June 15 after a two-day battle. Jeb Stuart's cavalry screened Lee's movements adroitly. Then on June 22 Lee ordered Stuart to circumvallate the Union forces and reunite with the Army of Northern Virginia in four days. Stuart took eight days, during which he raided, cut telegraph wires, captured 150 wagons, and left the Army of Northern Virginia blind. As he advanced through Maryland and into Pennsylvania, Lee needed intelligence on the Army of the Potomac. In hostile territory, cavalry provided such information. Without it, a commander could only make an educated guess about the whereabouts of enemy forces. Meade for his part received regular reports on Confederate troop movements from his cavalry patrols, telegrams from army headquarters in Washington, and an aerial signals system (flags).[24] Lee only learned of the location of the Union army on June 30, when a spy informed him that it had already crossed the Potomac and was coming toward him. By this time Ewell's corps had advanced all the way to Carlisle. Lee recalled it immediately and ordered Longstreet and Hill to turn east to face the threat. The three Confederate corps thus converged on Gettysburg.

Union forces won the race to the crossroads town. On June 30 Brigadier John Buford reached Gettysburg with two cavalry brigades (just over 2,000 men). A forward-thinking officer who understood that the day of lance and saber had passed, Buford employed his troops brilliantly as mounted infantry. With a keen eye for terrain, the brigadier quickly determined the importance of the high ground to the southeast of the town. Unfortunately, the Confederate main body was much closer than the lead Union infantry corps. Buford decided to fight a holding action along Seminary Ridge west of Gettysburg, sending a dispatch rider to summon help. A conventional cavalry officer would not have attempted such a feat, but Buford made skillful use of his smaller force and its technological advantage. Armed

Industrialization and the American Civil War

with Spencer repeating carbines (short-barreled rifles) capable of firing seven rounds from a tube magazine in the stock and light "horse artillery," his troopers could if properly managed hold off a larger force for some time. Firing 14 to 20 rounds per minute, as compared to 2 to 3 rounds per minute for the Minié rifled musket, Spencer carbines helped Buford hold off Harry Heath's division (a force three times the size of the two Union brigades) for three hours.[25] He bought enough time for John Reynolds's First Corps to arrive by dint of a forced march. While the rest of July 1 did not go as well for the federals, whom Ewell and Hill drove from the town, at the end of the day Union troops held the high ground along Cemetery Ridge, just as Buford had hoped.

On the morning of July 2, 1863, Robert E. Lee awoke to exactly the opposite situation he had hoped to face. Instead of forcing the federals to attack him on ground of his own choosing, he had to attack them in their strong position on a ridge linking two hills that could be easily fortified. To dislodge them, Lee devised a classic plan: a pincer attack in which Longstreet's corps on the right and Ewell's on the left would simultaneously outflank Meade on both ends of this line and envelope his army. Despite the failure of the two commanders to attack in unison, Lee nearly carried the day because of two colossal Union mistakes. First, Daniel Sickles moved his corps off the southern part of the ridge and forward into an exposed position a peach orchard. Second, Meade failed to adequately defend Little Round Top at the southern end of the Union line and the key to the whole defensive front. Fortunately, reinforcements arrived just in time to rectify both errors. Once Sickles was wounded, his successor pulled the exposed corps back to the ridge. Reinforcements reached Little Round Top just ahead of a Confederate assault that took hard fighting and clever tactics by the 20th Maine under Colonel Joshua Lawrence Chamberlin to repulse. Meanwhile, forces dug in on Culps and Cemetery Hills defeated Ewell's attack on the right flank of the Union line, while Union cavalry thwarted Jeb Stuart's effort to attack its rear.

By the evening of July 2, Lee faced a difficult situation. Two days' heavy fighting had weakened his army, while fresh Union forces kept arriving. Logistics had become a concern. He could feed his army by plundering the countryside, but he could not replenish its ammunition. He had two options: disengage and retreat back across the Potomac into Virginia or try another attack the following day. Disengaging and withdrawing with a large field army before him would be risky. Lee also felt that by reinforcing his flanks to repel the day's attacks Meade must of necessity have weakened his center. He therefore decided to mount a frontal assault by three divisions straight at the middle of the Union line. Confederate artillery would prepare the way with a massive cannonade to silence the enemy guns.

What came to be called "Picket's Charge," in dubious honor of General George Pickett, who commanded the division on the right of the Confederate line of attack, has been widely interpreted as one of the greatest blunders of the American Civil War. Sending 13,000 men across 1,400 yards of open ground into entrenched infantry armed with rifles and supported by artillery capable of both enfilading and direct fire seems foolhardy in retrospect and was deemed unwise even then. Longstreet had in fact pointedly disagreed with the plan. Both Union and Confederate generals had used such tactics so often, however, that they require considerable explanation. Lee, like virtually all Civil War generals on both sides, was a student of Napoleon, the great captain who had mastered the attack by columns. With few other examples to study, commanders naturally emulated him, although some did experiment with new approaches, such as advancing by rushes in extended order.[26] Even when they realized the problems of mass formations, generals often saw little alternative to using them. As so often happens in warfare, technology confounded tactics. An entrenched enemy could only be dislodged by outflanking him or breaking through his line, whatever the cost. The overwhelming advantage conveyed upon the defender by firepower would only be overcome when the tank and the airplane appeared on the battlefield.

These considerations notwithstanding, battlefield conditions at Gettysburg argued against Pickett's charge. Lee had orchestrated the slaughter of thousands of Union troops attacking Marie's Heights at Fredericksburg, where General Ambrose Burnside had sent rank after rank of infantry uphill into withering fire from Confederate artillery and riflemen ensconced behind a stone wall. Lee now launched an equally risky assault. He began with a preparatory barrage to destroy Union artillery and weaken Meade's line. He immediately encountered a difficulty common on Civil War battlefields: artillery proved largely ineffective at counterbattery fire and long-range bombardment of infantry. The rifle made it easy to keep enemy cannon outside the range from which they could deliver accurate fire. To make matters worse for Lee, faulty fuses caused many rounds to sail over the heads of the Union troops before exploding harmlessly in the rear. The preliminary bombardment thus killed few soldiers and knocked out few guns.

Pickett's charge encountered further problems once the infantry columns advanced. The Emmetsburg Pike Road crossed the space between the two armies at a 45-degree angle running southwest to northeast. Because the northern half of the road lay within range of Union rifles, the

Confederates could not take down the fence along the road. Furthermore, a grove of trees along the Confederate line created a gap between Pickett's division on the Confederate right and the divisions of Generals J. Johnston Pettigrew and Isaac Trimble on the left. To converge on the Union center, Pettigrew and Trimble would have to advance slightly southeast while Pickett would need to turn almost 45 degrees north, paralleling the road once he had crossed it. The northern two divisions faced enfilading fire from rifled cannon firing percussion rounds from Cemetery Hill as they crossed the open field. Once they reached the road, they had to climb over split rail fences, exposing themselves to rifle fire from front and flank. None even reached the stone wall that protected the Union line. Pickett's division fared almost as badly, taking enfilading fire from rifled canon on Little Round Top and canister shot fired into its flanks as it turned almost parallel to the Union line in order to close up with Trimble's division. A handful of men made it through to Meade's line, only to be cut down by Union reinforcements rushed in to close the gap.

The attack was a disaster. Half of those who stepped off from the Confederate line were killed, wounded, or captured. Meeting the shattered remnants of the three divisions as they staggered back, Lee proclaimed, "It was my fault." George Pickett sat in stunned silence. When Lee admonished him, "General, you must see to your division," Pickett responded, "General, I no longer have a division." In later years he became bitter, declaring, "That old man [General Lee] murdered my division." The attack was not, as some would later claim, the "high water mark of the Confederacy," an acme from which its fortunes would steadily decline. The South was already losing the war, and Gettysburg was a desperate gamble to reverse the deteriorating situation. The failure of the

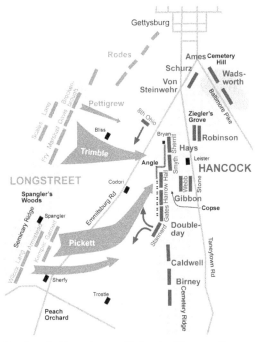

Battle of Gettysburg, Pickett's Charge. *Source:* Hal Jesperson.

attack did, however, confirm the loss of the battle. Lee could now hope for no more than to extricate what remained of his army.

Far from being lauded a hero for what would prove to be a significant victory, Meade faced scathing criticism for failing to pursue and destroy what remained of the Army of Northern Virginia. Lee withdrew to the Potomac only to find his bridges destroyed. He dug in while his engineers rebuilt them. Meade followed cautiously, and when he reached the bridgehead, declined to attack. History has been kinder to Meade than his contemporaries. He had taken command of the Army of the Potomac just days before the battle. Although victorious, he had suffered almost the same number of casualties as the Confederates, just over 23,000 killed, wounded, and captured. Casualties among his officers had been particularly high. Lee's bridgehead on the Potomac was too well fortified to take by storm.[27] Had Meade attempted such an attack, he might have turned victory into defeat. Meade faced the same frustration Lee had encountered at Fredericksburg and Chancellorsville, indeed what most commanders faced throughout the war. In the tactical stalemates that characterized Civil War battles, the victors were usually too exhausted to pursue a defeated enemy, who could easily dig in on better ground and repulse an assault. The size of armies and their division into autonomous corps made destroying them virtually impossible. The entire war saw no Napoleonic battles of annihilation.

Unconventional War

The American Civil War, like most conflicts during the modern era, was a hybrid war in which conventional and unconventional operations blended. Because the war took place predominantly on its soil, the South made the greatest use of irregular forces against the invading army. The Union countered such operations with harsh measures directed at the civilian population. As was the case in both the American Revolution and the Peninsular War in Spain, unconventional operations in hybrid wars could only succeed when incorporated into a comprehensive strategy in which the two forms of warfare complemented one another. Daniel Morgan had achieved this effective fusion at Saratoga and later at the Cowpens, as Wellington had at Salamanca in Spain. During the American Civil War, however, the Confederacy never achieved such synergy. Uncoordinated with conventional operations, unconventional activities proved worse than useless as they justified a harsh response from Union forces against the civilian population in the areas in which the guerrillas operated. Attacks by Confederate partisans followed by Union reprisals contributed to the increasing totality of the war.

Southern irregulars exhibited the same complex mix of organization, membership, and motives characteristic of their counterparts in the Peninsular War. Leaving out regular cavalry units temporarily engaged in unconventional operations such as raiding, these combatants fell into three broad groups: commissioned bodies of partisans wearing distinctive uniforms and operating within the Confederate chain of command, patriotic civilians formed into local bands operating on their own initiative as part-time guerrilla fighters, and outlaws taking advantage of the chaos of war for profit.[28] Conflict between pro-Confederate and pro-Union partisans added to the mayhem. Mini-civil wars between rival groups broke out in some areas, and personal vendettas mixed with political motives.

Although both the human and natural terrains of the theaters of war, particularly the western, favored guerrillas, partisan activities proved disastrous for the Confederacy. To be effective in a hybrid conflict, unconventional operations must support conventional ones as they had at key points during the American Revolution and on some occasions during Wellington's campaign against the French in Spain and Portugal. To a certain extent, southern partisan groups did aid Confederate armies, interdicting Union supplies, cutting telegraph and railroad lines, and ambushing small units. Because so many of them operated independently, however, partisans never amounted to more than a nuisance to federal forces. In two respects, though, they were worse than useless. First, they syphoned Confederate troops. As Union forces controlled more and more territory, Confederate soldiers deserted to defend their homes and families as members of local partisan groups, whose lax discipline they preferred to the tougher regimen of the army.[29] Second, and far worse, irregular operations encouraged Union reprisals against the general population.

The presence of outlaws and opportunists among Confederate irregulars led Union commanders to view all unconventional operations as banditry. Guerrilla activity also encouraged a belief that everyone in occupied territory was a potential insurgent. "There is no doubt but what every man in this state [of Tennessee] who has a gun is a guerrilla, and would shoot any of us down whenever he thought it safe," concluded Brigadier General Gordon Granger.[30] Sherman, whose name would become synonymous with war in extremis, had an even more inclusive view of the enemy. In September 1862 he told his brother it was about time the North understood "that the entire South, man, woman and child are against us."[31] This animosity toward a southern population deemed not only to be sympathetic to but actively supportive of irregular operations intensified as the war progressed.

Partisan units wearing no uniforms and operating outside the military chain of command were not protected by the laws and usages of war. Their activity inevitably provoked a harsh response, directed not merely against the partisans themselves but also against the communities from which they came. Union forces conducted reprisals against those communities, a tactic known as collective punishment, which would be used in colonial wars in the coming decades. Collective punishment presupposes that since the general population abets, harbors, or merely refuses to provide information on partisans, it bears some responsibility for their actions. Union commanders burned barns, destroyed crops, commandeered livestock, levied fines, destroyed homes, and sometimes razed entire villages in retaliation for guerrilla activities. Such reprisals inflicted greater damage on the Confederate war effort than the partisan raids inflicted on the Union campaign.

The Trend toward Total War

The reintroduction of ideology into warfare with the American and French Revolutions began a trend toward total war that intensified with the improved killing technology introduced by the Industrial Revolution. The Civil War represented a significant stage in that evolution. Partisan activity was an important factor in encouraging the federal government to make war, not merely against Confederate armies, but against the civilian population that supported them. Requisitioning also encouraged this trend. As Union armies drove deeper into the South, their supply lines became longer and more tenuous. Seizing crops and cattle to feed troops addressed this problem, although it inflicted considerable hardship on civilians, most of whom received no compensation for what the invading army took. The policy of reprisals for partisan activities and the need to requisition supplies eventually developed into a strategic imperative to wage economic warfare against the Confederacy. General Grant realized that because armies had become too large and too powerful to destroy in battle, they must be weakened by attacking the resources upon which they depended.[32] Shortly before Sherman's Atlanta campaign, Grant directed him to "move against [Joseph E.] Johnston's army, to break it up, and to get into the interior of the enemy's country as far you can, inflicting all the damage you can against their war resources."[33]

The Federal government provided a legal framework for such economic warfare with General Orders 100, otherwise known as the Lieber Code, for its author Francis Lieber, issued by President Lincoln in April 1863.

The code focused on governing occupied territory under martial law, but contained a broad caveat for dealing with a hostile population: "Military necessity, as understood by modern civilized nations, consists in the necessity of those measures which are indispensable for securing the ends of the war, and which are lawful according to the modern law and usages of war." The Code went on to outline what those measures might include:

> Military necessity admits of all direct destruction of life or limb of armed enemies, and of other persons whose destruction is incidentally unavoidable in the armed contests of the war; it allows of the capturing of every armed enemy, and every enemy of importance to the hostile government, or of peculiar danger to the captor; it allows of all destruction of property, and obstruction of the ways and channels of traffic, travel, or communication, and of all withholding of sustenance or means of life from the enemy; of the appropriation of whatever an enemy's country affords necessary for the subsistence and safety of the army.[34]

These instructions allowed commanders considerable latitude and along with other directives became the basis for waging war against the population of the Confederacy.[35] Sherman was the most famous (or infamous) practitioner of such operations, best known for cutting a 60-mile-wide swathe of destruction from Atlanta to Savannah and then northward into the Carolinas. He was not alone, however. General Philip Sheridan scorched the Shenandoah valley, and other Union commanders did the same throughout the theaters of operation. Confederate forces also targeted civilians, burning the town of Chambersburg, Pennsylvania, in April 1864 as retaliation for federal scorched earth tactics.

In one respect though, Union "hard war" strategy fell short of measures taken in 20th-century wars. It sanctioned destruction of property but not the deliberate taking of civilian life unless an individual were caught conducting an attack or engaging in sabotage. The Lieber code instructed soldiers to show humanity in implementing even the harshest measures. Some commanders destroyed only surplus foodstuffs that could supply the Confederate army, leaving people enough for themselves. Many others were less generous, and even those who wished to be humane could not always control their soldiers. Whatever the intent or the actual practice, it would be naïve to believe that a scorched earth policy had no lethal effects. Depriving women, children, and the elderly of food and shelter no doubt caused many to die of exposure, malnutrition, and disease. While no accurate records exist, an estimated 50,000 civilians perished in the Civil War.[36] The vast majority of these deaths occurred in the South and the border states, where most of the fighting occurred, and many no doubt resulted from the Union's economic warfare against the southern population. Still, civilian casualties represented a small percentage of the estimated 761,000 Civil War dead.[37] In World War II civilian deaths would exceed military ones. The American Civil War thus represented a significant step in the evolution of total war, but that process still had a long way to go.

The Experience of War

The experience of Civil War soldiers did not differ in many respects from that of combatants in previous wars. Soldiers spent most of their time in drill exercises, parades, sentry duty, camp chores, and marching. Battles occurred infrequently, and although the new weapons increased their lethality, more men still died of disease than were killed by bullets. Logistics and transport had improved considerably since Napoleon's day. The Union army enjoyed adequate, even ample supplies of food and clothing, while the Confederates usually subsisted on short rations and often went hungry. Many rebel soldiers marched barefoot.

What distinguished Civil War soldiers from their predecessors, however, were the reasons they fought. Patriotism motivated some French soldiers who defended the Revolution during its early days, but the vast majority of them were still conscripts. While both the federal government and the Confederacy eventually resorted to conscription, most Civil War soldiers volunteered. Many reenlisted even after battle and the monotony of camp life disabused them of any illusions about the glory of war. Since they chose to fight, understanding why is essential to comprehending the war. Because so many soldiers on both sides could read and write, the historical record contains many more of their letters, diaries, memoirs, and testimonials than exist for previous conflicts. More than 80 percent of white troops were literate, while almost half had at least some formal education.[38] The accounts they left reveal consistent themes. Patriotism motivated most soldiers, North and South. Northern men enlisted to preserve the Union, while Confederates joined up to defend their liberty, in some cases for the right to secede, and for a minority, the right to own slaves.[39] Some quite literally defended their own communities as they came under attack. The obligation to serve one's country, a sense of honor, and concern for one's reputation reinforced this patriotism.[40] Desire for adventure encouraged others to volunteer, while duty to comrades in arms helped men stay with their regiments after the disillusionment of camp life and combat had set in. Amid the reams of material written by Civil War soldiers, one passage from the diary of an officer in the 2nd Rhode Island

Volunteers captures all of these complex emotions. Explaining his decision to reenlist when his term expired in June 1864, Elisha Hunt Rhodes wrote:

> I decided without hesitation. The United States need [sic] the services of her sons. I am young and in good health, and I feel that I owe a duty to my country. I entered the Army as a private expecting that the war would end in a few months. It has dragged along, and no one can tell when the end will come. But when it does come I want to see it, and so I am going to stay. I like the soldier's life and without egotism I think I am doing some service. If I should go home I should be unhappy and want to come back. Our regiment is a good one and I prefer it to any other.[41]

Wars fought for an ideological cause tend to be more violent than those waged for narrow political objectives. The American and French Revolutions reintroduced ideology, largely absent since the end of the Thirty Years' War, into warfare, substituting nationalism for religion. Until the advent of free, compulsory public education, however, states had a limited ability to inculcate such feeling among their populations. Patriotism learned in school eventually replaced the knout as the prime motivator for ordinary soldiers. The American Civil War was a significant step in the process that has made modern warfare increasingly more total, but that process still had a considerable way to go. Widespread demonization of the enemy, which produced the genocides of the 20th century, was largely absent from the writings of Civil War soldiers and from the official literature of their governments.

CHAPTER SIX

Prussian Military Reforms and the Wars of German Unification

Despite its defeat in 1815, France remained the preeminent land power in Europe. It had taken a coalition of states more than a decade to bring Napoleon down, so even in defeat his reputation remained high. A new generation of military officers, including the generals who later fought the American Civil War, studied Napoleon's campaigns, primarily through the writings of Jomini. As so often happens, though, many of them focused on his campaigns rather than on the broad principles that underlay them. This tendency explains why generals such as Robert E. Lee continued to seek the battle of annihilation the French emperor had achieved at Austerlitz, even when changes in warfare made that impossible.

Prussia's military reputation, on the other hand, had declined considerably since the days of Frederick the Great. The rigid discipline and close-order maneuver that Frederick had so prized proved ineffective against the new formations and more flexible tactics of the French. Prussian armies suffered defeat after defeat at the hands of Napoleon until they copied his approach late in the war. As a result, few commanders in Europe paid much attention to a series of reforms that would transform the Prussian army into the most formidable fighting force in Europe. While officers in other armies studied the past, those in Prussia planned for the future.

Military Reform

Of all the armies that fought in the Napoleonic Wars, none took its lessons to heart more than the Prussian. Following crushing defeats at Jena and Auerstedt in 1806, Prussian generals and their political masters began a series of reforms that would continue through the middle of the 19th century and build the war machine that would defeat the Danes in 1864, the Austrians in 1866, and the French in 1870–71 to create the modern country of Germany. The reforms fell into three broad categories: reorganization of the army, creation of the general staff system, and improved tactics. Like all Western military establishments, the Prussian army benefited from the inventions of the Industrial Revolution, but its reforms enabled it to make better use of those changes than did its adversaries.

Late in the Napoleonic Wars the Prussian army had adopted the corps system, which helped it perform better at Leipzig (1813) and Waterloo (1815). More fundamental change, however, ensued during the postwar years. While other European states continued to employ the *armée de métier* (professional army), comprised of long-service professional soldiers, Prussia adopted the French revolutionary model of the nation in arms but adapted it to its own circumstances. Boyen's law, passed in 1814, made all young men liable for three years' service on active duty in the regular army (based on a lottery), followed by two years in the reserves, and seven years in the first levy of the *Landwehr* (local militias created in 1813), followed by another seven years in the second levy of the *Landwehr*, after which they might until the age of 50 be called upon to serve in the *Landsturm*, an inactive reserve that could be called upon to repel an invasion.[1] Adjusted over the years, this system allowed the Prussians to rapidly expand the standing army in time of war by feeding reservists into regular formations and using the *Landwehr* for rear-area duties. Corresponding social reforms ended serfdom and opened the officer corps to nonaristocrats, laying the groundwork for an army of citizen soldiers.[2] While critics worried that short-service "amateur" soldiers would perform poorly against long-service professionals, Prussia proved them wrong by building its conscript force around a core of highly trained career officers and NCOs.[3]

The second major Prussian reform occurred at the highest level of command. Armies of the Napoleonic age encountered two problems that limited their size: transport/logistics and command and control. Railroads solved the first problem, making it possible to move large numbers of men and supplies over great distance. The second problem required a fundamental shift in thinking about how armies should be led. As Napoleon himself had discovered, the span of control even the best commander could exercise was limited to his range of vision and his ability to transmit orders in a timely manner via mounted couriers. The corps system decentralized command and control to a significant degree, but it depended on competent commanders striking the right balance between obedience to orders and initiative. The larger the army, and the more complex the battle plan, the harder command and control became. The general staff addressed this problem. Generals had always had staffs, but these had consisted of adjutants who helped them draw up plans and draft orders in the field. The Prussian general staff coordinated the activities of the army as a whole. Located in Berlin, the Great General Staff developed doctrine, prepared war plans, and conducted military exercises.

To become a staff officer, a candidate had to graduate from the *Kriegsakademie*, the national war college. Applicants gained admission via competitive examination, and only about one-third of those who matriculated (approximately 150 per year) graduated. Graduates then spent a further two years with the Great General Staff in Berlin for further education and training in topography, map exercises, and war games. The three or four best of these officers stayed with this central body, while the rest served on the staffs of regular units, where the distinctive red stripe on their trousers identified them as the elite of the Prussian army.[4] As they rose through the ranks, these officers would rotate between the Great General Staff and field commands. The general staff system, consisting of a central staff and unit staffs, thus guaranteed that field formations included officers intimately acquainted with plans and doctrines who could advise their commanders on how to adapt to the fluid situation of combat. A corps commander could, for example, make an operational adjustment, confident that the corps commanders to his right and left would adjust their movements accordingly, because all three of them were acting on the best advice of staff officers trained and educated together.

The third major Prussian reform came at the tactical level. To be effective, the general staff system required considerable decentralization of command and control. Achieving this flexibility required a sea change in military thinking. The Prussian army of Frederick the Great had been renowned for its rigid discipline and authoritarian command structure. Necessary as such an approach may have been in the age of small, royal armies, the Napoleonic Wars had demonstrated its limitations during the era of the nation in arms. The reformers replaced the old approach with a flexible concept known as *Auftragstaktik*, "mission-based tactics." Rather than encourage slavish obedience to orders, this concept encouraged officers and even enlisted men to interpret a tactical situation and adjust their behavior accordingly. They would still be given plans and directives by their superiors, but they were empowered to use their judgment in implementing them. Field Marshal Helmuth von Moltke the Elder explained the concept:

> A favorable situation will never be exploited if commanders wait for orders. The highest commander and the youngest soldier must always be conscious of the fact that omission and inactivity are worse than resorting to the wrong expedient.[5]

Rigid obedience to orders when the tactical situation required adjustment was as reprehensible as wantonly disobeying them. A famous anecdote often repeated in the Prussian army down through the years illustrates the meaning of *Auftragstaktik*. A certain major being reprimanded for a tactical mistake defended himself with the argument that he was merely following orders. His commanding officer rejected this argument, pointing out that "his Majesty made you a major because he believed you would know when *not* to obey his orders."[6]

Clausewitz

The Prussians also benefited from the revolution in military thought occurring during the first half of the 19th century. No single writer has contributed as much to the theory and practice of war as the Prussian Karl von Clausewitz. Published after his death in 1831, *Vom Krieg* (*On War*) is a compilation of Clausewitz's writing. While Jomini confined himself to the art of war, Clausewitz took a more expansive view, examining the relationship between armed conflict and other elements of national power, what would later be called grand strategy. Clausewitz insisted that wars never occurred in isolation but served to further national objectives:

> War is not merely a political act, but also a real political instrument, a continuation of political commerce, a carrying out of the same by other means. All beyond this which is strictly peculiar to War relates merely to the peculiar nature of the means which it uses. That the tendencies and views of policy shall not be incompatible with these means, the Art of War in general and the Commander in each particular case may demand, and this claim is truly not a trifling one. But however powerfully this may react on political views in particular cases, still it must always be regarded as only a modification of them; for the political view is the object, War is the means, and the means must always include the object in our conception.[7]

To describe war as an instrument of politics is, it appears, to state the obvious. States go war to achieve specific objectives by force of arms. A close examination of military history before and after Clausewitz's time, however, reveals how often wars have become ends in themselves, guided less by rational considerations of policy than by the passion of kings and statesmen. Rulers had of course long understood that military power could be employed to achieve political objectives, but once a war began, they left it to generals who usually understood victory in purely military terms. In the case of kings and autocrats, one man served as political and military leader, often accountable to no one. For Napoleon and Hitler after him, war and conquest took on a life of their own beyond any reasonable political consideration. Even democracies would struggle with keeping military activity in check. It would take another 70 years and the bloodiest conflict to date for French Premier Georges Clemenceau to realize what Clausewitz could have told him: "War is too important to be left to the generals."[8]

Clausewitz argued that politics does not end when war begins but that war is merely an instrument of policy to be combined with the other elements of national power (diplomacy, economic activity, etc.) to achieve a desired outcome. The military means employed in any conflict should be commensurate with the nature and importance of the objective. By that logic, there could be no such thing, at least at the strategic level, as a purely military decision. The Austro-Prussian War ("Seven Weeks' War") of 1866 provides a good example of this principle. Following his decisive victory over the Austrian army at Königgratz, Field Marshal Helmut von Moltke (the Elder) argued on purely military grounds for capturing Vienna. The Prussian chancellor Otto von Bismarck overruled him, insisting that since the immediate political objective of forcing Austria to relinquish any claim to leading the North German states had been achieved, taking its capital served no purpose and would humiliate what might be a future ally.

The popularity of Clausewitz and particularly Jomini indicates another trend. Bearing arms was becoming a profession in which formal education mattered almost as much as field experience. The 19th century saw a proliferation of military educational institutions and an increase in the number of officers who attended them. Prussia placed the greatest emphasis on professional military education, but after its armies swept to victory in the wars of German unification, other states followed its lead. The system of education evolved until nations had academies for their new cadets, staff colleges for mid-career officers, and war colleges for those promoted to higher commands.

Moltke the Elder

Prussian military reforms, particularly the role of the general staff, met with considerable resistance from conservative senior officers. It would take war and a gifted general to reveal the validity of the new approach. Helmuth von Moltke the Elder became chief of the Prussian general staff in 1857, and in cooperation with the new war minister, Prince Regent Wilhelm and Chancellor Otto von Bismarck embarked on a new set of reforms. When Wilhelm became king of Prussia in 1861, he, War Minister Albrecht Theodor Emil Graf von Roon, and Chancellor Bismarck began expanding the regular army. Moltke concentrated on improving its quality.

Moltke was among the first European officers to grasp the importance of railroads. He realized that, surrounded by three powerful states (Russia, Austria, and France), Prussia could not easily defend its frontiers with linear systems of fortifications. Railroads could, however, allow army units dispersed throughout the country to concentrate at critical points to counter any threat.[9] To be of military value, though, railroads had to be laid out with strategic considerations in mind. Moltke diverted military funding from fortresses to rail lines and brought even private railroad companies under military control.[10] He understood that speed of mobilization, the calling up and deployment of reservists in conjunction with the regular army, might prove decisive in future wars. He created within the Great General Staff a Railroad Department, modeled on the office of the Director of U.S. Military Rail Roads, created by the federal government under the secretary of war during the American Civil War. The Prussian Railroad Department developed the elaborate timetables for mobilization necessary to move troops from their depots to the field. To facilitate this process Moltke replaced the extraterritorial structure of the army with a territorial system that grouped locally based battalions in regional corps areas.

Prussian willingness to embrace other technological changes of the Industrial Revolution was mixed. In the 1840s the army issued its infantry with the Dreyse breech-loading rifle, dubbed "the needle gun" because of its long steel firing pin. Although it had a shorter range than the rifled musket because of air leaking from its breech, the weapon could fire three to four times faster.[11] It could also be reloaded from the prone position, allowing infantrymen greater protection during combat. The Prussian army, however, did not replace its smoothbore bronze cannon with superior steel breech-loading rifled guns until much later. Although the army made limited use of the telegraph to communicate with units in the field during a campaign, it was probably ahead of its adversaries in this area.[12] The key to Prussian victories lay not in technology itself, however, but in the ability of the army to use it effectively. The wars of German unification make this point abundantly clear. The Prussians had better rifles but inferior cannon than the Austrians in 1866, inferior rifles but better cannon than the French in 1870. They won both wars decisively.

The Wars of German Unification

Half a century of military reforms came to fruition in the series of wars by which Prussia unified a collection of German-speaking states into the modern country of Germany, but this transformation did not happen all at once. At the outbreak of the war with Denmark over Schleswig-Holstein in 1864, the general staff functioned largely as a planning body outside the command structure of the field army. As chief of the Great General Staff, Moltke had limited influence until the king appointed him chief of staff of the Austro-Prussian invading army under Field Marshal Count Friedrich von Wrangel. Although the coalition defeated the Danes, the war revealed the deficiency of the Prussian command structure. Soon after the outbreak of war with Austria in 1866, the king decreed that Moltke could issue orders to units in the field without waiting for royal approval.

During the Seven Weeks' War with Austria (1866) Moltke fully employed the operational system he had been developing for years. His staff had already developed a war plan and worked out a mobilization schedule. These careful preparations helped to offset the Prussian numerical disadvantage in troops. Austria and its allies among the southern German states could deploy an army nearly twice the size of Prussia's, but its troops had to be brought together over considerable distances. To forestall this juncture of forces Prussia used its railroads to move rapidly against Austria's allies, Hesse, Hanover, and Saxony. These preemptive strikes eliminated all but a Saxon army of 32,000, which escaped to link up with the Austrians. The speed and audacity of the Prussian attacks intimidated the Bavarians into remaining on the defensive throughout the war.[13] Prussia's alliance with the kingdom of Italy prevented Austria redeploying forces from its southern front. Having thus diminished Austria's numerical advantage, Moltke was now free to deal with an anticipated Austrian advance toward Prussia through Bohemia in what is today the Czech Republic.

Moltke still needed promptly to inflict such a decisive defeat on the Austrians that they would sue for peace, since Prussia would be at a disadvantage in a long war of attrition. To achieve such a victory Prussia would have to go on the offensive. In doing so Moltke would encounter the same problem armies faced during the American Civil War: the tremendous advantage technological change conveyed on the defensive. The

Danish War had revealed the terrible cost of frontal assaults against troops armed with rifles.[14] Moltke found the answer to this tactical dilemma in the *Kesselschlachten*, "the battle of encirclement." To achieve such a double envelopment with the larger armies of his day required another operational innovation. Armies typically concentrated behind the front and then marched en masse into battle, a process that slowed their attack. Moltke proposed to concentrate his forces on the field. Such an approach increased speed of deployment but risked having individual units be defeated in detail. Superior planning, a better rail system, and *Auftragstaktik* made that risk acceptable.

The Battle of Königgratz near the village of Sadowa in what is today the Czech Republic proved the wisdom of the Prussian approach. Despite an almost two-week head start, the Austrians took twice as long to mobilize as the Prussians. The Austrian commander General Ludwig von Benedek moved his army northward using a single rail line, while Moltke had five tracks over which to transport his three armies into Bohemia. In keeping with his new approach, he would allow each army to engage the Austrians as it arrived on the field without waiting for the others. Committed to keeping his force together for greater shock power, Benedek missed an opportunity to defeat the Prussian forces before they combined. Once Moltke's three armies converged, hard fighting ensued. Prussian swarming tactics, which allowed units to advance in open formation in order to deliver maximum fire with their needle guns, proved decisive. Although Benedek managed to retreat across the Elbe before being encircled, he had suffered a decisive defeat. The Austrians lost 44,200 men killed, wounded, or missing (21.5 percent of Benedek's army) to the Prussian's 9,172.[15]

Following Königgratz Austria sued for peace, a decision made easier by the very generous terms Prussia offered. Austria paid no indemnity nor ceded any territory to Prussia, although it did surrender Venetia to Prussia's ally, Italy. Austria simply had to relinquish its leadership of the Confederation of German States, which now became the Confederation of North German States under Prussian leadership. Bismarck insisted on leniency because he understood that he had achieved the political objective of ending Hapsburg interference in Northern Germany. He also appreciated that Austria would be a future ally, provided that Prussia did not impose humiliating surrender terms upon it. From the outset the Iron Chancellor had managed with consummate skill the interplay of war and diplomacy, making certain that France and Russia would remain neutral and forming an alliance with the kingdom of Italy before going to war with the Hapsburg Empire. He employed just the sort of comprehensive strategy Clausewitz had envisioned.

Prussia completed the process of German unification with the Franco-Prussian War of 1870–1871. Although France proved a more formidable adversary than Austria, superior organization, planning, and tactics once again decided the matter in Prussia's favor. Both armies had analyzed Könniggratz, but each drew very different conclusions from it. The French realized the obsolescence of the rifled musket and replaced it with a breechloader of their own, the Chassepot, a weapon significantly better than the Dreyse rifle in range, accuracy, and rate of fire. A rubber ring fitted to the breech bolt addressed the problem of leaking air and the concomitant loss of propellant force and range. Unfortunately, French infantry tactics limited the advantage provided by the new rifle. Mistaking Prussian platoon level swarming tactics as lack of control and failing to understand the nature and importance of *Auftragstaktik*, the French army instructed its officers to assert tight control over their own troops, grouping them in close defensive formations and thus reducing their speed of reloading and at times even relying on outdated rolling fire by battalions.[16]

Even with inferior tactics, the Chassepot might have proven decisive had the Prussians not improved the branches of their army that had performed poorly against Austria: cavalry and artillery. Moltke replaced obsolete smoothbore cannon with rifled breech-loading steel guns. The Krupp six-pounder (designated for the weight of its shot) became the standard Prussian field gun. It was heavy enough to deliver significant firepower but light enough to be rapidly mobile. Rather than mass his cannon as the Austrians had done, however, Moltke distributed them in batteries large enough to support infantry formations but small enough to be moved forward quickly with an assault. With a range, accuracy, and rate of fire superior to their French counterparts, six-pounder batteries could more than compensate for the advantage the Chassepot had over the needle gun.[17] The experience of one Prussian artillery officer at the battle of San Privat revealed the value of the six-pounder as a close infantry support weapon. With a battery of just 30 guns and a handful of infantry he turned back an attack by an entire French infantry division.[18] Moltke also transformed the Prussian cavalry from an arm dominated by heavy horse arrayed for shock tactics to a force of light units prepared to swarm over the enemy countryside gathering intelligence and screening Prussian troop movements.[19]

Superior planning and staff work gave Moltke the advantage over the French from the outset. The Prussian mobilization went like clockwork, while the French encountered numerous difficulties. With its extraterritorial structure, French regiments had to form battalions and corps in the field, and many had trouble finding their units. The French railroad network proved inadequate for rapid mobilization and continuous supply of its troops once they had deployed.

Lack of a clear strategy further hampered French efforts. Napoleon III deployed 250,000 troops into two groups: a force of 100,000 near Strasbourg under command of Marshal Patrice MacMahon and 150,000 near Metz.[20] He thus split his armies in two, with the Vosges Mountains separating them. Based on the empty promise of an Austrian archduke that the Hapsburg Empire would back France in a war with Prussia, he planned to use the southern force to separate the Prussians from their Southern German allies (Bavaria, Württemberg, Baden, and Hesse) to support an Austrian offensive.[21] To make matters worse, he deployed the five corps of the western "Army of the Rhine" and the two corps of the eastern army along the entire frontier, blocking possible Prussian routes of advance but too far apart to mutually support one another.[22] The Prussians for their part deployed their troops efficiently in three mobile armies totaling 320,000 men by August 3.[23]

Despite its inferior numbers and mobilization difficulties, the French army opened hostilities with an attack across the frontier to capture Saarbrucken. Realizing he faced encirclement, however, Marshal Achille Baizane withdrew back to Spicheren on the French side of the border. The Prussian First and Second Armies followed and after hard fighting dislodged the French from their strong position on the heights. Baizane's forces withdrew into the fortress city of Metz, where the Prussians encircled them after several fierce battles. Meanwhile, east of the Vosges the Prussian Third Army had decisively defeated MacMahon's two corps at Wissembourg, causing him to retreat all the way to Chalôn. Alarmed by the deteriorating situation, Napoleon III took personal command of a new army forming around the remnants of MacMahon's corps and marched to relieve Metz.

With Prussian reinforcements pouring in and Baizane making only limited efforts to break out of Metz, Moltke could detach forces from the siege to pursue the relieving army, which he trapped in a bend of the Meuse River at Sedan. Occupying a depression surrounded by high ground, Napoleon III failed to realize the disadvantage of his position and did not try to move his army, even when one of his officers declared, "here we are at the bottom of a chamber pot and are about to be shitted upon."[24] Surrounded by a Prussian force of more than 200,000, some 130,000 French troops faced savage pounding from Prussian artillery. The six-pounder guns proved so devastating that Sedan has been described as "an artillery massacre."[25] On September 2 the emperor surrendered what remained of his army, just over 100,000 men, with all of their artillery, rifles, and equipment.[26] Metz capitulated at the end of October. All that remained was to take the capital, now in the hands of the newly proclaimed Third Republic. The Prussians besieged the city, hoping to starve it into submission. With the bulk of the professional French field army destroyed or captured, the garrison of Paris and newly mobilized conscripts were no match for the force of over one million Prussian and German allied troops now occupying France. After a month of bombardment, Paris capitulated, and the French signed an armistice on January 28, 1871.

Prussia's decisive victory made possible the unification of the remaining German states into modern Germany and saw that new nation supplant France as the preeminent land power in Europe. After 1871 the Prussian military system became the one to emulate. Unfortunately for the future peace of Europe, the victors were not as magnanimous to France as they had been to Austria, perhaps because the Franco-Prussian War had been more costly. Prussia had suffered 133,750 casualties to France's 238,000.[27] The cost of mobilizing over a million men and supplying them for five months of war was enormous, and the Prussian public believed France must be made to pay for it. Against his better judgment, Bismarck annexed the provinces of Alsace and Lorraine to the new Reich and imposed an indemnity of 5 million francs on France and made paying a portion of it a precondition of withdrawing Prussian troops from the country. While he may have desired a more conciliatory peace, Bismarck had to feed the demon of patriotic fervor he had invoked to fight the war. That popular feeling characterized warfare during the 19th century and would contribute to its increasing totality in the 20th century.

Unconventional Warfare

The Seven Weeks' War with Austria ended too quickly for unconventional operations to commence, let alone have an effect. The last phase of the Franco-Prussian War, however, did see significant partisan activity. The new republic proclaimed after Napoleon III had surrendered at Sedan tried to continue the struggle with a new *levée en masse* like the one that had saved the First Republic in 1793. In addition to raising new conventional forces, the provisional government recruited *francs-tireurs* (literally, "mavericks"), partisans operating out of uniform to attack supply lines, conduct ambushes, and murder Prussian stragglers. Had they been able to operate in close cooperation with effective field forces, these irregulars might have been effective. As it was, Moltke had to detach 105,000 troops to protect the vulnerable supply lines for his 500,000 frontline troops.[28] Serving merely to prolong the inevitable, however, *francs-tireurs* did nothing but add to the loss of life. Infuriated Prussians predictably responded much as Union officers had during the American Civil War. They summarily executed captured partisans (or men merely suspected of such activities), burned houses and sometimes entire villages, and levied collective fines on the civilian population. The experience of the *francs-tireurs* thus conformed to the pattern of previous hybrid wars that would be repeated in future ones. If partisans operate in cooperation with conventional forces, as they did during the American Revolution and would do in Eastern Europe during World War II and during the Vietnam War, they can be effective. Operating on their own, they do little but add to the misery of the civilian population because of the reprisals that their actions provoke.

Modern Warfare

The American Civil War and the wars of German unification fought during the mid-19th century were the first conflicts of the industrial age. Mass armies of citizen soldiers motivated by patriotism and armed with rifles deployed using railroads. In short wars victory went to the most skilled battlefield commander who made the best use of new technology. In long wars superior resources proved decisive. With its greater population, resources, and industrial capacity, the Union would be the inevitable winner of a war of attrition against a primarily agrarian Confederacy of southern states. Prussia, on the other hand, defeated Denmark, Austria, and France because of the effective way it organized its army and society to wage war. Lincoln and Bismarck understood the complex relationship among diplomacy, domestic policy, and war, without which they could not have been successful.

In one important respect, however, the wars of German unification differed markedly from the American Civil War. The Prussian advantages in organization, planning, tactics, and speed of mobilization were so decisive that the Danish, Austro-Prussian, and Franco-Prussian wars were very short. Had the adversaries been better matched, however, the Franco-Prussian War in particular might have been equally long and bloody an affair as the conflict between the northern and southern U.S. states. Two generations of future officers thus had two examples to study: the American and the Prussian. Unfortunately, European commanders had little regard for the American army. Moltke himself allegedly described the Civil War as "two armed mobs chasing each other around the country, from which nothing can be learned."[29] Whether or not the remark is apocryphal, it reflects the attitude of superiority held by many European officers.

Unfortunately the wars of German unification were atypical of industrialized warfare. Prussia enjoyed such a decisive advantage in planning, organization, speed of mobilization, and tactics that it achieved decisive victories in a very short time. It took seven weeks to defeat Austria. Just one month after the Prussians had massed troops on the French border, the emperor surrendered at Sedan. The war would drag on for several months, but its outcome had been decided. Had the adversaries in the Franco-Prussian War been more evenly matched, however, the constricted space of northeastern France would have made such a rapid victory very unlikely. The derisive views of Moltke and his contemporaries notwithstanding, the American Civil War was the more instructive example. With the two armies comparably equipped and the numerically inferior one enjoying the advantage of being on the defensive, neither side could achieve a knockout blow in a single battle or campaign. Grant and Sherman understood this situation and realized that only a grinding war of attrition could produce victory.

Focusing on the Seven Weeks' and Franco-Prussian Wars led European officers to a very different conclusion. They decided that victory belonged not to the side with the greatest ability to wage a long war of attrition, but to the one that could strike first and hardest. Planning for the next major war focused on how to achieve the result of 1871 with rapid mobilization and bold offensive action. General staffs spent considerable time working out precise timetables for getting their troops on trains headed for the frontier. Unfortunately, such an approach assumed that one state could mobilize significantly faster than the others. After 1871 all nations imitated the Prussians, developing their strategic rail networks and drawing up detailed mobilization plans. This approach made it very unlikely that any nation would have the advantage Moltke had enjoyed. Technological change in the decades following the Franco-Prussian War also militated against the next war being as brief. These changes benefited the defensive and thus made decisive battles much harder to achieve. Obsession with mobilization would introduce a disastrous rigidity into military planning. In July 1914 the tyranny of timetables would severely constrain diplomatic efforts to prevent war.

The Franco-Prussian War had another unforeseen consequence. The terms of peace left France so embittered as to make another war with Germany very likely. Loss of the war probably hurt less than the loss of Alsace-Lorraine. "Men more quickly forget the death of their father than the loss of their patrimony," Machiavelli had warned.[30] The loss of two provinces amounted to much more than one person's estate. It stood to reason that France would make every effort to recover them. Fear of embittering Austria had led Bismarck to offer that empire easy terms in 1866. As a result of his generosity, the Hapsburg Empire and Germany formed in 1879 an alliance lasting until 1918. The Iron Chancellor had also opposed taking Alsace-Lorraine from France in 1871, but he had been overruled. France never forgave Germany and taught two generations of its schoolchildren that the provinces must be recovered, which they were in 1919, but only after the most destructive war in human history to date.

CHAPTER SEVEN

The Long Peace

Forty-three years of peace followed the end of the Franco-Prussian War. For two generations none of the European powers fought with one another. These years saw tremendous political, social, economic, and technological change, which would profoundly affect the nature of warfare. The absence of conventional wars, however, prevented European militaries appreciating fully the impact of these changes. Only at the end of the period did a series of local conflicts in South Africa, the Far East, and the Balkans suggest what a major European war might be like. Even then, the circumstances under which these local wars were fought made it easy for observers to dismiss them as atypical. In the absence of more recent examples, military planners fixated on the Franco-Prussian War as the best guide to preparations for the next conflict. That example would prove to be very misleading.

Peace in Europe, though, did not mean peace in the world. Fighting took place throughout the period on the fringes of expanding European empires in Africa and Asia and in the American West. Colonial powers fought indigenous people to gain territory or suppress revolt, and the United States advanced steadily westward into Native American lands. The locals usually stood little chance against the superior weapons and organization of Western armies, although in some cases they did wage successful guerrilla campaigns to delay the inevitable. At the very least they forced Western armies to develop new strategies and tactics for combating irregulars. Since empires existed to provide markets and resources for the mother country, the wholesale slaughter of indigenous people was unprofitable. Colonial forces developed a combination of carrots and sticks to encourage and if necessary compel cooperation or at least quell unrest.

Technological Change

Technological development in the decades following the Franco-Prussian War consisted primarily of improvements to existing weapons and equipment. The breech-loading rifle remained the principle infantry weapon, and manufacturers worked to improve its range, accuracy, and rate of fire. The French had already addressed the problem of reduced range caused by gases escaping from the breech. The inventor of the Chassepot fitted the bolt with a rubber ring to produce a better seal when the bolt was closed. Brass cartridges tipped with lead or copper bullets replaced the less reliable paper or cloth ones. The brass jacket contained a percussion cap in its base and was filled with gunpowder. After firing the lead or copper tip, the soldier ejected the spent brass casing by opening the bolt.

Manufacturers increased rate of fire by adding a magazine to the gun, allowing a new bullet to be automatically chambered after the spent cartridge was ejected. After much experimentation, the clip magazine proved to be the most effective design. The clip was a metal box carrying several bullets fitted beneath the breech in front of the trigger. When the soldier opened the bolt after each firing, a spring mechanism ejected the spent cartridge and inserted another bullet into the chamber. The infantryman could now fire as fast as he could pull the trigger and open and close the bolt. When all the bullets in the clip had been fired, he simply replaced it with a new preloaded clip. The clip magazine rifle appeared in the 1880s and soon became the standard in Western armies. It has remained so ever since. The magazine increased the rate of fire dramatically. In the hands of a trained infantryman, the Lee-Metford rifle, which went into service in the British army in 1888, could fire 25 rounds per minute using an 8-round clip (increased to 10 rounds in 1892).[1]

The next stage in the evolution of rapid fire weapons was the machine gun. Inventors sought to create a weapon that could deliver a continuous volume of fire. Two prototypes had already been deployed: the Gatling gun of the American Civil War and the *Mitrailleuse* of the Franco-Prussian War. Both employed multiple barrels turned by a crank to produce continuous fire. Mounted on an artillery carriage, however, they were too heavy to be rapidly mobile and could not easily be turned for a wide field of fire. Their effectiveness as infantry support weapons was therefore limited.

In 1883 Hiram Maxim invented the first modern machine gun. Mounted on a small wheeled carriage or tripod, the weapon fired automatically using the force of the gun's own recoil to eject one shell and load the next from a belt fed through the breech. Because continuous fire overheated and eventually jammed the gun, the barrel had to be cooled by water in a hollow cylinder surrounding it.[2] The weapon could fire 450 rounds per minute and together with its tripod and cooling water weighed just less than 100 pounds.[3] It required three men to operate and could be moved and set up fairly rapidly. In the mid-20th century water-cooled machine guns were replaced by much lighter air-cooled models, including those small enough to be carried by individual soldiers. Modern military assault rifles combine the ability to fire individual rounds and automatic bursts. Although they may fire at the same rate as crew-serviced weapons, hand-held machine guns fire fewer rounds because of limitations on the size of magazine that feasibly can be carried by a soldier.

As weapons evolved, so did the ammunition they fired. In the 1880s chemists developed a new type of powder that created greater gas pressure without the clouds of smoke produced by traditional gunpowder. Smokeless powder allowed soldiers to fire without giving away their position. With battlefields no longer occluded by smoke, soldiers eventually adopted camouflaged uniforms to make them harder to spot. Inventors also made artillery more destructive. During the first decade of the 20th century trinitrotoluene, a high explosive, became the standard filling for shells. High explosives had their greatest immediate impact on naval warfare. Traditional powder would propel an armor-piercing round through the steel hull of a ship, and then the TNT would explode, causing maximum damage. In land warfare high explosives enabled heavy artillery to smash concrete fortifications and increased the destructive power of shrapnel and percussion shells.

Inventors improved not only the projectiles fired by cannon but the guns themselves. The Franco-Prussian War had demonstrated the superiority of the breech-loading rifled gun, but artillery still suffered from a problem that had existed since the invention of cannon. Newton's third law of motion states that "for every action there is an equal and opposite reaction." The explosive force that fired the shell caused the artillery piece to recoil. It then had to be rolled back into position and re-aimed. The larger the gun, the greater the recoil. A spade pit at the end of the gun carriage absorbed some of this motion, but the problem was only solved by the invention of an effective recoil mechanism. The new design mounted the gun barrel on a slide attached to a stationary carriage fitted with a hydro-pneumatic cylinder similar to the shock absorber on an automobile.

When the gun was fired, only the barrel retracted, compressing the gas inside the cylinder, which absorbed the force of the recoil. The stationary carriage kept the gun sited for the next firing. The French 75 mm cannon put into service in 1897 was the first recoilless artillery piece in European armies. Served by a skilled crew, the gun fired up to 15 rounds a minute with great accuracy at a maximum range of just over four miles.[4]

Recoilless artillery, smokeless powder, and TNT made much larger cannon possible. The German army would go to war in 1914 with massive 420 mm Krupp and 360 mm Skoda howitzers (guns firing shells on an arced as opposed to a flat trajectory). Designed to smash masonry fortifications, they would, along with larger mortars, also prove highly effective against entrenched infantry. Not all armies acquired heavy guns, however. Committed to a strategy of rapid offensive, the French made the lighter, more mobile 75 mm the mainstay of their army.[5] Their field guns would serve them well during the initial campaign when armies maneuvered in the open, but lack of heavy artillery became a huge liability once trench warfare took hold. By the end of World War I all armies had a broad range of artillery pieces designed for different purposes.

Another invention of the late 19th century not intended for military use would have a significant effect on warfare. In 1874 DeKalb, Illinois, native Joseph Glidden took out a patent for a new type of fence. Consisting of two strands of intertwined wire with twisted spurs evenly distributed along its length, "barbed wire" offered an inexpensive, easy-to-erect means of containing cattle on the vast American prairies, where wood was scarce and expensive to import.[6] Placed in front of entrenched infantry supported by machine guns and backed by artillery firing from concealed positions, however, barbed wire increased exponentially the advantage of the defensive over the offensive. The combination of new weapons with barbed wire would create the trench stalemate characteristic of World War I.

Another invention, which would in the long run revolutionize not only warfare but travel, transportation, and communication, appeared in the early 20th century. The Wright brothers' test of a successful airplane at Kitty Hawk, North Carolina, in 1903 ushered in the age of aviation. The primitive bi- and triplanes of World War I would have little impact on the conflict, but they foreshadowed the far greater destructive airpower that would be manifest during World War II. More than any other invention, the airplane would eliminate any remaining distinction between combatant and noncombatant. Strategic bombing of cities would kill far more civilians than soldiers ever could. The precursor of the large manned bomber was not, however, the airplane but the dirigible, a large canvas balloon stretched over a metal frame and filled with hydrogen gas. Militaries began using these lighter-than-air ships during the first decade of the 20th century.

Two additional inventions would also impact warfare, although neither was invented for that purpose: the internal combustion engine and the telephone. The implications of the automobile and its larger cousin the truck for logistics and transport immediately became clear. By 1908 all the major European powers except Austria-Hungary and Russia could field 50 motor vehicles at their annual maneuvers and had plans to commandeer civilian cars and trucks in time of war.[7] Telephones offered an improvement over telegraphs as they could transmit voice rather than just Morse code. Portable versions for use on the battlefield would make their appearance during the Russo-Japanese War (1902–1904).

Navies

Naval warfare also changed during the period from the middle of the 19th century to the outbreak of World War I. Ironclad warships began to replace wooden ones during the American Civil War. Sail disappeared as a means of propulsion when coal-powered, steam-engine-driven screw propellers became efficient enough for oceangoing vessels. Steel breech-loading rifled cannon became the norm at sea just as on land. During the first decade of the 20th century the evolution of naval warfare took a dramatic step forward. In 1906 the British launched HMS *Dreadnought*, the first of a new class of battleships equipped with steam turbine engines for greater speed and a main battery of 10-by-12-inch guns mounted in five turrets. HMS *Dreadnought* made all other battleships obsolete and led to a naval arms race with Germany, which contributed to the outbreak of World War I. Ironically, though designed for ship-to-ship combat, the new battleships rarely confronted one another. Their primary value lay in their ability to support a blockade of enemy ports.

Like the dreadnought, the submarine also came of age in the decades before the Great War. Inventors had experimented with prototype submersibles as early as the 18th century, but the first practical models did not appear until the end of the 19th century and were refined as warships in the decade before World War I. Conventional combustion engines powered them on the surface, and batteries propelled them underwater when combustion fumes would have suffocated the crew. They were armed with a combination of small deck guns and torpedoes. While Britain remained supreme on the surface of the seas, the Germans led the way in submarine warfare. Like surface fleets, submarines would be primarily weapons of economic warfare, preying on enemy commerce.

The HMS *Dreadnought*, a British battleship, in 1906. *Source:* U.S. Navy.

Social Change

The same process of industrialization that created new weapons transformed society. Roads, railroads, telegraph lines, and the development of modern bureaucracies helped turn nation states into modern nations, "imagined communities" whose citizens shared a common language, culture, and sense of history with millions of people whom they had never even met.[8] Creation of this new collective identity depended heavily on free, compulsory public education. State-funded schools taught students not only reading, writing, and arithmetic but civics, a combination of romanticized national history and instruction on the duties of citizenship. Fighting for one's country ranked first among those duties.[9] Public education thus did a great deal to promote the patriotic fervor that inspired millions of men to march enthusiastically to war in 1914.

Unconventional Conflict

The period 1871 to 1914 was predominantly an era of colonial warfare. European powers, particularly France and Britain, expanded their empires and suppressed revolts within them. During the same period the U.S. government facilitated settlement of lands west of the Mississippi River by relocating (forcibly if necessary) native American tribes living on those lands. All of these conflicts had much in common. To begin with, their outcome was never in doubt. Indigenous people stood no chance against the superior weapons, organization, and resources of the colonizers. They fought holding actions that did no more than delay the inevitable, often at great cost to their own people. While they used guerrilla tactics, they had no coherent strategy. They did not operate in support of regular forces like partisans, and they could not liberate territory like modern insurgents.[10] They fought a desperate, losing struggle to retain their land.

If the indigenous peoples of Africa, Asia, and North America were not acting like insurgents, neither were the conquerors conducting modern counterinsurgency campaigns. They faced few constraints on their use of coercive force save the decency of individual military commanders and the humanitarian sentiments of a public ill-informed about what really went on in colonies or along frontiers. Europeans and White Americans of the late 19th century subscribed to Social Darwinism (whether or not they understood the term), the inherent right of superior races to rule over inferior ones. "In every particular state of the world, those nations which are strongest tend to prevail over the others," wrote the British economist Walter Bagehot in 1872, "and in certain marked peculiarities the strongest tend to be the best."[11] For some thinkers, a humanitarian sentiment tempered this brutal ethic. The conquerors had an obligation to civilize and Christianize the savages whose land they appropriated. The British poet laureate Rudyard Kipling best expressed this mission in his 1898 poem, "The Whiteman's Burden," written as an epistle to the United States after victory in the Spanish-American War gave it an empire to govern:

> Take up the White Man's burden—
> Send forth the best ye breed—
> Go bind your sons to exile
> To serve your captives' need;
> To wait in heavy harness,
> On fluttered folk and wild—
> Your new-caught, sullen peoples,
> Half-devil and half-child.[12]

American Frontier and Colonial Warfare

The practical and humanitarian aspects of imperialism came together in American discussions of the "Indian problem." Conflict with native peoples dated to the earliest European settlements in North America, but in the decades following the Civil War westward expansion created new confrontations. Railroads opened the lands west of the Mississippi to settlement. As easterners moved into the prairies and plains seeking farm and grazing land, they inevitably encroached on tribal territory. Discovery of gold and other minerals in these areas intensified conflict. Wherever possible, the U.S. government sought to secure land by treaties, which were abrogated as convenience dictated. The Indians of course resisted the stealing of their land and resorted to raiding white settlements, often out of economic necessity. The government responded by herding Native Americans onto reservations, preferably by persuasion, but if necessary by force.

Some contemporary historians have characterized the treatment of Native Americans as genocide.[13] Mass killing certainly occurred, but neither the U.S. government nor the army had a policy of exterminating Indians. Some commanders certainly expressed genocidal sentiments. Not surprisingly, General Sherman was one of them. "We must act with vindictive earnestness against the Sioux, even to their extermination, men, women and children," he wrote General Grant following the massacre, scalping, and mutilation of 81 officers and men in an ambush.[14] He never of course got the chance to act on this impulse and probably in his calmer moments did not really wish to do so. Other officers had a more beneficent, albeit condescending, attitude toward the native population. General Alfred Terry, another Civil War veteran with extensive experience on the plains, delineated a two-step process for civilizing the Indian tribes:

> The first step, therefore, toward the successful solution of the Indian question is to give the Indians cattle and let them live a pastoral life, which is so closely allied to their own natural life, and which, I believe, they would gladly adopt and follow if properly managed. Then, after a few years, when they had become reconciled to the abandonment of their nomadic life and were content to settle down permanently at some peaceful occupation—in other words, when they had served an apprenticeship to peace and occupation—give them land and agricultural implements, and they will then adopt the agricultural life as readily as they did the pastoral, simply because they will have been educated up to that second step and will be prepared for it.[15]

Settlement of Indians on designated tracts of land known as reservations was official policy, although the government was seldom as generous with cattle, implements, and quality of land as Terry advocated.

Westward expansion and development combined with the policy of relocation to reservations led to a desultory type of frontier warfare. Although they loom large in the popular imagination, battles like the Little

Bighorn were rare. Even that engagement involved a single, understrength cavalry regiment (fewer than 700 men) divided into three columns, one of which (the one led by General George Armstrong Custer) was wiped out by a much larger force of Sioux and Cheyenne with the loss of all 209 officers and men.[16] Massacres like the infamous one at Wounded Knee Creek in December 1890, in which soldiers killed 145 Sioux (including 44 women and 18 children) did occur, but they were no more typical than the Little Bighorn.[17]

Most military operations involved small units of soldiers engaging small bands of Indians. In Texas alone from 1865 to 1881, 37 percent of engagements involved military units of 16 to 25 men, and only 7 percent involved a unit of more than 50.[18] Not only were engagements small, they were not particularly lethal. Estimates for Texas during the same period put the number of Indians killed in engagements with the army at 424.[19] Most military operations involved no hostile encounters at all. Patrolling represented the most common military activity. Again, the data for Texas reveal a pattern that was probably consistent for the frontier as a whole. From September 1878 to September 1879, cavalry units conducted 128 patrols from 13 posts over 40,100 miles, but fought only two engagements.[20] Such operations did not, however, need to be lethal to be effective. Wearing the Indians down over time with constant patrolling and reduction of their food supplies achieved the result of forcing native peoples onto reservations.[21]

Many tribes depended on hunting and could be conquered by depriving them of game. The American bison, commonly called buffalo, provided essential meat and furs for the nomadic tribes of the Great Plains. The transcontinental railroad made it possible for white hunters using high-powered rifles to slaughter the animals with ease, sometimes firing from the trains themselves. Profit motivated the hunters, but the army soon realized that their efforts contributed to the policy of forcing Indians onto reservations. General Philip Sheridan articulated the strategic value of destroying the buffalo herds. In defense of the hunters he observed:

> These men have done more in the last two years, and will do more in the next year, to settle the vexed Indian question, than the entire regular army has done in the last forty years. They are destroying the Indians' commissary. And it is a well-known fact that an army losing its base of supplies is placed at a great disadvantage. Send them powder and lead, if you will; but for a lasting peace, let them kill, skin and sell until the buffaloes are exterminated. Then your prairies can be covered with speckled cattle.[22]

While individual profit sufficed to promote hunting, the states of Texas and Kansas actively supported exterminating the buffalo.[23]

Besides fighting on its western frontier, the United States engaged in one counterinsurgency-style campaign outside the country. From 1899 to 1902 U.S. forces fought to defeat an insurgency in the Philippines, territory acquired following the Spanish-American War. Emilio Aguinaldo, leader of an anti-Spanish insurrection, launched a rebellion against the Americans, who refused to leave after "liberating" his country. The U.S. Army easily defeated his forces in open battle but faced a more serious challenge when he abandoned conventional operations and adopted guerrilla warfare. With just 24,000 troops it had to subdue an insurgent movement of 80,000 rebels operating in bands of 50–80 amid a population of 7.4 million.[24] Repression alone would not suffice, although American forces certainly tried it. To separate the insurgents from the population that supported them, the U.S. occupation government built schools and roads, inoculated people against smallpox, and doled out jobs to cooperative locals.[25] To defeat the guerrilla bands, the army divided its operational area into four districts, subdivided into zones in which small, mobile units conducted counter-guerrilla operations.[26] A generous amnesty reintegrated many former insurgents back into Philippine society. By no means flawless, the campaign nonetheless represented a good example of successful counterinsurgency. Unfortunately, the U.S. Army did not preserve its lessons for future generations, and by the time of the Vietnam War it had been all but forgotten.

European Colonial Warfare

During the era of frontier wars in the United States, the European powers expanded their empires in Asia and Africa. As in North America, a combination of pecuniary motives and humanitarian sentiment impelled them to conquest. Neither missionary zeal nor a civilizing mission, however, prevented the use of overwhelming force to seize territory or suppress revolt. At Omdurman on the Nile River in 1898, an army of 60,000 Dervishes armed with spears and rifles led by the charismatic Mahdi attacked an expeditionary force of 8,200 British and 17,600 Egyptian and Sudanese troops equipped with magazine rifles, 40 Maxim machine guns, and 50 pieces of artillery.[27] The British also used expanding bullets deemed inappropriate for "civilized" warfare in Europe. When the firing stopped, approximately 11,000 Dervishes lay dead at the cost of just 48 British, Sudanese, and Egyptian killed.[28] Omdurman, observed the war correspondent George Warrington Steevens, "was not a battle but an execution."[29]

Merciless in battle against nonwhites they sought to conquer, Europeans could be even more brutal in suppressing revolt by those they already ruled. The response of the German military to the Herero uprising in Southwest Africa in 1904 provides one of the most poignant examples of the destruction of native peoples. The Herero of what is today central Namibia resisted the seizure of their land and the destruction of their way of life by German colonists. In January 1904 some 8,000 warriors attacked farms and settlements. They killed approximately 125 German men, being careful to spare women, children, and non-German European men. Using local colonial forces, the governor drove the warriors back and might have negotiated a settlement with them had not Berlin determined on making an example of them. The government sent in nearly 19,000 regular troops, who defeated the rebel army in battle and caused the others to flee into the desert.[30] Unable to pursue them there, the Germans sealed off the area, intentionally causing many refugees to die of thirst.[31]

By the end of 1904 organized resistance had come to an end, but the Germans proceeded to round up the remaining Herero and Nama (another group who had rebelled) and herd them into concentration camps. In the camps the Africans suffered physical abuse, summary execution, and rape. Some were sold into slavery. German doctors even conducted experiments on the internees. By the time the rebellion ended in 1907, 80 percent of the Herero population (some 48,000 people) had died.[32]

With good reason, historians have described suppression of the Herero revolt as the first genocide of the 20th century and have seen in it an ominous foreshadowing of the Holocaust.[33] In military history it represents an equally important step towards total war.[34] Civilians had always died in wars, and commanders sometimes targeted them for supporting the enemy army or abetting guerrillas. They did not, however, kill women and children merely because they belonged to an enemy population. The German commander, Lieutenant General Lothar von Trotha, however, not only allowed his men to kill women and children but actually ordered them to do so. "Scientific" racism, which viewed subject peoples as less than fully human, made such brutal policy possible. Applied initially to Africans, this racial theory of warfare would be expanded to include all groups deemed inferior.

The Battle of Omdurman and the suppression of the Herero Revolt represent extremes in colonial warfare. Few large battles occurred, and most revolts ended with less loss of life. Indigenous people even won occasional victories. The Zulu wiped out a British battalion at Insandlwana in 1879, and Pashtun tribes along the Afghan frontier of British India successfully resisted conquest. Such limited successes, however, did little more than delay the inexorable advance of European colonialism. By the end of the 19th century, only a few states in Africa and Asia remained independent.

The impact of colonial warfare on the evolution of armies in Europe and the United States is difficult to gauge. The U.S. Army never captured its frontier experience in formal doctrine. Officers who had served in the West applied what they had learned to suppressing the Philippine insurrection (1899–1902), but the transfer of learning was never formalized.[35] The British, who had more colonial war experience than any other nation, did capture much of the practical wisdom of unconventional warfare, albeit in quasi-official form. In 1896 a young major named C. E. Callwell published *Small Wars: Their Principles and Practice*, based on his 1886 prize-winning essay on the lessons of colonial wars.[36] The book went through several editions and became a standard text in the British army.[37]

Small Wars is a vast compendium of strategic and tactical theory illustrated through historical examples and laced with practical wisdom based on a single premise:

> The conduct of small wars is in fact in certain respects an art by itself, diverging widely from what is adapted to the conditions of regular warfare, but not so widely that there are not in all its branches points which permit comparisons to be established.[38]

Much of the book's tactical information has long since become obsolete, but some of its broad principles remain timely. The chapter on guerrilla warfare in particular emphasizes the need for small, mobile forces led by junior officers empowered to take initiative, constant harassment of the enemy, a good intelligence organization, and destruction of the enemy's economic base (crops, livestock, etc.).[39] Callwell argued for the necessity of scorched earth policies and collective punishment under certain circumstances, although he had to admit that "wholesale destruction of the property of the enemy may sometimes do more harm than good."[40] By no means a modern counterinsurgency manual, *Small Wars* nonetheless showed greater understanding of unconventional conflict than any publication to date.

Conventional Conflicts in the Era of Colonial Warfare

The long era of peace from 1871 to 1914 did see some limited, localized conventional wars. Most occurred at the end of the period, and some taught valuable lessons about the changing nature of warfare, many

The Long Peace

of which were ignored by European armies. In 1898 the United States defeated Spain in just three months of a very one-sided war. Britain fought the Transvaal and the Orange Free State, two Boer republics in what is today South Africa, in two separate but related wars, first in 1880 and then from 1899 to 1902. Japan defeated Russia in a war over Manchuria and Korea (1902–1904), and several Balkan states fought Turkey (1912) and then quarreled with each other over the spoils (1913). The Boer War and the Russo-Japanese War provided some indication of what the approaching conflagration in Europe would be like, but because they occurred on the periphery of Western civilization, armies were quicker to absorb their tactical than their strategic lessons.

The Second Boer War was the first conflict in which armies equipped with magazine rifles faced one another.[41] Having abandoned their famous redcoats for khaki prior to the conflict, British soldiers soon learned that they had to paint over brass buttons and belt buckles, while British officers gave up swords, binoculars, and other insignia of rank that made them tempting targets for sharpshooters.[42] In the decade before the outbreak of World War I, all but the French, who clung tenaciously to their red trousers and blue coats, adopted uniforms that made them less visible. The Boer War also underscored the lesson of the American Civil War that frontal assaults against entrenched infantry had little chance of success. Volley firing in close formations, the British suffered frightful losses against Boer soldiers firing Mauser magazine rifles from concealed positions.[43] The British succeeded only when they changed their approach, pinning down enemy infantry with concentrated fire and conducting flanking attacks using mounted troopers, not as traditional cavalry, but as mounted infantry.[44] After the South African War the British army concentrated on training infantrymen to fire individual aimed shots in rapid succession to the point where they could discharge 30 rounds per minute.[45] This Second Boer War also saw extensive use of another ominous icon of 20th-century warfare: concentration camps, in which the British relocated women and children to isolate Boer guerrillas from their base of support.[46]

The Russo-Japanese War underscored the lessons of South Africa and taught some new ones. Both armies began the war in traditional brightly colored uniforms and ended it in drab ones. Two Western-style armies (though an Asian nation, Japan had Westernized its military) faced each other equipped with the full array of weapons that would make warfare so deadly in 1914: machine guns, rapidfire artillery, magazine rifles, barbed wire, and land mines.[47] The war demonstrated the necessity of indirect artillery fire and the superiority of shrapnel over high explosives in destroying infantry formations.[48] Both sides relied heavily on trenches to protect their soldiers from the rain of steel. The Japanese adapted to the new conditions better than the Russians. Their infantry advanced as close to the enemy line as possible by night and attacked, not in extended lines like the Europeans, but in small groups of a dozen or so men advancing independently and in rushes, making use of what natural cover the field afforded.[49] European military observers saw in the success of the Japanese not compelling evidence that frontal assaults would be at best costly and at worse futile, but proof that bayonet charges were still possible and even necessary.[50]

The Russo-Japanese War also saw the first widespread use of a new communication device, the field telephone. The advent of mass armies presented commanders with the vexing problem of how to control them. Prussian *Auftragstaktik* (mission-based tactics) and the general staff system helped by enabling highly trained officers to take initiative in applying a flexible plan, but the need for widely scattered units to communicate in a timely manner remained. The field telephone went a long way toward solving that problem. The Japanese kept their headquarters well to the rear, controlling operations via miles of telephone lines strung by their forces.[51]

Attitudes Toward War

The long era of peace in Europe and North America coupled with the dramatic expansion of free, compulsory public education shaped popular attitudes toward war. Very few people (including most soldiers) had any real experience of combat. The French relied on a mercenary force, the Foreign Legion, to fight most of their colonial wars, while the British had a small volunteer army comprised of the urban and rural poor led by middle- and upper-class officers. The Germans sent only volunteers to fight the Herero. War correspondents reported on some colonial conflicts, but their newspapers generally published sanitized accounts that spared readers the uglier aspects of battle. Fed a steady diet of patriotic pap in school and lacking any real experience or even knowledge of the horrors of battle, the general public in most countries proved receptive to the idea that war was good and ennobling.

The literature of the period both reflected and shaped attitudes toward war. The British writer George Alfred Henty wrote a series of popular books focused on young men going off to seek adventure and prove their manhood. *With Kitchener to Khartoum* contains a very heroic, rather romanticized view of the bloodbath at Omdurman. "The sight from the crest of Surgham Hill was grand," declared the novel's protagonist.

> The enemy's front extended over three miles. The lines were deep and compact, and the banners floated above them. They were advancing steadily and in good order, and their battle cries rose and fell in measured cadence. Their numbers were variously estimated at from fifty to seventy thousand—a superb force, consisting of men as brave as any in the world, and animated by religious fanaticism, and an intense hatred of those they were marching to assail.[52]

Even such a well-educated and widely traveled person as Winston Churchill presented this idyllic view of war. Despite having fought at Omdurman and seen the slaughter, he still described it in romantic terms:

> Nothing like the Battle of Omdurman will ever be seen again. It was the last link in the long chain of those spectacular conflicts whose vivid and majestic splendour has done so much to invest war with glamour. Everything was visible to the naked eye. The armies marched manoeuvered on the crisp surface of the desert plain through which the Nile flowed in broad reaches, now steel, now brass. Cavalry charged in close order, and infantry or spearman stood upright ranged in lines or masses to resist them.[53]

Popular poetry also extolled the ennobling virtues of war while ignoring its horrors. Alfred Lord Tennyson produced the most famous work in this genre, "The Charge of the Light Brigade," which celebrates the foolhardy and disastrous attack of British cavalry on a battery of Russian cannon during the Crimean War:

> When can their glory fade?
> O the wild charge they made!
> All the world wondered
> Honour the charge they made
> Honour the Light Brigade
> Noble six hundred.[54]

Such sentiments survived down to the outbreak of World War I. Written at the start of the conflict before its horrors became known, Rupert Brooke's "The Soldier" describes the coming war in heroic terms:

> If I should die, think only this of me:
> That there's some corner of a foreign field
> That is forever England. There shall be
> In that rich earth a richer dust concealed;
> A dust whom England bore, shaped made aware,
> Gave, once, her flowers to love, her ways to roam,

> A body of England's, breathing English air,
> Washed by the rivers, blest by the sons of home.
>
> And think this heart, all evil shed away,
> A pulse in the eternal mind, no less
> Gives back the thoughts by England given;
> Her sights, her sounds; dreams happy as her day;
> And laughter, learnt of friends; and gentleness
> In hearts at peace, under an English heaven.[55]

The sentiments expressed in literature help to explain why cheering crowds in the capitals of Europe welcomed news of war in August 1914.

Prevalent though they were, the voices extolling martial virtues were not the only ones speaking about war. Two groups espoused decidedly pacifist views: middle-class liberals who believed that civilization had progressed beyond the need for armed conflict and socialists who considered war a manifestation of bourgeois capitalism.[56] The socialists had sufficient support for governments to worry that, in the event of war, workers might disrupt mobilization by failing to answer the call to arms and/or stopping rail and other vital services with strikes.[57] The French government had in place a plan to arrest leading socialists upon the outbreak of hostilities should there be any sign of trouble.[58] Their fears proved groundless. In every country that went to war in 1914, patriotism trumped class consciousness.

While continuing to prepare for war during the long period of peace, the European nations also entered into a number of agreements to make war less destructive. The Brussels Declaration of 1874 articulated the customs of land warfare, which had begun to take shape in the 17th century. Because several nations did not ratify it, however, the declaration did not become a formal agreement. The International Law Institute did, however, use it to produce its 1880 manual *The Laws of War on Land* with the avowed purpose of codifying what had long been custom:

> War holds a great place in history, and it is not to be supposed that men will soon give it up—in spite of the protests which it arouses and the horror which it inspires—because it appears to be the only possible issue of disputes which threaten the existence of States, their liberty, their vital interests. But the gradual improvement in customs should be reflected in the method of conducting war. It is worthy of civilized nations to seek, as has been well said ([by] Baron Jomini), "to restrain the destructive force of war, while recognizing its inexorable necessities."[59]

The manual became the basis for the Hague Conventions of 1899 and 1907, which did become international law, being signed by all the European powers, the United States, and several non-Western nations.

The agreement consisted of three conventions: one calling for the peaceful settlement of conflicts; another on the laws of war; and a third, maritime agreement protecting hospital ships and wounded and shipwrecked sailors. The First Hague Convention was remarkable for its day. "With a view to obviating, as far possible, recourse to force in the relations between states," it proclaimed, "the Signatory Powers agree to use their best efforts to insure the pacific settlement of international differences."[60] The Second "Convention with Respect to the Laws of War on Land" dealt with a broad range of issues, including the nature and status of belligerents, the treatment of prisoners, the governing of occupied territories, and the protection of noncombatant persons and property.[61]

In addition to codifying the laws and customs of war, the meeting at The Hague also approved three declarations on weapons. One prohibited the dropping of bombs from balloons or "other new methods of a similar nature" for a period of five years.[62] The second prohibited the use of poisonous or asphyxiating gas.[63] The third prohibited use of expanding bullets in conflicts between two or more of the signatories to the agreement.[64] The agreement did not prohibit using such bullets against non-Europeans, as the British had done with such devastating effect at Omdurman. The belligerents in World War I abrogated the ban on gas as soon as they discovered how effective it was against entrenched troops.

The 1907 Hague Conventions built upon but did not substantially alter the 1899 accords. In addition to encouraging peaceful resolution of disputes, it devised a formal mechanism for arbitration, although participation remained voluntary.[65] Another convention detailed the rights and duties of neutral nations during wartime.[66] Unlike its predecessor, the 1907 meeting defined laws and customs of war at sea, devoting several of its 13 conventions to this subject. Whatever their individual accomplishments, the two Hague meetings were part of a growing desire to regulate warfare that has continued to the present.

Viewed as a whole, the attitudes toward war that developed during the four decades of peace in Europe present a curious collage of sometimes conflicting ideas. While free, compulsory public education inculcated patriotism and the duty to fight for one's country in young men, socialists viewed nationalism as at best suspect and at worst an ugly manifestation of bourgeois capitalism. At the same time that they engaged in an arms race, the nations of Europe agreed to try to resolve conflicts peacefully and, failing that, to fight wars more humanely. As events would prove, the hawks won out over the doves. Neither peace accords nor socialism prevented war in 1914, and the belligerents honored The Hague accords as expediency dictated. Everyone had an interest in treating prisoners humanely, as doing so helped ensure that one's own captured troops would be accorded the same consideration. The five-year ban on aerial bombardment expired just as the airplane was being developed, and in 1915 the belligerents discovered that heavier-than-air poison gas was particularly lethal when used against troops in trenches and bunkers.

The West on the Brink of Global War

The last decade of peace before the greatest conflict in human history to that point saw European armies accelerating preparations for war while few officers had any real experience of combat. The four decades of peace following the Franco-Prussian War had seen major technological changes whose impact on warfare had only been hinted at in the two conflicts that seemed to offer the best glimpse of the future: the Boer and Russo-Japanese Wars. As a result generals based their planning on 40-year-old assumptions about the nature of combat, modified only slightly by consideration of more recent events. None of them knew what war between mass conscript armies equipped with magazine rifles, machine guns, rapid fire artillery, and high explosives would really be like. Still, they planned for it in earnest.

For the vast majority of Europeans, war belonged to a distant, imagined past. Fed a steady diet of patriotism in school and then conscripted into the army, where they received even more indoctrination, they held romantic notions of war as an opportunity for adventure and a chance to prove one's manhood. Against the powerful emotive force of nationalism pacifist ideas could make little headway. Small wonder that in August 1914 men flocked to the colors for what the politicians and generals promised would be a short and glorious war.

CHAPTER EIGHT

World War I

The war that engulfed Europe and spread throughout much of the world from 1914 to 1918 was far more destructive than those who had so exhaustively planned for it could have imagined. A conflict that began between the Triple Entente of France, Russia, and the United Kingdom on the one side and the Central Powers of Germany and Austria-Hungary on the other expanded to include more than 25 other nations. During four years of war more than 65 million men took up arms, of which 8,528,831 million were killed and 21,189,154 were wounded.[1] At least 6.6 million and perhaps as many as 9 million civilians also died.[2] By the end of the war, four of the great empires that had fought it had ceased to exist, succeeded by a host of nations inhabited by their former subjects. The war cost an estimated $208 billion; caused an immediate postwar recession; and because of the debt it created, helped bring about the Great Depression that began in 1929.[3] With such an enormous cost in blood and treasure, it is difficult to see how any nation, save perhaps the United States, which sprang to world economic dominance afterward, truly won the war. The conflagration illustrates the wisdom of Carl von Clausewitz's maxim that "war is an instrument of policy" not an end in itself, which the Great War clearly became, as illustrated by the popular British slogan, "Damn the cost, we must win this war."[4]

Situated within the context of military history, the conflict represents a further step in the evolution of warfare. Since the time of the French

Revolution conventional conflicts had become increasingly more extensive (with the exception of the wars of German and Italian unification) and more lethal. This evolution had been driven by three factors. First, technology had facilitated the creation of mass armies and equipped them with ever more lethal weapons. Second, ideology (largely absent since 1648) had been reintroduced into warfare by the American and French Revolutions. Wars fought for a cause have tended to be bloodier than those fought for limited political objectives. Nationalism had replaced religion as the prime motivator for international conflict, and wars fought on its behalf would prove to be far more destructive than any fought in the name of faith. Third, the second half of the 19th century witnessed the creation of mass conscript armies made possible by widespread social and economic change. The Industrial Revolution and its corresponding impact on agriculture meant that more men could be spared from peacetime occupations to fight. Patriotic indoctrination provided by free, compulsory public education gave them a cause for which to fight and die.

Military Plans and the Outbreak of War

All strategists who had studied the Franco-Prussian War agreed on at least one of its most important lessons: the side that mobilized the quickest would enjoy a great, perhaps even a decisive advantage over its adversary. In 1870 the Prussians had begun their offensive before the French had even deployed enough forces to counter the attack. Rapid mobilization had resulted from careful planning. Moltke the Elder and the Prussian general staff had drawn up detailed railroad timetables to ensure that each unit embarked for the front as soon after it had gathered at the depot as possible. By the first decade of the 20th century, mobilization had become an even more complex task. The active duty army of each nation represented but one part of its fighting force. Mobilization required calling up reservists, equipping them, and then disembarking their units by train to concentration areas along the frontier, where they would be incorporated into larger formations for the advance into enemy territory. The military had to take control of railroads and telegraph offices, man fortresses, procure horses, and gather food for men and fodder for animals. With armies putting over a million men in the field in a matter of weeks, train schedules had to be worked out to the minute.

To prepare such a precise mobilization plan, general staffs had to know whom they would be fighting. The alliance system that had developed over the decades before the Great War made the most likely scenarios clear. Understanding that the defeated country would seek to recover its lost provinces of Alsace and Lorraine at the first opportunity, Bismarck constructed an alliance system to keep France isolated. He reached an agreement with Austria-Hungary in 1879 and Italy in 1882. A concord between Austria-Hungary and Italy the same year created the Triple Alliance. In combination with the Three Emperors' League of Germany, Russia, and Austria-Hungary first created in 1873, the Triple Alliance left France isolated and unwilling to risk war with a more powerful Germany. The only remaining great power, the United Kingdom, preferred to focus on its empire rather than become embroiled in continental affairs. In any case, France and Britain were longtime enemies.

The situation changed dramatically when the new German emperor, Wilhelm II, ascended to the throne in 1888. He replaced Bismarck in 1890 and allowed the Three Emperors' League to lapse. Russia had always had conflicting interests with Austria-Hungary in the Balkans and feared German dominance of the Continent. It also needed capital to industrialize, which France gladly offered in return for a military alliance in 1894. The naval race with Germany and the shock of the Anglo-Boer war revealed Britain's vulnerability as an isolated power. In 1904 it reached an entente cordiale (cordiale understanding) with France, agreeing to engage in joint military planning for a possible war with Germany. The entente developed into a de facto secret alliance by 1912, when Britain agreed to defend the French coast with its navy in time of war. Britain reached a similar informal agreement with Russia in 1907, leading to the creation of the Triple Entente. Given the small size and poor performance of the British army, however, continental general staffs did not factor it in as a major consideration in their military planning. Even its closest ally, France, relegated Britain's forces to the position of flank guard in its war plans. Diplomats and politicians, on the other hand, did worry about Britain's role in any future war.

With the battle lines in Europe drawn, the generals went to work devising strategies. Russia planned to attack Germany in East Prussia and Austria-Hungary in Galicia (present-day southern Poland). According to its Plan XVII, France would advance directly into Alsace-Lorraine. Austria-Hungary devised a two-option plan with the possibilities of mobilizing for an attack against its Balkan rival Serbia or for a war with Russia. Of all the great powers, Germany faced the most challenging strategic situation. Confronted with the prospect of a two-front war, precisely the scenario Bismarck had worked so hard to avoid, it had to devise a plan that would allow it to defeat a numerically superior enemy. The unyielding calculus of mobilization seemed to provide the answer. An industrialized nation with an extensive rail net and a good road system, France could mobilize much faster than Russia, which had to gather its troops from across a vast empire with a limited transportation network. Once it had mobilized, however, Russia would field a much larger army than Germany. It thus made strategic sense to defeat France first and then deal with Russia.

The man who gave his name to the German plan, Alfred von Schlieffen, Chief of the Imperial General Staff from 1891 to 1906, did not, however, actually develop it. His 1905 memorandum became the basis for the plan devised and implemented by his successor, Helmuth von Moltke the Younger. The memorandum addressed the scenario of a war with France only, not a two-front conflict with Russia and France. Recognizing the difficulty of breaking through the line of French forts along the Franco-German border and considering it unlikely that the French would leave these fortifications to attack Germany, he devised a bold plan for invading France. A small German force based on the fortress cities of Thionville and Metz would remain on the defensive while the bulk of the German army advanced westward through Luxembourg, Belgium, and the southeast corner of the Netherlands; swung south; and enveloped Paris from the West. The invaders would then drive the French field armies eastward, crushing them between the hammer of the German attacking force and the anvil of its defensive units on the border.[5] Schlieffen acknowledged that such a bold plan required a massive deployment of forces and raised doubts about whether Germany had enough troops to carry it out:

> We shall find the experience of all earlier conquerors confirmed, that a war of aggression calls for much strength and also consumes much, that this strength dwindles constantly as the defender's increases, and all this particularly so in a country which bristles with fortresses.[6]

Schlieffen's memorandum became the basis for the German strategy. Moltke, however, modified it considerably. Fearing that the French might actually attack Lorraine, he strengthened his forces there. He also had to deploy troops to the east to fight a holding action should Russia advance into East Prussia earlier than expected. In addition, he considered violating Dutch neutrality unnecessary. Because success depended on speed, Moltke created special assault brigades equipped with massive 360 mm and 420 mm howitzers to destroy the Belgian forts at Liege and Namur ahead of the advancing army. These units would cross the frontier as soon as the government issued mobilization orders. In its final form, the German plan deployed 1,360,000 troops in seven armies on the Western Front (a million of them committed to the offensive) and a single army of approximately 150,000 to fight a delaying action in East Prussia should the Russians attack sooner than anticipated.[7]

All the military plans of the great powers had one serious unforeseen consequence: their rigidity would seriously hamper diplomats trying to prevent the July 1914 crisis in the Balkans from escalating into a European war. They failed in large measure because actions by one state triggered a chain reaction in the others. When Austria-Hungary declared war on Serbia, Russia declared war on Austria-Hungary. Because it had no viable partial mobilization plan, however, Russia had to mobilize along its entire frontier, including the one opposite Germany. This move threatened to upset the Schlieffen Plan, which required the war to begin in the West. Germany had no plan for a war against Russia alone. France refused to remain neutral in a Russo-German war, which necessitated German mobilization and the immediate advance of the assault units into Belgian. This violation of Belgian neutrality brought Britain, which had been noncommittal, into the war on the side of France and Russia.

The failure of generals in every country to fully explain the implications of war plans with their civilian counterparts further hindered diplomatic efforts during the crisis. Tsar Nicholas II of Russia called for mobilization against Austria-Hungary alone, not realizing that such a partial mobilization was impossible. Kaiser Wilhelm II of Germany naively ordered Moltke to turn the trains headed for the Belgian frontier around and attack Russia, failing to understand that the general staff had no mobilization plan that would make such a deployment possible. Britain entered the war only when Germany violated Belgian neutrality, but any British general could have told Foreign Secretary Sir Edward Grey that such a violation was virtually inevitable, as Germany had no other feasible way to attack France. Had he been aware of this fact, Grey might have openly promised to back France earlier and so deterred Germany from encouraging Austria-Hungary to take strong action against Serbia and thus provoke Russia. In the end the tyranny of the mobilization timetables contributed to the outbreak of a European war.

Opening Campaigns

"No plan survives contact with the enemy," Helmut von Moltke the Elder had warned his officers.[8] The first four months of the Great War would underscore the wisdom of this observation. Every plan was quite literally shot to hell, every assumption upon which those plans had been based proven false. The German attack on France started auspiciously enough. The broad sweeping movement through Belgium caught everyone by surprise. Two armies (the Sixth and Seventh) held Lorraine on the German left while five armies (the First through Fifth deployed west to east) launched the broad flanking sweep through Luxembourg and Belgium. The French and British had considered that the right wing might sweep through part of Belgium, but none of their generals imagined that the Germans had the manpower to extend their line so far west of the Meuse River.[9] They were also shocked to see how easily the massive 360 mm Skoda and 420 mm Krupp howitzers pounded the Belgian forts into rubble. The frontal assault into Lorraine, which the Germans doubted France would be foolish enough to attempt, ended disastrously with the French suffering 300,000 casualties, their greatest loss in any single engagement in the entire war.[10]

As the Germans advanced westward, however, the Schlieffen Plan began to unravel. Instead of staying put after repulsing the French attack in Lorraine, the Sixth and Seventh Armies went over to the offensive only to suffer heavy casualties themselves and thus require reinforcement. The Belgians fought tenaciously, delaying the German advance and putting Moltke's timetable in jeopardy. Schlieffen's warning that an offensive force diminishes in strength as it advances was also proving true. General Alexander von Kluck, commander of the First Army tasked to envelope Paris from the west, had to detach troops to invest the port of Antwerp and the Belgian fortress town of Maubeuge. Far from being destroyed or routed, the French retreated in good order with most of their field armies intact.[11] The French Fifth Army and the British Expeditionary Force (BEF) on the left flank of the Anglo-French line fought effective rearguard actions before withdrawing to the southeast. More ominously, the situation on the Eastern Front grew precarious. Rather than await the completion of full mobilization the Russians began their offensive into East Prussia earlier than anticipated. The panic this advance created led Moltke to redeploy two corps from the west to bolster the Eighth Army in the east.

The turning point of the invasion came on August 28 when von Kluck made his infamous decision to change the First Army's axis of advance from southwest to southeast, swinging in front of instead of behind Paris. Kluck based his decision on the mistaken beliefs that the BEF had ceased to be a threat and that he could deal a crippling blow to the retreating French Fifth Army by striking its flank.[12] He may also have felt that he lacked sufficient troops to extend his line westward. Some historians have argued that additional troops would have done him little good, as the road system could not have accommodated such a large force with its logistics tail.[13] Whatever the reason for his change of plan, von Kluck exposed his flank to Paris, and French reconnaissance planes spotted the mistake. General

Joseph Gallieni, commander of the Paris garrison, assembled a sixth army to the northwest of the city. Recognizing the threat just in time, von Kluck turned to face it. In doing so, however, he opened a gap between himself and the Second Army under General Karl von Bülow, which the BEF and the French exploited at the Battle of the Marne, fought September 5–12. This victory forced the Germans to retreat and began what came to be called the "race to the sea." The two armies tried to outflank each other until they reached the coast in early October. They then had no choice but to dig in until they could find a way to break through the enemy line. Two months of fighting had cost the French 950,000 casualties and the Germans 700,000 and resulted in stalemate.[14]

The situation in the east developed unevenly, with the Germans scoring major victories over Russia while Austria-Hungary suffered setbacks. Mobilizing on two fronts, the Austro-Hungarians easily took Belgrade, but the Serbian army inflicted a major defeat on them at Cer Mountain in mid-August. The Russians also overran Galicia, driving the Austro-Hungarian forces back to the Carpathian Mountains. After the initial setback in East Prussia, the reinforced German Eighth Army under the new command of Paul von Hindenburg and Erich Ludendorff destroyed an entire Russian

Major battles on the Western Front.

army under General Alexander Samsonov at Tannenberg in late August and inflicted a decisive defeat on a second army under General Paul von Rennenkampf at the Masurian Lakes in early September.

Deadlock and Trench Warfare

By the end of 1914 all the belligerents faced the same problem. All had prepared for a short war decided by decisive battles following rapid mobilization. They had no plans for what to do once their opening gambits had failed. The two sides found themselves in a colossal stalemate that only expanded when Turkey entered the war on the side of the Central Powers in December 1914 and Italy joined the Entente in May 1915. Born of technology, the size of armies, and the terrain on which they operated, this deadlock would turn what had been foreseen as a war of maneuver to one of attrition. Victory went ultimately not to the side with the best strategy and tactics but to the alliance with the greatest manpower and economic resources. The cost in blood and treasure would be horrific.

The defensive networks developed by both sides produced a deadlock that would take four years to break. Following the race to the sea, the British, French, Belgians, and Germans on the Western Front had no choice but to dig in for a protracted conflict. From Nieuwpoort on the North Sea coast of Belgium to Pfetterhouse on the German border of Switzerland, the line ran for 450 miles along a jagged front. What began as hastily dug trenches quickly evolved into an elaborate system of fortifications exceedingly difficult to breech. Although the system varied depending on the army and the terrain, construction followed a definite pattern. A line usually consisted of three parallel trenches 100–200 yards apart: a fire trench, a support trench, and a reserve trench. To avoid enfilading fire in case of a breakthrough, the trenches either zig-zagged or had alternating fire bays and traverses. Concrete pillboxes with machine guns and dugouts to protect troops during shelling strengthened the works, and a second line of trenches several miles behind the first prevented deep penetration.[15] Barbed wire protected the fire trench, and artillery placed well to the rear covered the front line.

The trench system presented a virtually insurmountable obstacle to attacking troops. Before infantry could assault them, the enemy trenches, often a mere 50 yards away across "no-man's-land," had to be weakened and the barbed wire in front of them cut. To accomplish this purpose both sides relied on heavy bombardment, sometimes lasting days. This approach had several problems. To begin with, the shelling alerted the enemy of an imminent attack. The defenders could respond by moving troops back from the firing trench until the shelling stopped and then

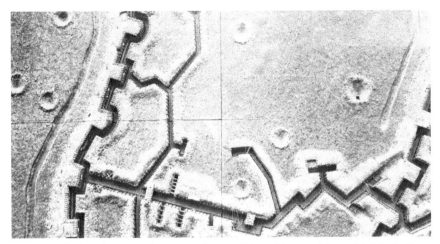

A model of a frontline trench system. *Source:* Edwin Tappan Adney, *Model of a Front Line Trench System.* Number 1. New series, 1917.

redeploy them before the infantry assault began. Lengthy bombardment also gave the enemy time to move reinforcements and supplies into the area behind the attack zone. The defender could then wait for the momentum of the charging infantry to weaken and drive out with a counterattack those troops who made it to the fire trench. Furthermore, high-explosive shells often did more harm than good. They flung the barbed wire about without destroying it and tore up the ground, making it difficult for infantry to cross at speed. Finally, attackers who did manage to break through an enemy line could not keep the advance going because of the difficulty of moving supplies over torn-up ground.

Striving for Breakthrough

As fighting in Europe slowed during the winter of 1914–1915, the belligerents worked to devise new strategies for winning the war. Circumstances dictated how the Germans would proceed in 1915. Austria-Hungary and its new ally Turkey both needed support, which meant shifting troops to the east and remaining on the defensive in the west. Russia advanced in Galicia, capturing the vital fortress of Przemysl in March. Austria-Hungary had to remain on the defensive until German help arrived. Turkey, meanwhile, suffered a disastrous defeat trying to invade Russia through the Caucasus. France, like Germany, had few options. Germany occupied just less than 4 percent of its territory, but the area contained 64 percent of the country's pig iron, 24 percent of its steel industry, and 40 percent of its coal capacity.[16] Furthermore, not trying to expel the invaders would have been politically unacceptable. The small British army deployed to France in August 1914 had lost most of its long service veterans in the Battles of Mons and the Marne and during the race to the sea. Britain would spend most of 1915 recruiting and training volunteers, and in 1916 it would be forced to institute conscription. Nonetheless, Britain looked for an alternative to bashing away at the formidable German defensive line on the Western Front. It sought to outflank the Central Powers by attacking their newest and weakest member, Turkey. An Anglo-Indian force advanced up the Tigris-Euphrates valley to Kut while another force landed on the Gallipoli Peninsula within striking distance of the Turkish capital, Istanbul.

Only the Germans enjoyed any real success in 1915. They created a new Eleventh Army comprised of four corps, 170,000 men, 702 field guns, and 300 pieces of heavy artillery under command of General (and in June Field Marshal) August von Mackensen and deployed it to the western end of the Carpathian front.[17] On May 2 the Germans smashed through the thinly held Russian line, and on May 10 the Austrian Third Army advanced toward Przemsyl. The Germans destroyed the Russian Third Army, taking 140,000 prisoners by the end of the first week of the offensive.[18] The battle forced the Russians out of Galicia and opened the way to Poland, which the Germans occupied almost completely by the end of August. On October 7 Mackensen led an Austro-German army across the Danube and, with the help of new ally Bulgaria, overran Serbia. By the end of the year Austria-Hungary had been secured, and the supply route to Turkey was opened. Italy's entry into the war on the side of the Entente in May could not offset these losses, as the Italian army could not break the easily defendable Austrian line along the Izonzo River, the Carnic Alps, and the Trentino.

While Germany's shift of emphasis away from the Western Front proved successful, Britain's was a disaster. On April 25 a British army landed on the Gallipoli Peninsula at the entrance to the Dardanelles in hopes of marching on Istanbul, knocking Turkey out of the war, and securing the water route to Russia. For a brief instant the way to the Turkish capital lay open, but reinforcements quickly closed the gap. Both sides dug in, and the peninsula became a mini-version of the Western Front. The Turks held the high ground and had a short, secure supply route, while the British clung precariously to the beaches below, supplied entirely by sea. They could make no headway against the entrenched enemy but kept trying until December 28, when they began an evacuation that concluded on January 8, 1916. The British had suffered 265,000 casualties to no purpose.[19] The offensive in Mesopotamia and a landing at Salonika in Greece intended to get help to Serbia fared no better. The Turks trapped the army advancing up the Tigris-Euphrates at Kut, where it surrendered after heavy losses (mostly to disease) in 1916. The Bulgarians hemmed in almost half a million Anglo-French troops at Salonika, which the Germans described as their "largest internment camp."[20]

Anglo-French efforts to break through on the Western Front also failed. Offensives in Champagne and St. Mihiel in February and in Arras in May cost 230,000 casualties for no strategic gain.[21] British attacks at Festubert and Aubers Ridge proved just as fruitless, but in April the Germans gave the allies their first taste of poison gas in a limited attack against Ypres. Despite these setbacks, Joffre planned an Anglo-French offensive in the Arras sector to begin in September. It resulted in nothing but more carnage: 50,000 British, 190,000 French, and 140,000 German casualties.[22]

Attrition

Futile though they certainly were, the offensives of 1915 did aim at breaking through the German lines, but their failure pointed the way to a new strategy. If the Entente could not defeat the Central Powers in a decisive engagement, they would have to wear them down. As early as January 1915, Lord Kitchener ordered Sir Charles Callwell, the War Department's director of military operations, to prepare a study on the relative strengthen of the belligerents. Callwell concluded that time favored the Entente:

> Germany can do no more in the way of increasing her armies, and will, a very few months hence, begin to feel the want of resources in men to keep her existing armies up to strength; Austria-Hungary is far more likely to go backwards in respect to numbers than to go forward. France, on the other hand, should find no difficulty in maintaining her field [army] constantly at its present strength for many months to come, and Russia ought to begin to get over her difficulties with regard to armament in about three months, and ought to have greatly improved her position within six months. Servia [sic] and Belgium can do little, but the great expansion of the British forces in the early future has to be reckoned with, and this should prove the decisive factor in the later stages of the contest.[23]

Lloyd George, then chancellor of the exchequer and later prime minister, recalled that this paper marked the first consideration of the strategy of attrition.[24] While they continued to strive for a breakthrough, the belligerents on both sides increasingly accepted that battles fought merely to inflict casualties in order to wear the enemy down might be the key to victory.

While the British may have been first to articulate a strategy of attrition, the Germans were the first to put it into effect. The new chief of the Imperial General Staff, Erich von Falkenhayn, devised a plan to draw French troops into a killing zone and destroy them with heavy artillery. He chose the fortress city of Verdun, a salient in the French line just east of the Meuse River, as the ideal place to implement his plan. Falkenhayn calculated correctly that even though it had little strategic significance and its forts had been stripped of most of their guns after the German pummeling of Liege and Namur called the value of such works into question, Verdun would be vigorously defended by the French for domestic political reasons. Giving up the fortress city without a fight would be bad for morale. After surrounding the salient with 1,400 guns, including the massive 420 mm and 360 mm howitzers, the Germans commenced their attack on February 21, 1916, firing 100,000 shells a minute into the salient.[25] Initially the attack went according to plan. The French poured more and more troops into the killing zone. Because the battle progressed so well, however, the Germans thought they might actually achieve a strategic breakthrough and sent in their own troops, turning the Verdun salient into a slaughterhouse.[26] With so many men blown to bits and buried in mass graves, the exact number of casualties remains unknown, but the combined total of dead, wounded, and missing for both armies may be over 700,000.[27]

The German offensive at Verdun forced the British to advance their own planned attack on the Somme to take pressure off the French. The Battle of the Somme, July to November 1916, has become the iconic example of the futility of warfare on the Western Front and of the ineptitude of the generals conducting it. The new Kitchener army of volunteers formed the bulk of the attacking force, with the French advancing in support to the south of the British position. To prepare for the attack the British bombarded the German lines for a week, hurling 1.6 million shells at the enemy trenches.[28] The Germans rode out the barrage in underground bunkers, some of them 60 feet deep. When the guns fell silent, the British stepped out of their trenches and marched shoulder-to-shoulder four ranks deep straight across no-man's-land. The Germans raced from their dugouts, set up machine guns, and mowed down the advancing infantry. The British suffered 60,000 casualties, including 20,000 dead on July 1, the greatest loss of life on any single day in British military history.[29] By the time the battle came to an end, it had cost the British approximately 420,000 casualties, the French 195,000, and the Germans 650,000.[30] The new British commander on the Western Front, Field Marshal Douglas Haig, had clearly been aiming at a breakthrough on the Somme. When that result could not be achieved, however, the War Office allowed the offensive to continue as, in the words of Haig's chief of staff, a "wearing out" battle.[31]

The one offensive that did achieve a significant breakthrough by attacking troops occurred not in France but on the Eastern Front. Ironically, this success came in what was supposed to be a diversionary attack to pin down Austro-Hungarian troops, tie up their reserves, and force the German southern front to pull back in preparation for an attack against German lines in the north. General Alexei Brusilov devised a plan to attack not in a narrow sector but in a series of concentrated blows along almost 200 miles of front. Instead of telegraphing his intentions with a lengthy bombardment, Brusilov unleashed an intense barrage just before specially trained shock troops, advancing in small groups instead of en masse, stormed the enemy trenches on June 4. By June 10, 1916, they had driven a wedge 90 kilometers wide and 60 kilometers deep into the Austro-Hungarian lines. Only the timely arrival of German troops, the failure of Russian General Alexei Evert to commence the northern offensive, and the inevitable problems of sustaining the advance with adequate supplies staved off disaster. Far from helping the Russians, Romania's entry into the war during the offensive forced Brusilov to extend his line eastward to protect the new ally. Finally, no matter how successful the offensive, the Russians could not afford the two million casualties they suffered in conducting it from June to November.[32]

The battles of 1916 established a pattern that would persist for the remainder of the war. Generals on all fronts would continue to strive for the elusive breakthrough that would lead to decisive victory; failing that, they sought to wear the enemy down with battles of attrition even when those proved incredibly costly to their own troops. The Italians and Austro-Hungarians fought each other in a dozen battles along the Isonzo River. The French and British repeated the slaughter of Verdun and the Somme at Arras, Champagne, and Passchendaele in 1917, with the same lack of results. The British general staff had of course calculated correctly; the numbers favored them. With their smaller aggregate population, the Central Powers had a harder time replacing losses. American entry into the war on the side of the Entente in April 1917 would tip the balance even further against them.

The commanders of the Great War have been subjected to intense criticism for their profligate wasting of human life in repeated futile offensives against formidable defensive positions. While many of them richly deserve the criticism heaped upon them, they all faced an almost insoluble problem. As the Brusilov offensive had demonstrated, the momentum of even a successful breakthrough eventually ground to a halt because the attackers could neither sustain the casualties suffered by men in the open nor keep supplies moving over torn-up ground. Eventually the enemy regrouped along a new defensive line, halted the advance, and often as not, regained the lost ground with a counterattack. Technology had created the impasse; it would take a technological solution to break it.

Innovation

Military and civilian leaders were not oblivious to the changed nature of warfare. Throughout the war they introduced technological and tactical innovations to try to break the trench deadlock. In April 1915 the Germans first used chlorine gas on the Western Front. Released from canisters, this heavier-than-air gas would settle into trenches and permeate bunkers, incapacitating troops within them. Chlorine is a vesicant or blistering agent that irritates all moist membranes (lungs, eyes, ears) it touches. In 1916 the Germans replaced it with dichloroethyl sulfide, dubbed "mustard gas" for its distinctive yellow color, a more effective agent fired from shells. The Entente quickly developed filter masks and began using their own poison gas against the Germans. Not only did gas fail to break the deadlock; it proved to be an unreliable weapon. A sudden change in wind direction might blow the toxin back on one's own troops. Far from being a wonder weapon, poison gas merely added to the suffering of soldiers. It killed relatively few but severely injured many others, who suffered permanent lung damage and shortened lives after the war.

Besides pioneering use of poison gas, the Germans developed new, more mobile weapons to aid attacking troops. They made flamethrowers, invented before the war, lighter and found them useful in clearing trenches and spreading fear. With tanks of flammable liquid strapped to their backs, however, the men equipped with flamethrowers were easy targets for riflemen, who concentrated on eliminating them.[33] The Germans also produced the first effective light or "sub" machine gun, the Bergman MP18, which fired a 9 mm bullet from a 32-round magazine.[34] The weapon would prove highly effective during the spring 1918 German offensive on the Western Front. These new weapons increased the amount of firepower infantry could concentrate on the point of attack.

Tactics evolved as the war progressed. Generals learned that massive bombardments lasting days accomplished little and forfeited surprise. They found that a short, intense "hurricane barrage" would do the same damage and often catch the enemy unaware, destroying many troops trapped in the fire trench. "Creeping" barrages required artillery to drop shells just in front of advancing infantry, thus clearing their way of enemy troops and obstacles. Creeping barrages had to be carefully planned to avoid attacking troops being killed by their own artillery.[35] Infantry assault tactics also changed over time. Brusilov made use of shock troops operating in small groups and advancing in rushes like skirmishers of old. The Germans made even more extensive use of such tactics in their spring 1918 offensive.

These new weapons and tactics allowed the belligerents to achieve some limited successes, but they failed to address the core problems that had caused the stalemate: how to overcome the tremendous advantage barbed wire, smokeless powder, the machine gun, and heavy artillery conveyed to the defense and how to maintain and supply an advance over torn-up ground once a breakthrough occurred. Armored tracked vehicles offered the best hope of solving both problems. The British pioneered the use of tanks in World War I. Discussion of such vehicles had begun before the war, but their value only became clear once trenches brought an end to mobile war. An early prototype had been covered with a tarp labeled "water tank" to disguise it, and for some reason the shortened version, "tank," stuck.

The tank was not the wonder weapon its proponents claimed it would be. The first model deployed on the Western Front, the British Mark I, was a ponderous beast 32 feet long and weighed 28 tons with a maximum speed of just under 4 miles per hour. One version mounted two six-pounder (57 mm) cannons in side bays known as "sponsons" and 4 machine guns; the other prototype replaced the cannon with two heavy machine guns. The Mark I had a range of 20–25 miles.[36] It also proved to be very unreliable. It frequently suffered mechanical failures, bogged down in mud, or got stuck in trenches too wide for it too cross. Tanks first saw action in September 1916 during the last phase of the disastrous Somme offensive. Although they initially frightened the enemy, the 36 Mark Is deployed by General Haig had no effect on the battle and alerted the Germans to the new weapon, allowing them to develop effective countermeasures.[37]

Like any new weapon, the tank was only as good as the tactics devised to use it, and those took time to develop. To be effective, tanks had to be employed en masse, which the British did not do until late 1917. At the battle of Cambrai, begun on November 20, 1917, they launched an attack with 378 improved Mark IV tanks. By foregoing the usually preassault artillery barrage, the British achieved total surprise and enabled their armored vehicles to advance over solid ground. They drove almost six miles beyond the German line along a seven-mile front in a single day, capturing 8,000 prisoners and 100 guns. Around the same time, an attack at Passchendaele without tanks took three months to advance the same distance and with much greater loss of life. Lack of reserves and supplies, however, prevented the British from exploiting the breakthrough at Cambrai.[38]

The success of Cambrai and its ultimate failure to achieve a lasting result highlight the strength and limitations of tanks during the Great War. The French and, belatedly, the Germans as well as the British would deploy increasing numbers of armored vehicles during the last year of the war. They contributed to but did not decide the outcome of the conflict. As Major General J. F. C. Fuller, the commander of the British Tank Corps, who had planned the Cambrai attack, later observed:

> To reinstate full mobility demanded that rapid penetration be followed by rapid exploitation, not by cavalry—the prevalent idea—but by tank forces, which could be supplied by cross-country transport—that is by vehicles mounted on caterpillar tracks. In 1918 they did not exist.[39]

To make armor effective, supply and troop transport would also have to be mechanized.

The St. Michael Offensive

Like the Battle of Cambrai, the last German offensive on the Western Front deserves attention, not for what it achieved, but because it foreshadowed how the next war would be fought. The roots of what would later be called blitzkrieg lie in the innovative tactics employed in a final German effort to break through the Entente lines in France. The key to the offensive lay in new tactics developed by General Oskar von Hutier in his attack on Riga in 1917. Hutier may have been inspired by Brusilov's shock troops, which had been so successful against the Austro-Hungarians the year before. The Germans created special storm trooper units. Divided into squads of 18 men with a light machine gun and a light mortar, the storm troopers bypassed fortified positions, driving deep behind enemy lines to disrupt communications, logistics, and command-and-control. Regular units following the elite forces would reduce strong points, concentrating on soft areas in which the storm troopers had achieved greatest success. "Hutier tactics" made careful use of creeping barrages, behind which the infantry advanced. Artillery would be "leapfrogged" forward in successive jumps to support the attack. Surprise and momentum were the keys to success. Preparation for the attack had to be kept secret and its momentum sustained by continuous movement forward.[40]

By the spring of 1918 the Germans knew they were running out of time. Unrestricted submarine warfare had not starved Britain into submission, but it had brought the United States into the war. Although the raw recruits sent from America thus far lacked the numbers and skill to tip the balance, in time they would certainly do so. Germany did, however, have a short-term advantage. The Bolshevik Revolution of October 1917 led to the new Soviet Union negotiating a peace agreement on German terms in December. Veteran German divisions on the Eastern Front had thus been freed for redeployment in the west. A successful offensive in France might lead the remaining members of the Entente to sue for peace.

Ludendorff deployed 210 divisions, including 1,559,000 infantry, on the Western Front.[41] He decided to concentrate the offensive against the British on the Somme, massing 67 divisions and 3,000 pieces of artillery against 26 divisions with fewer than 1,000 guns.[42] While the German general staff had great respect for the tenacity of individual British soldiers, they considered the British army inferior to the French.[43] The initial assault on March 21, 1918, caught the defenders completely by surprise. Within days the Germans had destroyed most of the British Fifth Army, and by June they had driven two salients 40 miles deep into the Entente lines. Like all World War I efforts, however, the offensive eventually petered out. The new Supreme Allied Commander, French General Ferdinand Foch, adopted a new approach of his own. Instead of throwing in his reserves in a massive counterattack, he conducted an orderly withdrawal, counterpunching as he pulled back. German troops in the open suffered more casualties than French and British soldiers firing from sheltered defensive positions. Most important, they could not sustain their attack over torn-up ground. Foch could move reinforcements forward by rail more rapidly than Ludendorff could advance men and equipment over a cratered battlefield.[44]

The spring offensive was Germany's last effort to achieve a breakthrough. In truth, it had little chance of success. Ludendorff later admitted that he lacked the troops to exploit a breakthrough, but that he hoped a series of tactical victories might lead to the sort of revolution that had occurred in Russia breaking out in France and/or Britain.[45] In the end, it was the German army that came near to collapsing. Soldiers suffering from severe shortages of food halted operations to loot British supplies. Once the force of the German wave had broken, Foch began a systematic offensive, not a concentrated blow at one weak point, but a series of short, sharp attacks up and down the line to keep the Germans off balance and in retreat until they sought an armistice in November 1918.

Total War

World War I was decided not by battles but by attrition, albeit a very different kind of attrition than the generals envisioned when they fought at Verdun and the Somme. Like the American Civil War, it was not merely a contest between armies but a struggle between societies. As long as the belligerents could maintain the political will to keep fighting, victory would go to the alliance with the greatest resources and manpower. At the outset of the war, the Entente had 51.7 percent of world manufacturing production; the Central Powers had only 19.2 percent.[46] The Triple Entente spent $40.6 billion on the war and mobilized 36.9 million men, while the Central Powers spent $24.7 billion and mobilized 25.1 million men.[47] American entry into the war tipped the balance even further, adding $17.1 million and 3.8 million men to the allied cause.[48] The U.S. contribution was, in fact, much greater than these numbers reveal, as the French and British borrowed money from American banks and bought equipment from American factories.

War between societies of course produced significant civilian casualties. During the Great War the belligerents usually did not directly target noncombatants. German Zeppelin raids on London and the long-range shelling of Paris produced relatively few casualties. Civilians traveling on passenger ships like the *Lusitania* died in U-boat attacks, but as these ships also carried military supplies, they could be considered legitimate targets, and the German consulate in New York warned passengers that ships might be attacked. Civilians in occupied areas suffered the worst, but even so, noncombatant deaths from direct military action numbered only 950,000.[49] Disease and famine caused by the war, on the other hand, killed six million civilians.[50]

Some of this loss of life was an unintended consequence of disrupting agriculture by putting farmers in uniform and diverting resources to armaments production, but both sides used starvation as a weapon. Overwhelming naval superiority allowed the British to keep the German High Seas fleet in port for most of the war and impose an effective blockade on Germany that produced real hunger by 1918. For its part Germany sank British shipping throughout the war and in 1917 declared unrestricted submarine warfare against ships of any nation headed for British ports. Because the island nation could not feed its population, this tactic very nearly worked. Only an increase in escort vessels produced by American entry into the war and use of convoys defeated the U-boat campaign.

Unconventional Operations

Like all modern conflicts, World War I involved unconventional operations, although they had virtually no impact on the outcome of the conflict. In German East Africa (modern Tanzania) Colonel Paul von Lettow-Vorbeck conducted a brilliant guerrilla campaign against British forces that lasted the entire war. Never defeated in the field, von Lettow-Vorbeck agreed to surrender only after he had been informed of the armistice a week after it had been signed. Interesting though the East Africa campaign may be to students of irregular warfare, it had no strategic importance to either side. However romantic it may have seemed, it did nothing but add in a very small way to the butcher bill of the Great War.

A far better known episode of irregular warfare occurred in Arabia from 1916 to 1918. After the Ottoman Empire joined the Central Powers in December 1914, the British engaged them in Mesopotamia and Palestine. As both campaigns got off to a bad start, British headquarters in Cairo sought to foment an Arab revolt against Ottoman rule. They sent a young subaltern fluent in Arabic to liaise with Emir Feisal, the Sherif of Mecca. Thomas Edward Lawrence helped lead the Arabs in a classic guerrilla campaign, raiding, cutting rail lines, and springing ambushes. During General Edmund Allenby's advance to Jerusalem in 1917, an Arab force of 3,000 tied down 150,000 Turkish troops dispersed throughout the region to counter its operations.[51] Lawrence of Arabia, as he came to be known, captured the imagination of people in a war largely devoid of heroes, but the Arab Revolt had limited strategic value. He did help Allenby defeat the Turks more rapidly, but the outcome of the campaign would have been the same without the revolt. British operations in the Middle East had more to do with achieving postwar imperial objectives than with defeating the Central Powers. The Arab Revolt has been appropriately described as a "side-show within a side-show."[52]

The Experience of War

Few conflicts have been so thoroughly documented by those who fought them as the Great War. A ream of letters, memoirs, novels, and poems documents the experiences of men and women on the Western Front. Fought by large numbers of illiterate peasant soldiers, the war in the east produced a much less abundant record. The experience of Russian, Austro-Hungarian, and Turkish soldiers probably resembled that of their French, British, and Italian counterparts. Military reports provide further evidence of the nature and experience of trench warfare. A plethora of primary sources thus allows historians to reconstruct the experience of war and learn something of what soldiers felt about it. Some of the literary accounts have also perpetuated myths about the nature of trench warfare.

Desirous of dispelling romantic illusions about war and capturing the horror of life and death in the trenches, the war poets and novelists have helped, unintentionally, to create and perpetuate some major misunderstandings. Foremost among these is the notion that soldiers spent uninterrupted weeks and even months in the squalor of the trenches, when in fact units rotated in and out of the front lines on a regular basis.[53] Although the exact dispositions differed from country to country, the experience of one British officer illustrated a typical pattern: from December 1914 to August 1916, he spent 141 days in trenches, 90 days in support, 114 days in reserve, 19 days in the hospital, and 12 days on leave.[54] Only when a soldier was in the trenches or in support was he in immediate danger, some 231 out of 424 days in the case of the British soldier in question, although during an offensive the time spent in harm's way might be considerably greater.[55]

As in previous wars, major battles occurred infrequently. Soldiers in the trenches spent most of their time in a broad range of routine activities. They repaired trenches, built up parapets, dug latrines, and maintained their equipment. They stood for inspection and prepared and ate meals. At night they went into no-man's-land to repair existing lines of barbed wire and/or lay new ones. They might engage other wiring parties or agree to "live and let live." Frontline troops would conduct periodic raids on enemy trenches, and patrols might fight one another in no-man's-land. Snipers on both sides picked off anyone who rose above the level of the forward parapet.[56]

Conditions in the trenches varied considerably. For the Germans occupying the high ground in France and Belgium, they could be dry and reasonably comfortable. For the British in waterlogged Flanders during spring rains, they were cold, wet, and miserable. Soldiers in all armies had to deal with lice, trench foot, and dysentery. The stench of rotting corpses, excrement, and unwashed men was awful. Soldiers faced death or injury from shrapnel, bullets, and poison gas. Without antibiotics and in the unsanitary conditions of the trenches, wounds easily became infected. Gangrene was common. Many of the wounded went through the rest of their lives horribly disfigured and/or missing limbs.

Attitudes toward War

A large body of literature documents how men felt about the war in which they fought. Poems, novels, and memoirs from both sides contain remarkably consistent themes and ideas. Soldiers railed against the utter futility of the war, which they portrayed in vivid, unvarnished terms contrasting sharply with Victorian tripe about honor and glory. They had deep respect for the enemy across no-man's-land, with whom they felt a closer kinship than they did with friends and family back home. Loyalty to comrades kept them fighting after loyalty to country became meaningless. Disillusionment with the glib certainties and the smug confidence of the prewar world permeates the literature of the Great War. Watching men die by the thousands to gain worthless yards of mud made it difficult to sustain belief in any cause or the nation for which one fought. "How senseless is everything that can be written, done, or thought when such things are possible," wrote the German Erich Maria Remarque in his epic novel *All Quiet on the Western Front*. "It must all be lies and of no account when the culture of a thousand years could not prevent this stream of blood being poured out."[57] As the French writer Henri Barbusse observed, men fought not for God, king, or country, but merely to survive:

> This, evidently, is the creed of men who, a year and a half ago, left all corners of the land to mass on the frontier: Give up trying to understand, and give up trying to be yourself. Hope that you will not die and fight for life as well as you can.[58]

Beyond merely struggling to survive, though, soldiers supported one another. Virtually all accounts of the Great War speak of the camaraderie of the uniform. Soldiers in all wars have tended to bond with those in their unit, but during the Great War those ties were strengthened by alienation from friends and family at home. World War I was the first conflict in which entire societies mobilized for war. Women replaced men in factories and service jobs. Civilians endured food rationing and other shortages. To justify these sacrifices on top of the loss of sons, husbands, and fathers, governments launched propaganda campaigns to proclaim the justness of their own cause and demonize the enemy. Soldiers home on leave had difficulty understanding, let alone relating to, those who had not fought and yet hated the enemy more than they did. "England looked strange to us returned soldiers," wrote Robert Graves.

> We could not understand the war madness that ran about everywhere, looking for a pseudo military outlet. The civilians talked a foreign language; and it was newspaper language. I found serious conversation with my parents all but impossible.[59]

Small wonder that Graves, Remarque, and so many other writers related how relieved and even happy they were when leave ended and they could return to their comrades at the front.

Not only did soldiers not hate the enemy with the intensity of civilians, they often demonstrated a deep respect for the men on the other side of no-man's-land. The most famous manifestation of this attitude occurred during Christmas 1914. British and German troops declared a series of informal truces at various places along their line. They sang Christmas carols and in some cases walked into no-man's-land to fraternize with the enemy and even play informal soccer matches. The French, who had more reason to hate the Germans who occupied their land, did not join in, and nothing like the Christmas truce happened again.[60] Nonetheless, small acts of kindness toward the enemy occurred throughout the war. Barbusse describes an informal truce in which a German unit smuggled a French soldier behind the lines to see his wife.[61] At news of the armistice and despite strict orders not to fraternize with the enemy, soldiers from both sides met in no-man's-land to embrace one another.

The difficulty soldiers had in talking with civilians stemmed in part from a natural disinclination to trouble loved ones with the horrors of war. Strict censorship kept not only the truth about defeats, but even realistic descriptions of battle, from civilians. Only after the war did its true horrors become apparent to all. Wilfred Owen's vivid poetry presented unvarnished images of war wholly absent from Rupert Brooke's "The Soldier." In "Dolce et Decorum Este," Owen used the victim of a gas attack to challenge the unquestioning patriotism of the home front:

> If you could hear, at every jolt, the blood Come gargling from the froth-corrupted lungs,
> Obscene as cancer, bitter as the cud
> Of vile, incurable sores on innocent tongues,
> My friend, you would not tell with such zest
> To children ardent for some desperate glory,
> The old lie; *Dulce et Decorum est*
> *Pro patria mori.*

"Dulce et Decourm est Pro patria mori," was a famous saying from the Roman poet Horace, meaning "how sweet and right it is to die for one's country."[62]

Although women in general had no experience of combat, nurses saw the carnage of war. They too could describe its futility and their disillusionment with official patriotism. None did so as forcefully as Vera Brittain. Her war diary became the basis of *A Testament of Youth*, in which she describes her exhilaration at the outbreak of war; anxiety over her loved ones at the front; and her bitter disillusionment following the death first of her fiancé, then of a close friend, and finally of her only brother. She described "God, King and Country," the cause for which Britons fought, as a "voracious trinity" that had taken from her everyone whom she had loved.[63]

Aftermath

Those who fought in the Great War took some solace from the hope that a better world might emerge from it. That hope proved forlorn. The victorious allies did not follow the Armistice with a just peace but with a vindictive settlement that left Germany broken, embittered, and yearning for revenge, just as France had been in 1871. Forced to cede territory, pay a crippling indemnity, and accept full responsibility for the war, Germany harbored a latent desire for revenge, which the National Socialists exploited. In 1919 an influenza epidemic spread by returning soldiers killed more people than the war itself. Recession added to the hardship. The Great War thus takes its place as the next to last step in the evolution of total war that began with the French Revolution and would end with the atomic bombing of Japan.

CHAPTER NINE

The Interwar Period

Future historians may view World War II as a continuation of World War I, just as those who study ancient history now see the Punic Wars between Rome and Carthage spanning more than a century as part of the same struggle for hegemony in the western Mediterranean. In Europe the same belligerents faced one another, with the exception of Italy, which switched sides, and Turkey, which remained neutral. Once again fears over German hegemony on the Continent led to an alliance to oppose it. To a significant degree, the conflict resulted not from World War I itself, but from the vindictive peace that had ended it. Germany resented the loss of territory in 1919 just as much as France had in 1871. Humiliating disarmament, crippling indemnity payments, and the infamous war-guilt clause of the Treaty of Versailles (1919) forcing Germany to accept sole moral responsibility for the war piled insult on top of injury. These factors did not make another war inevitable, but they certainly made one more likely and guaranteed that if it did occur, Germany would seek revenge.

As the dominant power in Asia, Japan sought to build an empire. While it had the population and military strength to expand, lack of vital resources such as oil, iron ore, and rubber left the country vulnerable to an embargo. Those resources, however, lay in territories controlled by European empires. To gain unfettered access to them would bring Japan into conflict with the world's two greatest naval powers, Great Britain and the United States. If Japan stood any chance at all in such a contest, it could only be under circumstances in which the other powers found themselves facing conflict far closer to home. Conditions in Europe and Asia thus guaranteed that the next conflict would truly be a world war, unlike the previous one fought primarily in Europe.

These disturbing trends and conditions, however, did not make World War II inevitable. Many people in Europe viewed the Great War as a terrible tragedy that must not be repeated. The victors made some effort to mitigate the harsh terms of the Versailles Treaty. The former belligerents formed an international body to arbitrate disputes and entered into agreements to limit armaments. That these measures failed to preserve peace owed as much to what began in 1929 as to what took place in 1919. Without the debilitating effects of the Great Depression, the right-wing National Socialist Workers Party, a fringe party throughout the decade, would probably not have come to power. The interwar years must thus be seen as a complex era in which military development continued as at least some leaders sought to avoid war.

Technological Change

The weapons that would dominate World War II were in their infancy during the previous war. Tanks evolved rapidly. The effectiveness of armored vehicles depended on a number of characteristics: armor, speed, armament, and cruising range. Designers had to balance these characteristics to produce the type of vehicle necessary for a specific purpose. The thicker the armor and the larger the main battery, the heavier and therefore slower the vehicle would be, thus the decision to categorize tanks as heavy, medium, or light. Two innovations made tanks much more effective: turrets and radios. Mounting the vehicle's main battery in a rotating turret instead of in the hull allowed its cannon to be fired at a target no matter which way the tank faced and to change field of fire rapidly. Two-way radios made it possible to coordinate the actions of groups of tanks in battle.

Military aircraft also developed apace. The primitive bi- and triplanes of World War I had had little effect on the fighting beneath them. Despite the romance of one-on-one aerial combat, the main value of airplanes lay in reconnaissance. They could carry only small payloads, so their effectiveness as bombers remained limited. Larger engines and better designs based on a single-wing model had addressed these problems by the outbreak of World War II. Improvement necessitated specialization. Engineers developed small, single-engine fighters with multiple machine guns to engage other aircraft. They designed multiple-engine bombers to carry heavier payloads and smaller dive bombers to support infantry and armor. The accoutrements of aviation also improved: better instruments, parachutes, and oxygen masks for high-altitude flying.

Military aviation had as profound an impact on naval warfare as it did on land operations. Airplanes could drop torpedoes as well as armor-piercing bombs, both capable of sinking even the largest battleships. The technological challenge in using them effectively lay not merely in designing airplanes but also in developing a platform for launching them at sea. Single light biplanes could be launched from catapults on conventional battleships and cruisers, land on water using pontoons, and be retrieved with cranes. To be effective, however, naval aircraft had to be deployed en masse, and that required a larger launch platform, a floating airfield. The aircraft carrier solved the problem. Carriers allowed fleets to engage one another without ever coming into visual range and enabled navies to bomb land targets from far out at sea. With the invention of the aircraft carrier, the days of the battleship as the primary arm of naval warfare were numbered. Engagements between vessels mounting massive guns did occur during World War II, but the real value of battleships lay in their ability to bombard coastal fortifications preparatory to amphibious landings.

Allied Planning and Land Warfare Doctrine

Weapons are only as effective as the doctrines devised for employing them. Those doctrines develop from national defense policy and planning. Each nation assessed the threats it faced, distilled the lessons from the last war, and made plans for how to deal with the next conflict. The United Kingdom, France, the Soviet Union, and the United States approached this process with differing assumptions and drew different conclusions, which in turn led them to employ new technologies in different ways. It should come as no surprise that having lost the Great War and been stripped of most of its military equipment, Germany proved the most innovative.

Unhappy at being dragged into a costly land war and unable to afford both a large navy and a large army, Britain reverted to its historic "deepwater strategy," relying on the navy as its first line of defense and using the army as a small imperial police force. Policing a vast empire purely with infantry, however, was neither feasible nor cost effective. Technology seemed to offer a solution. In what came to be called the "air control" method of imperial policing, the War Office proposed to use light armored cars with wheels rather than tracks, supported by light biplanes, to control remote areas. Armored cars could convey soldiers to hotspots while airplanes kept indigenous populations in remote areas under control through punitive bombing.[1] Air control had mixed results in colonial warfare, but it inhibited development of tank and armored warfare doctrine in the British army. Armored cars worked well enough against lightly armed colonial peoples, but they would be of little use in a conventional land war.

The British did study the use of tanks in World War I, but they focused on how they were employed and how they actually performed rather than on a more imaginative assessment of their potential. The ponderous, slow-moving machines of 1916 to 1918 served primarily as close infantry support weapons capable of destroying fixed positions. The British army thus planned to use them in the same role in future wars. This decision led them to emphasize armor and armament over speed and range. Instead of using motor transport to allow infantry to move at the speed of tanks, they slowed the tanks to the speed of the foot-slogging soldier. They thus went to war in 1939 with too few armored vehicles and tanks of a less than optimal design, with an ineffective doctrine of armored warfare.

The French also based their strategy on a mistaken assessment of the Great War, just as they had entered that war with incorrect ideas based on a misunderstanding of the Franco-Prussian War. Committed in 1914 to the cult of the offensive, they now embraced defensive warfare. This decision led them to devote much of their defense budget during the interwar period to constructing the Maginot Line, a system of bunkers, gun emplacements, tank traps, and other fortifications linked by underground tunnels and lifts along the German frontier from the Ardennes Forest to the Swiss border. This massively expensive project left few resources for other weapons systems, and in any event, French doctrine relied on infantry supported by heavy artillery for its offensive punch. Although the French army did develop tanks that could compete one-on-one with their German counterparts, they did not embrace the concept of armored warfare. Like the British, they viewed the tank primarily as a close infantry support weapon, and so in 1940 they had few armored divisions.

The Soviet Union did not emerge from the throws of civil war until 1922. From 1919 to 1921, it had fought and lost a border war with the newly reconstituted country of Poland. A power struggle followed Lenin's death in 1924, which Joseph Stalin eventually won. He then launched the country on a campaign of rapid industrialization that succeeded at the cost of millions of lives due to artificial famines created by his decision to export grain for capital to buy machinery. The Soviet Union did produce one of the pioneers of armored warfare. Soviet Marshal Mikhail Tukhachevsky advocated "deep battle" using armor and aircraft. Unfortunately,

The Interwar Period

Tukhachevsky fell victim to Stalin's purges, making his military ideas politically incorrect. Perhaps more important, the Soviet military made decisions based on incorrect analysis of the Spanish Civil War (1936–1939), in which Soviet officers advised the Republican forces, and on their own Winter War with Finland (1939–1940).[2] Like the French, the Soviets had trouble conceptualizing how mobile forces fit into a mass conscript army. In the Russo-Finnish War they faced an enemy with few tanks and virtually no air force, but one who made excellent use of fortified lines. This experience led the Soviets to concentrate on training troops in mass assaults against pillboxes and other fixed positions.[3] The Soviets did, however, develop what would turn out to be the best medium tank of World War II: the T34.

The United States ended World War I disillusioned with European affairs. The Republican-controlled Senate had refused to ratify the Versailles Treaty, so the United States never joined the League of Nations. The army shrank to the status of the garrison force it had been before the war. Many Americans believed that the ocean separating them from Europe and a powerful navy offered sufficient protection from foreign aggression. They wanted nothing to do with Europe and Europe's problems. Force reduction and budget cuts limited equipment purchases and hampered innovation. These decisions and an inherent conservatism inhibited formulation of effective armored warfare doctrine and the development of tanks.

The official literature of the interwar period reflects a failure to understand the importance of armored units in the future of war. The U.S. Army abolished its Tank Corps in 1920 and relegated armor to the role of close infantry support. The 1923 *Field Service Regulations* stated:

> The tank constitutes an armored infantry element possessing protective properties that enable it to close with intrenched [sic] defensive groups protected against the effects of ordinary infantry fire. Its essential mission is to assist in the progression of the infantry by overcoming or neutralizing resistances or breaking down obstacles that check the infantry advance.[4]

The 1939 version of the same manual still tied armor to infantry, noting that tank units should be assigned to General Headquarters, which allocates them to "[infantry] divisions operating in terrain favorable to the employment of tanks." The manual still insisted that

> [a]s a rule, tanks are employed to assist the advance of infantry foot troops, either preceding or accompanying the infantry assault echelon. They attack

successive objectives which coincide with those of the supported infantry foot troops.[5]

The 1941 *Field Service Regulations*, written after the battle of France, finally acknowledged the importance of armored units exercising a more independent role. "When widely distributed or engaged piecemeal," the publication warned, "tanks suffer rapid destruction from the concentrated fire of artillery and antitank weapons." They also untethered armor from infantry, noting, "Tanks should not be tied too closely to foot troops. If so restricted, their mobility is sacrificed and they become a vulnerable target for antitank weapons."[6]

Like its French and British counterparts, the U.S. Army of the interwar period failed to appreciate the potential of tanks. Farsighted officers did challenge this official orthodoxy in papers and articles, but their ideas had little impact on official doctrine, although their efforts may have contributed to the army's steep learning curve once war broke out.[7] Not surprisingly, the limited role the army assigned tanks affected their design. In 1938 its armored units consisted of two types of tank: the M2 light tank, mounting 1 × 30 caliber and 1 × 50 caliber machine guns in separate

Put into service in 1942, the M4 Sherman was the main U.S. battle tank of World War II. *Source:* Library of Congress.

turrets, and the M2 medium tank, mounting a 37 mm antitank gun and five machine guns.[8] The campaigns in Poland and France revealed the obsolescence of both models before they could even be deployed. The army had to design new, more suitable models at the same time that it produced realistic doctrine.

Germany and the Origins of Blitzkrieg

Although the Germans led the way in developing armored warfare doctrine during the interwar period, they did so with at least some help from their future enemies. The earliest pioneers of mechanization were not German but British. J. F. C. Fuller, who had commanded the British Tank Corps during World War I and planned the successful attack at Cambrai, became a postwar advocate of armored warfare. Fuller argued for using massed tanks supported by aircraft to drive deep through enemy lines to disrupt command and control. He helped draft "Plan 1919" (never employed because of the armistice), which took this approach. Fuller later claimed that "in modified form, this tactical theory was first put to the test in 1939, and became known as *Blitzkrieg*."[9] His assertion contains an element of truth wrapped in a lot of braggadocio. He was a pioneer of armored warfare, but he did not invent blitzkrieg. Forward-thinking officers in other armies articulated similar theories. British Captain Basil Liddell Hart, a protégé of Fuller, expanded on his ideas, devising the strategy of the indirect approach. Colonel Charles De Gaulle in France, Soviet Marshal Tukhachevsky, and American General George Patton also supported an expanded role for tanks. Nonetheless, Fuller's ideas enjoyed the widest circulation outside of Britain. His *Lectures on Field Service Regulations III: Operations between Mechanized Forces*, first published in 1932, was translated into Russian and German.[10] The British rejected Fuller's ideas, opting for motorization based on light armored cars equipped with machine guns.[11] Better suited for colonial warfare, these vehicles would be of little use in a conventional European war.

While many German officers contributed to the development of mechanized warfare doctrine, one in particular best explained the evolution of German doctrine. In 1937 General Heinz Guderian published *Achtung Panzer!*, a lengthy treatise on armored warfare.[12] While Guderian acknowledged the contribution of British theorists, he improved upon their ideas. Fuller and Liddell Hart envisioned armored formations as the successors of cavalry, which should be allowed to range far afield, free from the encumbrance of foot soldiers. "To combine tanks and infantry," Fuller argued, "is tantamount to yoking a tractor to a draught horse."[13] Guderian, however, understood the vulnerability of tanks to natural obstacles, mines, artillery, and infantry throwing grenades at their treads.[14] Armor had to operate with support elements, but instead of slowing the tanks to the speed of the infantry, he proposed motorizing the infantry:

> I became convinced that tanks working on their own or in conjunction with infantry could never achieve decisive importance. My historical studies, the exercises carried out in England and our own experiences with mock-ups had persuaded me that tanks would never be able to produce their full effect until the other weapons on whose support they must inevitably rely were brought up to their standard of speed and of cross-country performance. In such a formation of all arms, the tanks must play the primary role, the other weapons being subordinated to the requirements of the armour. It would be wrong to include tanks in infantry divisions: what was needed were amoured divisions which would include all the supporting arms needed to allow tanks to fight with full effect.[15]

All elements of the mechanized division (infantry, engineers, artillery, and support units) would be transported by trucks or half-tracks. Guderian also equipped each tank with a two-way FM radio to facilitate coordinated action among vehicles in a unit. Grouped into corps, armored divisions would function like the steel tip of a spear, puncturing the enemy line so that the nonmotorized infantry and the slower foot soldiers could exploit the gap.

Guderian did not, of course invent mechanized warfare. No single individual did. The concept developed out of careful analysis of World War I. General Hans von Seeckt, Chief of the General Staff, which met covertly in contravention of the Versailles Treaty, oversaw writing of the after-action report on the Great War. Blitzkrieg had its origins in a realistic assessment of the Great War, which focused on the St. Michael Offensive of 1918 as the harbinger of the future. Captured in *Die Truppenführung* (Troop leading), first published in 1924, this doctrine advocated mobility, flexibility, and surprise. "The weaker force," the manual proclaimed, "through speed, mobility, great march accomplishments, utilization of darkness and terrain to the fullest, surprise and deception, can be the decisive area."[16] The manual also reiterated the time-honored principle of *Auftragstaktik* (mission-based tactics). "In the vicissitudes of war an inflexible maintenance of the original decision may lead to great mistakes," the manual instructed. "Timely recognition of the conditions and the time which call for a new decision is an attribute of leadership. . . . The commander must permit freedom of action in his subordinates insofar that this does not endanger the whole scheme."[17] Mechanized warfare thus evolved out of established concepts applied to new equipment to implement innovative approaches to warfare.[18]

Airpower

Airplanes developed dramatically during the interwar period, and their potential as weapons of war drew the attention of military planners. As with tanks, a debate arose as to how best to employ them. Advocates of strategic bombing argued for the creation of fleets of bombers capable of carrying large payloads to attack industrial sites and cities. Proponents of mechanized warfare wanted aircraft that could provide close air support for ground troops. Fuller and other proponents of mechanized warfare considered this tactical role vital to the success of armored attacks. To have any role at all, of course, air forces would have to protect their planes from enemy aircraft trying to shoot them down, hence the need for dedicated fighter aircraft.

Most designers realized that specific combat roles required specialized aircraft. Multi-engine heavy bombers could carry heavy payloads and enough fuel to reach distant targets, but they lacked speed and maneuverability. Fast, highly maneuverable fighters could not carry heavy payloads, but they could shoot down bombers and other fighters and strafe ground targets. Dive bombers usually lacked sufficient armament for aerial combat, but they could strike targets on the ground with considerable precision. To save money engineers experimented with models capable of performing more than one role. However, multipurpose planes such as the French Potez 630, capable of bombing, reconnaissance, and aerial combat, did not excel at any of these tasks.[19] Ideally, militaries needed a range of functional types, but budget constraints usually forced them to make difficult choices. The British focused on strategic bombing, while the Germans emphasized close air support. Both developed excellent fighters, notably the German Messerschmitt 109 and the British Spitfire. The United States developed a broad range of specialized aircraft for warfare on land and sea. The Soviets concentrated on air superiority fighters and dive bombers, while the Japanese focused on naval aviation.

Military planners chose strategic or tactical aircraft based on the type of war they expected to wage. Strategic bombing could produce decisive results only in a long war of attrition. The prophet of this new type of warfare, the Italian Guilio Douhet, described how bombing campaigns would be conducted. "In general," he declared in his 1921 treatise *The Command of the Air*, "aerial offensives will be directed against such targets as peacetime industrial and commercial establishments; important buildings, private and public; transportation arteries and centers; and certain designated areas of civilian population as well."[20] Douhet also recognized that strategic bombing would destroy the already blurred line between combatant and noncombatant:

> The battlefield will be limited only by the boundaries of the nations at war, and all of their citizens will become combatants, since all of them will be exposed to aerial offensives of the enemy. There will be no distinction any longer between soldiers and civilians.[21]

Having won the long war of attrition against Germany, Britain and the United States embraced the concept of strategic bombing.

Germany, on the other hand, decided that strategic bombing would take time that it could not afford. Published in 1924, the general staff's study of World War I concluded that the country could not win a war of attrition against a coalition of nations such as it had faced in 1914–1918. It must fight a short, decisive war to defeat its enemies before they could mobilize their superior manpower and resources. This emphasis on brief, decisive campaigns explains the willingness of Adolf Hitler and his generals to embrace mechanized warfare with its corresponding emphasis on tactical aircraft. While the Luftwaffe (air force) developed a range of types, the JU87 Stuka Diver bomber stands out as its premier tactical aircraft. Once again, however, it was not merely the machines but how the Germans used them that mattered. During the first two years of the war, the French, British, and Americans parceled out aircraft to ground commanders in much the same way they allotted tanks. Planes were to provide close infantry support as "flying artillery." The Germans understood that to be effective planes, like tanks, had to be massed. They concentrated them to support the mechanized spearhead and assigned forward air controllers to army units to coordinate air and ground operations. When the Panzers encountered stiff resistance, these controllers called in the Stukas to clear the way.

Naval Warfare

The evolution in aviation had as much of an impact at sea as it did on land. The idea that planes could sink ships became obvious once designers made it possible for them to drop bombs or torpedoes. During World War I conventional ships were retrofitted to carry a small number of pontoon planes capable of taking off from and landing on water. Two such aircraft sank three Turkish merchant ships in the Dardanelles Straits in 1915.[22] It

The Interwar Period

became apparent, though, that to be effective naval weapons, airplanes would have to be launched in large numbers from ships designed to carry them. The first aircraft carrier or "flattop" was the British ship HMS *Argus*, completed in 1918. During the interwar period development of aircraft carriers and the planes they carried progressed rapidly. Engineers designed dive bombers, torpedo planes, and the fighters necessary to protect them.

Not only did the aircraft carrier transform naval warfare, but it had profound implications for land warfare as well. Navies had traditionally contributed to war by disrupting trade and commerce and imposing blockades. Their ability to project force onshore had been limited to the range of their guns and the troops they could land. Combat between warships had been conducted to gain naval supremacy so that fleets could perform these functions. Now warships could deploy aircraft to hit targets hundreds of miles inland. Although the full implications of naval aviation had yet to manifest themselves, all maritime powers began acquiring aircraft carriers. By 1939 Britain had seven and France one.[23] Germany, which probably realized it could not match Britain's surface fleet, opted for submarines and raiders (fast cruisers), although it did build two powerful battleships, *Bismarck* and *Tripitz*.

Although few at the time realized it, Japan and the United States would fight an extensive naval war based on aircraft carriers. As an island nation bent on establishing an East Asian empire, Japan concentrated heavily on naval aviation. It built 10 aircraft carriers during the interwar period and developed an impressive array of naval aircraft. The Mitsubishi Zero (an air superiority fighter), the Kate torpedo plane, and the Val diver gave the Japanese an initial advantage in the Pacific. The United States recognized the importance of naval aviation, especially since it occupied Hawaii, the Philippines, and Guam. The American navy, however, had to divide its fleet between two oceans. On December 7, 1941, only three of its seven aircraft carriers were deployed in the Pacific.[24]

In retrospect the importance of carriers seems clear, but at the outbreak of World War II they were untested. In all navies but the Japanese, battleships outnumbered carriers, and battleships and heavy cruisers together outnumbered them considerably. Skeptics still conceived of naval warfare as a contest between capital ships mounting massive guns. Some officers questioned the value of naval aircraft, just as their counterparts on land questioned the importance of tanks. The program for the November 30, 1941, Army-Navy football game featured a bow-shot of the battleship *Arizona* accompanied by the later bitterly ironic statement: "It is significant that despite the claims of air enthusiasts no battleship has yet been sunk by bombs."[25] Just a week later a single armor-piercing bomb went through the ship's forward deck,

The U.S. Navy aircraft carrier USS *Enterprise* served in the Pacific throughout World War II. *Source:* U.S. Navy Naval History and Heritage Command.

detonated its magazine, and sent the proud battle wagon to the bottom of Pearl Harbor along with almost 1,200 of its crew. Even then a few diehards would insist that the *Arizona* and its sister ships had only been sunk because they had been trapped in harbor and unable to maneuver. The Japanese shattered that myth three days later when they sank the British battleships *Repulse* and *Prince of Wales* in just over an hour off the coast of Malaya. The aircraft carrier was now the undisputed queen of the sea.

Interwar Conflicts

Although the period between the two world wars saw no conflict between major powers, numerous small wars occurred around the globe. From 1919 to 1921 Poland fought a successful war against the fledgling Soviet Union to expand its border eastward. The Russian Civil War did not end until 1923, the same year that the Turks drove the Greeks from their territory. Japan invaded Manchuria in 1931 and China in 1937, actions that would put it on a collision course with the United States.

One conflict had a significant impact on the development of conventional warfare. The Spanish Civil War (1936–1939) pitted Republicans against monarchists and ended with the dictatorship of Francisco Franco.

The Interwar Period

The Soviets sent advisers to support the Republicans, and the Germans sent both men and equipment to aid Franco. While the Soviet military derived little benefit from its participation in the conflict and in fact drew incorrect conclusions based on it, the Wehrmacht used the Civil War as a live-fire exercise. It bombed the Basque village of Guernica to test the effectiveness of the Stuka dive bomber. The Germans also learned that their primary antiaircraft gun, the famous FLAK 88 mm, was highly effective as an antitank gun. These lessons would be put to good use in the coming world war.

The first stirrings of anticolonialism also began during this era. From 1919 to 1921 the Irish Republican Army fought a protracted insurgency against the British government. From the outset it was clear that the conflict differed from previous colonial revolts. In the election of 1918 a legitimate Irish political party, Sinn Fein (Gaelic for "Ourselves Alone") won almost every seat outside Protestant Ulster. Rather than take the seats in the British Parliament in Westminster, however, they formed their own legislative body and declared independence. When London refused to recognize them, the Irish formed their own paramilitary force, the Irish Republican Army (IRA), under the leadership of Michael Collins. The IRA assassinated police, soldiers, and Irish collaborators. In the countryside they formed guerrilla "flying columns" to ambush British patrols. By the end of 1920 one IRA commander boasted that the British dared not venture forth in bodies of less than 100.[26] The government augmented the Royal Irish Constabulary with demobilized soldiers, known as "Black and Tans" for their khaki military trousers and dark green police shirts, and sent in regular troops. Having no experience fighting irregular warfare in a Western country where they could not get away

The FLAK 88. *Source:* Library and Archives of Canada.

with the exemplary violence meted out to colonial peoples, the security forces became frustrated. They retaliated against the general population, which undermined their legitimacy and increased public support for the IRA. One British officer summed up this frustration:

> We've all been slandered, tarred, and maligned until the public will believe anything about the military, RIC, or Auxiliaries in Ireland till we are utterly sick of trying to win this most difficult of wars.[27]

These sentiments would be echoed by countless regular soldiers in counterinsurgency campaigns throughout the 20th century.

In 1921 the British adopted new tactics. They created their own flying columns, small groups of soldiers lightly equipped, wearing rubber-soled shoes, and operating across country. Irish Republican Army units now found themselves being surprised and ambushed. Constant patroling, better intelligence, and good police work began to wear down the guerrillas.[28] By this time, however, the British had decided upon negotiations, especially since they had the power to set conditions. The resulting Irish Free State was less than the fully independent republic Sinn Fein had demanded but rather more than the Home Rule government Britain had promised.

The Anglo-Irish War did not start a wave of revolutionary wars. The French and British successfully suppressed revolt whenever and wherever it occurred. Most nationalists had to accept that the colonial powers were still too strong for them to overthrow. The IRA did, however, provide a valuable lesson on just how that might be done. Once World War II had weakened European states, a wave of insurgencies would sweep Africa and Asia. In the brief span of 25 years (1945–1970) most former colonies would become independent states.

Changing Attitudes toward War

While the interwar period saw unprecedented advances in military technology, it also witnessed a growing aversion to war among many politicians and the general public in most Western nations. The Versailles settlement included creation of the League of Nations, whose members agreed "not to resort to war" to resolve disputes.[29] Failure of the United States to join and lack of any power to punish aggressors weakened the league, but it nonetheless represented a genuine effort to avoid war. The league successfully supervised the 1935 Saar plebiscite and the return of the territory to Germany. It failed, however, to prevent Italian aggression against Ethiopia or the Japanese invasion of Manchuria.

The Interwar Period

The major powers considered limitations on armaments to be one way to prevent war. In November 1921 the League of Nations convened the Washington Naval Conference. The meeting sought to preserve the existing balance of power among world navies. Disarmed by the Versailles Treaty, Germany could not participate, but Great Britain, the United States, France, Japan, and Italy reached an agreement in February 1922. The Washington Naval Treaty established an agreed-upon ratio of battleships and aircraft carriers. It allowed Great Britain and the United States battleships totaling 525,000 tons and aircraft carriers totaling 135,000 tons. Japan could build battleships totaling 315,000 tons and aircraft carriers totaling 81,000 tons. France and Italy could each build a battleship fleet totaling 165,000 tons and aircraft carriers totaling 60,000 tons.[30] As with all such agreements, the signatories could ensure compliance only by going to war, the course of action they sought to avoid. Japan chafed at the treaty's restrictions and soon abrogated it.

Perhaps the most optimistic of all interwar period accords was the 1928 Kellogg-Briand Pact, named for Secretary of State Frank Kellogg of the United States and Foreign Minister Aristide Briand of France. Signed by representatives of France, the United States, Germany, the United Kingdom, Italy, Belgium, Poland, Czechoslovakia, and Japan, the agreement outlawed war. "The High Contracting Parties solemnly declare in the names of their respective peoples," the agreement proclaimed, "that they condemn recourse to war for the solution of international controversies, and renounce it, as an instrument of national policy in their relations with one another." The signatories would resolve their disagreements solely by peaceful means.[31] The irony embedded within this agreement can have been lost on no one: the only way for the signatories to enforce the prohibition against war was to go to war.

It would be tempting to dismiss the agreements of the interwar period as cynical or naïve, but considerable evidence suggests that most nations genuinely wished to avoid war, or at least an international war between alliances of the great powers. Their great reluctance to confront Japanese and German aggression in the 1930s reflects this sentiment. By the time Hitler came to power in 1933, few of the victors save France had any great interest in upholding the terms of the Versailles Treaty. Many in the West considered a strong Germany a useful buffer against the Soviet Union, so they did nothing when Germany rearmed and then in 1936 occupied the Rhineland. When Hitler annexed Austria in 1938, many statesmen dismissed the move with the comment that the country was "Hitler's backyard," and noted that the Austrians had voted for the *Anschluss* in a plebiscite. Only when he demanded control of the Sudetenland in Czechoslovakia did the allies begin to take the German threat seriously. Even then, they acceded to his wishes with the Munich Accord in September 1938. The United States was equally slow to respond to Japanese aggression.

In what came to be called a policy of appeasement, politicians may have been in sync with their electorates, who genuinely desired to avoid conflict. With the possible exception of Japan, little evidence suggests that ordinary people wanted another major war. Even in Germany and Italy ordinary folk welcomed its outbreak not with the enthusiasm with which their parents and grandparents had greeted World War I, but with grim resignation and acceptance of a duty that had to be performed. They certainly hoped that if a war must be fought, it would at least be short. That hope would prove forlorn.

CHAPTER TEN

World War II in Europe

Although the Great War has been retroactively dubbed a "world war," most of the fighting took place in Europe. Indeed, during the interwar period American libraries catalogued books on the subject under the heading, "European War, 1914–1918." World War II, on the other hand, was a truly global conflict. It involved 1.7 billion people (three-quarters of the earth's population) from 61 countries and was fought in locales ranging from jungle atolls in the South Pacific to the snow-covered steppes of Russia.[1] In addition to being more extensive, World War II was far more lethal than its predecessor. The increased destructive power of weapons, especially bombs, combined with virulent ideologies, whose intensity had not been seen since the wars of religion three centuries earlier, made the conflict the deadliest in human history. It claimed the lives of 60 million people, three quarters of them civilians.[2] When the belligerents saw each other not as soldiers in opposing armed forces, but as members of alien races bent on one another's destruction, they made no distinction between combatant and noncombatant, man, woman, or child, old or young. World War II completed the evolution toward total war.

Blitzkrieg

On September 1, 1939, two German army groups invaded Poland from three directions: north from East Prussia, northwest from Pomerania, and southwest from Silesia and occupied Czechoslovakia. In a week they had broken the back of Polish resistance and were driving toward Warsaw, which capitulated on September 28 after savage bombing. The Soviets, who invaded from the east on September 17 per an agreement with the Germans that also gave them the Baltic States, contributed nothing to the German victory but took their share of the spoils. Reporting on the campaign, *Time* magazine gave a new word to the English language:

> This was no war of occupation, but a war of quick penetration and obliteration—Blitzkrieg, lightning war. Even with no opposition, armies had never moved so fast before. Theorists had always said that only infantry could take and hold positions. But these armies had not waited for the infantry. Swift columns of tanks and armored trucks had plunged through Poland while bombs raining from the sky heralded their coming. They had sawed off communications, destroyed stores, scattered civilians, spread terror. Working sometimes 30 miles ahead of infantry and artillery, they had broken down the Polish defenses before they had time to organize. Then, while the infantry mopped up, they had moved on, to strike again far behind what had been called the front. By week's end it mattered very little whether Warsaw stood or fell. The Republic of Poland, aged 20, was lost.[3]

The German army had never formally used "blitzkrieg" in any of its official publications, preferring the term *Bewegungskrieg* ("mobile warfare").[4] Whatever one called it, though, the Polish campaign introduced the world to a new type of war, one that proved the prophets of armor and airpower to be frighteningly right.

Since becoming chancellor of Germany in January 1933, Adolf Hitler had propelled his country on an inexorable course toward war. He had pulled Germany out of the League of Nations almost immediately. By 1935 he had given up the pretext of democracy, declared himself *Führer* ("leader"), and commenced a program of rearmament in violation of the Versailles Treaty. In March 1936 he had occupied the Rhineland, yet another violation of the peace accord. In 1938 Hitler began his campaign of expansion, annexing Austria in March, the Sudetenland in October, and the rest of Czechoslovakia in March 1939. The British responded by joining France in guaranteeing Polish neutrality and signed a military alliance with Poland on August 6. London tried to persuade the Soviet Union to join then, but Stalin signed the "German-Soviet Nonaggression Pact" on August 23 instead. Secret clauses in the treaty promised him eastern Poland and the Baltic states. On September 3, two days after the invasion of Poland, France and Britain declared war on Germany, and the European conflagration everyone had feared began.

The Battle of France

The British and French knew that they could get no material help to Poland but hoped the threat of war might force Hitler to back down. When he did not, they understood that Poland would probably fall, although the speed of the German victory shocked them. The two allies prepared for the inevitable German invasion of France. They also reached out to Belgium and the Netherlands, certain that any thrust westward must go through the Low Countries. The Battle of France would epitomize the new type of warfare and in many ways represents Germany's greatest victory of the war.

In retrospect it seems as though France and Britain should have been alerted to the effectiveness of blitzkrieg by Germany's rapid defeat of Poland. Viewed from the vantage point of late 1939, however, the Polish campaign did not appear to be incontrovertible evidence of the superiority of German doctrine and tactics. In the first place, few military observers had given Poland much of a chance. Defending a flat country with few natural barriers from invasion by an enemy with greater numbers and superior equipment attacking from three sides would be extremely difficult. The Polish army's decision to defend the entire length of its western frontier made a bad situation worse. Observers may have been surprised by the speed of the German campaign, but not by its outcome. Furthermore, the invasion was hardly a flawless example of lightning war. Panzer spearheads often outran their trailing infantry and in some cases their own fuel and supply columns. Polish antitank guns proved more effective against thin-skinned light tanks than anticipated. Finally, French and British officers had good reason to believe that mechanized divisions would have a much harder time maneuvering through the confined space of the Low Countries than they had over the open plains of Poland.[5] In any event, seven months was hardly enough time to overhaul doctrine and strategy that were 20 years in the making.

The Allies dubbed the period from the surrender of Poland on October 6, 1939, to the invasion of Denmark and Norway on April 9, 1940, the "phony war" or the "Sitzkrieg" (sitting war) to describe the long period of seeming inactivity. The French, supported by the British, adopted a strategy designed to halt the German assault and allow the Allies to mobilize their manpower and resources for a protracted struggle. Seeking to avoid a war of attrition it could not win, Germany needed to take the offensive. The Wehrmacht spent the respite following the Polish campaign preparing for an invasion of France. Its initial plan, code-named "Case Yellow," replicated the Schlieffen Plan, except that this time the Germans would invade the Netherlands as well as Belgium. This plan, however, had one glaring weakness: the French and British anticipated it. They planned to forestall the flanking move by advancing northward to join forces with the Belgian and Dutch armies. This weakness and the fact that a copy of "Case Yellow" fell into Allied hands following the crash of a German plane in Belgium led the general staff to alter its strategy. Initially devised by Major General Erich von Manstein, "Sickle Stroke" focused on an armored thrust through the Ardennes Forest, an obstacle the French considered impenetrable by mechanized forces.

Before the Battle of France unfolded, however, the Germans struck north. On April 9, 1940, German forces invaded Denmark and Norway. Hitler may have feared that the British planned to occupy Norway, which would have threatened iron ore shipments from neighboring Sweden.[6] Denmark had no choice but to surrender almost immediately, and German troops successfully occupied Oslo and the Atlantic ports of Norway after limited resistance, although Oslo's harbor forts did sink the German heavy cruiser *Blücher*. The British navy sank 10 German destroyers in Narvik Fjord, but landings at Narvik and Trondheim in May failed to reverse the German conquest. Control of Norway gave Germany access to excellent bases for launching submarine attacks against North Atlantic convoys headed for Britain. The Scandinavian campaign, however, was only a preliminary to what everyone knew would be the decisive campaign in the west. By the first week of May both sides had completed preparations for the coming battle.

The two belligerents were more closely matched in men and equipment than might be imagined judging by the outcome. Approximately 2.9 million Allied troops faced 3.5 million Germans.[7] The Allies had a slight advantage in tanks (3,000 to 2,600)[8] and a significant edge in artillery (11,200 to 7,000 pieces), although the French had deployed many of their guns in the Maginot Line, but a serious deficit in anti-aircraft guns.[9] The Germans did enjoy a considerable advantage in aircraft (3,700 to 1,400).[10]

Contrary to popular belief, Germany did not have vastly superior tanks. Comparing specific vehicles requires weighing the relative merits of armor, armament, speed, fuel consumption, cruising range, and crew size, and these factors vary depending on whether the tanks are heavy, medium, or light. A category-by-category analysis of Allied and German tanks is beyond the scope of this work. Suffice it to say that neither side enjoyed a decisive advantage. The British Matilda IIs and the French SOMUA S35s performed well against the Panzer Mark IIIs and IVs. Indeed, at Hannut, Belgium, the first tank battle in history, the SOMUAs temporarily halted the German advance, destroying 165 enemy tanks for the loss of 105 of their own.[11] At Arras on May 21, a British Expeditionary Force (BEF)

World War II in Europe

counterattack with Matildas even forced the Germans to retreat temporarily. German success came not from superior weaponry but from superior doctrine and tactics.

In the air, however, Germany did enjoy a qualitative as well as a quantitative advantage. In the French air force only the Dewoitine D520 could match the ME109, and only 80 of these planes were available by May 1940.[12] The British Spitfire was also the equal of its German counterpart, but Spitfires made up only a third of the Royal Air Force (RAF) in 1940, and most were based in Britain. Neither the British nor the French had developed dive bombers. These ground attack aircraft proved highly effective during the German advance. Every time the Panzers stalled, Stukas came out of the sky to destroy whatever lay in the way of their advance. Lack of dive bombers and sufficient numbers of effective fighter aircraft hurt the Allied cause, but the disparity in air forces alone could not explain the German conquest of France. The disposition and handling of the men and equipment available had more to do with the outcome than did the quantity and quality of machines.

The French deployed their forces in three army groups. Army Groups 2 (27 divisions) and 3 (7 divisions) covered the Maginot Line. Army Group 1, consisting of four armies (37 divisions), including the best French field forces and most of the French armor, deployed along the Belgian border from the English Channel to the western end of the Maginot Line at Montmedy. The BEF of 9 divisions supported them. As soon as German forces crossed the Belgian frontier, the Allies planned for the French Seventh, First, and Ninth Armies, along with the BEF, to advance northeast to link up with Belgian forces along the River Dyle and, if possible, extend their line northward to join with the Dutch army at Breda. The French left the Second Army, composed primarily of older reservists and lacking armor and antitank guns, to cover the Ardennes and defend the line of the River Meuse.

The German plan aimed to take advantage of the Allied deployment and strategy. In the south Army Group C (19 divisions) covered the Maginot Line. In the north Army Group B (29½ divisions, including 3 Panzer divisions) would invade the Netherlands and Belgium. Army Group A (45½ divisions, including 7 Panzer divisions grouped into 3 Panzer corps) in the center was to provide the main thrust of the invasion. Its Panzers would advance through the Ardennes and cross the Meuse near Sedan. They would then drive west toward the English Channel, unhinging the Allied line and trapping most of the French First Army and the BEF in Belgium.

Early on the morning of May 10 the campaign began with German air attacks, followed by the advance of ground forces. In the north infantry and paratroopers of Army Group B overran the Netherlands. Despite putting up stiff resistance, the Dutch had no answer to aerial bombardment, especially when the Germans targeted Rotterdam, so they surrendered after just five days. As the Germans advanced into Belgium, the French and British moved northeastward to meet them, little suspecting that they were stepping into a carefully laid trap. The three Panzer corps of Army Group A, one of which was commanded by General Guderian, drove through the Ardennes and forced a crossing of the Meuse on May 13. Most of the Allied air forces had deployed to Belgium, and the Second French Army, which bore the brunt of the German onslaught, had no armor or antitank guns. The French deployed the 3rd Armored Division to seal the breach, but the Second Army commander, General Charles Huntzinger, deployed its tanks along his entire front instead of massing them for a counterattack. Once he found himself in the open, Guderian drove deep into French territory, spreading panic as he went and threatening to resign when his superiors ordered him to halt until the infantry could catch up with him. Allied counterattacks against the widening Panzer corridor failed due to lack of coordination. By May 20 Guderian had reached the coast, cutting the Allied forces in two. The British fell back on Dunkirk, from whence they evacuated most of their troops and some of the French as well, but they had to leave most of their equipment behind. Belgium capitulated on May 28. France fought on until June 22, but the outcome of the campaign was no longer in doubt.

Miracle, Myth, or Stroke of Genius?

Virtually every observer was shocked by the speed at which French resistance collapsed in the face of the German onslaught. On its March 6 cover, *Life* magazine had featured the picture of an old *Poilu* (literally "hairy one," the common nickname for French soldiers) with the caption describing him as "about the best soldier European civilization has developed."[13] Two months later he and his colleagues were routed in less than three weeks of fighting. Military analysts around the world sought to explain the stunning victory. Had the Germans developed a new, unstoppable form of warfare and created a formidable fighting force to conduct it? Or had they simply been lucky that the Allies had not detected their long columns of tanks and other vehicles wending their way through the narrow roads of the Ardennes, lucky that the French had not better defended the south bank of the Meuse? Was it French incompetence rather than German brilliance that had decided the outcome? How generals in every army answered these questions would determine the further course of World War II. Historians have debated the matter ever since.

No single explanation suffices. The Germans had developed doctrine that allowed them to make the most effective use of the new weapons of war, and they had devised a bold operational plan that correctly assessed and exploited Allied weakness. They had created an army with at least a 20 percent "combat effectiveness superiority" over its enemies (i.e., 100 German soldiers were the combat equivalent of 120 Allied soldiers).[14] By May 1940 many Wehrmacht recruits had spent as much as six years in paramilitary youth movements and undergone rigorous training after conscription. By any measure, they had conducted a brilliant campaign. On the other hand, success blinded many observers to how precarious the advance through the Ardennes really had been. Had Allied planes spotted the long, slow-moving columns on the narrow forest roads, they might have called in devastating airstrikes.[15] Even against second-line, poorly led French troops lacking armor and antitank guns, crossing the Meuse had proven more difficult than anticipated and the margin of victory slimmer than many realized.[16]

French commanders made serious mistakes, which contributed to the German victory, but they were not all as incompetent as they are sometimes portrayed, nor did they design the Maginot Line as an impregnable wall behind which they could sit passively waiting to be attacked. They built the fortifications to free up troops for an effective, mobile field army.[17] The real weakness of the French lay in their doctrine and strategy. They subscribed to the idea of the "methodical battle." Based on the assumption that firepower conferred greater advantages on the defender than on the attacker, this doctrine dictated that engagements must occur only after careful preparation and that spontaneous "encounter battles" must be avoided. They thus emphasized highly centralized command and control, which made it very difficult for local commanders to react to rapidly changing circumstances such as those of the Battle of France.[18] This doctrine led to a flawed strategy: the British and French decided that they should fight the Germans to a standstill and then allow blockade and superior resources to wear Germany down, as they had during World War I.[19] They advanced into Belgium, not to engage German forces in mobile battles, but to link up with the Belgians and the Dutch along prepared defensive lines. This approach left the Allies vulnerable to the flexible mobile war the Wehrmacht planned to fight.

When criticizing the French approach and praising the German one, it must be noted that the armed forces of the two countries reflected the societies that created them. An authoritarian regime like the Third Reich could devote extensive resources to rearmament without answering to an electorate. The French Republic could not. Many German soldiers had spent several years in the paramilitary Hitler Youth. France had no such organization to train future conscripts. The French had devised not the ideal doctrine, but the doctrine best suited to the kind of military establishment they had. As Julian Jackson observed in his excellent study, *The Fall of France*, "the 'methodical battle' was what the [French] military considered necessary for an army composed primarily of short-service conscripts, badly prepared reservists, and overworked professionals."[20]

The myth of invincible blitzkrieg was invented and promulgated by the Germans themselves. Following the Polish campaign the German high command had undertaken a rigorous after-action assessment of the operation. They then spent the next seven months fixing the problems they had identified. Following their stunning victory over France, they conducted no such study.[21] As a result most German generals never considered what might happen if they encountered a more flexible enemy with better doctrine operating under different circumstances. Instead they made more grandiloquent plans based on the assumption that what they had accomplished in France they could accomplish virtually anywhere, including the vast and populous Soviet Union.[22] In January 1941 Chief of the General Staff Alfred Jodl declared that the "Russian colossus will prove to be a pig[']s bladder; prick it and it will burst," and Hitler compared a war with the Soviets to a "child's game in a sandbox."[23]

If blitzkrieg was not a miracle, however, neither was it a myth. After the Battle of France the Germans continued to rack up impressive victories, but only until their enemies adopted new doctrines and tactics. Like Napoleon using the flexible corps system to win battles of annihilation against opponents wedded to cumbersome mass armies, German generals could achieve deep penetration and win battles of encirclement against opponents committed to linear defensive tactics. Like Napoleon, that victory did not come so easily when those opponents adopted the same tactics or adjusted to them.

Barbarossa

Virtually all historians consider Hitler's invasion of the Soviet Union his greatest mistake, the single decision that, more than any other, led to Germany's defeat. Had he been content to consolidate his gains instead of attacking his erstwhile ally, Hitler might not have lost the war in Europe. His worldview, however, necessitated such a move. Nazi ideology rested on two principles: race and space. According to its Social Darwinist view of the world, human populations were dynamic groups: they either expanded or contracted but never remained static. Germany needed lebensraum, "living space," into which its growing population could expand, displacing or enslaving "inferior" peoples as needed. In addition to living space, the Nazis also sought autarchy, economic self-sufficiency. The Soviet Union offered the possibility to achieve both goals. The natural axis of German expansion had always been eastward, the historic *Drang nach Östen*, "drive to the east," which predated the Nazis. With its vast agricultural lands and extensive resources defended by an army that had struggled against Finland, the Soviet Union seemed ripe for conquest. The Nazis' fanatical hatred of "Jewish Bolshevism" provided another incentive for advancing eastward.

Hitler also had another strategic reason for attacking the Soviet Union. As long as Britain refused to make peace, the Battle of France remained a marred victory. Furious that the British would not accept a negotiated settlement that left them with their empire intact and Germany master of the Continent, Hitler had his general staff draw up plans for Operation Sea Lion, the invasion of Britain. Failure of the Luftwaffe to destroy the RAF, however, made an invasion impossible. Hitler believed that only the hope of Russian and/or American intervention was keeping Britain in the fight. An invasion of the Soviet Union would not only eliminate the Bolshevik threat but would give Germany the resources for a long struggle with the United States and Britain, a struggle with nothing less than world hegemony as its goal.[24]

The urgency Hitler felt in launching his attack may have stemmed from Soviet assertiveness. The 1939 alliance was an uneasy marriage of convenience, which the Kremlin exploited to the fullest. In addition to annexing eastern Poland and the Baltic states, it demanded that Romania surrender to it the provinces of Bessarabia and Bukovina (present-day Moldova), asserted its right to guarantee Bulgaria's borders, insisted on greater access to the Mediterranean via the Turkish straits, and even raised questions about the neutrality of Sweden, thus challenging Germany's vital source of iron ore.[25] In July 1940 Hitler told his generals to prepare Operation Barbarossa, the invasion of the Soviet Union.

Before he could move east, however, Hitler had to secure his southeastern flank. Following victory in France, Germany had extended its power through alliances. It had been allied to Italy since 1936, which led Italian dictator Benito Mussolini to declare war against France and Britain on June 10, 1940, and to invade southeastern France the same day. On September 27 the two allied with Japan to create the Rome-Berlin-Tokyo Axis. Hungary and Romania joined the Axis in November, and Bulgaria became a member in March 1941. The Italian alliance proved a mixed blessing, as Italy dragged Germany into a campaign against the British in North Africa and a war against Greece. Hitler needed to secure the Balkans, but he had hoped Mussolini would be able to conquer Albania and Greece, leaving Germany to deal with the central Balkan states.[26] The Italians occupied Albania but failed in Greece and had to be bailed out by their more powerful German ally. A military coup overthrew the pro-German Yugoslav government. As a result, the Germans invaded Yugoslavia and Greece on April 6, 1941, defeating the former in 11 days and the latter in 3 weeks.

Barbarossa had an achievable strategic objective, but it faced significant challenges and entailed enormous risks. The Soviets had a numerical advantage in troops, but the Germans enjoyed a qualitative edge in training, organization, and doctrine. Like the French, the Soviets committed themselves to a linear defense of their frontier, parceling out armored and air units to their ground commanders. This deployment gave the German strategy of destroying the bulk of Soviet forces in the western Soviet Union a reasonable chance of success. To achieve this goal, however, the Wehrmacht had to overcome an enormous logistics challenge. Despite its emphasis on mechanization, the army remained heavily dependent on horses to haul its supplies. Despite scouring occupied territories for trucks, the German high command barely scraped together enough motorized transport to support its mechanized units. Even then it remained unclear how far and for how long an advance could be sustained. The army's chief logistics officer, Major General Eduard Wagner, warned that the logistics system could sustain an advance of only 500 kilometers along the Eastern Front, well short of Moscow and Leningrad.[27] Even then the advance units would have to halt at 300–400 kilometers to restock and resupply.[28] Besides being overly optimistic about their logistics capability, the Germans seriously underestimated the strength of Soviet reserves, the quality of Soviet equipment, and the determination of Soviet troops to keep fighting even in hopeless situations.

These risks notwithstanding, the Germans mounted the largest invasion force to date: three million German troops in 146 divisions supported by perhaps a million more Axis troops (Romanian, Hungarian, Slovak, and Italian) and the Finnish army, 2,000 aircraft, and 3,500 tanks organized in three army groups.[29] The invasion plan called for a three-pronged attack. Army Group North would clear the Baltic states and take Leningrad; Army Group Center would drive toward Smolensk and then capture Moscow; and Army Group South would seize Kiev and occupy Ukraine. Launched on June 22, 1941, Barbarossa caught the Soviets completely by surprise. The Luftwaffe destroyed most aircraft in the western Soviet Union on the ground, and all three army groups made rapid progress, fighting massive battles of encirclement at Minsk, Kiev, and Smolensk. By September they had taken Kiev, occupied the Baltic states, and besieged Leningrad; Moscow lay within reach. By December 1941 Soviet losses were staggering: 800,000 killed and three million captured.[30] The Red Army had lost 22,000 pieces of artillery, 18,000 tanks, and 14,500 aircraft.[31]

Despite these impressive results, by October Barbarossa was in serious trouble. The Soviets had taken a beating but had not capitulated. The Wehrmacht's logistics system could not keep up with the fighting, and frontline units faced serious shortages of fuel, ammunition, and supplies. Although the Germans had inflicted serious losses on the Red Army, their own casualties were mounting. Units caught in the German encirclements exacted a high price before surrendering or being annihilated. By the end of November the invasion force had suffered more than 25 percent casualties.[32] Heavy fighting and long advances over rough roads had taken a toll on tanks and transport vehicles. In early October the *rasputitsa* ("time without roads") had begun, the annual fall rains that turned the Russian plains to mud.[33] This respite allowed the Soviets to catch their breath. Marshal Georgi Zhukov, one of the most able commanders of the entire war, took charge of the defense of Moscow. Reinforcements poured into the capital along with new equipment from factories the Soviets had built in the safety of the Urals and those relocated from the west. Many of the troops were reservists with little training, but a sizable number came from Soviet forces in Siberia, troops equipped for and accustomed to fighting in winter. Expecting the campaign to be over before the cold set in, the German army had not equipped its forces with winter clothing and winterized fuel for the vehicles. In the Soviet Union winter temperatures dropped to -20 Fahrenheit or lower. Guns froze up, vehicles failed to start, and men suffered frostbite. On December 5 the Soviets counterattacked in front of Moscow, and in a month of hard fighting they drove the Germans back. Then both exhausted armies waited out the winter. Two days after the start of the Soviet offensive, Japan bombed Pearl Harbor. On December 8, the United States declared war on Japan. Three days later Germany declared war on the United States, a mistake that would prove as grave as had invading the Soviet Union.

Entry of the United States

Any citizen of an Allied nation who picked up the morning paper on New Year's Day 1942 could be forgiven a glum mood. The Axis powers in Europe controlled an empire stretching from the Atlantic Ocean in the west to Orel in the east and from Norway in the north to Sicily in the south. In North Africa Erwin Rommel's Africa Corps was poised to drive the British Eighth Army back into Egypt. Much of the U.S. Pacific fleet lay at the bottom of Pearl Harbor. Japan had conquered vast areas of East Asia and was knocking at the door of British India.

Despite the gloomy outlook, Britain's decision to fight on, the survival of the Soviet Union, and American entry into the war combined to make an Axis victory virtually impossible. Germany, Italy, Japan, and the smaller Axis nations now found themselves in a war of attrition they could not win. The Allies had more of everything: people, raw materials, and industrial capacity. A single indicator, aircraft production for the year 1942, reveals the huge disparity between the two blocs. The United States alone out produced the Axis, 47,836 to 26,670, and together the Allies produced 101,519 aircraft.[34] In 1943 the Allies spent $62.5 billion on armaments, while the Axis could afford just $18.3 billion; the disparity would increase as the war progressed.[35] Germany tried to offset quantity with quality.[36] To a certain degree they succeeded, especially with tanks, but they never achieved a qualitative edge great enough to offset their quantitative deficit. Hitler also hoped to recoup the situation by inventing wonder weapons, like the V2 rocket, but although they pointed the way to the future of warfare, these inventions never provided significant help in the present.

Given the enormous advantages in production and manpower American entry into the war bestowed on the Allies, Hitler's decision to declare war on the United States requires considerable explanation. What seems folly in retrospect had a certain strategic logic to it at the time. The U.S. Navy was already waging an undeclared naval war against Germany by protecting convoys in the Atlantic against U-boats. Hitler thus considered a declared war between the two powers inevitable, and his submarine fleet commander wanted permission to attack American shipping more aggressively, even sinking ships along the east coast of the United States. Hitler also believed that the American military would be too busy fighting in the Pacific to devote significant resources to Europe. He overestimated the strength of Japan and underestimated the speed with which the United States would bring its resources to bear on Europe.[37]

American military officers had considered the possibility of a two-front war long before the Japanese bombed Pearl Harbor. They had concluded that a "Germany-first" strategy made the most sense given the relative threat posed by their two potential adversaries.[38] If Hitler had not declared war on the United States, however, President Roosevelt would have had a hard time selling that strategy to the American people. Even then, only after the U.S. Navy's victory over the Japanese in June 1942 removed the threat of Japan attacking the continental United States could he safely implement the "Germany-first" strategy.[39]

Eastern Front, 1942 to 1944

The entry of the United States into the war did not, of course, immediately produce a dramatic change in Allied fortunes. Conscription had been introduced and rearmament begun in 1940, but it would still take time for the country's war-making potential to be fully realized. Until then, the U.S. military had to content itself with limited operations on the periphery of the European theater. Not until October 1942 would American troops engage German forces, and that would only be in North Africa after General Bernard Law Montgomery had beaten Rommel at El Alamein in July. Stalin repeatedly pushed the Allies to open a second front in Western Europe, but that would not be possible until the United States had enough troops and equipment ready to deploy.

In the meantime, intense fighting continued on the Eastern Front. Throughout most of 1942 the Germans maintained the initiative. On May 8 they began an offensive in the Crimea, which they completely subdued by July 5. This operation was part of a massive summer offensive, a southern campaign against the Volga region and the Caucasus, areas rich in farmland and oil respectively, which Hitler had long coveted. Operation Blue involved a two-pronged attack: Army Group A would advance toward Stalingrad, while Army Group B drove into the Caucasus. As in 1941, the German offensive got off to a good start, once again catching the Red Army by surprise and driving deep into Russia. On May 22 the Germans encircled yet another Soviet Army, and by the end of June they had taken 239,000 prisoners and destroyed 1,240 tanks.[40] As they advanced further east, however, the situation changed. The Red Army continued to retreat, but the Panzers no longer achieved any great encirclements. The Soviets had reverted to the traditional Russian strategy of trading space for time.

The southern wing of the offensive advanced to the foothills of the Caucasus, where it ground to a halt at the end of long supply lines and in difficult terrain, but the real disaster came at Stalingrad, the juncture of the Don and Volga Rivers. The city had little strategic value in and of itself, but Hitler became obsessed with taking it, probably because it bore the name of his nemesis. Once they entered it, the Germans found their advantage in mechanized warfare neutralized. Although they took most of the city, they failed to dislodge the Soviet defenders, who clung tenaciously to the districts along the Volga. With winter approaching, casualties mounting, and supplies tenuous, the German commander in Stalingrad, General Friedrich

Paulus, requested permission to retreat. Hitler refused. The Soviets meanwhile had been preparing a counterattack against the exposed corridor into the city. On November 19 Zhukov launched his attack against weak Italian and Romanian divisions on the German flanks, and on November 23 the northern and southern pincers closed at Kalach west of Stalingrad. Assured by Air Marshal Hermann Goering that the Luftwaffe could supply the city, Hitler refused to let Paulus break out, even when von Manstein shortened the escape route with a counterattack in December. On February 2, 1943, Paulus (belatedly promoted to field marshal in hopes that this honor would prevent his giving up) surrendered what remained of the beleaguered garrison. He had lost 147,000 killed and another 91,000 taken prisoner, only 10,000 of whom would ever return home.[41]

After encircling Stalingrad and beating back von Manstein's break-in effort, the Red Army continued to counterattack westward. Only a skillful fighting withdrawal kept the Soviets from encircling the retreating Germans. They lost Kharkov on February 15, but managed to stabilize their line and prepare for a counterattack of their own. Von Manstein launched his offensive on Feburary 19 and recaptured Kharkov on March 15. Soon afterward the spring thaw turned the steppes into a quagmire and provided both armies a much-needed respite. Operation Blue had been a disaster. Whether or not Stalingrad was the decisive battle some have claimed, it certainly punctured the myth of blitzkrieg.

While Hitler's micromanagement of the campaign contributed to the defeat, Soviet victory owed much to a complete overhaul of the Red Army. To begin with, Stalin turned the war into a patriotic struggle to defend the fatherland, a task made much easier by Nazi brutality in occupied areas. The Orthodox Church temporarily came back into favor. In July 1942 the government created three new military honors named for the heroes of past wars: the Order of Alexander Nevsky, who had fought the Teutonic Knights in the 13th century, and the Orders of Suvorov and Kutuzov, who had battled Napoleon. The Kremlin reduced the power of the political commissars in the army, thus allowing officers the much-needed freedom to take the initiative without worrying about the political correctness of their decisions. Marshals Zhukov and Semyon Timoshenko finally convinced Stalin to relax his "not-one-step backward" order, thus making possible the tactical withdrawals that led to the strategic victory at Stalingrad. While Hitler increasingly made poor strategic and even operational decisions, Stalin increasingly allowed his generals to fight the war, although he would later claim credit for their victories.[42] The most important change, however, may have been the Soviet embrace of mechanized warfare. In the spring of 1942 the Soviet high command reorganized its forces into "tank armies." Each consisted of two tank corps, a mobile infantry division, and support elements. A tank corps had 168 tanks plus antitank battalions, Katyusha rocket batteries, and its own anti-aircraft guns. Each tank army was roughly equivalent to a German Panzer division. This reorganization allowed the Red Army to match German mobility and striking power.[43]

Defeat at Stalingrad did not spell defeat for the Wehrmacht, at least not in the short run. The general staff planned another major offensive for the summer of 1943. They targeted the Kursk salient, a bulge in the Russian lines, approximately 150 miles wide and 100 miles deep, between Orel in the north and Belograd in the south. Operation Citadel would be a pincer movement to pinch off the salient and trap the Soviet forces inside it. The Germans massed 435,000 troops, 9,960 artillery pieces and mortars, and 3,155 tanks, including the new Panther medium tank and the massive Tiger heavy tank.[44] This time, however, the Soviets were ready. Having learned of the impending attack, they fortified the Kursk salient and deployed one million men with 13,013 pieces of artillery and mortars, as well as 3,275 tanks with additional reserves behind the front.[45] The Red Army blunted the German pincers and then counterattacked.

Operation Citadel was the last major German offensive in the east. From that point on the Soviets marched inexorably west. They liberated Kiev on November 6, 1943, and entered Poland in January 1944. That same month they lifted the siege of Leningrad. Over the next year the Red Army delivered a series of hammer blows up and down the entire front. The Germans could do little more than delay the inevitable. The Red Army swept through central Europe toward Budapest and moved into the Balkans; by the middle of April 1945 Zhukov stood poised to take Berlin.

Air and Naval Campaigns against Germany

As the Germans were locked in a life and death struggle with the Soviets, more and more American troops and equipment poured into Europe. Not until the invasion of Italy in September 1943 did they gain a foothold on the Continent, but their impact on the war occurred long before that in two distinct arenas. Upon its entry into the war the U.S. Navy immediately committed more ships and airplanes to the battle of the Atlantic, and American planes added to the growing armada of bombers flying from Britain and North Africa to strike Germany and its allies.

Britain had of course been dealing with the U-boat threat since September 1939. While American entry into the war helped turn the tide of battle in the Atlantic in the long run, loss of merchantmen to U-boats actually increased during 1942. After Pearl Harbor, Admiral Karl Dönitz deployed his Wolf Packs (groups of U-boats working together) along the Atlantic Coast of the United States, where they did considerable damage until the United States organized convoys for coastal shipping. Submarine attacks were also highly effective in a region known as the "air gap," an area in the middle of the North Atlantic out of range of land-based planes from North America or Britain. A concerted, coordinated effort by the U.S. and British navies along with new equipment turned the tide of the battle. Sonar (British ASDIC), which could locate submarines using sound waves; improved depth charge launchers; long-range patrol bombers; and small aircraft carriers with antisubmarine planes gave the convoys a decisive advantage over the U-boats. Along with these improvements, a dramatic increase in the number of escort vessels and the ability of American shipyards to replace losses and even increase the number of merchant ships plying the Atlantic allowed the United States to supply Britain and send troops and equipment to Europe. By May 1943 the Allies were sinking U-boats faster than the Germans could replace them, and Dönitz had to withdraw his submarines to European coastal waters, later admitting that he had lost the battle of the Atlantic.[46]

All historians acknowledge the vital importance of winning the convoy war, but the efficacy of strategic bombing remains a controversial subject. American entry into the war increased the air campaign against Germany, but strategic bombing had been part of military operations from the beginning of the war. The Luftwaffe had bombed Warsaw to force Poland to surrender in 1939 and did the same to Rotterdam in 1940. Given these successes, its decision to launch an air campaign against Britain came as no surprise. After concentrating on shipping in the English Channel, followed by attacks on airfields to defeat the RAF, Hitler decided to bomb London. From mid-August to mid-September 1940 waves of German bombers rained death and destruction on the city, laying waste to vast areas of the East End and killing approximately 40,000 Londoners but failing to break British morale. German aircraft losses forced Hitler to end the air campaign and shelve his plan for the invasion of Britain.

The British meanwhile launched their own bombing campaign against Germany. The RAF began attacking industrial targets in Germany in May 1941 and would continue to do so until the summer. When a study revealed that only 20 percent of bomber crews got within five miles of their targets, RAF Bomber Command switched from "precision" to "area" bombing, a euphemism for deliberate targeting of civilians.[47] Heavy bombers capable of flying at higher altitudes and improved navigation equipment allowed the RAF to do extensive damage to German cities, most notably Cologne (May 1942), Hamburg (July 1943), and Dresden, a joint

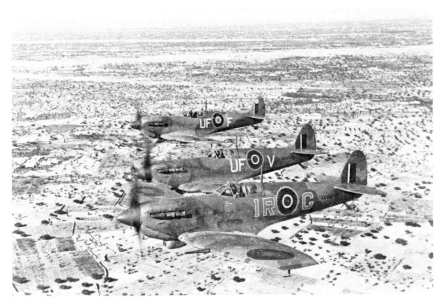

The RAF Spitfire helped win the Battle of Britain. *Source:* Library of Congress.

operation with the U.S. Army Air Force (USAAF) (February 1945). The British also switched from daylight operations to night raids, which made German air defense more difficult.

The United States shared Britain's commitment to strategic bombing, but disagreed on the approach. Beginning with the June 1942 raid on the oil fields at Ploesti, Romania, the USAAF continued with daylight bombing of industrial targets, concentrating on vital elements of the German war machine: oil, aircraft manufacturing, and ball bearing plants. The Norden bombsight gave American planes a greater degree of accuracy than their British counterparts, but "precision bombing" hardly existed in World War II. American B17s and B24s dropped their payloads from well above 20,000 feet. Clouds obscured targets while flak (an acronym formed from *Flugabwehrkanonen*, "anti-aircraft gun") further impeded accuracy. Only a fraction of bombs dropped hit their targets, although that was often enough to do considerable damage.

After the war the U.S. military conducted an extensive survey of strategic bombing. It determined that the Allies dropped 2,700,000 tons of bombs in 1,440,000 sorties, primarily against targets within Germany but also against German assets in occupied and other Axis countries. According to the survey, Allied bombs killed 300,000 German civilians, wounded

A B-17F (Flying Fortress) led the American strategic bombing campaign in Europe. *Source:* Library of Congress.

780,000, and left 7.5 million homeless because of the destruction of 3.6 million "dwelling units."[48] Other estimates put the German death toll at 600,000 and added 58,000 Frenchmen (most of whom died in bombing associated with the Normandy invasion) to the butcher bill.[49] With the British bombing at night and the Americans during the day, the Germans never got a respite from attacks. The results of strategic bombing, though, came at a high price: 79,265 American and 79,281 British airmen lost their lives in the air war, and the two countries lost a total of 40,000 planes.[50]

Strategic bombing was clearly lethal, destructive, and costly in Allied blood and treasure, but was it effective? That question has been the subject of intense debate since 1945 and may never be answered to everyone's satisfaction. Contrary to Douhet's prediction, bombing of their cities did not break the will of civilians, nor did more focused attacks degrade industry sufficiently to bring the German war effort to a halt. On the contrary, German productivity in July 1944 was 3.2 times greater than it had been in January/February 1942.[51] Even the U.S. assessment concluded that strategic bombing "had little effect on German production before July 1944."[52] However, the Allies dropped 72 percent of all their bombs after July 1944.[53] Increased bombing with greater efficacy resulted in large measure from the deployment of long-range fighters, particularly the P51 Mustang, capable of escorting bombers deep into Germany. By the time strategic bombing was having a demonstrable effect on production, though, Germany was already losing the war. By mid-1944 it was no longer a question of *if* but *when* Germany would surrender. On the other hand, a case can be made that without strategic bombing, German war production would have increased even more than it did and the war would have lasted longer. This assertion is impossible to prove or disprove. Despite declining production, the Wehrmacht never ran out of equipment, but it did run out of fuel, indicating that the American focus on oil production was correct.[54] Even so, the direct effect of strategic bombing was probably to hasten the end of the war rather than to determine its outcome.

The indirect effects of strategic bombing, however, may have been even more important, though they are harder to measure. Both area and precision bombing forced Germany to divert valuable resources from its fighting fronts to defend the homeland. By 1944 Germany had deployed more than 10,000 anti-aircraft guns manned by half a million men and women.[55] In 1940 Germany devoted only 17 percent of its aircraft production to fighters; by late 1944 that figure had risen to 42 percent.[56] In 1941 the Luftwaffe deployed 65 percent of its aircraft on the Eastern Front; by 1944, it could only afford to deploy 32 percent.[57] Hitler's desire to retaliate for the devastating bombing raids may explain his emphasis on the costly but largely ineffective V-1 and V-2 rocket programs, another diversion of resources that would have been better employed elsewhere.[58]

The morality of strategic bombing has generated even more debate than its effectiveness. Subsequent conflicts, especially the Vietnam War, have influenced this debate. Any discussion of the ethics of the air campaign during World War II must consider the context in which it took place. RAF Bomber Command and the USAAF had no way of ascertaining the effectiveness of strategic bombing. They certainly knew they were killing civilians, but they had no reliable data on the degree to which precision or area bombing was degrading Germany's ability to wage war. Intense disagreements over the meaning of data collected after the war suggest that those making decisions during the conflict did so in a very ambiguous environment.

From D-day to Victory in Europe

By the beginning of 1944 the United States and Britain finally had the troops and equipment necessary to consider invading France. Stalin had been pushing the Allies to open a second front in Western Europe from at least 1942 and blamed the delay on Allied foot dragging. It seemed to him and many in the Kremlin that the United States and Britain were perfectly willing to allow the Red Army to bear the brunt of the fighting so that the Soviet Union would be less of a threat in the postwar world. In truth, the Allies probably could not have mounted a massive invasion of Europe any earlier than they did. Previous attempts at even limited amphibious assaults had enjoyed only mixed success. Allied forces had successfully landed in North Africa, Sicily, and southern Italy, but the British landings at Trondheim, Norway (1940) had failed, and the landing at Dieppe, France (1942) had been a disaster. More recently the landing at Anzio, Italy, in January 1944 had been fraught with problems. The troops established a beachhead in February but could not break out until May. To make matters more difficult, British Prime Minister Winston Churchill opposed a landing in France, arguing that the Allies should attack through the Balkans, what he called the "soft underbelly of Europe." The difficulty Allied forces were having advancing up the mountainous Italian peninsula, however, dissuaded American commanders from that approach.

Operation Overlord, the amphibious invasion of France, would require an unprecedented effort. The Germans knew an invasion was coming and had ample time to prepare. They covered the coasts of northern France with landing obstacles, mines, barbed wire, gun emplacements, and tank traps. They did not, however, have enough troops to defend every landing area, so they needed to determine where the invaders would come ashore. To confuse them, the Allies mounted one of the most brilliant strategic deception campaigns in military history: they created a dummy army complete with inflatable mock-ups of tanks and trucks across from the Pas de Calais region of France to convince the Germans that the landings would occur there. The ruse worked well enough to cause the diversion of German forces to that region and away from the real landing site on the Normandy coast.

The Allies also devoted considerable energy to developing technological solutions to the problems posed by such a massive amphibious landing. They designed flotation skirts and duel drives for tanks so that they could "swim" ashore" and flail tanks to clear mine fields. Specially designed landing crafts fitted with rocket launchers would blast holes in beach fortifications. The Allies even constructed artificial harbors whose components could be floated across the channel and assembled at the beachheads. They built a floating pipeline to carry fuel from depots in England to the landing points in France. Not all of these inventions worked as well as hoped, but in the aggregate they facilitated the operation.[59]

A successful amphibious landing required air superiority over the beachhead and the area behind it, which in turn required the destruction of as much of the Luftwaffe as possible well before the invasion. Beginning in

February 1944, the goal of strategic bombing expanded from destruction of German industry (which the allies still wanted) to forcing the German air force to fight on terms favorable to the Allies. New long-range escort fighters, the American P51 Mustang and P47 Thunderbolt, not only defended the bombers but went on the offensive against the Me109s.[60] Allied air forces also concentrated on destroying airfields in western France, forcing the Germans to withdraw their aircraft to bases in Belgium, eastern France, and western Germany, farther away from the landing areas.[61] Air raids also targeted radar installations, so that by D-day only 18 percent of German radar installations in France were still operational.[62]

As D-day approached, the Allies shifted their air assets away from Germany itself to conduct a highly successful interdiction campaign in France. Despite its commitment to mechanization, the German army remained throughout the war heavily dependent on railroads to move supplies to a theater and upon horses to distribute them to forces in the field. Logistics tied the Wehrmacht to railheads, which reduced its mobility and made it vulnerable to interdiction.[63] In the weeks before D-day, Allied air forces systematically bombed rail lines, rolling stock, bridges, and military infrastructure in western France. To support the deception campaign they targeted both the intended landing area and the Pas de Calais region. By June 6 rail traffic in the affected area had declined to 30 percent of its January 1944 total, after which it declined to 10 percent.[64]

Although the Germans knew the invasion was coming, the Allies succeeded in deceiving them about its exact location and timing. The campaign began around midnight on June 6 with landings by paratroopers, supported by gliders a few hours later. These airborne troops moved to secure strategic points behind the beaches to facilitate a breakout and delay German counterattacks. Around 6:30 a.m. the first Allied troops hit the beaches along a 50-mile stretch of the Normandy coast between Cherbourg and Le Havre. The Americans came ashore at Utah and Omaha Beaches in the west, the British and Canadians at Gold, Juno, and Sword Beaches to the east. Only at Omaha did invaders meet substantial sustained resistance. Fortunately, just 18 percent of the Germans' Atlantic Wall, an elaborate system of coastal defenses, had been completed by D-day. The Allies also benefited from a strategic mistake made by Hitler arising out of a dispute between two of his generals. Rommel wanted to contest the landing at the water's edge while Gerd von Runstadt, German Commander in the West, wished to let more troops land so that they could be destroyed. The two quarreled over control of the Panzer reserve, and Hitler resolved the issue by keeping control of it himself. He remained convinced for some time after D-day that a landing might still occur in the Pas de Calais region and so did not release the armored units until it was too late.

Hitler's mistakes, combined with Allied deception, left only two German mechanized units in position to attack the Allied beachhead. Around 10:00 a.m. General Erich Marks ordered his 21st Panzer Division to drive into the gap between Juno and Sword Beaches, telling his spearhead commander, "If you don't succeed in throwing the British into the sea, we shall have lost the war."[65] After a day of hard fighting, a few of his tanks reached the coast by nightfall, but unsupported they had no choice but to withdraw. Arguably, the Germans had already lost the war, but Marks may have been right about the coming battle for France. Once the Allies had a secure lodgment on the French coast, an inexorable calculus came into effect. With virtually complete air and naval supremacy and the destruction of the French rail system, the Allies could move troops and equipment across the English Channel more rapidly than the Germans could move them across France.[66] By the end of D-day, the Allies had landed 155,000 troops by air and sea; more than half a million would deploy within the first two weeks of the invasion, and by early July one million men and 190,000 vehicles had landed in France.[67]

Much hard fighting lay ahead. Caen did not fall to the British until July 9, and they did not reduce the Falaise Pocket until August 20. From July 3 to July 25, the Americans faced tough fighting in the *bocage* (hedgerow) country of Normandy, but once they broke out west of St. Lo, they rapidly advanced, threatening to encircle German forces. The new German commander in the west, Field Marshal Walter Model, managed to extricate his forces, but they had been too badly damaged to form a new defensive line on the Seine. Paris fell to the free French on August 25, while the Germans retreated into the Low Countries and the Reich itself. They could do no more than delay the inevitable. Despite a limited local victory at Arnhem in September and a fierce counterattack in December, the famous "Battle of the Bulge," the Western Allies marched inexorably toward Germany. They crossed the Rhine River at Rhemagen on March 7, and American and Soviet troops met on the Elbe River on April 25.

Meanwhile, in the east the Red Army juggernaut continued its drive westward. In June the Soviets launched Operation Bargration, their major summer offensive. By the end of September they were at the gates of Warsaw, which they took in January 1945. The Red Army captured Bucharest on August 31 and then moved into Hungary, Bulgaria, and Yugoslavia. It continued the advance throughout the winter, clearing the Baltics and driving deep into Germany and Austria. On April 16 Zhukov commenced his assault on Berlin, defended by what remained of the Wehrmacht along

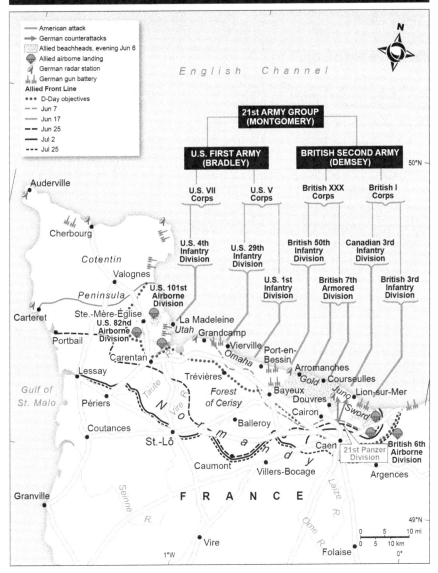

D-day, invasion of Normandy.

with hastily conscripted boys and old men. Hitler committed suicide on April 3, and the city surrendered on May 2. Five days later the Germans surrendered unconditionally to the Allies, and World War II in Europe came to an end.

Who Won the War in Europe?

The history of World War II in Europe quickly became subsumed in the propaganda battle of the Cold War that followed. The Soviets insisted that they had won the war in Europe, engaging in the heaviest fighting, suffering the worst destruction, and taking the most casualties. They would, the argument continues, have won the war even without the Allied invasion of Normandy. The Soviets further insisted that they manufactured the majority of their own equipment and that what U.S. aid they received had come after the tide in the east had turned.

There is considerable but not complete truth to Soviet (and later Russian Federation) claims. The Soviet Union did suffer more than any other Allied or Axis nation. The best estimates put its military deaths at 8.6 million and civilian loss of life at 17 million.[68] The scorched earth policy of both armies caused widespread destruction and a housing shortage that would not be alleviated until the 1960s. If the Soviet Union had suffered the most, it had also done the most to destroy the Wehrmacht. Eighty percent of German battle casualties occurred on the Eastern Front.

The Soviets thus deserve much, perhaps even most, of the credit for defeating Nazi Germany, but they did not win the war single-handed. Had Britain not chosen to fight on alone for an entire year after the fall of France, the outcome of World War II might have been very different. There would have been no convoy war to drag the Americans into the conflict and no bomber bases in England to hammer German industry. The Germans came very close to defeating the Soviets in 1941. Without the losses sustained by the Luftwaffe during the Battle of Britain and the need to concentrate resources on air defense, Barbarossa might well have succeeded. In addition to confronting Germany with a two-front war, the British provided the Soviets valuable intelligence gathered from their code-breaking operation at Bletchley Park, including warning about the German buildup for the battle of Kursk.

Leaving aside this counterfactual argument, the contribution of Western aid to the Red Army was far more important than the Soviet argument acknowledges. While the Soviets did manufacture 96 percent of their own arms, the most important aid did not come in the form of weapons and ammunition.[69] The Western allies, particularly the United States, supplied the Soviet Union with trucks, boots, radio sets, locomotives, freight cars, rails, food, and a host of other important supplies. In a bugged 1963 conversation released in the 1990s, Zhukov admitted that without foreign aid the Soviet Union "could not have continued the war."[70] The trucks may have been the most important lend-lease item. By 1945 the Soviet Union had 665,000 motor vehicles, almost two-thirds of which (427,000) were manufactured abroad, most in the United States.[71] "Just imagine," Nikita Khrushchėv later reflected on the war, "how we would have advanced from Stalingrad to Berlin without [American transport]."[72]

In addition to what they contributed to the war effort, the Western Allies helped shape the postwar world. By June 6, 1944, the Soviets were advancing rapidly toward Berlin and probably would have defeated the Germans even without the Normandy landings. The invasion of France hastened but did not cause the defeat of Germany, although probably no one on the Allied side was certain of victory at the time. It did, however, serve a far more important purpose: it guaranteed that Western Europe would remain free as Eastern Europe fell under the Soviet yoke for almost 45 years.

Unconventional Operations

Like all wars in the modern era, World War II involved both conventional and unconventional operations. Resistance movements sprang up in almost every country occupied by the Germans. Throughout the war these irregulars engaged in a broad range of activities, including sabotage, assassination of German officers, and intelligence gathering for the Allies. Following the war, national mythologies exaggerated the activities of resistance groups, perhaps to divert unwanted attention from those who collaborated with the enemy.

In truth, resistance groups varied widely in capabilities and effectiveness. Their strength waxed and waned with circumstances. Asked about the number of fighters in his underground group, one commander in Milan, Italy, cynically responded, "600 if things are difficult, 6,000 if things are less difficult, and 60,000 if things are easy."[73] As the Allied armies advanced, things became easier. Much of the sabotage carried out by the French Resistance took place around the time of the D-day landings.

Brutal occupation policies discouraged resistance. For each of their soldiers killed by the French underground, the Germans shot 100 hostages. As a result, the *Maquis*, as the French resistance called itself, resorted to targeting collaborators, whose deaths invoked no such harsh penalties. In other occupied countries the reprisals could be even more brutal. When Czech partisans assassinated SS-Obergruppenführer Reinhard Heydrich in

Prague in 1942, the Germans responded by leveling the village of Lidice and murdering its inhabitants. Even the most dedicated resistance fighters found it difficult to operate under threat of such reprisals.

In the East European theater the largest and most famous resistance movements developed in Yugoslavia and the Soviet Union. In ethnically divided Yugoslavia, two resistance movements diametrically opposed to one another formed during the German occupation. The Chetniks under General Dragoljub Mikhailović consisted primarily of former members of the regular army, most of them Serbians. Josef Broz Tito formed an alternative, ethnically diverse Communist resistance movement known as Partisans. The two did carry out some limited operations against the occupation forces, but they never cooperated fully and indeed spent much of their time fighting each other. This internecine conflict diminished their effectiveness. The Partisans performed somewhat better than the Chetniks, who at times collaborated with Axis forces to fight their rivals. Based on the performance of the two groups rather than their ideologies, the British abandoned Mikhailović and supported Tito. The Yugoslav resistance never seriously threatened the occupation forces nor significantly hampered Axis operations in Eastern Europe.[74]

Resistance groups in the Soviet Union were larger, better armed, and more effective than their counterparts elsewhere. Comprised of troops trapped behind German lines during the invasion of 1941 (augmented by volunteers and conscripts), partisan units operated in the marshes and forest of the western Soviet Union. They began with a collective strength of 30,000 during the summer of 1942, which grew to 150,000–175,000 by the summer of 1944.[75] During the course of the war, Red partisans may have killed as many as 50,000 Axis troops, but this tally came at a terrible price, as the Germans killed perhaps 500,000 Soviets in antipartisan sweeps and reprisals.[76] The Germans wove antipartisan operations into their campaign of genocide, killing thousands of innocent civilians because of their ethnicity or religion.[77]

Until late in the war, partisan operations never amounted to more than a nuisance for the Axis powers. Contrary to the myths created after the war, resistance movements did not tie down large numbers of German troops who might otherwise have been available for conventional operations. Of 300 German divisions deployed in early June 1944, fewer than 20 were assigned to internal security duties.[78] Many of those conducting antipartisan and internal security operations were older men less fit for frontline duty, so detaching them from combat forces had even less of an impact on conventional operations than their numbers might suggest.[79]

CHAPTER ELEVEN

World War II in Asia

If Germany had little chance of success in a war against the United States and its allies, Japan had virtually none. No one understood this better than the man responsible for planning the attack on Pearl Harbor. "In the first six to twelve months of a war with the United States and Great Britain," he told a Japanese cabinet member in 1940, "I will run wild and win victory after victory. But then, if the war continues after that, I have no expectation of success."[1] Admiral Isoroku Yamamoto had lived in the United States and understood its tremendous military potential. Given that his prediction would prove profoundly accurate, why did Japan attack the United States?

Like all such plans the decision to go to war in 1941 grew out of perceived strategic necessity and assumptions about the nature of the enemy. An island nation of 60 million people, Japan lacked sufficient land to feed its population and the natural resources necessary to sustain its heavy industry, particularly iron ore, oil, and rubber. Under normal circumstances it could import these resources, but Japan had imperial ambitions in East Asia, which brought it into conflict with the United States and the European colonial powers. These nations could impose a crippling embargo on Japan. The answer to this dilemma lay in gaining control of strategic resources through conquest. The tentativeness of the Western response to its initial imperial moves may have emboldened Japan. When it conquered Manchuria in 1931 and invaded China in 1937, the United States and the European colonial powers criticized Japan but took no definitive action against it.

Much as it desired to gain control of Indochina, Malaya, and Indonesia, Japan lacked the military power to challenge the United States and the Europeans. That situation changed dramatically with the outbreak of World War II in Europe. The German conquest of France and the Netherlands and Britain's need to defend its homeland created a power vacuum in East and Southeast Asia that Japan could exploit. The 1941 German invasion of the Soviet Union left that country's Asian possessions vulnerable to Japanese conquest. During the summer of 1941 the Japanese cabinet considered a northern strategy of attacking the Soviet Union, but rejected that option as too risky until it became clear that Germany would win.[2] In July 1941 Japan occupied Indochina with Vichy French acquiescence, a move that gave it bases capable of striking at the Burma Road supply route to China and oil-rich Indonesia. In response, the United States imposed an oil embargo on Japan. The Japanese military had to either back down or attack the United States. Japanese Prime Minister General Hideki Tojo summed up Japan's predicament:

> Two years from now we will have no petroleum for military use. Ships will stop moving. When I think about the strengthening of American defenses in the south-west Pacific, the expansion of the American fleet, the unfinished China Incident, and soon, I see no end to difficulties.[3]

The decision to bomb the U.S. Pacific fleet at Pearl Harbor, Hawaii, was a bold gamble but not an irrational one. The Japanese knew they could not win a war of attrition against the United States, but they believed they would not have to do so. A devastating blow against the American navy, followed by rapid conquest of territory within a string of barrier archipelagos protecting Japan, Tokyo reasoned, would present the United States with a fait accompli that it would deem not worth the cost in blood and treasure to reverse. If this calculation proved correct, Yamamoto's promised six months would be enough to create the "East Asia Co-prosperity Sphere." The Japanese failed to anticipate the degree to which a sneak attack prior to a formal declaration of war would enrage the American public and end its isolationist lethargy.

The attack on Pearl Harbor on December 7, 1941, has been appropriately described as a brilliant operational and tactical success but a strategic failure. Despite the U.S. Navy having broken the Japanese code, the Japanese achieved complete surprise. At 7:55 a.m. aircraft from four carriers more than 200 miles north of Oahu swooped down on an undefended harbor, dropping armor-piercing bombs and torpedoes modified for the harbor's shallow water. In less than an hour, they put all eight U.S.

battleships out of action, destroyed 188 planes on the ground, and killed 2,403 Americans. Fortunately the two U.S. carriers stationed at Pearl Harbor were at sea, and the Japanese failed to bomb the dry docks, fuel tanks, or other harbor facilities. The sunken battleships were obsolete World War I designs, and six of them were repaired and put back in service. As Yamamoto had predicted, the Japanese did "run wild" for the six months after Pearl Harbor, capturing all the territory within the designated "Co-prosperity Sphere" and threatening New Guinea and Australia, which had sent most of their land forces to support the British in the Middle East. They also occupied a string of islands running from the western Aleutians through Wake Island to the Solomon archipelago in the south, as well as all the islands within that perimeter. Their only disappointment was the failure to catch the American aircraft carriers at Pearl Harbor. The importance of this failure became clear in May 1942, when a task force consisting of the carriers *Yorktown* and *Lexington* confronted a Japanese invasion force headed for Port Moresby in southern New Guinea. In the ensuing Battle of the Coral Sea, the Japanese won a tactical victory, sinking the *Lexington* and damaging the *Yorktown* for the loss of a light carrier and damage to a heavy one, but suffered strategic defeat because the invasion fleet had to turn back.

Yamamoto determined to finish the destruction of the U.S. Pacific fleet by sinking its three remaining aircraft carriers. He developed an elaborate plan to launch a diversionary attack against the Aleutians and his main thrust against Midway, the westernmost of the Hawaiian Islands, to draw the Americans into a trap. Because they had broken the Japanese naval code, the Americans learned of the plan and deployed the *Yorktown*, *Hornet*, and *Enterprise* to counter it. On the morning of June 4, 1942, American dive bombers caught three of the four Japanese carriers at their most vulnerable as they were refueling planes, loading bombs, and landing aircraft. In a matter of minutes they left all so badly damaged that they had to be abandoned and scuttled. Later that afternoon, U.S. planes found and sunk the fourth carrier.

It would be difficult to exaggerate the importance of the battle of Midway. For the loss of one carrier (*Yorktown*, damaged by bombs and later sunk by a submarine) and a destroyer, the U.S. Navy sank four Japanese carriers. The Imperial Navy lost 228 aircraft and 3,057 sailors and airmen, while the Americans lost 145 planes and 340 men.[4] The victory removed any perceived threat to the West Coast of the United States, thus making it easier for the American public to accept the "Germany first" strategy. At a single stroke, Japan lost its decisive advantage in aircraft carriers, which it would never recover. From 1942 to 1944 Japan added 6 new fleet carriers to its navy, while the United States added 14 to its navy.[5] The victory also allowed the United States to go on the offensive in the Pacific Theater.

Land War in Asia

The Japanese strategy required compelling the United States to withdraw its forces from East Asia and accept Japanese hegemony in the region. With France and the Netherlands already defeated and occupied and Britain engaged in a life and death struggle with Germany, their colonies in Asia would be ripe for conquest. By themselves Australia and New Zealand could not oppose Japanese expansion. The weakness in this strategy lay in the assumption that a single decisive defeat or even a series of defeats would force the Americans to sue for peace. Should that assumption prove incorrect, Japan could find itself overextended, defending a vast empire against indigenous resistance and Allied attacks on multiple fronts. Following initial success, this overextension is precisely what happened. Long before the U.S. Army and Marines began their campaign in the Pacific, the Japanese Imperial Army got bogged down in a major campaign on the Asian mainland.

Since 1937 Japanese forces had been at war with China, expanding out of their base in the puppet state of Manchukuo on China's northern border. They had little trouble defeating poorly equipped, badly led, and internally divided Chinese forces, which performed poorly against the invaders. By the end of 1938 the Japanese had overrun most of north China and captured the country's ports and major cities, including Beijing, Shanghai, and Nanking. Despite these stunning victories, the Chinese refused to surrender, and Japanese forces made little headway into the south and west of the country. The Nationalists under Chiang Kai-shek moved their capital to Chongqing, while the Communists operated out of Yan'an. The two groups formed a United Front against the Japanese, although they did not always cooperate effectively. They operated largely in parallel, using limited conventional operations and guerrilla warfare. Neither won major battles, but they both fought an effective defensive campaign.

What stymied the Japanese in China was not, however, the Nationalist and Communist armies, but the size and population of the country. China covered 3.7 million square miles, nearly one and a half times the size of the continental United States, and had a population of 400 million people.[6] While the Japanese easily overran the plains and river valleys of the northeast, they had difficulty penetrating the mountainous interior of the country, with its few roads and railroads. The Chinese could not expel the Japanese, but neither could they be destroyed by them. The stalemate did have one overwhelmingly negative effect on the invaders: it tied down a large number of troops. The China campaign occupied half of the Imperial Japanese Army. In 1941 the Japanese managed to severely weaken Nationalist and Communist forces by moving to cut off their sources of supply. After France fell to Germany, the Japanese occupied French Indochina and cut the vital rail line from Haiphong to Chongqing. They also pressured the British to close the supply route from Burma to China. Unwilling to risk a two-front war, London shut down the famous Burma Road in July 1941.[7] At the same, the German invasion of the Soviet Union threatened Soviet supplies to the Communists. Fortunately for the Chinese, the Japanese occupation of Indochina prompted the U.S. oil embargo, which led the Japanese to attack Pearl Harbor. Once the United States had entered the Pacific War, it began flying supplies to China from India.

While American entry into the war boded well for an Allied victory in the long run, the short-term picture in Asia looked bleak. Within three months the Japanese had captured Hong Kong, overrun most of the Philippines, and occupied the Dutch East Indies. They launched an amphibious assault on Malaya and drove the British down the peninsula into Singapore, which surrendered on February 15. The Japanese invaded Thailand and secured base rights from its compliant government. They then advanced into Burma, crossed the Sittang River, and moved toward Rangoon, which the British evacuated on March 7. Over the next two months Anglo-Indian forces conducted a fighting withdrawal northward. Even with two Nationalist Chinese divisions Chiang sent to Burma, the British could not stem the Japanese tide. Mandalay fell on May 1, and what remained of British forces in Burma limped into Imphal, India, on May 20. The Nationalist troops returned to China.

Burma was but the latest in a long string of humiliating defeats. The advance to the borders of British India, however, represented the highwater mark of imperial Japan. Its forces conducted a final offensive against Imphal in March 1944, but the hard-pressed British and Indians held them off until the attack lost its momentum. The Allies then went on the offensive. General William Slim's Anglo-Indian forces advanced from the west, while Chinese troops commanded by American General Joseph ("Vinegar Joe") Stillwell attacked from the northeast. By the end of January 1945 the Allies had reopened the Burma Road. Fighting continued until the end of the war, but by 1944 Burma had become a sideshow. The American advance through the South and Central Pacific, which brought heavy bombers in striking range of Japan, offered a quicker road to victory.[8]

Island Hopping

The naval victory at Midway allowed the United States to go on the offensive in the Pacific. That advance took place along two axes. The army under General Douglas MacArthur advanced northward through the South Pacific to the Philippines, while the Marines under Admiral Chester Nimitz moved northeast through the Central Pacific. The two commanders first had to cooperate to remove the threat to Australia posed by the Japanese in New Guinea. They accomplished this task by January 1943 and spent the rest of the year securing the Solomon Islands, where the Marines had landed on Guadalcanal in August 1942. In November the Central Pacific drive began in earnest when the Marines invaded Tarawa in the Gilbert Islands. Nimitz then advanced in succession from Kwajalein in the Marshalls (February 1944), to Saipan in the Marianas (June 1944), to Iwo Jima (February 1945) and Okinawa (April 1945). Supported by the Marines, who took Peleliu (September 1944), Macarthur returned to the Philippines in October 1944.

This "island-hopping strategy" bypassed many Japanese garrisons while securing islands large enough for airfields that could accommodate bombers. Saipan gave the U.S. Army Air Force (USAAF) its first base from which the new B29 Super Fortress could attack the Japanese home islands. The B29 had a maximum range of 5,800 miles, a ceiling of 31,850 feet, and a payload of 20,000 pounds.[9] At maximum range, the plane had to carry 9,000 gallons of fuel, which significantly reduced the weight of bombs in its payload.[10] Each step closer to Japan thus increased the ratio of bombs to fuel. Under the command of General Curtis "Bombs-Away" Lemay, the USAAF adopted low-level flying tactics to drop incendiaries on Japanese cities built largely of wood. Because the Japanese did not construct factories in concentrated industrial zones as did the Americans and Europeans, industrial sites could not be destroyed without a massive loss of civilian life.[11]

Conventional strategic bombing of Japan did not, however, win the Pacific war any more than it had won the European one. Limited strategic bombing began in June 1944, with raids by planes launched from bases in China. However, even the U.S. Strategic Bombing Survey conducted after the war admitted that raids only started to become effective in March 1945, when B29s launched from the Marianas adopted low-altitude bombing.[12] The USAAF dropped 160,800 tons of explosives and incendiaries on Japan, far less than the 1.36 million tons dropped on Europe.[13] The bombing destroyed vast areas of Japanese cities and by July 1945 had caused industrial output in some sectors to decline as much as 45 percent from its 1944 high.[14] The raids killed 240,000 to 300,000 civilians, depending

World War II in Asia

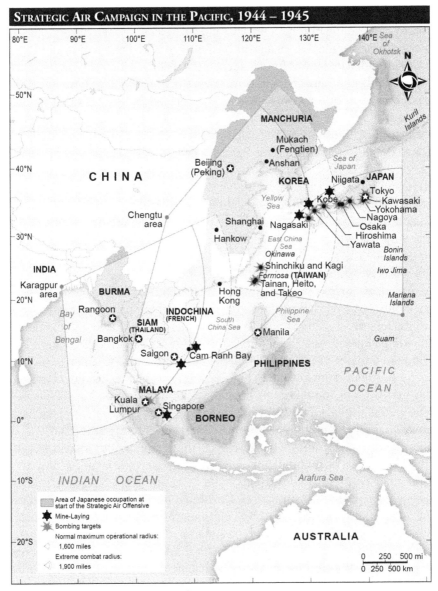

Strategic air campaign in the Pacific.

on whether one accepts the lower Japanese or the higher American estimates.[15] Whether continued conventional strategic bombing would have shortened the war became a moot point after the United States dropped the atomic bombs in August 1945.

The decision to bomb Hiroshima and Nagasaki remains one of the most controversial in the history of warfare, indeed in all of human history. Critics of the decision argue that Japan was on the verge of collapse and would soon have surrendered anyway. Its defenders insist that the action saved hundreds of thousands of American and Japanese lives that would have been lost during an invasion of the home islands. The debate has been clouded by the ideological struggle of the Cold War, the trauma of the Vietnam War, and the benefit of hindsight. More Japanese died in the conventional bombing of Tokyo (89,000) than the atomic bombs killed in either Hiroshima (78,000) or Nagasaki (25,000).[16] Those who wish to add subsequent deaths from radiation and cancer to the total of atomic carnage should bear in mind that no one in 1945 understood the effects of radioactive fallout.

Like all historical events, the decision to drop the atomic bombs must be evaluated within the context of the times in which it was taken. In August 1945 the outcome of the war was no longer in doubt. The only questions were how soon and at what cost the Allies would defeat Japan. As American forces approached the home islands, their Japanese defenders increasingly refused to surrender even after they had lost a battle. The willingness of so many troops to fight to the death, attacks by kamikaze suicide planes on American ships, and the mass suicides of civilians on Okinawa convinced military planners that an invasion of Japan would be costly. Casualty estimates ran as high as 500,000 U.S. troops, not counting the hundreds of thousands of Japanese military personnel and civilians who would also be killed and wounded.[17] Concern for Japanese casualties, however, probably did not factor into American thinking at the time.

Some of the scientists who developed the atomic bomb argued that it should be tested on an uninhabited island to frighten the Japanese into surrendering. With only two weapons built, however, that would have been a risky choice. Even the bombing of Hiroshima on August 4 did not induce the Japanese military to capitulate. Only after the bombing of Nagasaki four days later, and at the insistence of the emperor, did the high command agree to unconditional surrender. Even then, hard-line officers attempted a coup to prevent capitulation. From a strictly military point of view, it is thus difficult to condemn the decision to drop the bombs. It is also difficult to see why two atomic bombs were any more or less immoral than thousands of conventional ones, which in aggregate were more lethal and destructive.

Unconventional Operations

Although conventional operations dominated World War II in the Pacific, unconventional warfare also occurred. Some of the British forces in Malaya and the Americans in the Philippines went into the jungle rather than surrender to the Japanese. These groups never amounted to more than a nuisance to the Japanese, and not a very big one at that. Cut off from supplies and often even outside information, they spent most of their time struggling to survive in the harsh conditions. Two groups, though, deserve special attention because they supported major conventional operations and were thus at least somewhat more effective: the British Chindits and the American "Merrill's Marauders." These elite units conducted deep penetration operations behind the Japanese lines in Burma.

The Chindits were the brainchild of a very eccentric British officer named Orde Wingate. Wingate had served in Palestine, where he developed special small-unit "night squads" to pursue insurgents during the Arab Revolt of 1936–1939. In 1940–1941 he commanded another special unit known as the Gideon Group. He had also worked with long-range desert groups in Libya. In each case, Windgate employed the same strategy: strike deep behind enemy lines to disrupt supply and communications in order to compromise the effectiveness of forward units. His commander in the Middle East had been General (later Field Marshal) Archibald Wavell, who became commander in chief of British forces in India and as such responsible for Burma at the outbreak of World War II. Windgate arrived in India in May 1942 and set to work creating another special unit, dubbed the "Chindits" from the Burmese word for "lion."

Wavell appointed Wingate to command a mixed brigade (approximately 2,500 men) of British, Gurkha, and Burmese troops, which he trained in jungle warfare tactics. In February 1943 Wingate divided his brigade into six columns and crossed into central Burma, evading large Japanese units along the Indian frontier. The Chindits sought to cut the major north-south rail line from Rangoon and so disrupt supplies to Japanese forces threatening India. Although they successfully infiltrated Japanese lines, conducted some successful ambushes, and cut the line, the high command considered the Chindit expedition a failure. Of the 3,000 men Wingate deployed, only 2,182 returned to India, a casualty rate of 27 percent for a mission that produced an interruption of rail traffic lasting only a few days.[18]

The second Chindit operation, using multiple brigades and launched in February 1944, proved more successful. As one Chindit brigade advanced south into Burma on foot, American gliders flew more brigades to three separate landing zones in north Burma. These units were to link up with a Chinese force advancing southwest, preceded by the American special unit Merrill's Marauders and supported by Karin irregulars attacking from the northeast. From their landing zones the Chindits conducted successful ambushes and then marched north to link up with Stillwell, an advance that took four months of tough jungle fighting. They helped capture Mogaung in June and continued to operate until they returned to India in August.

In addition to their own accomplishments, the Chindits spawned an American counterpart. In 1943 Wingate had requested additional forces from the United States to support his deep penetration operations. President Franklin Roosevelt requested 2,830 volunteers (officers and men) form the regular army for a "dangerous and hazard[ous] mission."[19] The army formed the 3,000 volunteers into a three-battalion special unit codenamed "Galahad Force," but known by its popular name "Merrill's Marauders" for the unit's commander, Brigadier General Frank Merrill. Wingate trained the Marauders, but contrary to his expectations, Stillwell took them over to support his own operations.[20] Stillwell used the Marauders to spearhead his drive into North Burma. Operating well ahead of his Chinese "X Force," they helped create strategic deception, misleading the Japanese about the number and whereabouts of the main Allied body.[21] As part of the offensive that involved the Chindits and Stillwell's Chinese regulars, the Marauders helped capture the towns of Maingkwan in early March and Myitkyina in May 1944.

The Chindits and Marauders certainly contributed to the Allied victory in Burma, perhaps even decisively since they fixed Japanese units in place until Stillwell's slow-moving conventional forces could be brought to bear. By 1944, however, Burma had become a sideshow. The steady advance of U.S. Army and Marine units across the South and Central Pacific brought the Japanese home islands in range of American aircraft. Island hopping and strategic bombing, not jungle warfare, would ultimately decide the outcome of World War II in Asia.

Attitudes toward War

No cheering crowds greeted the declarations of war in 1939 and 1941 as they had in 1914. Memories of Verdun, the Somme, and Passchendaele were too fresh in the minds of far too many Europeans for visions of a glorious war to have much appeal. Most Americans felt shock and anger, not excitement, after Pear Harbor. Those who went off to fight World War II did so with a grim determination to accomplish an odious task as quickly as possible. Paul Fussell has demolished the myth of the "good war," a Manichean struggle in which Allied soldiers flocked to the colors to take arms against the evils of fascism. Most of the young men who fought, he determined, had little understanding of the issues at stake. The evils of the Third Reich became clear only as the war progressed.[22]

Nationalism and ethnocentrism did play a role in motivating men to fight. On active duty in 1943, the poet Randall Jarell confided to a friend that "99 out of 100 people in the army haven't the faintest idea what the war is about. Their two strongest motives are a.) nationalism . . . and race prejudice [against the Japanese]."[23] Avenging Pearl Harbor mattered most to Americans. Even then, just over a third of those in the American armed forces (38.8 percent) volunteered; the rest had to be drafted.[24] Much the same pattern occurred in the other Allied nations. Men and women fought out of necessity to defend their countries, not because of lofty ideals. Stalin acknowledged as much when he admitted that his people would fight for mother Russia but not for Communism. The "greatest generation" was a myth embraced by the children and grandchildren of those who fought in World War II, not by the combatants themselves.

Nationalism and racism also motivated those who fought for the Axis states. The Japanese felt superior to the Asian peoples they conquered and the Americans who defeated them. The code of Bushido ("the way of the warrior"), stressing honor and duty to country and family, explains why so many Japanese soldiers, sailors, and airmen preferred death in battle to surrender.[25] Ardent Nazis and perhaps ordinary German soldiers felt superior to Jews and Slavs, but loyalty to the army and the fatherland, not National Socialism, kept them fighting even after they had grown disillusioned with Hitler.

However soldiers at the front viewed the war, governments fed people at home a steady diet of propaganda. The Germans excelled at what today would be called "information warfare," creating a specialized Propaganda Ministry under the leadership of Nazi stalwart Josef Goebbels. The ministry made use of all existing media (print, poster art, radio, and film) to convey its message of militarism and Aryan supremacy. The government even provided radios to families that could not afford them. Because the radio was preset to the official channel and could not be changed, people referred to it as the "Goebbels snout."

The Nazis commissioned the brilliant young filmmaker Leni Riefenstahl to make movies extolling the virtues of the Third Reich. Her tour de force, *Triumph of the Will*, celebrated the 1934 Nuremburg Party rally. It received an Academy Award for "Best Foreign Film of 1935." Riefenstahl insisted to the end of her life that the *Triumph of the Will* was a documentary, her artistic interpretation of a historical event. Whatever its merits as a piece of cinematography, however, both the victorious allies and virtually all historians have regarded it as brilliant propaganda.

The United States conducted its own information campaign to promote the war effort. After Pearl Harbor, Americans needed no convincing to fight Japan, but they did not understand the war against Germany. Even after Hitler declared war and the German navy began sinking American ships, people believed the major U.S. effort should be directed at Japan, even though the War Department had decided Germany posed the greater threat. The army turned to Major Frank Capra, a successful Hollywood director, to produce a series of motivational films explaining the war. From 1942 to 1945, Capra made a series of seven films: *Prelude to War* (1942), *The Nazis Strike* (1943), *Divide and Conquer* (1943), *The Battle of Britain* (1943), *The Battle of Russia* (1943), *The Battle of China* (1944), and *War Comes to America* (1945). Capra drew on a deep pool of talent, including Walt Disney's animators, who made many of the interactive maps for the films. Interestingly, only the last two films focused on the Pacific war.

Outside official channels, Hollywood beat the drum for war on its own accord. Of the 1,700 films made during the war years, 500 dealt with the conflict or fascism.[26] Although it promised to respect freedom of expression, the U.S. government provided guidelines for wartime films, suggesting that they should focus on

(1) The Issues of the War: what we are fighting for, the American way of life;
(2) The Nature of the Enemy: his ideology, his objectives, his methods;
(3) The United Nations: our allies in arms;
(4) The Production Front: supplying the materials for victory;
(5) The Home Front: civilian responsibility;
(6) The Fighting Forces: our armed services, our allies and our associates.[27]

Hollywood complied without any need for coercion or even pressure, producing films that served as "a weapon of democracy," just as Washington wanted.[28] These films did much to promote the image of World War II as the "good war."

Total War

The conflict that engulfed the world from 1939 to 1945 was the nearest to total war that humanity had ever come and perhaps the farthest it could go if it wished to survive. "I know not with what weapons World War III will be fought," Albert Einstein observed in 1949, "but World War IV will be fought with sticks and stones." The physicist whose work had made the atomic bomb possible understood full well the implications of the new weapon. Although they foreshadowed what a future war would be like, the bombings of Hiroshima and Nagasaki caused a mere fraction of the casualties suffered during World War II. The death toll from the conflict is staggering. No one knows precisely how many people died, but a conservative estimate puts the loss of life at 60 million and notes that civilian deaths outnumber those killed in battle by three to one (45 million vs. 15 million).[29] Factoring in loss of life from indirect causes brought about by the war, such as disease and famine, the death toll may have been much higher. As many as 50 million people may have died in China alone.[30]

The numbers, however, fall far short of telling the whole story. World War II was not only the most lethal conflict in history; it was also the most brutal. Soldiers in all armies committed atrocities, but the worst abuses occurred when the belligerents saw the conflict as a racial struggle. On Europe's Eastern Front, the belligerents gave little quarter and expected none. Three out of five Soviet prisoners died in German captivity, most from starvation. The Schutzstaffel (SS) used Red Army captives to test the gas chambers at Auschwitz before using them on the Jews. *Einsatzgruppen* (special action squads) carried out mass executions of Jews at places like Babi Yar in Kiev, Ukraine, long before the death camps opened. Historians have debunked the myth that only the ardent Nazis of the SS did the killing. Ordinary Germans formed into police battalions, and members of the regular army joined in the orgy of slaughter. The Soviets also used exceedingly brutal methods. Following the defeat of Poland, the NKVD (Soviet secret police) murdered approximately 10,000 Polish officers in the Katyn Forest. Only about 10,000 of the more than 90,000 Germans who surrendered at Stalingrad ever returned home.

Racism also led to brutality in the Pacific war. During the "Rape of Nanking" in 1937, Japanese soldiers murdered some 300,000 men, women, and children. Not satisfied with simply killing them, they tortured many and burned others alive. Women were systematically gang raped.[31] After the fall of Malaya, Japanese troops used British prisoners of war for bayonet practice. They forced American soldiers captured in the Philippines on the infamous "Bataan Death March." Like the Nazi doctors in the death camps, Japanese physicians conducted human experiments on Chinese prisoners. These behaviors deepened American racial hatred of the Japanese. Seeing the wreckage of Pearl Harbor from the bridge of the USS *Enterprise* on December 8, 1941, Admiral William Halsey exclaimed, "Before we are through with them, the Japanese language will be spoken only in hell."[32] General Curtis LeMay, who led the strategic bombing campaign against Japan, later remarked that "killing Japanese never bothered me much at the time."[33]

As so often happens in war, women and children suffered the most. They were shot and gassed by Nazi executioners, suffocated in Hamburg air raid shelters, and incinerated in the streets of Tokyo. Soldiers raped women in every battle zone, but German women suffered the worst during the Red Army's assault on the Reich, when some two million were sexually assaulted, the majority by Soviet troops. A worse fate awaited thousands of Korean "comfort women," forced into sexual slavery to service Japanese soldiers. The process of reducing the enemy to a subhuman "other," arguably begun with the rise of nationalism during the French Revolution, had come to its logical, horrific conclusion.

The American Way of War

The American approach to fighting World War II conformed to what Russell Weigley dubbed "the American Way of War." The American Civil War, Weigley argued, had been carried on by generals like Grant and Sherman waging a campaign of annihilation against the Confederate army and the war-making capability of the South. They had employed the superior resources and manpower of the North to overwhelm the Confederacy. Lincoln would accept nothing but unconditional surrender from the rebels. In waging this type of war, the Union generals established a precedent for how future wars would be fought.

American involvement in World War I was too brief to make a strong impression on the U.S. military, although the country's resources, manufactures, and money certainly helped to overwhelm the Germans. World War II, however, presented the United States with precisely the type of war it was best suited to fight: a no-holds-barred conflict in which wealth, resources, and human capital would prove decisive. American forces aimed for the annihilation of German and Japanese armed forces and the destruction of both nations' capacity to make war. They insisted on unconditional surrender and considered the enemy's will to resist a legitimate target, just as General Sherman had during his march to the sea.[34]

Weigley also noted that because of its relative isolation, the United States did not have to think about national defense policy or strategy. It approached each crisis on an ad hoc basis, expanding its armed forces to fight a war and then demobilizing them when it was over.[35] This tendency encouraged the American public and perhaps the military as well to view war as a distinct activity unrelated to peacetime politics. Contrary to French Premier Georges Clemenceau, Americans believed that war *should* be entrusted to generals. This naiveté, coupled with the commitment to employing overwhelming conventional forces, would prove disastrous when the United States went to war in Vietnam.

CHAPTER TWELVE

The Cold War: A New Era of Limited Conflicted?

The post-1945 world has been characterized as a new age of limited war not unlike the period 1648 to 1789. In both eras political leaders tacitly agreed that the costs and consequences of war had become unacceptably high. They took definitive steps to keep armed conflict within bounds. There, however, the similarity ends. Limitations on warfare between the Treaty of Westphalia and the outbreak of the French Revolution stemmed in large measure from the decline in ideology as a motivating factor in international conflict. During the post–World War II era, on the other hand, ideological differences intensified, especially during the era of the Cold War (1949–1989). The limitation of armed conflict during this period was also deceptive. While war between states diminished and war between major powers disappeared, other forms of political violence increased dramatically. Between 1945 and 2000 approximately 120 million people died as a result of all forms of conflict, as opposed to 70 million who died during the two world wars.[1] Most of these deaths occurred in a wide range of unconventional intrastate conflicts. Wars were much smaller, but they occurred almost continuously. Discussion of this most recent period in the history of warfare must therefore consider how and why these changes occurred.

Technological Change

Advances in military technology during the postwar era have consisted primarily of improvements to existing weapons systems. Many of the items that dominated the new era were invented during World War II. German jets and V-2 rockets developed into the aircraft and intercontinental ballistic missiles of the Cold War. Indeed, Werner von Braun, the German scientist who had developed the V-2, helped to build the rockets that eventually carried U.S. nuclear warheads and sent American astronauts into space. The most awesome weapon of World War II, the atomic bomb, also evolved during the postwar era. For four years the United States had a monopoly on the new weapon. Then in August 1949 the Soviet Union exploded its first nuclear weapon, followed by Britain in 1952, France in 1960, and China in 1964. As of this writing, India, Pakistan, and North Korea have tested nuclear weapons; Israel is presumed to have them; and Iran has been working to acquire them.

Nuclear proliferation led to an arms race. The United States vied with the Soviet Union to acquire larger and more lethal stockpiles of more effective weapons, followed belatedly by China. Once the Soviets had an atomic bomb, President Harry Truman launched a program to produce an even more destructive weapon, the hydrogen (fusion) bomb, a thousand times more powerful than its predecessor.[2] The United States successfully tested its first hydrogen bomb in 1952, followed by the Soviet Union in 1953. From then on the arms race would focus on numbers of nuclear weapons and delivery systems. Long-range bombers remained the primary means of deploying nuclear weapons until intercontinental ballistic missiles (ICBMs) and submarine-launched ballistic missiles (SLBMs) augmented them in the 1960s. By 1970 the United States had deployed the first multiple independently targetable reentry vehicle (MIRV), which allowed a single missile to carry multiple nuclear warheads, each aimed at a different target. The Soviets and the Chinese, once again, followed suit. Tactical or "battlefield" nuclear weapons fired from cannon or launched via cruise and other short-range missiles rounded out the nuclear arsenals of the three superpowers.

Conventional weapons also evolved in the postwar era. Tanks became larger, faster, and better protected with reactive armor, and they mounted heavier cannon. Antitank guns gradually disappeared, replaced by shoulder-fired antitank missiles. Man-portable air defense systems (MANPADs) reduced the need for anti-aircraft guns. Increasingly specialized helicopters made it possible to rapidly deploy "air cavalry" and provided highly effective close-infantry support with rockets and/or machine guns.

Beginning of the Cold War

As World War II drew to a close, many people hoped that the alliance that had defeated the Axis would continue into the postwar era. That hope quickly faded as the Soviet Union began setting up Communist puppet governments in the countries occupied by the Red Army. Former British Prime Minister Winston Churchill was among the first to spot the danger. "From Stettin in the Baltic to Trieste in the Adriatic, an iron curtain has descended across the Continent [of Europe]," he told an audience at Westminster College in Fulton, Missouri, on March 5, 1946, "[b]ehind that line lie all the capitals of the ancient states of Central and Eastern Europe. Warsaw, Berlin, Prague, Vienna, Budapest, Belgrade, Bucharest and Sofia, all these famous cities and the populations around them lie in what I must call the Soviet sphere, and all are subject in one form or another, not only to Soviet influence but to a very high and, in many cases, increasing measure of control from Moscow."[3]

On April 1, 1948, tension between the Western allies and the Soviet Union escalated to confrontation when Stalin closed the land routes into Berlin, deep in the Soviet occupation zone, to force France, Britain, and the United States to withdraw from their sectors of the city. Instead the Allies conducted a yearlong aerial relief operation, flying supplies into Tempelhof Airport around the clock. The Berlin crisis established the pattern for the Cold War. The Soviets calculated that the Western allies would not risk war by forcibly reopening the land route into the city. The Americans, British, and French for their part considered that the Soviets would not risk war by shooting down transports flying in the designated air corridor between West Germany and Berlin. Victory would depend on whether or not they could keep the city supplied until Stalin relented and reopened the land routes, which he did on May 12, 1949. Thus began a game of brinkmanship that would continue for the next 40 years.

The Cold War was shaped by two factors: an unprecedented strategic stalemate and an intense ideological struggle. For the first time in history two countries had the ability to destroy one another and take the rest of the world with them. At the time, East and West embraced diametrically opposed ideologies. The April 1950 National Security Council Paper 68 (NSC 68), "United States Objectives and Programs for National Security," succinctly described the situation. The Soviet Union, the report declared, "is animated by a new, fanatical faith, antithetical to our own, and seeks to spread its absolute authority all over the rest of the world." This ideological confrontation made conflict endemic but the prospect of total war unacceptable. "With the development of increasingly terrifying weapons of mass destruction," NSC 68 concluded, "every individual faces the ever-present possibility of annihilation should the conflict enter the phase of total war."[4] The Soviets drew a similar conclusion.

What came to be called "the balance of terror," however, took time to develop. Initially the United States had too few weapons to completely deter Soviet aggression, but Soviet acquisition of the bomb could not immediately offset the U.S. head start. Stalin concluded that not until 1955 would the United States have enough nuclear weapons to threaten the Soviet Union, and U.S. intelligence set the same date for when the Soviets would have enough weapons to threaten the United States.[5] Once they reached equilibrium, though, the two sides waged an aggressive arms race, seeking to gain enough of an edge in weapons and delivery systems to mount a "first strike" capable of wiping out all or at least most of the other's nuclear force before it could retaliate. Not until the 1960s did the United States and the Soviet Union admit that they had achieved a state of "mutually assured destruction" (with its appropriate acronym, "MAD"), in which neither side could mount a first strike. Fear of a nuclear holocaust deterred them from going to war with each other. When China joined the nuclear club, its leaders too wished to avoid a major war. By that time, the Soviets and Chinese had come to distrust each other so much that each had a significant number of warheads aimed at the other.

Nuclear weapons did not make conventional forces obsolete. The paucity of bombs through the mid-1950s meant that both sides had to maintain large conventional establishments. The Soviets did not demobilize as many of their troops at the end of World War II as did the United States. The Berlin crisis prompted the West to create a new defensive alliance, the North Atlantic Treaty Organization (NATO), comprised of the United States, the United Kingdom, France, Belgium, the Netherlands, Italy, Portugal, Norway, Iceland, Luxembourg, Canada, and Denmark. Signed on April 4, 1949, the Washington Treaty proclaimed:

> The Parties agree that an armed attack against one or more of them in Europe or North America shall be considered an attack against them all and consequently they agree that, if such an armed attack occurs, each of them, in exercise of the right of individual or collective self-defense recognized by Article 51 of the Charter of the United Nations, will assist the Party or Parties so attacked by taking forthwith, individually and in concert with the other Parties, such action as it deems necessary, including the use of armed force, to restore and maintain the security of the North Atlantic area.[6]

The Cold War   243

A treaty could not, however, immediately remedy the huge disparity in conventional forces. In 1950 NATO had 14 divisions in Western Europe, only 4 of which (2 U.S. and 2 UK) were deployed in West Germany. The Soviets had 22 divisions in East Germany and 2 each in Poland, Austria, and Hungary.[7] Faced with a two to one Soviet advantage, NATO leaders determined that in the event of a Soviet attack, they could perhaps hold the line of the Rhine River. The American promise to defend Europe with nuclear weapons rang hollow, given that any attack on the Soviet Union would result in World War III and the use of even tactical nuclear weapons would devastate Germany. Following the outbreak of the Korean Conflict in June 1950, therefore, the United States rapidly built up its armed forces, not just in Asia but also in Europe. In 1955 NATO made the controversial decision to rearm West Germany. To allay the fears of its own allies, though, it denied the Bundeswehr (federal defense forces) their own general staff, keeping them under the oversight of Supreme Headquarters Allied Powers Europe (SHAPE). The Soviets responded by creating the Warsaw Pact, an alliance of Soviet bloc nations, in 1956. Although NATO never achieved parity of troop strength with the Warsaw Pact, it did reduce the Soviet advantage to the point at which Western forces could halt an attack long enough for the nuclear option to be exercised, thus making the risks associated with an invasion unacceptably high. The two sides thus achieved conventional as well as nuclear stalemate.

Stalemate did not, of course, end conflict, but it did keep it in check.

AMERICA UNDER COMMUNISM!

American propaganda took many forms during the Cold War, including comic book covers like the one seen here. *Source:* Magnus Manske.

The United States and the Soviet Union came close to war only once during the Cuban Missile Crisis of October 1962. That confrontation arose in part through failure to communicate strategic intent clearly enough, and Washington and Moscow resolved it peacefully. They then installed a hotline for direct communication in the event of another crisis. For the most part, the two adversaries preferred to spar with one another indirectly through a series of proxy conflicts. The Soviets (and after 1949 the Chinese) backed Communist "wars of national liberation," while the United States supported threatened democracies and even propped up corrupt dictatorships as long as they promised to fight Communism. Almost every conflict during the Cold War involved the superpowers, however indirectly.

The Korean Conflict

The first conflict of the Cold War occurred not, as might have been expected, in Western Europe, but half a world away on the Korean peninsula. At the end of World War II the Allies divided Korea at the 38th parallel. Soviet forces occupied the north and the United States the south, each supporting a rival government. In 1948–1949 the United States reduced its troop strength in South Korea, despite signs of increasing Communist guerrilla activity sponsored by the North.[8] Supported by Stalin and Mao Zedong, the new premier of Communist China, North Korea believed that the South Korean regime would collapse in the face of an attack and that if the United States intervened at all, its efforts would be delayed and ineffectual.[9] According to Politburo member and later Soviet Premier Nikita Khrushchev, Stalin worried about U.S. intervention but was convinced that a swift victory would eliminate that threat.[10] It was the first of several mistaken assumptions that would escalate the crisis.

Early on the morning of June 25, 1950, 135,000 North Korean troops attacked across the 38th parallel. They advanced in two broad thrusts, one directed at the capital, Seoul, and from thence down the east coast of the country, and the second down the center of the peninsula. They overwhelmed the Republic of Korea (ROK) Army and a small number of American troops rushed from Japan, forcing them to fall back toward Pusan in the southwest. By August 1 these forces were clinging to a toehold within the "Pusan perimeter." The United Nations (UN) Security Council branded North Korea the aggressor and authorized the first UN police action to repel the invasion. The Soviet representative would have vetoed such a decision, but he had removed himself in protest against the decision to allow Taiwan to keep the seat that Moscow claimed should go to Communist China. As the UN internationalized the crisis, more

The Cold War

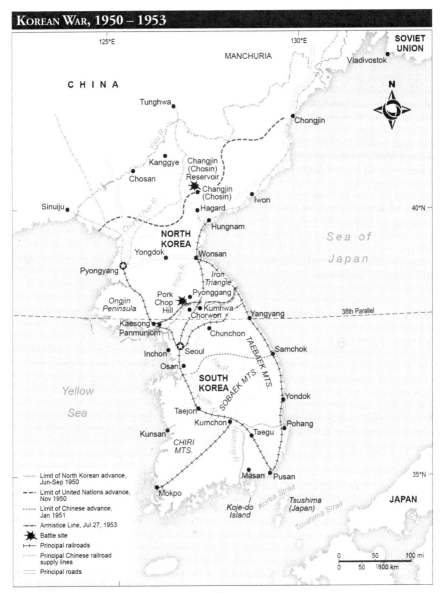

Major engagements of the Korean Conflict.

troops arrived from the United States, and the Pusan perimeter held. The commander of UN forces, General Douglas MacArthur, eschewed a conservative strategy of simply driving the North Koreans back from Pusan and devised a bold plan involving an amphibious landing at the port of Inchon east of Seoul. Allied forces landed on September 15 and recaptured

Seoul on September 27. Meanwhile U.S. forces attacked out of the Pusan perimeter. With attenuated supply lines and battered from two directions, the North Koreans fell back. By the first week of October the allies had reached the 38th parallel.

Now it was Washington's turn to misinterpret the situation. Instead of being satisfied with a return to the status quo ante, MacArthur saw an opportunity to unite the Koreas under a democratic, pro-Western government. President Truman worried about the risks of Chairman Mao sending in troops to support the North. MacArthur assured him that China would not dare intervene, an assertion he would continue to make even as American advanced units were capturing Chinese prisoners.[11] If Beijing did intervene, MacArthur arrogantly proclaimed, "There will be the greatest slaughter."[12] Chinese Foreign Minister Zhou Enlai had, however, already made Beijing's intentions crystal clear. Because China had no direct relations with the United States, Zhou sent a stern warning via the Indian embassy. "If the United States or United Nations forces cross the 38th parallel," he told the Indian ambassador on October 3, "the Chinese People's Republic will send troops to aid the People's Republic of [North] Korea. We shall not take this action, however, if only South Korean troops cross the border."[13] Although passed on promptly to UN headquarters and the U.S. government, the warning went unheeded. Truman authorized MacArthur to advance to the Yalu River, the border between North Korea and China.

Allied forces moved rapidly north until they reached the Yalu at the Chosin Reservoir on October 27. True to their word, the Chinese sent in the People's Army. The UN forces had an overwhelming advantage in naval and airpower, but the Chinese diminished their effectiveness by marching at night and holing up in caves by day. MacArthur wanted to bomb not only the bridges over the river but the Chinese mainland as well. Realizing that the situation had escalated dangerously and fearing that the war in Korea might be a diversion to cover a Soviet attack against Western Europe, Truman refused MacArthur's request and ultimately relieved the petulant general of his command. The Chinese drove allied forces back across the 38th parallel to a defensive line south of Seoul, where they regrouped, counterattacked, and this time halted at the old border in late July 1951. A desultory form of trench warfare dragged on for two more years until both sides agreed to an armistice on July 27, 1953, a truce that has held to his day without a formal peace treaty ever being signed.

Unconventional as well as conventional operations played a significant role in the Korean Conflict. Communist organizers created insurgent cells in the South long before the invasion. The ROK Army, supported by American advisers, employed a strategy consisting of two elements. First they relocated civilians from affected areas to remove any source of support from the local population. Then they conducted search-and-destroy operations, cordoning off large areas and systematically clearing them of guerrillas.[14] In other circumstances, such a heavy-handed approach might have been counterproductive, but in Korea it made the guerrillas desperate for supplies.[15] Ironically, though, the initial success of the conventional invasion doomed the insurgents, who came out of hiding to support the North Koreans only to be destroyed in the allied counteroffensive.

People's War

The insurgents in South Korea adopted a strategy developed and successfully employed by the Chinese Communists during their long struggle (1927–1949) with the Nationalists and the Japanese invaders. Based in part on the writings of the sixth-century CE Chinese strategist Sun Tzu, Mao Zedong developed a theory of revolutionary war ideally suited to conditions in China. Sun Tzu emphasized careful preparation, choosing to fight only when one had a significant advantage, and maneuvering to achieve surprise. "Attack when they are unprepared, make your move when they do not expect it," he counseled.[16] Mao recognized that although the Communists started from a position of weakness, they had long-term strengths, which they could exploit, particularly their ability to win the support of the Chinese people in an anticolonial struggle against the Japanese followed by a revolution against a Nationalist Chinese government inattentive to the needs of its own people.

Mao called for "protracted war" progressing through three distinct phases. During the first phase, when enemy strength precluded direct confrontation, the Communists would concentrate on building up their strength. They would engage in "primarily mobile warfare, supplemented by guerrilla and positional warfare," harassing the enemy with hit-and-run operations but avoiding conventional engagements. They would also use this period to expand their base of support among the people. The second phase would begin when the enemy had been stalemated and forced to divert more and more troops to defend fixed positions. The Communists would establish base areas behind the enemy lines and expand the guerrilla campaign. During the third stage they would go over to the offensive, escalating conventional operations to clear and hold the country.[17]

Although Mao initially developed his theory of protracted war to expel the Japanese from China, he adapted it to overthrowing the Kuomintang, the Nationalist party led by Chiang Kai-Shek, who governed China before and after the Japanese invasion. Unlike traditional partisan warfare, in which guerrillas operate in support of conventional armies, people's war sought to gain control of a country from within using indigenous forces. To succeed Communists needed to win the support or at least the acquiescence of the people among whom they lived. Mao compared his guerrillas to fish swimming in a sea of peasant support.[18] In order to secure that support, though, the Communists had to treat ordinary people with decency and respect. Mao laid down strict rules for how his followers should conduct themselves. "Be courteous," he instructed his fighters. "Be honest in your transactions, return what you borrow, replace what you break, do not bathe in the presence of women."[19] These and other instructions required Communists to treat people with consideration not shown them by either the Japanese or the Nationalists.

The Chinese Communists had contributed to the Allied victory over Japan by tying down large numbers of Japanese troops, but American naval and airpower ultimately won the war in Asia. Without the U.S. offensive in the Pacific and Soviet aid, people's war would probably not have succeeded in liberating China. It did, however, work brilliantly against the Nationalists. The Nationalist Chinese Army remained holed up in cities and garrisons while the Communists controlled the countryside and eventually overwhelmed government forces. Chiang fled to Taiwan, and on October 1, 1949, Mao declared the establishment of the People's Republic of China.

Mao Zedong articulated what may be the first complete theory of modern insurgency. Although the terms "insurgent" and "guerrilla" have often been conflated, a clear distinction must be made between them. As previously discussed, guerrilla warfare is a tactic that has been employed by irregular forces for centuries. Small units of various types, in or out of uniform, engage in hit-and-run tactics, attacking supply lines, ambushing small parties, and avoiding engagements with larger conventional units. While insurgents make use of guerrilla warfare, insurgency involves much more than these irregular operations. To succeed, insurgents must win sufficient popular support to secure safe areas in which to operate against the government. They win this support through a combination of effective governance and coercion. Insurgencies often start because a government fails to meet the needs of its own people. The insurgents offer an alternative, promising to do a better job than the existing state. They also intimidate anyone who cooperates with the government through selective use of terror. Insurgency is thus a complex form of conflict involving guerrilla warfare, terrorism, and political action.[20]

Anticolonial Insurgency

The two decades following the end of World War II saw a wave of insurgencies by local people against the colonial powers occupying their countries. Not all of these revolutions were Communist inspired, but the superpowers nonetheless incorporated them into the Cold War struggle. The Kremlin vowed to support "wars of national liberation," as did Beijing, and Washington promised to aid friendly regimes threatened by revolution. Many local conflicts thus became proxy wars between the superpowers. This ideological framework led the United States to back some undemocratic, even oppressive regimes, largely because they claimed to oppose Communism.

While most anticolonial campaigns succeeded, few sought to establish Communist regimes. They won not by inflicting decisive military defeats against the imperial powers, but by convincing them that the benefits of remaining did not outweigh the costs. From 1945 to 1947 Zionist insurgents forced the British to withdraw from Palestine. Indonesian revolutionaries compelled the Dutch to quit that colony in 1949. Nationalist insurgents forced the French to grant Algeria independence in 1962. Other imperial powers faced similar revolts or, anticipating them, granted their colonies independence. By 1970 virtually all of the European empires in Africa and Asia had disappeared. Colonial powers were not, however, alone in facing insurgencies. In 1959 Fidel Castro overthrew the corrupt government of Fulgencio Batista and established a Communist regime in Cuba, just 90 miles from American shores.

Counterinsurgency

The success of so many revolutions led analyst Robert Taber to conclude that insurgency represented a new, irresistible form of warfare. "Guerrillas who know their trade and have popular support cannot be defeated by means available to most governments," he wrote in 1965. "And on the other hand, few governments can stand the political, psychological, and economic stresses of guerrilla war, no matter how strong they may be militarily."[21] This sweeping conclusion invited a sharp rebuttal from J. Bowyer Bell, who noted in *The Myth of the Guerrilla: Revolutionary Theory and Malpractice* that most insurgent victories had been against "soft" colonial targets, European states weakened by World War II and unable to afford the continued cost of colonialism.[22] Each argument has merit, but they both overlook the importance of the response by the threatened state in determining the success or failure of an insurgency.

Counterinsurgency (COIN) consists of those measures taken by a threatened state to combat a violent revolutionary movement. Since insurgency usually results from legitimate grievances (economic, social, and/or political), the government must address the root causes of unrest. At the same time that it undertakes reform, it has to combat the insurgent guerrillas through military and police operations. Regimes overthrown by insurgents lost primarily because they focused on the purely military aspects of COIN. In doing so they encountered the same problem faced by the French in the Iberian Peninsula. Conventional forces are designed to fight other conventional forces. Their structure, organization, equipment, and logistics needs make them ill-suited to pursue bands of lightly armed, highly mobile guerrillas who hide among the general population, who actively or tacitly support them. Frustration at their inability to come to grips with the illusive enemy often leads soldiers to carry out reprisals against the population accused of aiding them. These reprisals encourage more people to support the insurgents. If, however, the government can win the support of people by meeting their needs, foremost of which is security, it might induce them to provide information on the whereabouts of the insurgents. The examples of the Algerian Civil War and the Malayan Emergency illustrate the dynamics of failure and success in COIN campaigns.

France acquired Algeria in 1830, and by the middle of the 20th century approximately one million white, French Algerians ruled some eight million indigenous people, who had few political rights.[23] Caught up in the wave of nationalism that swept Africa and Asia after World War II, native Algerians demanded change. The French answered their demands with token reform and repression. In 1954 Algerian opposition groups joined to form the National Liberation Front (NLF) and launched an insurgency against French rule. The NLF's strength reached 40,000 active fighters by 1957.[24] Enjoying safe havens in neighboring Tunisia and Morocco, the insurgents conducted effective guerrilla operations, assassinating white French *colons* and pro-French Muslims.

The French response to the insurgency made a bad situation worse. France armed the *colons*, who conducted reprisals against Arab Algerians and thus encouraged them to support the NLF.[25] As the conditions deteriorated, Paris sent in more French troops, which reached peak strength of 500,000, but deployed them ineffectively in static defensive outposts.[26] Beginning in 1957, however, the security forces adopted a better approach. They divided the countryside into operational zones and regrouped the rural population into new settlements in which the military made at least some effort to improve living conditions.[27] They also built a defensive line along the Tunisian border and backed it with artillery and mobile infantry units capable of pursuing infiltrators. In the Battle of Algiers the French secured the capital through registration of the population, control of movement, and extensive use of detention and torture to gain information on the NLF. This heavy-handed approach allowed them to construct an *organogram*, a detailed map of the NLF organization in the city. In a matter of weeks the security forces destroyed the insurgent organization in Algiers.

In winning the Battle of Algiers, however, the French army lost the war. Its methods provoked a crisis in France, which led to defeat in Algeria. French people who had only recently suffered Nazi occupation would not tolerate abusive behavior by their own troops. The crisis led to the collapse of the Fourth Republic and the election of a new president, Charles de Gaulle. Contrary to military expectations, de Gaulle conducted a referendum on independence in which Algerians as well as *colons* could vote. When the Algerians chose independence, the French granted it to them in 1962. While France could probably not have prevented Algerian independence indefinitely, liberal reforms at the outset of national unrest might have prevented a long and costly war, fostered better relations with the postcolonial government, and prevented much of the violence that has plagued Algerian politics in the years since independence.

The successful British campaign against Communist insurgents in Malaya (future Malaysia) contrasts markedly with the French efforts in Algeria. From 1948 to 1960 the British conducted what has become the classic example of effective COIN. The insurgents had an active strength of approximately 6,500, with another 50,000 supporters in a population of some 4.3 million.[28] Fortunately for the government, the insurgency remained confined to the Chinese population, approximately 38 percent of the total, and the Malayan peninsula isolated the guerrillas from outside support. Nonetheless, the British faced a formidable task, as much of the sympathetic Chinese population lived a marginal existence in squatter villages along the jungle fringe, ideally located to support insurgents operating in the jungle. At the height of the emergency, they deployed no more than 30,000 troops to support 28,000 police in protecting the threatened population and pursuing the insurgents.[29]

The British approach rested on two broad principles: minimum force and hearts-and-minds. English common law required that soldiers and police conducting internal security operations use deadly force in a limited, focused manner. They employed considerable coercion and atrocities did occur, but not on anything like the scale of the French in Algeria. The legal requirement limiting use of force required the British to develop a strategy aimed at garnering intelligence on the whereabouts of the insurgents. Winning hearts and minds consisted of efforts to improve people's quality of life to the point at which they would no longer support the guerrillas and might provide information on the insurgents. In Malaya the British forcibly relocated Chinese squatters from settlements along the jungle fringe to "new villages" in more secure locations. Relocation required considerable coercion, both to move people and to keep them in the resettlement communities, but over time the British provided schools, piped-in water, medical clinics, and other amenities. An offer of Malayan citizenship to the Chinese squatters and generous amnesty for insurgents who surrendered further induced cooperation, which provided actionable intelligence. Granting independence to Malaya eliminated the cloak of anticolonial legitimacy the insurgents had thrown over their campaign.[30]

The British also employed effective civil-military coordination mechanisms and flexible military tactics. They created a system of district, state, and federation emergency committees attended by military, police, and civil officials to plan and conduct joint operations. Decentralization of command and control made it easier to conduct those operations. COIN has often been described as a subaltern's (second lieutenant's) and a corporal's war, since most engagements occur at platoon and section level. Allowing junior officers and senior NCOs considerable latitude in carrying out orders was thus crucial to success in operations against insurgent guerrillas. This approach applied German conventional war *Auftragstaktik* to unconventional conflict.

The British army had not discovered a magic formula for COIN, but it enjoyed greater success than most Western militaries. It failed in Palestine (1945–1947) and South Arabia (1964–1967) and would fail again in Basra, Iraq (2003–2011). It defeated insurgencies in Kenya (1952–1956) and Cyprus (1955–1959), but nonetheless withdrew from those colonies. British seconded officers and Special Forces helped the sultan of Oman defeat an insurgency in Dhofar Province (1970–1975). Perhaps its greatest success came in its longest and most difficult campaign, Northern Ireland (1969–1998). It took more than 25 years to fight the Provisional Irish Republican Army to a stalemate that created the opportunity for a negotiated settlement, largely on British terms. All in all, though, the British established an impressive record for COIN campaigns, suggesting that their approach had much to commend it.

Like all such doctrine, British COIN lays out broad principles that must be turned into strategies for specific situations. As the Americans discovered in Vietnam, simply copying methods from a previous campaign does not work. A powerful enough regime can sometimes crush an insurgency with brute force, as Guatemala did after a civil war lasting over 30 years.

Aiding a state threatened by insurgency adds another level of complexity to a campaign. The U.S. efforts to help the government of El Salvador during the 1980s initially had little success because the Americans could neither persuade nor compel the Salvadoran government to stop human rights violations and engage in meaningful reform. Only at the end of the Cold War, when fighting Communism no longer mattered, could the United States make military aid contingent upon a less brutal approach to COIN.[31]

Vietnam

The Vietnam War, more accurately known as the Second Indochina War (1958–1975), deeply divided American society and left an indelible mark on the U.S. military. Ironically, its domestic significance far outweighed its international importance.[32] The United States inherited the conflict from the French, who lost a decade-long struggle with Communist insurgents led by Ho Chi Minh. The 1954 Geneva Accords divided the country into a Communist north and a democratic, pro-Western south with the promise of eventual unification based on popular elections. When it became clear these elections would not take place, Ho Chi Minh launched an insurgency against the south. Interpreting the conflict not as an anticolonial revolution but as a Communist crusade, the United States supported the Saigon government.

During the 1950s and 1960s the United States based its Cold War strategy on the principle of containment. That strategy dictated the need to oppose Communism whenever and wherever possible. Ironically, a principal architect of containment, George Kennan, argued that the concept did not apply to Vietnam, an unimportant country outside the U.S. security perimeter in Asia and one whose fall seemed unlikely to have any serious impact on international affairs no matter which group governed it. "Vietnam is not a region of industrial-military importance," he told Congress in February 1966. "It is difficult to believe that any decisive development of the world situation is going to be determined by what happens on that territory."[33] Proponents of the war insisted that the fall of Vietnam would trigger a domino effect: Laos, Cambodia, and perhaps even Thailand would become Communist. Both Kennan and his critics proved correct. Laos and Cambodia did go red, though Thailand did not, but these developments had no significant impact on the Cold War.

American intervention may well have been based on a false premise, but that error in judgment alone does not explain why the United States and the government it backed lost the war. The nature of the conflict and

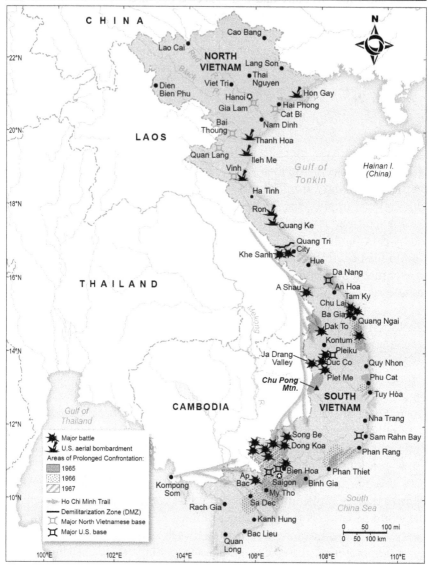

Major engagements of the Vietnam War.

how the U.S. military approached it help to explain that defeat. Like most wars in the modern era, Vietnam was a hybrid conflict with a conventional and an unconventional dimension. The People's Army of Vietnam (PAVN) conducted conventional operations along the demilitarized zone separating north and south, while the government in Hanoi sponsored an insurgent organization known as the National Front, dubbed the "Viet Cong" by the Americans and the South Vietnamese. By establishing a supply route from the north through nominally neutral Laos, the North Vietnamese could move men and supplies to the insurgent cells in the south. Because the Saigon regime governed in the interests of an elite class established during colonial days, it lacked support and even legitimacy in the eyes of many South Vietnamese. Poor governance by the official state thus made it easier for the insurgents to subvert the local population.

Arguably the United States stood little hope of success in backing such a corrupt government, but the manner in which the U.S. military fought the war made matters worse. American involvement began not with the deployment of combat troops, but with the training and equipping of a new Army of Vietnam (ARVN). Unfortunately, the Pentagon created the South Vietnamese military patterned on its own force structure, a conventional establishment reliant upon firepower. Between 1956 and 1958 the United States spent $85 million to reorganize the ARVN into a conventional fighting force of 150,000 grouped into six heavy and four light divisions.[34] Within a few years, however, the ARVN had disbanded its light divisions, leaving its force well-suited to repel a conventional invasion by the north but ill-suited to combat insurgent guerrillas.[35]

The inability and in some cases the unwillingness of ARVN commanders to take the fight to the Viet Cong even with American advisers on the ground to encourage them led the United States to commit its own forces to the fight. In 1965 Military Assistance Command Vietnam (MACV) assumed direct control of operations. Because it had begun as an advisory mission, however, MACV had a low tooth-to-tail ratio: only 80,000 of its peak strength of 543,000 consisted of combat troops, far too small a number to fight an insurgency in a country the size of South Vietnam while at the same time protecting that country from invasion by the PAVN.[36] The U.S. military relied on mobility and firepower to make up for numbers.

The American approach did enjoy some initial success. The first test came in November 1965 when the 1st Battalion, 7th Cavalry, numbering approximately 1,000 men under the command of Colonel Harold Moore, faced a PAVN unit at least twice its size at Ia Drang Valley in the Central Highlands.[37] Custer's old unit flew into battle aboard Huey helicopters in one of the first applications of air mobile warfare. In a four-day battle the Americans defeated the larger PAVN force, thanks largely to Moore's ability to call in artillery and air support. In his after-action report on the battle, Moore stressed the importance of such support. "Fire support to be effective must be close in," he noted. "Aerial rocket artillery is extremely effective."[38] Other commanders asserted the value of firepower even more aggressively. An officer at the Marine Command in Staff College in the early 1960s responded derisively to a lecture by a British officer on the long-haul, low-cost approach employed successfully in Malaya. The Marine saw no point in the gradual approach against the enemy because, he said, the U.S. military would "work them over with so much steel that six months will see the end of it."[39]

Ia Drang Valley seemed to validate the American reliance on firepower and mobility. Indeed, throughout the war neither the PAVN nor the Viet Cong could defeat American units in large engagements. The same approach that worked for conventional operations, however, proved disastrous in the COIN campaign. Lacking the troops necessary to clear and hold territory, the U.S. military under the command of General William Westmoreland adopted an attrition strategy, known as "search and destroy." American and ARVN forces would deploy to "fix," enemy formations so that they could be destroyed by airstrikes and/or artillery bombardment. This approach, combined with strategic bombing of North Vietnam, would wear down Hanoi until it sued for peace. Westmoreland based this strategy on the false premise that the PAVN and Viet Cong would oblige him by concentrating their forces in large formations as they had at Ia Drang Valley. Instead they reverted to traditional guerrilla operations, which frustrated the Americans. Search-and-destroy had the added disadvantage of killing innocent civilians and thus encouraging them to support the Viet Cong.

These concerns led some officers and civilians to challenge the search-and-destroy strategy. They argued that the key to defeating the insurgency lay in "pacification," clearing and holding areas to prevent the Viet Cong from returning. Westmoreland resisted pacification on two grounds. He insisted that the PAVN represented a greater threat to South Vietnam than did the Viet Cong, and he believed the South Vietnamese should handle pacification since they spoke the language and understood the culture of their own people far better than did the Americans.[40] Westmoreland was not entirely wrong about the conventional threat, as the Tet Offensive would demonstrate, but his approach did not take into account the intimate connection between insurgency and conventional operations. The period 1965 to 1968 has been described as Phase II Maoist revolutionary war, a combination of conventional and unconventional operations.[41] Furthermore, the ARVN proved incapable of conducting pacification operations on their own. They created strategic hamlets based on the model of the Malayan new villages, but failed to adequately protect them from Viet Cong infiltration.

Some Americans did understand COIN and made a concerted effort to devise and implement an effective strategy. Marine Corps Major General Viktor Krulak argued for pacification programs in the coastal plane and the Mekong Delta, areas in which 90 percent of South Vietnamese lived.[42] To implement this strategy, the Marine Corps developed combined action platoons (CAPs), which paired a 12- to 15-man Marine rifle squad with a 30-member South Vietnamese militia unit to live in and defend local villages.[43] CAPs proved effective, but they were never employed widely enough to make a strategic difference, nor could they offset the overemphasis on firepower employed by the U.S. military.

The dénouement in Vietnam came at the beginning of 1968. On the night of January 29–30, the North Vietnamese launched a countrywide offensive against the cities of South Vietnam employing PAVN regulars and Viet Cong in hopes of triggering a national uprising. American and ARVN forces inflicted a decisive defeat on the Communists, killing 45,000 of 84,000, and the anticipated uprising failed to occur.[44] This military victory, however, turned into a major political defeat for the administration of President Lyndon Johnson. After months of being told that the United States was winning the war and that victory was at hand, the American people were shocked at the extent and intensity of the Communist onslaught. Iconic *CBS Evening News* anchor Walter Cronkite provided the most damning epitaph of the battle. "We have been too often disappointed by the optimism of the American leaders, both in Vietnam and in Washington, to have faith any longer in the silver linings they find in the darkest clouds," he told the American public on February 27, 1968. "For it now seems more certain than ever that the bloody experience of Vietnam is to end in a stalemate."[45]

It would take another five years to reveal the truth in Cronkite's prophecy, but those years did nothing but add to the loss of life. An end to college deferments made the sons of white, middle-class Americans eligible for the draft and thus increased opposition to an already unpopular war. Intensified bombing of North Vietnam by the administration of President Richard Nixon failed to have a decisive effect. At the end of the day, even the most die-hard hawks had to admit that no possible gain could justify the cost in blood and treasure of continuing the war. Washington negotiated what it called a "peace with honor" and withdrew its combat forces in 1973. The Saigon regime held out for another two years and then collapsed in the face of a North Vietnamese invasion. Even in the aftermath of defeat some American officers never grasped the true nature of the conflict. Several years after the war had ended, Colonel Harry Summers told a North Vietnamese colonel, "You never defeated us on the battlefield." "That may be so," the Vietnamese responded. "It is also irrelevant."[46]

For the American people, the traumatic effect of the Vietnam War stemmed in no small measure from the idealistic view of war they had held at its outset. They believed that American military might must be exercised only in a moral conflict.[47] Many had grown up with the idea of World War II as the "great crusade," a belief made credible by what soldiers liberating the death camps in Europe discovered. American forces had then defended South Korea from Communist aggression. Surely, people reasoned, America would go to war only for a just cause. Newly elected President John F. Kennedy had begun the decade of the 1960s proclaiming as much. "Let the word go forth from this time and place, to friend and foe alike, that the torch has been passed to a new generation of Americans," he proudly declared, "born in this century, tempered by war, disciplined by a hard and bitter peace, proud of our ancient heritage—and unwilling to witness or permit the slow undoing of those human rights to which this Nation has always been committed, and to which we are committed today at home and around the world."[48] Although 60 percent of the American public supported the Vietnam War, they did so with little enthusiasm, giving President Johnson the benefit of the doubt that the war would be just despite evidence even at the outset that the United States was propping up a corrupt regime, which had little popular support.[49] As that hope grew more and more forlorn, a profound disillusionment replaced it.

Afghan-Soviet War

The Soviet Union could take satisfaction in the American defeat, which it had facilitated by supplying North Vietnam. The Soviets would not, however, be able to gloat for long. In 1979 they became embroiled in a similar conflict. During their 10-year occupation of Afghanistan, the Soviets made the same mistakes the Americans had made in Southeast Asia. The war also ominously foreshadowed what the United States would encounter after it invaded the country in 2001. Moscow sent in troops to support a regime that lacked legitimacy. It showed little awareness of, let alone regard for, the ethnic diversity and cultural complexity of Afghanistan and as a result alienated local people. The Soviet military had even less experience of counterinsurgency than its American counterpart and shared the U.S. military's faith in the efficacy of firepower. The result was the same: a long, enervating war of attrition that wore the Soviets down to the point where they had to accept that no conceivable benefit could outweigh the cost of continuing the war.

The Soviet-Afghan War progressed in a manner similar to the American intervention in Vietnam. On December 25, 1979, the Soviet 40th Army entered Afghanistan to support establishment of a Communist government in Kabul. Moscow considered this move to be a limited, short-term effort in which Soviet forces would provide urban security and protect key points in order to free the Afghan army for operations in the countryside.[50] Communist reforms, however, alienated the Afghan people and increased support for the insurgency. The Soviets found themselves being dragged deeper and deeper into a quagmire as Afghan forces proved incapable of winning the war. In fighting the insurgents, the Soviet military faced the same dilemma the Americans had encountered in Vietnam: too few troops to cover a vast country with challenging terrain. Like the U.S. military they tried to overcome this deficit with mobility and firepower. Their strategy was to hold the major centers, prevent infiltration, and destroy insurgent strongholds with massive air and ground assaults to minimize Soviet casualties.[51] They burned crops and destroyed villages to clear areas, practicing what one analyst described as "migratory genocide."[52] This strategy caused untold human suffering, but did not turn the tide of the war. By 1984 Soviet forces had suffered 20,000 casualties (killed and wounded), but the insurgents controlled 75 percent of the country.[53]

The Soviets changed their approach in ways, once again, eerily reminiscent of the Americans in Vietnam. They first escalated the war, only to realize that military operations alone would not suffice. In 1985 the new Soviet premier, Mikhail Gorbachev, sent in an additional 26,000 combat troops (bringing the total to 105,000), expanded the war into eastern Afghanistan, and used airpower with even less discrimination.[54] Within a year another 1,868 Soviet soldiers had died without bringing the insurgents closer to defeat.[55] In a February 25 speech to the Soviet Communist Party, Gorbachev described Afghanistan as a "bleeding wound" and expressed a desire to withdraw from the country.[56]

As with all such interventions, exiting Afghanistan would prove harder than entering it. Gorbachev advised Afghan President Babrak Karmal to "widen your social base. Pursue a dialogue with the tribes. Try to get the support of the clergy. Give up on the leftist bent in economics."[57] Without using the term, the Soviet premier was encouraging his Afghan counterpart to adopt a hearts-and-minds strategy. He had as much success as the United States had in persuading the Saigon government to engage in reforms. In May 1986 the Soviets replaced the hard-liner Kamal with the more pragmatic Mohammad Najibullah.

With a new Afghan leader in place, the Soviet Politburo decided to adopt a two-part strategy to accelerate withdrawal of Soviet forces.[58] First, they began a policy of "Afghanization," placing greater emphasis on training and equipping the Afghan army and police while continuing to provide economic aid to the country.[59] Second, Najibullah engaged in a policy of "national reconciliation," a series of political, social, and economic reforms to win the support of the Afghan people.[60] It soon became clear, however, that whatever token reforms he had undertaken, Najibullah was more interested in consolidating his hold on power than in building a national consensus.[61]

The Kremlin also pursued a negotiated settlement of the conflict, which would allow it to withdraw from Afghanistan while leaving the Najibullah government in power—a Soviet version of "peace with honor." After long, tortuous negotiations involving the United States and Pakistan, the Soviets got a deal that allowed them to withdraw while giving the Afghan government a fighting chance for survival. The Geneva Accords, signed on April 14, 1988, included a timetable for Soviet withdrawal, which began on May 15, 1988, and ended when the last elements of the 40th Army crossed the Freedom Bridge back into the Soviet Union on February 15, 1989. The Gorbachev government had hoped to continue providing aid to Najibullah, but the collapse of the Soviet Union brought that to an end. Whether the Afghan regime would have survived with more aid is a moot point, although the poor performance of its army without direct Soviet military support suggests that it would not have. Najibullah fell from power soon after Soviet aid stopped in January 1992.

The Vietnam and Afghan Wars occurred under very different circumstances, but the similar, ultimately futile approach taken by the two superpowers at opposite ends of the ideological spectrum reveals a great deal about the limitations of counterinsurgency. The precept that conventional armies have difficulty conducting COIN campaigns has become a truism. The nature of both the U.S. and Soviet militaries, however, exacerbated this problem. During World War II the American and Red armies had relied on overwhelming firepower and mobility to defeat their adversaries. They applied the same approach in combating insurgents. In addition to exposing the inefficacy of that approach, the Vietnam and Afghan Wars reveal an even more important lesson: an intervening power cannot win the hearts and minds of someone else's people. Intervention in support of a threatened government can only succeed if that government has some degree of legitimacy among its own people. If it does not have such

The Cold War

legitimacy at the outset, it must engage in meaningful reform to acquire it. Foreign military aid and even direct military support will seldom save a corrupt regime that lacks the trust of its own people. As counterinsurgency expert Bernard Fall concluded, a state defeated by insurgents has not been "out-fought but out-governed."[62] The United States would confront this hard lesson again when it invaded Afghanistan in 2001 and Iraq in 2003.

UN Peacekeeping

The Cold War stalemate and the tacit agreement by all concerned that nuclear war must be avoided made possible a new type of military activity: UN peacekeeping. The deployment of soldiers to prevent conflict has become such a common activity that most people would be surprised to learn that the UN Charter does not mention such activity, let alone sanction it. The victorious World War II allies created the international body to prevent war and, when necessary, combat aggression. Chapter 7, Article 42 empowers the Security Council to "take such action by air, sea, or land forces as may be necessary to maintain or restore international peace and security."[63] Because the UN Charter gave the permanent five members of the Security Council (the United States, the Soviet Union, Nationalist China, Great Britain, and France) veto power, the organization engaged in only one enforcement action during the Cold War: the Korean Conflict. The Security Council could take such a decision because the Soviet ambassador was boycotting its meetings to protest Communist China not being given the seat held by Nationalist China, reduced to the island of Taiwan. The Soviets never made that mistake again.

The Security Council deadlock seemed to preclude the UN ever taking military action, but a conflict in the Middle East changed the situation. In 1956 Israel attacked Egypt in the Sinai in collusion with France and Britain. The United Kingdom planned to intervene, ostensibly to separate the belligerents but in reality to regain control of the Suez Canal, nationalized by the Egyptians. France supported the plan in return for British support for its COIN campaign in Algeria. With the Soviet Union backing Egypt against two NATO members, the conflict risked escalating to a superpower confrontation that neither Moscow nor Washington wanted. Seeing the transparent imperialist design behind the affair, the Eisenhower administration pressured Israel and Britain to withdraw. They complied, but then the international community needed a way to separate the Egyptians and Israelis and create a buffer zone between them. Out of this need grew UN peacekeeping.

The idea of using neutral troops to supervise a cease-fire or provide stability was not new. The League of Nations had deployed more than 3,000

British, Italian, Dutch, and Swedish troops to provide security for the 1935 Saar plebiscite. In 1948 the UN had deployed the UN Truce Supervision Organization (UNTSO) to oversee the cease-fire between Israel and the Arab states and the UN Military Observer Group (UNMOG) to the India-Pakistan border the following year. With fewer than a hundred soldiers at some times, these missions could do little more than report on truce violations, although in that capacity they performed a valuable function.

The situation in the Sinai required a more robust deployment. Secretary-General Dag Hammarskjold and Canadian Foreign Minister Lester Pearson conceived of a new type of UN mission based on Chapter 6, which calls for peaceful settlement of disputes, and Article 40 of Chapter 7, which calls for "provisional measures" short of military action to stop international conflict.[64] Hammarskjold called this legal rational "Chapter 6½." He and Pearson conceived of peacekeeping missions in which a large force (1,000 or more) of lightly armed troops from nonaligned nations would be interposed between belligerents who had agreed to its presence. They would prevent a recurrence of hostilities through an accidental encounter between belligerent units. Peacekeeping missions would operate under a UN Security Council mandate, which defined their composition and activities. Members of the mission could use force only in defense of themselves, their position, or "the mandate," which Hammarskjold interpreted as the ability of peacekeepers to perform their duties.[65]

The UN Emergency Force (UNEF), the first peacekeeping mission, deployed 6,073 troops from Canada, Brazil, Yugoslavia, Norway, Sweden, Finland, Denmark, Colombia, and Indonesia to the Sinai.[66] It helped preserve peace until the Six-Day War broke out in June 1967. During the entire period of the Cold War the United Nations deployed only five peacekeeping missions. In 1964 the Security Council created the UN Force in Cyprus (UNFCYP) to separate Greek and Turkish Cypriots. It sent UNEF II back to the Sinai after the 1973 Yom Kippur War, and the UN Force in Lebanon in 1978 to separate Israeli and Lebanese forces. These four missions conformed to the model of blue-helmeted soldiers providing a buffer zone between belligerents

The fifth mission did not. The UN Mission in the Congo (ONUC from its French name) escalated from a peacekeeping mission to an enforcement operation. Following independence from Belgium in 1960, civil war broke out in the country. The Belgians sent in troops to protect their nationals and, many Congolese believed, to reassert neocolonial control. Mineral-rich Katanga province seceded, and Congolese President Patrice Lumumba requested UN assistance to resist what he described as "external aggression"

(Belgian intervention).[67] A confluence of East-West interests led the United Nations to approve a mission with a very expansive mandate to

> assist the central government of the Congo in the restoration and maintenance of law and order throughout the territory of the Republic of the Congo and to safeguard its unity, territorial integrity and political independence in the interests of international peace and security.[68]

Clearly an internal security operation tenuously connected to "international peace and security," ONUC arguably violated the terms of the UN Charter, which addressed only conflict between sovereign states. Nonetheless, the peacekeeping force deployed almost 19,828 troops (maximum strength in July 1961) to the Congo, where they engaged in conventional operations to suppress revolt, end the secession of Katanga, and supervise withdrawal of Belgian forces.[69] As the subsequent turbulent history of the Congo bears witness, the mission did not produce lasting peace and stability. It cost the United Nations U.S.$400.1 million and the lives of 250 peacekeepers as well as that of Secretary-General Hammarskjold (killed in a plane crash), and created a crisis that nearly wrecked the UN. No other such mission would be approved for the remainder of the Cold War, but ONUC foreshadowed the complex UN interventions of the 1990s.

Insurgency and Counterinsurgency in Latin America

During the last decade of the Cold War the United States found itself in the odd position of supporting one insurgency while helping to suppress another. In July 1979 the Marxist revolutionary Sandinistas seized power in Nicaragua. Two years later newly elected U.S. President Ronald Reagan determined to fight Communism more aggressively. He therefore decided to aid a counterrevolutionary movement known as the Contras, providing funds, weapons, and perhaps covert operatives. The Central Intelligence Agency rather than the U.S. military mounted this intervention.

The U.S. campaign to support the government of El Salvador, on the other hand, involved American military advisers working with the Salvadoran armed forces. As in Nicaragua, an authoritarian government ruling a desperately poor country in the interest of a wealthy elite faced a Marxist insurgency. With the memory of Vietnam still painfully fresh, however, the United States would not deploy a large combat force to engage in operations. The U.S. military had eschewed direct participation in foreign COIN campaigns in favor of "foreign aid for internal defense," otherwise known as the "Nixon doctrine." First articulated during President Nixon's visit to

Guam in July 1969 and then formally stated in his November 3 address to the nation, this doctrine asserted:

> [I]n cases involving other types of aggression, we shall furnish military and economic assistance when requested in accordance with our treaty commitments. But we shall look to the nation directly threatened to assume the primary responsibility of providing the manpower for its defense.[70]

Convinced that the Vietnam War had been a costly diversion from its proper role, the U.S. military embraced the new doctrine. The U.S. mission in El Salvador would have a small footprint.

The greatest obstacle to success in El Salvador, though, proved to be the Salvadoran government, which steadfastly refused to reform. Instead, it deployed paramilitary death squads to eliminate insurgents and anyone else perceived to be a threat, including Archbishop Oscar Romero, who had advocated for the poor. Under these circumstances, the 15,000-strong Salvadoran armed forces, organized and equipped for conventional war and comprised largely of conscripts, did poorly against an insurgency with at least 7,000 guerrillas and widespread support among the Salvadoran people.[71] American advisers notified Washington that without a massive infusion of aid, the Salvadoran government would lose the war.[72] Beginning in 1981, the Reagan administration readily supplied the aid but did not make it contingent upon adopting new tactics and respecting human rights. The Salvadoran military continued to rely on heavy-handed conventional operations while its death squads murdered more civilians. With the election of the moderate José Napoleón Duarte in 1984 and under growing U.S. pressure, human rights violations by the Salvadoran security forces declined. American-supplied aircraft and helicopters forced the FMLN to abandon large-scale operations and revert to guerrilla warfare, but the insurgents still managed to control much of the countryside and the urban slums of San Salvador.[73] They remained strong enough to launch a major offensive against the capital in November 1989.

The Salvadoran conflict ended in compromise rather than a clear-cut victory for either side. The end of the Cold War made opposing Communism in Latin America less of a priority, so the new administration of President George H. W. Bush (1988–1992) could put more pressure on the Salvadoran security forces to clean up their act. The FMLN realized it could not defeat the government. A strategic stalemate opened the way for a negotiated settlement, which demobilized the Salvadoran army, gave insurgents land, and recognized the FMLN as a legitimate political party.

Changing Attitudes toward War

Popular attitudes toward the Cold War changed over its long course. In the United States, during the 1950s people generally accepted the legitimacy of the ideological struggle. Europeans shared the American fear of the Soviet Union, but with their long experience of socialism, they did not become as hysterical about Communism. As awareness of the futility of nuclear war became clear, however, a growing cynicism crept into popular culture. Neville Schute's 1957 novel *On the Beach* described the last days of human life on earth as an American submarine crew and their hosts awaited the arrival of fatal radiation in post–World War III Australia. Hollywood also reflected changing attitudes. The scathing satirical comedy *Dr. Strangelove or: How I Learned to Love the Bomb* (1964) mocked military notions that a nuclear war could be fought and won. The grim postapocalyptic movie *The Day After* portrayed America's descent into survivalist barbarism after a nuclear exchange. Produced in 1983 during the height of the cruise missile crisis, the film challenged the dangerous notion that a first strike could succeed.

Musicians too pointed out the absurdity of preparing for nuclear war. Tom Lehrer's "Who's Next?" (1965) drew attention to the growing threat of nuclear proliferation:

> Luxembourg is next to go,
> And (who knows?) maybe Monaco.
> We'll try to stay serene and calm
> When Alabama gets the bomb.[74]

The same album contained "So Long Mom (A Song for World War III)," which ends with the biting verse:

> Remember Mommy, I'm off to get a Commie,
> So send me a salami, and try to smile somehow.
> I'll look for you when the war is over,
> An hour and a half from now.[75]

Censorship in the Soviet Union and Warsaw Pact countries prevented such overt criticism of the government, but Russians had a long tradition of sardonic humor that helped them cope with brutal realities even under the tsars. One Cold War joke mocked civil defense posters. "In the event of nuclear war," it proclaimed, "Wrap yourself in a sheet and crawl slowly to the nearest cemetery." "Why slowly?," someone asked. "To avoid spreading panic." Had they been freer to express themselves, Soviet citizens would probably have shared American views.

Caught between the two superpowers, Western Europeans grew even more cynical. Realization that use of even tactical nuclear weapons would devastate Germany led many to quip that the Americans and Soviets would fight World War III "to the last European." Concerned British subjects launched The Campaign for Nuclear disarmament in 1958. The movement reflected a growing awareness of the danger of nuclear weapons, which may have encouraged the signing of the 1963 Nuclear Test Ban Treaty and the 1968 Nuclear Non-proliferation treaty. Protests flared up again with the deployment of nuclear-tipped cruise missiles in the mid-1980s.

What the men and women who fought during the Cold War era thought and felt varied with the conflict in question. Vietnam, the most controversial war of the era, inspired a large volume of fictional and nonfictional literature, as well as songs and movies. Michael Herr's *Dispatches* (first published in 1968) reflects the sentiments of many Vietnam War authors. A reporter covering the conflict in the field, Herr lived with and understood the average American soldier. His book captures their sense of futility about fighting what seemed a pointless, never-ending war:

> Year after year, season after season, wet and dry, using up options faster than rounds on a machine-gun belt, we called it right and righteous, viable and even almost won, and still it went on.[76]

Musicians produced a whole genre of antiwar songs in the 1960s and 1970s. Bob Dylan, Pete Seeger, John Lennon, and a host of other artists and groups sang of peace generically and criticized the war specifically. Barry McGuire's "Eve of Destruction" reached number one on the charts in September 1965:

> The eastern world it is exploding
> Violence flarin', bullets loadin'
> You're old enough to kill but not for votin'
> You don't believe in war but what's that gun you're totin'?
> And even the Jordan River has bodies floatin' [a reference to conflict in the Middle East][77]

In 1970 Edwin Starr wrote an iconic song condemning war:

> Oh war, is an enemy to all mankind
> The thought of war blows my mind
> War has caused unrest within the younger generation
> Induction, then destruction who wants to die . . .

War, it ain't nothin' but a heartbreaker
War, it's got one friend that's the undertaker[78]

None of these artists spoke for all Americans, but they represented a wave of dissatisfaction unprecedented in American history.

Hollywood produced a spate of films critical of the war, most of which came out after the conflict had ended. One film, however, cast the war in a favorable light. Released in 1968, *The Green Berets*, starring John Wayne, treated Vietnam as a struggle for freedom. In one scene the iconic actor repeated a line from his 1945 movie *Back to Bataan*, telling a young Vietnamese boy, "You're the reason we're fighting this war." The film, along with Barry Sadler's 1966 song "Ballad of the Green Berets," reflects American fascination with its new Special Forces, but they would remain among the few works of art portraying a positive image of that war until the 2002 film *We Were Soldiers* told the story of Ia Drang Valley from a pro-American perspective. Beginning in 1978, Hollywood released a series of scathingly critical films. *Coming Home* (1978), *The Deer Hunter* (1978), and *Apocalypse Now* (1979) were followed in the 1980s by *Platoon* (1986), *Full Metal Jacket* (1987), and *Born on the Fourth of July* (1989).

The vast body of popular literature, music, and film produced during the Cold War suggests that attitudes toward war shifted dramatically during this era. Two disastrous conflicts during the first half of the 20th century left Europeans heartily sick of conflict and determined to avoid it. Governments found it difficult even to sustain small wars to preserve their empires in a climate of opinion that had come to reject war as a legitimate means of resolving disputes. Americans clung to notions that their country went to war only in defense of noble causes, until Vietnam shattered that illusion. People on the other side of the Iron Curtain seemed as averse to conflict as their Western counterparts, although they could not say so openly.

CHAPTER THIRTEEN

Conflict in the Post–Cold War World

The Post–Cold War Era

As George Kennan predicted, the fall of South Vietnam had no significant impact on the course of the Cold War, even though Laos and Cambodia went Communist as the proponents of the domino theory had said they would. Less than a decade and a half after the American defeat in Southeast Asia, however, Communism in Eastern Europe collapsed. The United States ultimately spent the Soviet Union into bankruptcy. Amid a host of domestic problems and with the realization that he could not keep up with the arms race, Premier Mikhail Gorbachev withdrew Soviet support from Warsaw Pact regimes, allowing them to collapse in bloodless revolutions (with the exception of Romania, which suffered a short internal conflict) in November 1989. The Soviet Union broke up two years later. China remained Communist in name, but its free market reforms and openness to travel, trade, and study abroad hardly conformed to Marxist, Leninist, or Maoist thought.

Unfortunately, the end of the Cold War did not usher in the new era of peace and prosperity for which many had hoped. On the contrary, the vacuum created when first Moscow and then Washington stopped treating every conflict as a proxy war between them increased the number of flashpoints around the world. Without the Soviet Union to oppose it, though, the United States could intervene in places it would not have gone previously. In August 1991 Iraqi dictator Saddam Hussein invaded neighboring Kuwait. With UN approval the United States led a coalition of 15 nations fielding 750,000 troops, 540,000 of them American, in Operation Desert Storm to oust him.[1] After a month of intense aerial bombardment beginning January 17, 1991, a ground offensive defeated the Iraqi Army in less than 100 hours of fighting, killing 8,000–10,000 at a cost of 300 coalition soldiers.[2] The Gulf War demonstrated the enormous advantages conveyed by technology on conventional forces. Stealth aircraft entered Iraqi airspace to attack at will with virtual impunity. Cruise missiles launched from far out at sea struck targets in Baghdad with pinpoint accuracy, and laser-guided bombs went through the doorways of Iraqi bunkers. While some American analysts proclaimed that Desert Storm had exorcised the ghost of Vietnam, that optimism faded as it became clear that civil conflict and asymmetric warfare would plague the post–Cold War world.

Technological Change

During the last quarter of the 20th century technological advances provided weapons with greater stealth and precision. The United States developed laser-guided munitions capable of striking a target with pinpoint

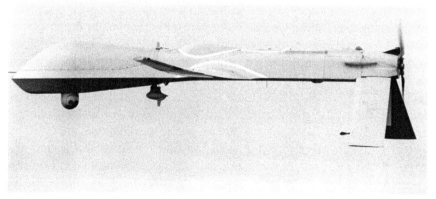

A Predator. *Source:* Department of Defense.

accuracy. It had first used laser-guided bombs in 1968 during the Vietnam War. By the time of the 1991 Gulf War the accuracy of such weapons had increased even further. The United States also developed cruise missiles capable of flying at constant speed, often at low altitude guided by terrain-following radar, making them difficult to detect and destroy. Remotely piloted vehicles (commonly called "drones"), in use since the Vietnam War, improved in range, accuracy, surveillance capability, and payload.

Military engineers have devoted considerable effort to developing stealth technology. Stealth planes are not designed to be invisible to the naked eye, but to fool radar. Radar operates by bouncing radio waves off objects. The object reflects the waves back at the radar set, creating a blip on its screen. The British employed radar effectively for the first time during the Battle of Britain in World War II. To create a stealth aircraft, engineers reconfigured its shape and coated its surface with special paint. These alterations cause radio waves to scatter rather than be reflected back, making the airplane "invisible." The United States began developing stealth technology in 1975 and first deployed stealth aircraft in operations against Panama in 1989. Since the 1990s the United States has employed two types of stealth aircraft: the F-117 fighter and the B-2 bomber. The Russians have designed similar stealth planes.[3]

Development of cheaper, more powerful computers along with the Internet has made

A two-ship formation of Lockheed F-117A Nighthawk Stealth fighter aircraft. *Source:* Department of Defense.

societies more dependent on them for communication and information storage as well as control of vital systems such as power grids. This dependence creates vulnerabilities that foreign states and nefarious groups and individuals can exploit. Attacks thus far have concentrated on stealing information and disrupting Internet services. At least one case, however, involved a cyber-attack doing physical damage to a secure facility. In 2009 the Stuxnet virus, allegedly produced by the United States, disrupted the operation of centrifuges at an Iranian nuclear plant by targeting the computers that controlled them. Although all major powers have developed cyber-warfare capability, both offensive and defensive, it is as yet unclear whether such activities belong primarily in the military proper or the intelligence services.

Yugoslavia, from Peacekeeping to Peace Enforcement

The end of the Cold War had two immediate effects on international security. The power vacuums it created around the world made local conflicts more likely, and the break in the Security Council deadlock allowed the United Nations to intervene more easily in some of these conflicts. The end of the Cold War also meant that the superpowers could participate in UN missions. The United Nations readily embraced its new role, and the United States showed a willingness to deploy forces in UN missions, although it would never allow American soldiers to serve under any but U.S. command.

This enthusiasm notwithstanding, the United Nations immediately encountered serious difficulties with conflicts in the post–Cold War world. Traditional peacekeeping had involved separating belligerents in a war between sovereign states or two sides in a civil war, provided a geographic line could be drawn between them, as was the case on the island of Cyprus. In the post–Cold War world, however, the conflicts requiring intervention occurred within states and often involved several groups of combatants who could not be easily separated into containable geographic areas. Furthermore, the United Nations faced a serious jurisdictional problem in such cases. Arguably it had no legal authority to intervene in civil conflicts, as its charter enshrined the sovereignty of member states. In June 1992 the new secretary-general, Boutros Boutros-Ghali, expanded the scope of the organization with "An Agenda for a Peace." "The foundation-stone of this [the UN's work] is and must remain the State," this document insisted. "Respect for its fundamental sovereignty and integrity are crucial to any common international progress." It then drew a radically new conclusion, insisting that "the time of absolute and exclusive sovereignty, however, has passed."[4] The secretary-general was arguing that the international community had the right to intervene in a civil conflict when a party or parties involved grossly violated human rights. This argument provided the justification for three major interventions during the 1990s.

Finding legal grounds for intervention was one thing, mounting a successful operation quite another. The UN Mission in the Congo (ONUC) provided the only precedent for such an operation, and that mission had gone badly. Traditional peacekeeping depended on the neutrality of the peacekeepers. As the blue helmets deployed to the Congo discovered, however, neutrality is virtually impossible to achieve in an intrastate conflict. Aid or security provided to one party would invariably be interpreted as hampering the cause of the others. In addition to compromising the principle of neutrality, ending civil conflicts also required larger troop deployments than traditional peacekeeping. Furthermore, in such conflicts peacekeepers would not be operating in the permissive environment that had characterized missions like UNEF I and II, since at least some of the belligerents would object to their presence. Most significantly, lightly armed forces operating under a highly restrictive self-defense mandate would prove wholly inadequate to deal with intrastate conflict involving heavily armed forces. However, these and other challenges only became clear as the new missions unfolded.

The first test for what some analysts in the early 1990s were calling the "new world order" came in the Balkans. Yugoslavia had been struggling to manage the ethnic differences among its component republics since the death of the country's founder, Josip Broz Tito, in 1980. Following months of mounting strife, Slovenia declared its independence from what it saw as an increasingly Serbian-dominated country on June 25, 1991. Macedonia declared independence on September 8, and Croatia followed suit on October 7. Bosnia-Herzegovina, the most multi-ethnic Yugoslav republic, seceded on March 3, 1992, after a referendum showed a majority in support of independence. Yugoslavia, consisting now of just Serbia and Montenegro, controlled most of the Yugoslav military and the bulk of its equipment. Following a 10-day struggle to prevent Slovenia from seceding, Serbian President Slobodan Milošević realized he could not hold the country together by force of arms. He opted instead to control as much Serbian-occupied territory as possible. This decision unleashed a bloody three-year civil war.

Serious fighting began in Croatia, which had .5 million ethnic Serbs among its 4.5 million people. Because the Serbs in Croatia lived in two ethnic regions, the Krajina bordering Bosnia-Herzegovina and Eastern

Slavonia along the Serbian border, conquering this territory proved relatively easy. Milosevic used local militias to launch offensives and then sent in the regular army, allegedly to restore order but in reality to consolidate Serb gains. Fighting raged from June through November, leaving thousands dead and many more homeless. Serb paramilitaries added a new term to the lexicon of war: "ethnic cleansing." Paramilitary forces made systematic use of rape and murder to terrorize people into fleeing territory so that it could be annexed. By the end of 1991 Serbian forces controlled all of the Krajina, which became a self-proclaimed republic, and most of Eastern Slavonia.

Growing international concern over the fighting in former Yugoslavia led the United Nations to get involved. A de facto cease-fire in effect in Croatia created the opportunity to deploy a peacekeeping mission. In his February 15, 1992, report to the Security Council, Boutros Boutros-Ghali recommended troops be deployed to create safe areas for civilians. On February 21 the Council approved establishing the United Nations Protection Force (UNPROFOR) with a mandate to "create the conditions of peace and security for a negotiation of the overall settlement of the Yugoslav crisis."[5] The resolution creating UNPROFOR failed to spell out exactly what this vague mandate meant. This ambiguity would plague the mission throughout its tenure, leading to serious mission creep and putting the lives of peacekeepers in danger.

Initially, the United Nations planned to deploy 10,000 lightly armed troops to secure the safe areas and supervise the cease-fire in Croatia.[6] Before it could even complete this deployment, however, the war had spread to neighboring Bosnia. Instead of redesigning the mission, the Security Council simply expanded it and extended its jurisdiction to cover the new conflict. This approach would prove highly problematic. In Croatia the United Nations had the approval of the two warring factions, Croatian regular forces and Serb paramilitaries (albeit operating with support from the Yugoslav armies), which had agreed to a cease-fire.

The Bosnian War involved three ethnic groups as well as factions within them. With a population of approximately 4.4 million, Bosnia-Herzegovina was the most ethnically diverse of the Yugoslav republics. Muslims formed the largest group (43.7 percent), followed by Serbs (31.4 percent) and Croats (17.3 percent).[7] To make matters worse, the ethnic groups did not live in large, concentrated areas. The patchwork quilt of the republic's ethnic communities virtually guaranteed that the civil war would be bloody and destructive. It also meant that UN peacekeepers would face an extraordinarily difficult task, since there would be no clear line of separation between the belligerents. At no time during its mission did

UNPROFOR ever have approval for its deployment from all parties to the conflict.

The newly proclaimed Bosnian Republika Serbska enjoyed an overwhelming military advantage, having inherited most of the equipment from Yugoslav Federal Army units, who conveniently left it behind when they withdrew after secession. The Army of the Republika Serbska had 330 tanks, 800 pieces of artillery, and 400 armored personnel carriers (APCs); the Bosnian Muslims, 40 tanks, a few artillery pieces, and 30 APCs; the Bosnian Croats, 75 tanks and 200 pieces of artillery.[8] An arms embargo prevented the Bosnian government (a federation of Muslims and Croats) from getting heavy weapons to offset the Serb advantage. It thus had to rely on UNPROFOR to protect it, a task for which the peacekeeping mission proved ill-equipped and ill-prepared.

Throughout the conflict the United Nations responded to the evolving crisis in an ad hoc manner, always one step behind events. During the second half of 1992 and throughout 1993, regular Serb forces and paramilitaries drove Muslims and Croats from large areas of Bosnia and besieged several cities. The United Nations declared these besieged enclaves "safe areas" and then struggled to protect and supply them. A new Security Council resolution empowered UN troops to defend humanitarian aid convoys traveling to the beleaguered cities.[9] The ability to enforce such a mandate depended on the resources of the local commander and his willingness to take resolute action. The Serbs often stopped and even looted aid shipments, but in some instances local commanders punched convoys through. The British used their Warrior armored cars to attack Serb positions, and in one celebrated instance a Swedish officer threatened to blast his way through with Leopard II tanks, which caused the Serbs to back down.[10] The Security Council also declared a no-fly zone over the enclaves.

Although they undoubtedly saved lives, these measures did not stop the fighting. UNPROFOR hovered between peacekeeping and enforcement and thus performed neither task well. Fighting intensified during the summer of 1993, when release of a partition plan signaled that the international community had given up on preserving the territorial integrity of Bosnia. An uneasy alliance between Bosnian Muslims and Bosnian Croats broke down, and the conflict became a three-way competition for land. With its preponderance of military might, Republika Serbska did the most damage, caused the greatest loss of life, and seized the most territory. UNPROFOR continued to protect and supply the enclaves as best it could, but it could not stop the fighting. NATO airpower linked to the UN mission, however, did have an effect. Air strikes were launched against

Serbska forces besieging the Bihać pocket in northwest Bosnia. As winter set in a de facto cease-fire took hold, but no one expected it to last beyond the spring thaw.

In 1995 the Bosnian War moved toward a decisive resolution, with an end to hostilities, but not due to the presence of UN peacekeepers. Croatia had rearmed itself and created an effective modern army capable of successfully engaging Serbian forces. On May 1, 1995, the new Croat army recaptured Western Slavonia in 30 hours of fighting. In late May Bosnian Serb forces shelled Sarajevo, and the new UNPROFOR commander, British General Rupert Smith, issued an ultimatum on May 24. If the Serbs did not stop the shelling, he would commence NATO air strikes against them. The Serbs called his bluff, and the air strikes began, escalating to attacks on ammunition dumps at the Bosnian Serb capital of Pale. In retaliation for the attacks, Bosnian Serb General Radko Mladić took 400 peacekeepers hostage, chaining some to bridges as human shields. Once again, UNPROFOR backed down and stopped the air strikes.

Following the hostage incident, events in Bosnia moved rapidly to a dénouement. The Security Council approved deployment of a 12,500-man rapid reaction force to Mount Igman above Sarajevo. Comprised of British paratroopers, French Foreign Legionnaires, and Dutch Royal Marines and equipped with heavy artillery and mortar-locating radar, this force had the means to act decisively, but it still operated under a limited, peacekeeping mandate. Perhaps emboldened by lack of political will on the part of the United Nations and the NATO allies, the Bosnian Serb army and Serb paramilitaries perpetrated the worst massacre in Europe since World War II. In early July they brushed aside the Dutch battalion protecting the safe area in Srebrenica and captured the city. They then rounded up and executed 7,000–8,000 unarmed Muslim men and boys.[11] Serbian forces also raped Bosnian Muslim women. These genocidal acts strengthened the resolve of the United Nations. UNPROFOR sent Mladić an ultimatum: further attacks on any of the safe areas would result in NATO air strikes. At the same time, UNPROFOR pulled its scattered forces into protected bases to prevent them being taken hostage.

Before international resolve could be tested in Bosnia, however, the situation in Croatia changed dramatically. Buoyed by success in Western Slavonia, Croatian President Franjo Tudman launched his army against the occupied Krajina on August 6. Croat forces recaptured all the territory lost in 1991. Neither the Bosnian Serb forces nor the Yugoslav army moved to help the self-proclaimed Republic of Krajina. Unfortunately, the Croats perpetrated a new round of ethnic cleansing against Krajina Serbs, which sent them streaming toward Serbia proper. Most had probably done nothing against their Croat neighbors. Operation Storm, as the offensive was dubbed, also helped lift the siege of the Bihać pocket, in northwest Bosnia.

Matters in Bosnia came to a head on August 28, 1995, when a mortar shell landed in the Sarajevo marketplace, killing 37 people. UNPROFOR claimed it had been fired from Bosnian Serb positions, but some evidence suggests a bomb had been placed in a fruit stand as a staged pretext.[12] After Srebrenica, however, few cared to give the Serbs the benefit of the doubt. NATO aircraft began flying sorties in the early morning of August 30, and the guns of the rapid reaction force destroyed Serb artillery positions around Sarajevo, lifting a three-year siege. Bosnian Federation forces took advantage of the situation to attack out of the Bihać pocket. A month of sustained bombing forced Republica Serbska to accept an armistice on UNPROFOR's terms on October 6. The Dayton Peace Accords, signed on December 14, 1995, confirmed partition of Bosnia-Herzegovina into a Muslim-Croat Federation and a Serb Republic.

The wars of Yugoslav succession, as they are now called, represent a low point in the history of UN peacekeeping and provide a poignant example of how much and yet how little had changed since the end of the Cold War. UNPROFOR reiterated the lessons of ONUC that a lightly armed force operating under a Chapter 6 peacekeeping mandate cannot stop a civil war. The mission also revealed that a clear resolve to use force early on might have done so. Throughout the conflict, whenever UN forces showed at the tactical level a firm determination to use force, the aggressor backed down. The same determination demonstrated earlier at the strategic level might have saved a lot of lives. The Bosnian War alone killed an estimated 167,426.[13] Estimates of the number of women and men who suffered sexual assault run as high as 60,000, but given the reluctance of victims to report such incidents, it is impossible to arrive at a precise number.[14] A huge percentage of houses was destroyed or severely damaged, and thousands of people fled their homes. In its violence, the war conformed to the pattern of 20th-century ethnic conflicts.

Somalia

As the Bosnian War was unfolding, the United States and the United Nations became embroiled in another intrastate conflict. In January 1991 the east African country of Somalia disintegrated into civil war after the ouster of President Mohammed Siyadd Barre. The collapse of government and a severe drought brought famine to the war-torn land. From November 1991 to January 1992, 300,000 died and another 4.5 million, more than half the country's population, faced severe malnutrition.[15] Humanitarian organizations rushed in to deal with the crisis, only to discover that aide cannot be distributed in an atmosphere of anarchy. To safeguard food deliveries, the United Nations approved the UN Mission in Somalia (UNISOM) with an initial strength of 500.[16] These lightly armed troops could not stand up to Somali warlord Mohammed Farrah Aidid, who controlled much of the capital, Mogadishu. Efforts to reinforce the mission failed as Aidid prevented deployment of the UN troops.

The Somali famine might have played out to its tragic conclusion had it not drawn the attention of President George H. W. Bush. Having lost the November 1992 election to Bill Clinton, Bush had the luxury of acting purely on principle, which seemed to be his sole motive in intervening in Somalia in 1993. Although Secretary-General Boutros-Ghali would have preferred a robust enforcement operation under UN command, he realized that neither the support nor the troops would be forthcoming. The Security Council approved creation of a Unified Task Force (UNITAF) to "use all necessary means to establish as soon as possible a secure environment for humanitarian relief operations in Somalia."[17] The Council had provided an open-ended mandate but with clear Chapter 7 enforcement authority. The U.S. Marines provided the bulk of the 28,000 U.S. troops in the 38,000 personnel mission. Operation Restore Hope, the American name for the mission, interpreted its mandate narrowly, protecting delivery of aid but leaving the warlords and local militias alone provided they did not interfere with food convoys or bother U.S. troops. Brisk firefights early in the mission demonstrated UNITAF's determination to complete its mission with force if necessary. In addition to robust rules of engagement and armament suitable to the task, UNITAF benefited from the Civil-Military Operations Center it created to keep in regular contact with the Somali warlords.[18] By the spring of 1993, the intervention had guaranteed delivery of sufficient aid to end the famine.

Had the United States disengaged from Somalia following the end of the UNITAF mandate in May 1993, the mission would have been deemed a great success. Unfortunately, the new administration of William J. Clinton chose to leave a much smaller contingent to support the follow-on mission created by the United Nations to stabilize Somalia after the parties reached a cease-fire in January. On March 26, 1993, the Security Council approved expanding UNSOM (which would henceforward be designated UNSOM II) with a Chapter 7 enforcement mandate.[19] The resolution gave UNSOM II an extensive list of tasks, including disarming the warring factions and apprehending those who violated international humanitarian law. Although given a much broader mandate, the UN mission would have 10,000 fewer troops than UNITAF and occupy the whole of Somalia instead of the 40 percent the U.S.-led force had controlled. UNSOM II suffered a further weakness. While UNITAF had been built around a core of 28,000 well-trained and -equipped American troops, the largest national contingent of UNOSOM II's 20,000 was a Pakistani contingent of 4,973.[20]

The UNOSOM II mandate threatened to embroil the mission in precisely the sort of open-ended commitment Operation Restore Hope had vowed to avoid. Instead of disengaging from such a dangerous commitment, the Clinton administration kept a small force of 3,000 troops in country along with a 1,150-man rapid reaction force aboard ships offshore. The American troops did not come directly under UN command, but they were yoked to the mission via Admiral (ret.) Jonathan Howe, who served as special representative of the UN secretary-general, and U.S. Major General Thomas Montgomery, the deputy force commander. A mission with too few troops of very uneven quality trying to implement a very ambitious mandate, with a small American contingent promising to intervene in support as needed, provided a formula for disaster.

The crisis did not take long to materialize. Trying to disarm the belligerents got UNISOM II into trouble. On June 4, 1993, a contingent of Pakistani soldiers insisted on inspecting one of Aidid's weapons depots near the radio station in Mogadishu, which the warlord also controlled. The inspection produced a violent backlash the next day. In a series of ambushes, Aidid's forces killed 27 Pakistani soldiers and wounded 54 others as well as 3 U.S. members of the rapid reaction force, which had been sent to rescue them.[21] UNSOM II and its American supporters moved to seize the radio station with an air and ground assault. A mission to relieve famine and police a cease-fire in an impartial manner thus went to war with the main Somali faction. UNSOM II lacked the troops and resources for such an aggressive move. Violent confrontations occurred throughout the summer, including an attack that killed 4 Americans on August 8. Meanwhile an investigation into the June attack on the Pakistanis concluded that Aidid had violated international law. Boutros-Ghali determined he should be arrested, and the Clinton administration agreed to take the leading role in apprehending him.

The operation that resulted in the disastrous October 3 incident featured in the book and movie *Blackhawk Down* was profoundly flawed from the outset. The American contingent in Somalia had been reduced to 1,120, and it had no tanks or armored personnel carriers. Other UNSOM II contingents had armored vehicles, but given the lack of communications between the Americans and the UN force, calling upon these assets in an emergency would prove problematic. Nonetheless, Washington deployed a combined unit of U.S. Army Rangers and members of Delta Force, the elite interservice Special Operations Force. The raid on Aidid's headquarters proceeded without a hitch, although the warlord himself was not there. On the way back, however, the Somalis shot down a Blackhawk helicopter. Eighteen Americans and 300 Somalis were killed in the ensuing rescue mission. Lack of armored vehicles necessary to reach the trapped American unit hampered the rescue. UNSOM II had such vehicles, but failure of the United States to alert the mission about the planned raid, combined with command and control problems, delayed their arrival. Americans watched in horror television footage of the charred body of the helicopter pilot being dragged through the streets of Mogadishu.[22] The disaster led the United States to withdraw entirely from Somalia by the end of 1993. UNSOM II continued to operate until March 1995, albeit under a much restricted mandate with no ability to facilitate an end to the conflict.

The Somali debacle underscored the lessons of the former Yugoslavia. UNITAF succeeded because it consisted of a large body of heavily armed troops, most from the United States, operating under robust rules of engagement to accomplish a limited mission. It safeguarded deliveries of humanitarian aid and pacified the areas it occupied. American forces refused to be drawn into the civil war by trying to disarm any of the factions. UNISOM II, on the other hand, tried to implement a much broader mandate with fewer troops. Instead of steering clear of such a problematic deployment, the United States kept a limited presence, too small to shape the course of the mission, but large enough to get into trouble. UN missions suffer a serious, sometimes fatal weakness due to their polyglot nature. Small detachments from several nations do not add up to a cohesive fighting force. When the United States or any nation deploys, especially for an enforcement operation, it must have under its own control all the assets it will need to carry out a mission, without having to borrow them. Finally, Somalia underscored the lesson taught by Bosnia and destined to be reiterated in Afghanistan and Iraq. Short-term interventions can alleviate a crisis like famine, but nation building takes a long time.

Chechen War

The Russian Federation, heir to what remained of the Soviet Union, encountered its own problems in the aftermath of the Cold War. In 1991 the oil-rich Soviet Republic of Chechnya in the Caucasus declared its independence. Three years later Russian forces invaded to force it back into the Russian Federation. On paper at least Russian forces enjoyed an overwhelming advantage in numbers and firepower, but they encountered the same problem the Americans had faced in Vietnam and they themselves had confronted in Afghanistan. Heavy armored units organized for conventional war are not effective in fighting mobile guerrillas who know the land and enjoy the support of the people. The collapse of the Soviet Union exacerbated Russian problems. High-quality Special Forces did exist, but regular units comprised of poorly trained conscripts lacked supplies, funding, and experienced NCOs.

The battle for the Chechen capital Grozny revealed the weakness of Russian forces and deficiencies in their approach to intrastate conflict. During World War II the Red Army had been very proficient at urban warfare, but it had failed to pass on what it had learned to new generations of Soviet soldiers. Poor intelligence led Russian commanders to underestimate the strength and effectiveness of rebel forces. They believed that a show of force would be sufficient to induce the city to surrender. The 6,000 Russian troops who attacked Grozny on New Year's Eve 1995 faced a highly organized, well-equipped rebel force, many of whom had served in the Red Army. Divided into small mobile units equipped with rocket-propelled grenades, shaped charges, and light automatic weapons, the rebels sprang carefully laid ambushes for Russian tank columns, trapping them in narrow streets by disabling the lead and trailing vehicles. By firing from hospitals, schools, and other such locations, the Chechens baited the Russians into killing civilians in order to win international support for their cause.[23]

Russian forces gradually adjusted, recalling past lessons of urban warfare and learning from recent experience. They secured Grozny by early March. Taking the capital did not, however, end the conflict as Moscow had hoped. The Chechen rebels continued to mount successful attacks. In June they attacked the Russian town of Stavropol, seizing the hospital and taking hostages. After failed attempts to recapture the building, the Russians negotiated for release of the hostages, allowing the insurgents to flee. The rebels attacked Gudermes, the second largest city in Chechnya, in December, fought the Russians to a stalemate, and negotiated safe withdrawal of the insurgents. They conducted a raid on Grozny in March and launched a full-scale offensive against the city with 6,000 fighters on August 6.[24] By the time negotiators reached a settlement of the First Chechen War on August 22, rebels controlled most of the city.

Russia had suffered a humiliating defeat by insurgents in a tiny former Soviet republic. Under such circumstances both sides considered the agreement for withdrawal of Russian troops nothing but a truce, especially since it called for the final status of Chechnya to be determined by 2001. During the three years between the first and second Chechen Wars both sides prepared for a renewal of hostilities. Foreign fighters, many of them Islamists, entered Chechnya to train and fight alongside the Chechens. Their presence would, after 9/11, make it possible for the Kremlin to claim that the separatist conflict was part of the larger Global War on Terror (GWOT). For its part, the Russian military analyzed its performance during the First Chechen War and identified three problems: failure to seal off Grozny before entering it, poor coordination among units and between air and ground forces, and lack of an effective information campaign.[25] The military tried to address these issues. It also prepared units for counterinsurgency and urban warfare. In 1998 Russian forces carried out in the north Caucasus a large-scale training operation based on the scenario in which insurgent groups conducted widespread, simultaneous attacks coupled with individual acts of terror.[26]

The conflict reignited in 1999, following a number of provocative incidents attributed to Chechens. Criminal groups kidnapped Russian soldiers and officials, demanding high ransoms. In August 1999 a Chechen commander launched several raids into the neighboring Russian Federation Republic of Dagestan. In September terrorist attacks killed nearly 300 people in three separate attacks on Moscow apartment buildings. Investigative journalists have claimed that the FSB (state security service) staged the bombings to provide a pretext for war and to enhance the reputation of Vladimir Putin.[27] Nonetheless, the Russian public supported stronger military action against the Chechens. This time, however, the Russians proceeded methodically. They secured villages in Dagestan and Chechnya, closing in on the capital, which they carefully mapped and methodically reduced from December 1999 to February 2000. Russian forces used small unit tactics and did a better job of coordinating infantry, armor, artillery, and air elements. It still took heavy fighting and many casualties to seize the capital against stiff, well-coordinated resistance, but Russian forces performed much better than they had in 1999. They also made effective use of pro-Kremlin Chechen militias, who proved more effective at sweeping rebel-held areas than did their Russian counterparts.[28] After the fall of Gozny, Russian forces reduced other rebel-held villages. By 2002 major hostilities ceased. A low-level counterterrorism campaign would continue until 2009, when the war formally ended.

The Chechen Wars were a brutal affair. Estimates of the number of Chechen war-related deaths range from 35,000 to 50,000 (5 percent of the country's prewar population).[29] The Russians lost 5,500 troops from 1999 to 2008[30] as well as at least 5,000 in the First Chechen War.[31] The military made some effort to reduce noncombatant casualties, including warning civilians to leave Grozny prior to attacking the city and creating safe-passage corridors through which they could travel. They also set up soup kitchens in the city after the fighting ended.[32] Despite these token efforts, credible evidence of widespread atrocities surfaced despite Moscow's censorship. Testimony by a member of Human Rights Watch included allegations of summary executions and the use of rape and torture.[33] After 9/11, however, U.S. criticism of Russian operations in Chechnya declined markedly as Washington wooed the Kremlin to support the GWOT. The presence of foreign mujahedeen in Chechnya fighting alongside the insurgents made this request easier to support.

Kosovo

As Russia prepared to reenter Chechnya, the United States found itself embroiled once again in a Balkan crisis. The Kosovo conflict was the final episode in the wars of Yugoslav succession. The crisis that had led to that series of wars actually began in Kosovo in 1989, when Serbian President Slobodan Milsoević revoked the autonomy of the province, sending a ripple of fear through the Yugoslav republics. Albanians, who comprised 83 percent of the province's population of 2.1 million, suffered systematic discrimination by ethnic Serbs in all areas of social and economic life.[34] Preoccupied with events in Croatia and Bosnia, the international community could do little to address the situation in Kosovo, where little actual violence was occurring.

With the might of the Yugoslav government ranged against them and the rest of the world indifferent to their plight, the Kosovars could do little to resist. That situation changed dramatically in 1997 when the government of neighboring Albania collapsed, losing control of some of its arsenals. Weapons poured over the border into the hands of a small resistance group known as the Kosovo Liberation Army (KLA). Facing a weakened and isolated Yugoslavia, which now consisted of just Serbia and Montenegro, the KLA escalated to armed conflict. The insurgents knew that they could not defeat the Yugoslav army, which supported the federal police and paramilitary groups. They could, however, provoke Serbian forces into overreacting, which might in turn lead to international intervention as it had in Bosnia.

Milosević took the bait. Beginning in January 1998 Serbian forces began a sweep through Kosovo's central Drenica region. The operation, which lasted until March, killed 136 people, including 23 women and 11 children.[35] These and other operations, which continued into 1999, sparked an exodus of 250,000 Kosovars from the province, nearly a quarter of its entire population.[36] With memories of ethnic cleansing perpetrated by Serbs in Bosnia still fresh, the NATO allies led by the United States determined to intervene in Kosovo. The problem they faced, however, was how to mount an effective intervention. A proposal for a UN peacekeeping operation would almost certainly face a veto by Serbia's supporter, Russia. The NATO allies themselves did not wish to launch a ground invasion of Kosovo. Given this reluctance, air attacks offered the best alternative.

The NATO air campaign began on March 23, 1999, and lasted 78 days. It faced difficulties from the outset and came very close to failing. Knowing that his allies had refused to sanction a ground war, President Clinton announced in an address to the American people that no such action would take place. Assured that it would not face invasion, the Serbian military could disperse its tanks and other vehicles, making them harder to destroy. Because the United States did not wish to lose aircraft, it conducted less-accurate, high-altitude bombing. Milosević calculated that under such circumstances he could simply hold out until NATO's political resolve weakened. He failed to consider, however, that the mission objective might change from forcing Serbian withdrawal from Kosovo to preserving the credibility of the NATO alliance.[37]

The air campaign ultimately succeeded, but it nearly resulted in a major power confrontation when Russian troops temporarily occupied Pristina airport. Once the Yugoslav army withdrew, a follow-on mission had to secure the province and facilitate rebuilding it. Rather than repeat the fiasco of UNPROFOR, the NATO allies deployed nearly 50,000 troops as part of Kosovo Force (KFOR), while the United Nations approved its own UN Mission in Kosovo (UNMIK). Separating the humanitarian effort from the NATO mission created liaison problems but guaranteed that the military force would have the necessary resources and a robust mandate for enforcing the peace settlement without constantly reporting to the Security Council.

The Kosovo crisis underscored the lessons of Croatia, Bosnia, and Somalia. Achieving international consensus for intervention in a civil conflict is very difficult. Mounting such an intervention is even harder. Stopping the conflict does not always end the intervention. KFOR, albeit much reduced in size, still operates in Kosovo. Getting into an intrastate conflict is much easier than getting out of one.

The Global War on Terror

As the new millennium dawned, the instability of the immediate postwar world appeared to be over. The wars of Yugoslav succession had ended with independence for most of its member states. NATO had expanded into Eastern Europe to stabilize the region after the collapse of Communism. An embargo and no-fly zones over the north and south of Iraq kept Saddam Hussein in check, and the rest of the Middle East remained relatively quiet. Newly elected President George W. Bush had campaigned on a promise not to commit American forces to "nation building" missions like those in Bosnia and Somalia. Less than a year after he took office, however, the United States suffered the worst attack on its homeland since the War of 1812. The country and its allies found themselves embroiled in a new, entirely different type of warfare for which their conventional armed forces were ill-suited.

During the decade of the 1990s few Americans, however, had any idea that a new threat was developing in Afghanistan. In the aftermath of the Soviet defeat an Islamist organization committed to violent global jihad had emerged. Al-Qaeda ("the base") began as an agency to facilitate recruitment of Arab mujahedeen (foreign fighters) to oppose the Soviet invaders. Under the leadership of Osama bin Laden it continued as a movement to aid Muslims under attack anywhere in the world. Bin Laden saw secular or "apostate" regimes in Muslim countries as the primary enemy. During the 1991 Gulf War he refocused his rage on his native Saudi Arabia and the United States. The Saudi monarchy had allowed the infidel Americans onto the sacred soil of the Prophet Mohammed's land. The United States also backed Israel and President Hosni Mubarak in Egypt, two other enemies of traditional Islam as bin Laden saw it. The Americans were thus the "far" enemy who had to be attacked so that al-Qaeda could defeat its "near" enemies in the Muslim world.

The al-Qaeda threat became manifest for the first time on August 7, 1998, when al-Qaeda detonated car bombs outside the U.S. embassies in Darussalam, Tanzania, and Nairobi, Kenya. The United States conducted a limited and ineffectual response, attacking a pharmaceutical plant in Sudan, where bin Laden had lived, and al-Qaeda training camps in Afghanistan. In October 2000 al-Qaeda struck again. Two small boats filled with explosives attacked the destroyer USS *Cole* in Aden harbor, Yemen. Although the terrorist group claimed responsibility, neither the outgoing President Bill Clinton nor his successor, George W. Bush, took military action against al-Qaeda. This perceived weakness may have emboldened the terrorist organization to carry out its most daring and successful attack to date, the September 11, 2001, attacks on the Twin Towers of the World Trade Center in New York City and the Pentagon in Washington, DC, which together claimed the lives of nearly 3,000 Americans.

In a televised address to both houses of Congress on September 20, 2001, President Bush declared what came to be called the "Global War on Terror (GWOT)." "Our war on terror begins with al Qaeda," he told the

American people, "but it does not end there. It will not end until every terrorist group of global reach has been found, stopped and defeated."[38] The president may merely have been preparing the nation for a protracted struggle and the sacrifices it would entail, but the idea of a "war on terror" took on a life of its own. Many analysts disliked the term GWOT for two reasons. First, it created the impression that terrorism could be eradicated, and second, it put the military in the forefront of operations against al-Qaeda and its affiliates. GWOT has since given way to "long struggle," a recognition that fighting terrorism requires a concerted, combined effort by military, law enforcement, and the intelligence community.

Afghanistan

In his address to the nation following 9/11 President Bush announced that he had demanded that the Taliban, the party ruling Afghanistan, turn over bin Laden to the United States and allow the U.S. military full access to al-Qaeda training camps.[39] The demand was in fact an ultimatum. If the Taliban did not comply, the United States would take military action. Mullah Mohammed Omar, the Taliban leader, refused to give up bin Laden, so the Pentagon prepared to invade Afghanistan. The mountainous, landlocked country in Central Asia presented a unique set of challenges, especially since the United States had no close allies in the region. Once it overcame these challenges, however, the U.S. military would discover what previous invaders had learned: conquering the country is a lot easier than occupying and controlling it.

The Pentagon devised a bold, innovative strategy. It exploited Afghanistan's ethnic civil war, backing the Northern Alliance of Tajiks, Uzbeks, and Hazaras against the Pashtun Taliban regime. The army deployed 300 Special Forces grouped in eight 12-man "A" teams, four company-level "B" teams, and three battalion-strength "C" teams to advise and fight alongside 10,000 Northern Alliance troops.[40] With the soldiers came a massive influx of military and humanitarian aid and the awesome firepower of the U.S. Air Force and Navy. Special Forces forward air controllers with satellite-uplinked laptops directed precision tactical air strikes in support of Northern Alliance operations while American cruise missiles and long-range bombers struck strategic targets in Kabul and other areas. Approximately 5,000 U.S. Army troops, including Rangers, and Marines operating from ships at sea conducted airborne assaults to seize airbases and other installations and to support the Northern Alliance as necessary.[41] Operation Enduring Freedom, which began on October 7, 2001, achieved rapid results. Northern Alliance forces entered Kabul on November 14 and

Kandahar on December 6. By the end of the year, the Taliban controlled only enclaves in the southeast and along the Pakistan border. The campaign demonstrated how a small-footprint American land force with air assets supporting a determined local group could defeat a numerically superior enemy.

Impressive though the Afghan invasion certainly was, it did not lead to the creation of a functioning democratic state capable of defending itself and preventing terrorists using its territory as a staging area. Eager to move on to what it considered the more important business of invading Iraq, the Bush administration handed over responsibility for Afghanistan to the NATO-led, UN-approved International Security Assistance Force (ISAF), formed after 9/11 under Article 5 of the organization's founding treaty, which declared an attack upon one to be an attack upon all. The American contingent in ISAF focused on pursuing the leadership of al-Qaeda and the Taliban, a counterterrorism strategy, instead of conducting a COIN campaign to gain and consolidate control of the country. Comprised of contingents from over 30 NATO and non-NATO nations with differing capabilities and mandates, ISAF could not easily carry out such a mission. As a result, the allies missed a window of opportunity from 2002 to 2005 during which they might have consolidated control of the country. Instead the Taliban had a chance to regroup, and when the United States refocused its attention on the country after the invasion of Iraq, it faced an intransigent insurgency. Afghanistan remains to this day a fragile state propped up by U.S. aid and dependent on American military support.

The Iraq War

Desire to deal once and for all with the Iraqi dictator Saddam Hussein prompted the United States to prematurely shift its focus from Afghanistan to Iraq. President Bush and several of his advisers considered the 1991 Gulf War a truncated victory because it had left the dictator in power and Iraq a continuing threat to its neighbors. The 9/11 attacks heightened that anxiety, especially when the administration made the case that Saddam might have been working toward getting weapons of mass destruction, claims that have since been debunked. Much as it wished to oust Saddam Hussein, though, the Bush administration had no desire to engage in a protracted nation-building mission in Iraq. Secretary of Defense Donald Rumsfeld in particular wished to transform the U.S. military, replacing outdated equipment with new technologically advanced weapons systems. A long-term, labor-intensive mission in Iraq would create personnel costs, diverting funds from transformation. These concerns led the Pentagon to devise a short-term, low-cost strategy. Making use of air power and a relatively small invasion force, the United States planned to liberate the country, hand control over to a democratic regime, and withdraw as soon as possible. The Pentagon based this strategy on overly optimistic assumptions and a failure to consider that, deprived of its dictator, the fragile state of Iraq might degenerate into civil war and insurgency.

"Cobra II," the final version of the invasion plan, adopted an approach that would be dubbed "shock and awe." Instead of a long preparatory aerial bombardment, the United States and its principal ally, Great Britain, would engage in a short, intense air campaign followed by a blitzkrieg drive by 115,000 U.S. mechanized forces from Kuwait up the Tigris-Euphrates valley to Baghdad and a simultaneous advance by 26,000 British troops northeast to take the southern Iraqi city of Basra. Meanwhile the 4th U.S. Infantry Division (18,000–20,000 troops) would invade northern Iraq from Turkey, while a Joint Special Operations Task Force based in Jordan would support the invasion with attacks deep inside Iraq.[42] Because of its aversion to nation building, the Rumsfeld Pentagon gave short shrift to Phase IV (postconflict stability operations) of the plan. Rumsfeld envoy Lawrence Di Rita told one colonel working on a paper addressing this part of the plan to "forget it" because the United States would win the war and be out of Iraq in 120 days.[43]

The invasion went off largely according to plan, although Turkey withdrew permission for the 4th Infantry Division to use its territory. The air campaign began on March 19, 2003, just two days before the ground invasion. It included 1,500–2,000 sorties per day and deployed 1,500 sea- and air-launched cruise missiles as well as bombs and rockets to take out command and control, air defense, and artillery installations. As the ground attack got under way on March 21, tactical air strikes made up the bulk of the sorties. Air action became so intense during the darkest hours of March 21–22 that the military dubbed the period "the night of shock and awe."[44] The Iraqis stood no chance against the Anglo-American assault, which brushed them aside. Many Iraqi soldiers surrendered without fighting. The British took Basra on April 7, and the United States had secured most of Baghdad by April 9, while elements of the 101st Airborne, U.S. Special Forces, and Kurdish Peshmerga captured Kirkuk on April 11. On April 14 the Pentagon declared major ground operations over. The United States and its allies had conquered Iraq in just over three weeks of fighting for the loss of 138 Americans killed and 542 wounded.[45]

Impressive though the conventional operation certainly was, its aftermath did not go according to plan. Contrary to expectations, Iraqi government officials failed to remain at their posts to maintain order and provide vital services. With the fall of Saddam Hussein, central authority collapsed, and with it went law and order. Widespread looting rocked the capital and other major cities, destroying much of the country's already fragile infrastructure. Neither equipped nor trained to handle such lawlessness, U.S. soldiers and Marines watched helplessly as looters ransacked government buildings. Throughout the summer and fall the occupation forces faced growing unrest from Shi'a militias and disgruntled former Ba'athist army officers. Nonetheless, the Coalition Provisional Authority (CPA) set up in June proceeded with plans for elections, a new constitution, and an orderly transfer of power. The CPA unwisely dismissed without compensation Ba'ath Party members above a certain rank, depriving the country of badly needed administrators, military officers, and civil servants. These disgruntled former party members combined with other Iraqis unhappy with the invasion to attack coalition forces. By the spring of 2004 the United States and its allies faced a full-blown Sunni insurgency supported by foreign fighters connected to the al-Qaeda affiliate, "al-Qaeda in the Land of the two Rivers," commonly known as al-Qaeda in Iraq, as well as a Shi'a uprising in Baghdad and other cities.

The U.S. Army was ill-suited for COIN. Most of its equipment had been designed in the late 1970s for use on the Central European battlefront. Its senior officers had either experienced Vietnam or come of age in its shadow and thus loathed unconventional war as something to be at best avoided or at worse delegated to Special Forces. Once they occupied Iraq, the human environment neutralized many of the advantages of technology and firepower their equipment gave them. Separating insurgents from the general population, which tolerated or even supported them, would be a slow, painstaking task, which they would have to learn how to perform through trial and error and study of past campaigns. The result of that effort was a new COIN manual, *FM 3-24: Counterinsurgency*. Based in large part on wisdom gained in Vietnam and other Cold War conflicts as well as two bitter years of experience in Iraq, the manual advocated a comprehensive, unified approach in which the United States partnered with the host nation to regain control of the threatened country area by area over a long period. It contained sound theory as well as practical advice on all aspects of COIN. "Long-term success in COIN depends on the people taking charge of their own affairs and consenting to the government's rule," the manual declared. "Achieving this condition requires the government to eliminate as many causes of the insurgency as feasible."[46] Military operations against insurgent guerrillas required small unit tactics and a high degree of decentralization, what it called "empowering the lowest level," and the application of "appropriate" levels of force.[47]

Doctrine alone does not win wars, conventional or unconventional, but it can help governments create an effective strategy for doing so. In Iraq that strategy was the "Anbar Awakening," a local initiative by sheiks, the U.S. military, and the Iraqi Army and police in Anbar Province starting in the fall of 2006. Fed up with the tyranny of al-Qaeda in Iraq, the sheiks agreed to work with the Americans, provided intelligence on the insurgents, and encouraged members of their tribes to join the police. The United States provided equipment and pay for the police and funds for urban renewal.[48] Working together, the Americans and Iraqis cleared the cities and countryside of al-Qaeda fighters. The Awakening, in combination with the "surge" of approximately 20,000 additional U.S. combat troops to Iraq, a truce with Shi'a leader Muqtada al-Sadr, and monthly remittances to Sunni sheiks, caused violence in Iraq to decline dramatically from 2007 through the end of the U.S. mission in December 2011. A new constitution, fair elections, and local autonomy for the Kurds of the north, along with the U.S.-trained and -equipped Iraqi Army and police force gave Iraq a fighting chance for stability. Mismanagement, corruption, and the decision to favor the Shi'a by the government of Nuri al-Maliki squandered this opportunity and allowed for the rise of the Islamic State in Syria and Iraq (ISIS).

Libya

The experience of the Balkans and Somalia, coupled with the Afghanistan and Iraq wars, made the administration of President Barack Obama and the NATO allies leery of becoming embroiled in civil conflicts. Like his predecessors, however, Obama soon discovered that events often overtake intentions. In December 2010 a democratic movement known as the Arab Spring exploded across North Africa and the Middle East. In February an uprising in Benghazi, Libya, pitched the country into a civil war to topple Muammar Gadhafi. The longtime dictator responded with a savagery that led the UN Security Council to condemn his "gross and systematic violation of human rights, including repression of peaceful demonstrators."[49]

When economic sanctions failed to compel Gadhafi to halt the aggression, the United Nations imposed a no-fly zone over Libya. As had happened so often in the past, the Security Council worded the resolution ambiguously. It authorized "member states that have notified the Secretary-General . . . to take all necessary measures . . . to protect civilians." The mandate also precluded "a foreign occupation force of any form on any part of Libyan territory."[50] The Russians and the Chinese understood the mandate as limited to enforcing a no-fly zone, but the United States, France, the United Kingdom, and Italy interpreted it broadly. Their 4,500 sorties targeted Gadhafi's ground forces, providing air cover for the rebels who eventually overthrew him.

Once again, NATO air action had determined the outcome of a civil war. This time, however, no follow-on mission would ensure stability in Libya. The country is now a fragile state whose eastern area provides a haven for Islamic State terrorists. As the experience of Iraq had already shown, overthrowing a dictator does not automatically lead to democracy. Chinese and Russian anger over what they considered a manipulation of the no-fly zone mandate has made them very reluctant to support Security Council resolutions endorsing intervention in civil conflicts. Whether the Libya mission has made things in the country and the region better or worse remains to be seen.

The Face of Battle and the Experience of War

For most of the wars covered by this study it has been possible to identify a single battle or campaign that in some way typifies warfare during the conflict as a whole. The post–World War II era, however, has been remarkable for the absence of decisive engagements. In that regard, warfare has resembled the limited affairs of the 18th century. In other respects, though, it has differed dramatically from fighting during that period or any other. Nonstate actors (insurgents, extremist groups, ethnic separatists, and even criminal organizations) using guerrilla tactics and terrorism have played an unprecedented role in organized violence around the world. Much of that violence has come in the form of asymmetrical conflicts in which the political stakes of one party were significantly greater than those of the other. Vietnam was a total war for the Vietnamese but a limited one for the United States. The political will of the North Vietnamese and Viet Cong exceeded that of the United States, which gave them the ability to outlast Washington.

The number, type, and diversity of combatants make it very difficult to generalize about their attitudes toward war and their reasons for fighting. Conscription has disappeared from most advanced armies. The high-tech nature of modern warfare requires unprecedented levels of education and training and thus diminishes the effectiveness of short-term conscripts. All-volunteer forces have attracted soldiers who find the work rewarding and see the military as an opportunity for education and training. Patriotism also motivates many who serve, but to what degree it matters compared to careerism cannot easily be determined. The virulent ideology of ethnocentrism has motivated combatants in civil conflicts, which explains why those conflicts have been so deadly and the violence in them so indiscriminate. Religious extremists are the most fanatical in their willingness to kill in the name of their cause. In virtually all types of post–World War II armed conflict, camaraderie and a sense of duty have motivated men and women to carry on, even when they no longer believed in the cause for which they were fighting, just as those values have inspired soldiers for centuries.

While individual beliefs and feelings show some striking similarity with those of the past, social attitudes toward war have progressed considerably, at least in the Western world. Greater efforts have been made both to avoid war and to limit its destructiveness. The UN Charter, the *Universal Declaration on Human Rights*, and a host of conventions and accords have delegitimized armed conflict as a means of settling disputes; outlawed genocide; and restricted or forbidden the use of chemical, biological, and nuclear weapons. The absence of global or even large-scale regional conflict since 1945 suggests that these measures have had some effect. In smaller, local conflicts, however, they have been honored in the breech.

Considerable evidence does indicate, though, that the world is becoming less violent. Harvard psychologist Steven Pinker has calculated the lethality of armed conflict based on the annual number of deaths per 100,000 people worldwide over time. During World War II the number was 300. It dropped into the 20s during the Korean War, the teens in the era of Vietnam, and single digits during the 1980s and 1990s. Since the turn of the 21st century it has fallen to .5 and then risen to 1 because of the Syrian conflict.[51] Humans are killing each other in smaller numbers, at least in armed conflicts. That is certainly a hopeful note on which to end a study of modern warfare.

Conclusion

Historical surveys must come to an end even if their subject matter does not. The Cold War ended 26 years ago, so it is difficult to say to what degree the term "post–Cold War era" still makes sense. Future historians may see September 11, 2001, as the beginning of a new era of international security (or insecurity). The reemergence of Russia and a more assertive China have restored some balance to a world that for about a decade seemed to have only one superpower. The freedom of NATO led by the United States to intervene almost at will in civil conflicts with or without UN support appears to have been curtailed. Whether this and other recent changes in international affairs herald the dawn of new era remains to be seen and will probably only become apparent in hindsight. "Something," to quote Samuel Beckett, "is taking its course."

Conclusion: The New Security Environment and the Future of Warfare

A study of war tracing developments over three and half centuries would be incomplete without some consideration of how the past can help people understand the present and prepare for the future. Predictions about the future can, of course, only be tentative, but recognizing trends over long periods of time does allow for some reasonable if cautious conclusions about what the future holds. Governments regularly engage in such rational speculation about the future. In order to devise national strategies and craft defense budgets, every state has to look at contemporary events, weigh past experience, and conduct a realistic threat assessment based on present trends. Unfortunately, domestic politics, interservice rivalry, and bureaucratic inertia often impede efforts to match force structure with actual threats. Politicians must pander to voters, while generals are prone to prepare for past wars rather than future ones.

Historians are no better than anyone else at prognostication, and like everyone else they are enmeshed in their own world to a degree that makes complete objectivity impossible. Unlike those who vote on defense budgets and plan wars, however, they are beholden to no one. Perhaps that gives them an important measure of detachment. With that hope in mind, I conclude this study with a recapitulation of its main conclusions, followed by reasonable speculation about the nature of armed conflict for the foreseeable future.

Evolution of Warfare

As with so many areas of study, the road to the future runs through the past. Before considering current trends and future possibilities, it is necessary to review the historic trends revealed by this survey of military history. These trends can shed light on the nature of organized violence in today's world. They may also lead to some reasonable predictions about how armed conflict will continue to evolve.

Hybrid War

As the title of this work attests and its content makes clear, modern wars have consistently been hybrid affairs. The distinction between conventional and unconventional conflict is problematic in most cases and very misleading in others. Some conflicts during the modern era have seen a preponderance of conventional operations, while others have been characterized by a higher degree of unconventional activity. Few were exclusively one or the other. Eighteenth-century monarchs used designated units of irregular forces to conduct out-of-area operations, disrupting supply lines and attacking enemy units. During this period French and English colonists in North America developed ranger units to fight Native Americans and one another. These irregular forces figured prominently in the French and Indian and American Revolutionary Wars. In both conflicts they conducted independent operations and fought alongside regular forces. The American Revolution in particular saw one of the most synergistic uses of conventional and unconventional forces. At Saratoga, Cowpens, and Guilford Courthouse, American commanders combined riflemen, colonial militias, and Continental regulars to great effect.

The French Revolution and Napoleonic Wars were overwhelmingly conventional affairs, but unconventional operations played a significant role in those conflicts. The Vendee uprising had elements of peasant revolt and modern insurgency, as did irregular operations in the Iberian Peninsula. The Spanish guerrillas were not terribly effective in engaging French forces, but they tied down significant numbers of troops that might have been deployed elsewhere. Cossack irregulars harried Napoleon's troops out of Russia in 1812. By the time they deployed, Napoleon's invasion had already failed, but they made sure fewer of his troops survived the long retreat from Moscow.

Most wars of the 19th century were also hybrid. Large conventional armies battled one another during the American Civil War, but the Confederacy did make use of irregular forces, particularly in the western theater. Their activities, however, proved counterproductive. Many of the bands operated independently of one another and did not cooperate effectively with either the Confederate armies or the Confederate government. Partisan operations provoked Union reprisals, which contributed to their decision to wage war against the entire southern population. The wars of German unification were too short for partisan operations to have an effect, although Prussian units suffered attacks from *francs-tireurs*.

The period 1871 to 1914 saw no major conventional wars but a host of unconventional conflicts. American cavalry battled Native Americans in irregular campaigns on the western frontier. European states with empires in Africa and Asia battled indigenous forces along the fringes of their empires and quelled revolts within existing colonies. They did not combat partisans operating in support of conventional forces, but rather fought indigenous insurgents seeking to regain control of their territory. This pattern of warfare continued during World War I. T. E. Lawrence's Arab Revolt had little effect on the course of the war, and German resistance in East Africa had none at all.

The interwar period saw the emergence of modern insurgency and counterinsurgency. Britain granted self-rule to Ireland following a three-year conflict that revealed the limitations of conventional forces combating unconventional ones. The spread of nationalism to Africa and Asia increased the number of rebellions colonial powers faced. While the Europeans suppressed them, these uprisings foreshadowed the successful anticolonial struggles of the post–World War II era in which insurgents conducted successful campaigns for independence. The Second World War itself was the largest conventional conflict in human history, but even it had an unconventional dimension. Partisans in Eastern Europe engaged German forces in support of the Soviet Army, and specialized units conducted out-of-area operations in Burma.

The nuclear stalemate put an end to large-scale conventional war between superpowers, which recognized that the danger and costs of escalation were unacceptably high. Small wars occurred throughout the period of the Cold War. Many of these involved a blend of conventional and unconventional activities. Vietnam was the quintessential hybrid war. American and South Vietnamese troops had to battle North Vietnamese regulars and National Front (Viet Cong) insurgents. The Soviets faced a similar challenge in Afghanistan. Both countries found their conventional forces ill-suited to the task. On a smaller scale, the Salvadoran civil war taught the same lesson.

Hybrid war has also been the norm in the post–Cold War world. Chechnya was a hybrid affair. The 1991 Gulf War was a short, decisive conventional operation, but the 2003 invasion included a conventional phase followed by an unconventional one. The occupation of Afghanistan followed the same pattern. Peace enforcement operations are by nature unconventional, but the missions to Somalia, Bosnia, and Kosovo employed conventional means to intervene in those conflicts.

Technology

Since the invention of gunpowder weapons in the 14th century, technology has impacted the conduct of war. From then until the middle of the 20th century, the evolution of weaponry has made warfare increasingly lethal. Improved firing mechanisms and the addition of a bayonet made the smoothbore, flintlock musket the standard infantry weapon until the Minié rifle replaced it in the mid-19th century. Improvements to the rifle then focused on loading and rate of fire. Artillery went through a similar evolution.

Not all technological change that affected warfare dealt with weaponry, however. Designed for commercial purposes, railroads did more than anything else to make modern mass armies possible. They could move large numbers of troops over great distances and supply them. None of the belligerents in the American Civil War, the wars of German unification, or the two world wars could have fielded the forces they did without rail transport. Steam locomotion also made possible larger, faster ships with greater cruising range, capable of carrying larger cannon. Like the railroad and the steamboat, the airplane was not invented for military purposes, but its application to warfare became immediately apparent. Its ability to drop ever-larger bomb loads increased exponentially the lethality of warfare and its impact on civilians. Intercontinental ballistic missiles made it possible to hit targets with nuclear or conventional warheads anywhere in the world.

The nuclear arms race notwithstanding, technological advances in the second half of the 20th century focused less on the lethality of weapons than on their accuracy. Laser-guided munitions could strike targets with great precision. Stealth technology made it possible for aircraft to enter enemy airspace undetected by radar. Satellites could identify military installations from space. Unmanned aerial vehicles could be deployed from far away and stay over a target for a prolonged period. The cumulative effect of these changes was to diminish the loss of civilian lives in war.

Ideology, Warfare, and the Limitation of Conflict

The extent and destructiveness of wars have been closely linked to the reasons for which they have been fought. Ideology usually makes warfare deadlier. The impact of religion and ethnic nationalism on conflict has created a clearly discernible pattern to warfare in the modern era. After the end of the Thirty Years' War in 1648 religious wars in Europe came to an end. For the next century and a half monarchs fought one another to gain territory or affect the balance of power. This pragmatic approach and a tacit agreement to limit the impact of warfare on civilians limited the destructiveness and lethality of armed conflict. Long-service professional armies maintained year-round at state expense and tightly controlled by their officers could not as easily perpetrate the brutal and destructive acts committed by their predecessors during the Thirty Years' War.

The American and French Revolutions reintroduced ideology into warfare. Nationalism would prove to be an even more deadly force than religion. Love of country often leads to feelings of superiority, which in wartime can degenerate into demonization of the enemy. The advent of "scientific racism" and Social Darwinism during the second half of the 19th century increased this tendency. It also blurred the line between combatant and noncombatant. Free, compulsory public education introduced during the same period inculcated ideas of patriotism and racial/ethnic superiority into the soldiers who would build European empires in Africa and Asia and then fight one another in Europe.

The American Civil War and the two world wars were fought for ideological causes as well as pragmatic considerations. Each was in turn deadlier than its predecessor. From 1789 to 1945, warfare became increasingly total. Sherman's March to the Sea aimed to inflict economic hardship on the civilian population of the Confederacy. The next logical step would be to attack civilians directly, which occurred with unrestricted submarine warfare and aerial bombardment of cities, albeit very limited in scope, during World War I. Development of long-range heavy bombers during the interwar period made destruction of entire cities possible. All the belligerents in World War II targeted civilians in their strategic bombing campaigns. The Germans perpetrated genocide against Jews and other "undesirables," and the Japanese committed large-scale atrocities in the countries they occupied. Any remaining distinction between combatant and noncombatant disappeared in the mushroom clouds over Hiroshima and Nagasaki.

The evolution of total war ended with World War II. To escalate conflict any further would be to risk annihilation of the human race. Ironically, as war between them became unthinkable, the ideological struggle between the Soviet bloc (and later China) and the Western allies became intensified as a Manichean struggle between capitalism and communism. At the same time, both sides in the Cold War understood that no one could win a military conflict once "mutually assured destruction" became a reality. Neither Moscow nor Washington abandoned the quest for first-strike capability, a sufficient edge to guarantee destruction of enough enemy bombers, missiles, and submarines to prevent effective retaliation. Military leaders on both sides of the Iron Curtain, however, realized that they would never enjoy such an advantage. The total destruction of even a handful of cities was deemed unacceptable. This realization led to a new era of limited war in which the superpowers used allies and nonaligned states as proxies against one another while at the same time avoiding direct confrontation.

The end of the Cold War has not eliminated the balance of terror, since the three superpowers as well as several smaller states still possess their nuclear arsenals. The greatest risk of nuclear war, however, comes not from a confrontation between two of them but from a rogue state such as North Korea using its limited nuclear arsenal. The possibility that a religiously motivated terrorist group, which has no compunction about killing civilians, could get hold of weapons of mass destruction (radiological, biological, chemical, or nuclear devices) is worrisome.

War and Human Society

This study began with a question that remains unanswered: Are humans innately violent? The number of wars fought over the past 350 years suggest that they are. On the other hand, the last half century has seen a decline in the number and lethality of wars. The desire of people in most countries to engage in armed conflict only as a last resort and then to keep wars as short and limited as possible is encouraging. The restraint shown by many nations and their willingness to enter into arms limitations agreements suggests that societies as a whole are becoming less violent, even if individuals are not.

Throughout history armed forces and the nature of the wars they have waged have reflected the societies that created them. During the first age of limited war, monarchs recruited soldiers from two elements of society. Officers came primarily from the aristocracy, for whom fighting had long been their raison d'être. Vagabonds, criminals, and the poorest of the poor whose absence would have little impact on the economy formed the rank and file of royal armies. Some men volunteered, while press gangs forced others into service, which could last as much as 20 years. Mercenaries also played an important role in 18th-century armies. Monarchs of the ancien régime avoided arming the masses for fear that doing so might encourage them to rebel. Iron discipline kept the rank and file in line, but desertion plagued all armies.

Conclusion

The French Revolution expanded the recruitment base of armies dramatically. Given a stake in a country that finally showed some interest in their well-being, ordinary Frenchmen came forward to defend it. Once the initial enthusiasm for revolution faded, however, the government had to institute a draft, the infamous *levée en masse*. Recruits were no more eager to die than had been their predecessors, but the army reinforced patriotism inculcated in ordinary French people by the Revolution. Soldiers who fought for a cause in which they believed could be employed more flexibly, as they were less likely to run away at the first opportunity. More men could be conscripted into the army without fear that they would overthrow the state.

The French established the pattern for the future. After the fall of Napoleon, European monarchs reverted to the long-service professional armies of the ancien régime. Prussian victories won by a short-service conscript army led by professional officers and NCOs convinced all European states to adopt some variety of universal conscription. Volunteers initially filled the ranks of Union and Confederate armies, but when the war did not end quickly, both sides had to resort to conscription. Free, compulsory public education instilled the importance of patriotism and civic virtue in boys who would eventually serve in the military. Massive conscript armies of every major power in Europe would march to war in 1914. Most of the Americans who joined them in 1917 would also be conscripts.

Conscripts also filled the armies that fought World War II. The size of these forces, the length of the war, and the hardships soldiers faced meant that no government could count on volunteers to fill the ranks of its armed services. Conscription continued for most armies through the era of the Cold War. By the last quarter of the 20th century, however, professional armies came back into their own. The United States halted the draft in 1973 and has never reinstituted it. The Vietnam War revealed the limitations of short-service conscripts in protracted irregular conflicts. As warfare became more technical, requiring a higher degree of training for even enlisted personnel, it became clear that men and women drafted for two years would barely have completed their training when their term of service ended. All-volunteer forces have, however, made militaries more expensive. To attract qualified men and women, armed forces have had to offer good pay and benefits as well as opportunities for education and advancement.

Changing Attitudes toward War

What groups and individuals have felt about armed conflict has also changed over the past three and a half centuries, although the changes have not unfolded in the linear manner of some other developments. Civilians in the path of marauding soldiers suffered greatly during the Thirty Years' War. For the soldiers comprising the free companies of mercenaries who fought, however, the opportunity for plunder may have attracted them to military life in the first place. Military life offered an opportunity for advancement or at least for income few mercenaries would otherwise have had.

Creation of full-time royal armies during the second half of the 17th century significantly reduced opportunities for plunder and rapine. Indeed, monarchs created such armies in part to eliminate the destructiveness of free companies. Establishing full-time regular armies, however, removed a powerful incentive for enlistment. The boredom of barracks life and the rigors of campaigning attracted few rank-and-file recruits willing to serve the typical 20-year term required in most armies. Men had to be pressed into service and kept in line with stern discipline. These illiterate soldiers left no record of what they felt, but high rates of desertion in every army indicate that many did not want to be in the army. Like rankers in any age, however, they may have felt some loyalty to the men with whom they served, especially during wartime.

Few in the early modern era questioned the necessity of armed conflict. Save among members of small sects such as the Quakers, pacifism did not exist. Nonetheless, the 17th and 18th centuries witnessed a concerted effort to make warfare more humane. This period saw the creation of modern just-war theory, which insisted that wars must be fought for a just cause and waged by just means. The laws and usages of land warfare, which emerged out of this thinking, distinguished between combatants and noncombatants, stipulating that the latter should not be attacked provided they did not aid enemy forces. They also called for humane treatment of prisoners and laid down other provisions to reduce the damage caused by war. Although not always honored, these laws and customs attest to a growing realization that wars should be fought by rules.

Attitudes toward war underwent further changes as a result of the French Revolution. Patriotism motivated soldiers to enlist and inspired even conscripts to fight for a cause in which they believed rather than for hope of plunder or out of fear of punishment. Continued, even expanded use of conscription throughout the 19th and into the middle of the 20th centuries, however, indicates that love of country alone did not motivate enough people to enlist in time of war. Once it drafted them, though, armies appealed to the recruits' patriotism to inspire them to fight. That commitment, along with loyalty to comrades, helps explain why so many endured the hardships of war. Ideology motivated Civil War soldiers, two-thirds of whom had volunteered.

Ironically, as armies grew larger and weapons more deadly, the trend toward regulating war continued apace. The Hague conventions of the late 19th and early 20th centuries further specified the proper treatment of prisoners and outlawed certain types of weapons such as poison gas. They even called for the peaceful settlement of disputes. These agreements did little to prevent or mitigate the ferocity of either world war, but they represent an important step in the evolution of attitudes toward war. The UN Charter, the Universal Declaration of Human Rights, the Geneva accords, and the Nuclear Test Ban and Non-proliferation Treaties embrace the notion that war should be avoided and, failing that, be conducted in such a manner as to minimize loss of life and destruction of property. This change in consciousness has not prevented war, but it helps explain why the annual loss of life from armed conflict has declined over the past several decades.

Current Trends and Future Prospects

The evolution of warfare over the past three and a half centuries helps explain patterns of conflict in the contemporary world. Past trends and present patterns in turn suggest future possibilities. Several tendencies in the contemporary world seem likely to continue for the foreseeable future.

Continued Avoidance of Global and Large-Scale Regional War

While most armed forces devote the bulk of their resources to preparing for large-scale conventional war, the experience of the past 70 years suggests that the probability of such a conflict actually occurring will remain low. The United States, the Russian Federation, and China are still the only superpowers capable of waging war on such a scale, and all three have powerful incentives not to do so. Russia has been reasserting its claim to influence if not control in its near abroad, as evidenced by its 2008 incursion into Georgia, its 2014 seizure of Crimea, its subsequent support for eastern Ukrainian separatists, and its repositioning of military assets to its western border. The United States and NATO have responded by moving equipment to the Baltic States and increasing support for Poland. Russia has also been asserting its rights in the Arctic, and the United States and its allies have moved to counter the Russian buildup with deployments of their own. Russia and the United States have intervened in Syria, where they often operate at cross purposes. These actions suggest the threat of a renewed Cold War, but not an open conflict, from which neither country would benefit. China seeks to dominate the maritime territory inside the ring of islands running from Japan through Taiwan to the Philippines and claims the South China Sea as its exclusive domain. This assertion has led to some confrontations with ships of other nations operating in those waters, and to counter this threat the United States has promised a "rebalancing to Asia," shifting military assets to East Asia. China and Russia share a potentially troublesome border, but neither has made disturbing moves along it, although that could change. If it does, both powers would probably posture but stop short of outright war.

One factor that increases the danger of conflict, however, is the proliferation of nuclear states. The United States, Russia, China, the United Kingdom, and Israel were the first members of the nuclear club, but none of them is likely to use a nuclear weapon except in the extreme case of an existential threat. India, Pakistan, and North Korea also have nuclear weapons and may be more likely to use them in a local conflict that could easily escalate. A 2015 agreement might delay if not halt Iran's nuclear program altogether.

Increase in Local Conflicts

If the chances of a major war remain, the possibility of local ones will increase, especially in the developing world. Borders drawn in the interest of colonial powers a century ago continue to plague the Middle East and Africa, as do ethnic and religious divisions that cross them. The conflict between the Islamic State in Iraq and Syria (ISIS) and its regional opponents is a struggle within Sunni Islam, a struggle between Sunni and Shi'a, and an ethnic conflict between Arabs and Kurds as well as a conflict among neighboring states. The Sahel, running along the border between Saharan and sub-Saharan Africa, demarcates a divide between Christianity and Islam and is a fault line for existing conflicts in Mali, Nigeria, and Sudan as well as for potential ones in several other countries. Scarcity of water and other resources may also fuel local and regional wars.

Migration as a Major Source of Conflict

Uncontrolled migration is a major source of insecurity in the developing world and a growing problem for the developed one. It will only get worse. The flood of refugees into Europe from the Middle East and Central Asia as a result of the conflicts in Syria and Afghanistan and economic migration from Africa to Europe is a harbinger of things to come. The earth's population has reached seven billion and is still growing. The great disparity between poor and prosperous areas of the world, coupled with conflict in the former, will impel more people to migrate to the West.

Conclusion

North America and Europe, however, have a finite capacity to absorb immigrants and refugees. Illegal immigration has fueled anti-immigrant movements in many destination countries. The United States and several countries in Europe have already used their militaries to stem the flow of migrants. The NATO allies may find themselves intervening in conflicts for the sole purpose of preventing refugee crises. The alternative would be using force to prevent refugees, asylum seekers, and economic migrants crossing their borders.

Persistence of Nonstate Actors and Unconventional Conflict

Unconventional conflict will continue to be the most prevalent if not the most lethal form of organized violence for the foreseeable future. Large areas of the globe have been described as "ungoverned," "loosely governed," or "alternatively governed" spaces. The states in which these areas lie exercise little or no sovereignty over them and provide few if any services for the people living in them. In many cases nefarious groups have moved in and govern them more effectively than does the official state. For example, the Taliban in Afghanistan has thrived because it has in many cases provided better local governance than does the government in Kabul. While they may help local people, though, such groups also use the areas they control to carry out criminal activity and/or wage war with the official state and one another, to the detriment of society as a whole. Terrorist groups also make use of ungoverned or loosely governed spaces, sometimes with the acceptance or even the tacit agreement of the legitimate state. The Taliban and al-Qaeda have both operated from within the border area of Pakistan with relative impunity. The United States has limited ability to strike at these groups without provoking a conflict with the host (unwitting or otherwise) nation. Only by violating Pakistani sovereignty without warning and apologizing later did the United States eliminate Osama bin Laden.

The Islamic State represents the most sophisticated unconventional threat to date. Although it lacks international legitimacy and enjoys only limited support in the areas it occupies, it has many of the attributes of a state. It organizes itself into departments headed by what could be called ministers. It taxes, has a legal system (however harsh), and provides some services to the people it rules. It also behaves like a terrorist organization, intimidating local people and encouraging attacks against its enemies abroad. Finally, ISIS belongs to the Islamist extremist ideological movement, and it engages in criminal activity. Although ISIS behaves with such brutality that it probably will not survive in the long run, hybrid groups like it will probably continue to crop up in the future. The nightmare scenario is that such an organization or even a more limited terrorist group would get hold of a nuclear, radiological, biological, or chemical weapon of mass destruction.

Increasing Role of Special Forces

Unconventional threats must be combated by unconventional forces that operate with the same flexibility as their adversaries. The way to get rid of an alley cat that keeps you up at night is not to unleash a pack of hounds but to send in a bigger, tougher, meaner cat.[1] Special Forces of various types will thus become a larger percentage of military establishments. These forces include elite hostage rescue units like the U.S. SEAL (Sea, Air Land) Team 6 and Special Forces Groups like the British Special Air Service or the American Green Berets, capable of living in threatened countries and training, advising, and fighting alongside local security forces. Striking the proper balance between conventional and unconventional forces may be the greatest challenge facing contemporary military establishments.

The Privatization of War

Afghanistan and Iraq saw the emergence of a trend that, however disturbing, seems likely to continue. The U.S. military began relying heavily on contractors during the 1980s and 1990s, but initially they outsourced activities such as logistics and support services (cleaning, laundry, food preparation). As the security situation in Iraq deteriorated, the Bush administration found it expedient to rely increasingly on private security companies to perform essentially military tasks such as personnel and base protection. These armed contractors operated outside the military chain of command with little public accountability. Their actions sometimes interfered with the COIN campaign. Despite these problems, some analysts and even government officials find the use of contractors cost effective and even consider their ability to operate below the radar and outside the rules an advantage in certain circumstances. The serious implications of outsourcing a sovereign state's traditional monopoly on legally sanctioned coercive force outweigh any advantages they might have. That reservation notwithstanding, private military contractors are probably here to stay. At the very least, they must be brought under closer supervision by the states that employ them. The fact that many serve private corporations is even more worrying.[2]

Triumph of Technology over Numbers

The technology of warfare has evolved almost continuously throughout the modern era. This evolution has accelerated since the end of World War II. While previously the trend had been toward increasing the lethality of weapons, more recent developments have focused on improving their precision. Improved satellite surveillance and remotely piloted aircraft, commonly called drones, have allowed the United States to carry out focused strikes against terrorist leaders with significantly reduced collateral damage and loss of innocent life. Use of such weapons will increase, but as drones have become commercially available, the danger of them falling into terrorist hands must also be considered. Wherever technology takes military establishments, the 9/11 attacks serve as a grim reminder of what can happen when faith in machines leads them to ignore the human element in warfare. Low-technology attacks have frequently defeated high-technology security.

Abhorrence of War Will Continue

The increasingly more stringent regulation of armed conflict over the past half century and its formal condemnation by most states as a legitimate means of resolving international disputes bodes well for humanity. The devastating effect of two world wars has left European states extremely reluctant to fight. Vietnam had a similar effect on the United States. Americans will support foreign wars when politicians make a compelling case that vital U.S. interests are at stake, but they have little patience for protracted conflicts. The long engagements in Afghanistan and Iraq, conducted at a high cost with dubious results, have produced both war weariness and caution among the electorate.

The governments of the other two superpowers do not have to answer to voters to the same degree as does a U.S. president, but even they must pay some attention to public opinion. Their publics would be no more willing to support a major conflagration than would Americans. China has become assertive within its regional sphere of influence, but further abroad it prefers economic competition to military confrontation, trading aid and infrastructure projects throughout Asia and Africa and even South America for resources. It too realizes that wars are in the long run bad for business. The Russian Federation under Vladimir Putin will probably absorb eastern Ukraine and may use Russian minorities in the Baltics to stir up trouble there, but as long as NATO shows a firm determination to defend those countries, he will probably not risk war over them.

Unknowns

All of these predictions are, of course, based on a rational assessment of what nations should do based on their own self-interests. If the study of war teaches us anything, however, it is that human beings often behave quite irrationally. States have frequently tried to control war, to use it to their advantage, only to discover that, once started, it takes on a life of its own and produces a host of unforeseen consequences. Warfare has evolved to the point where humans now have the power to annihilate themselves. Fortunately that evolution has been accompanied by a growing trend toward avoiding war if possible and limiting how it is conducted if not. Which of these trends, the rational or the irrational, will prevail remains to be seen.

Notes

Introduction

1. George Santayana, "Tipperary," in *Soliloquies in England* (New York: Scribners, 1924), 102.

2. Chris Hedges, "What Every Person Should Know about War," *New York Times*, July 6, 2003, http://www.nytimes.com/2003/07/06/books/chapters/0713-1st-hedges.html?pagewanted=all, accessed January 4, 2013. The thirteen years since Hedges wrote this article have been marked by continuous war in Iraq, Afghanistan, and elsewhere.

3. Richard Leakey, *The Making of Mankind* (New York: Dutton, 1981).

4. Sir Basil Liddell Hart, *Strategy* (Westport, CT: Praeger, 1967), 25.

5. Julian Jackson, *The Fall of France: The Nazi Invasion of 1940* (Oxford: Oxford University Press, 2003).

6. Paul Kennedy, *Rise and Fall of the Great Powers: Economic Change and Military Conflict from 1500 to 2000* (New York: Vintage Books, 1989).

7. Theodore Ropp, *War in the Modern World* (New York: Collier, 1962), 33.

8. The definition of insurgency is based on Thomas R. Mockaitis, *The "New" Terrorism: Myths and Reality* (Stanford, CA: Stanford University Press, 2008), 5.

Chapter 1

1. Gerald of Wales, *Itinerary through Wales* (1191), 49, http://www.archive.org/stream/itinerarythroug00girauoft/itinerarythroug00girauoft_djvu.txt (accessed February 23, 2012).

2. Thomas Esper, "The Replacement of the Longbow by Firearms in the English Army," *Technology and Culture* 6, no. 3 (Summer 1965): 390.

3. Clive Pointing, *Gunpowder* (London: Chatto & Windus, 2005), 147.

4. Much academic debate surrounds the size of the two armies. For a summary of the arguments and the rationale for current figures, see James Glanz,

"Centuries after Henry V, Henry V's Greatest Victory Is Besieged by Academia," *New York Times*, October 25, 2009, sec. A, col. 0, Foreign Desk, 6.

5. Ibid.

6. Christopher Phillpotts, "The French Plan of Battle during the Agincourt Campaign," *The English Historical Review*, vol. 99, no. 390 (Jan., 1984), 62.

7. Ibid., 59–66

8. Ibid., 62.

9. Web Archive, "The Battle of Agincourt," http://web.archive.org/web/20091027132428/http://geocities.com/beckster05/Agincourt/AgAftermath.html (accessed February 24, 2013).

10. Cliff J. Rogers, "The Military Revolutions of the Hundred Years' War," in *The Military Revolution Debate: Readings on the Military Transformation of Early Modern Europe*, ed. Cliff J. Rogers (Boulder, CO: Westview Press, 1995), 58–61.

11. Details on different gunpowder mixtures are from Pointing, *Gunpowder*, 26–27.

12. Ibid., 18.

13. Ibid., 101.

14. Rogers, "Military Revolutions of the Hundred Years' War," 73.

15. Pointing, *Gunpowder*, 86–88. The Turks had a number of smaller guns as well.

16. Ibid., 142.

17. Esper, "Replacement of the Longbow by Firearms," 393. Esper's study focuses on England, but his conclusions seem reasonable for Europe in general.

18. Paul Kennedy, *The Rise and Fall of the Great Powers* (New York: Vintage Books, 1989), 19.

19. Details on evolution of naval warfare are from Geoffrey Parker, *The Military Revolution: Military Innovation and the Rise of the West* (Cambridge, UK: Cambridge University Press, 1996), 82–114.

20. Sebastian LePestre de Vauban, *A Manual of Siegecraft and Fortification*, trans. with an introduction by George A. Rothrock (Ann Arbor: University of Michigan Press, 1968).

21. Ibid., 140–141.

22. Michael Roberts, "The Military Revolutions, 1560–1660," in *Military Revolution Debate*, ed. Rogers, 13–36; Rogers, "Military Revolutions of the Hundred Years War," in ibid., 55–94. The rest of this edited volume explores most aspects of the debate.

23. C. R. L. Fletcher, *Gustavus Adolphus and the Thirty-Years War* (New York: Capricorn Books, 1963), 111.

24. Details of the Swedish financial system are from Robert A. Doughty et al., *Warfare in the Western World*, vol. I, *Military Operations from 1600–1871* (Lexington, MA: DC Heath, 1996), 14.

25. Guy Rowlands, *The Dynastic State and the Army under Louis XIV: Royal Service and Private Interest* (Cambridge, UK: Cambridge University Press, 2002), 29.

26. Ibid., 29.

Notes

27. Ibid., 173.
28. Discussion of administrative system is from M. S. Anderson, *War and Society in Europe of the Old Regime, 1618–1789* (New York: St. Martin's Press, 1988), 100.
29. John A. Lynn, "Recalculating French Army Growth," in Anderson, *War and Society in Europe of the Old Regime*, 132.
30. Rowlands, *Dynastic State and the Army*, 202.
31. Anderson, *War and Society in Europe of the Old Regime*, 86.
32. Ibid., 106.
33. For a discussion of these reforms see C. Jones, "Professionalization of the French Army under the Ancien Regime," in *The Military Revolution and the State, 1500–1800*, ed. Michael Duffy (Exeter, UK: Studies in History, 1980), 149–167.
34. Pointing, *Gunpowder*, 164–165.
35. Ibid., 161–167.
36. Paul Kennedy, *The Rise and Fall of the Great Powers: Economic Change and Military Conflict from 1500 to 2000* (New York: Vintage Books, 1989), 3–30.

Chapter 2

1. M. S. Anderson, *War and Society in Europe of the Old Regime* (New York: St. Martin's, 1988), 145.
2. Quoted in Jones, "Professionalization of the French Army," 156.
3. Details on ships of line dimensions and armaments are from John Dull, *The Age of the Ship of the Line: The British and French Navies, 1650–1815* (Omaha: University of Nebraska Press, 2009), 1–10.
4. Details are from "HMS Victory," http://www.stvincent.ac.uk/Heritage/1797/Victory/index2.html (accessed July 27, 2015).
5. Dull, *Age of the Ship of the Line*, 2.
6. Brent Nosworth, *The Anatomy of Victory* (New York: Hippocrene Books, 1992), 55–58.
7. Paul Kennedy, *The Rise and Fall of the Great Powers* (New York: Vintage Books, 1989), 98.
8. Ibid.
9. Details of the Prussian recruiting system are from Franza J. Szabo, *The Seven Years War in Europe, 1756–1763* (New York: Pearson/Longman, 2008), 21.
10. Ibid.
11. Ibid.
12. Frederick the Great, "Les Principes Généraux de Guerre," in *Œvre de Frédéric le Grand*, 28:art. XXVI, 95 (Berlin: Deckersche Geheime Ober-Hofbuchdrucherei, 1846–1856), Digitale Ausgabe Universitätsbibliothek Trier, http://friedrich.uni-trier.de/de/oeuvres/28/toc/ (accessed March 7, 2014). Frederick the Great wrote in French. The translation is mine.

13. Estimates of the size of the two armies vary. David Chandler, *Marlborough as Military Commander* (London: Penguin, 1973), 144. Charles Spencer, in *Blenheim, Battle for Europe* (London: Phoenix, 2004), 226, puts the French strength at 60,000 and credits them with 100 artillery pieces.

14. Chandler, *Marlborough*, 142.

15. Robert A. Doughty et al., *Warfare in the Western World*, vol. I, *Military Operations from 1600–1871* (Lexington, MA: DC Heath, 1996), 48.

16. Spencer, *Blenheim*, 254.

17. The number of units engaged around Blenheim comes from Chandler, *Marlborough*, 145.

18. Ibid., 259.

19. Theodore Ropp, *War in the Modern World* (New York: Macmillan, 1962, 1959), 51.

20. See Spencer, *Blenheim*, for a detailed discussion of Marlborough's handling of Blenheim.

21. Beatrice Heuser, "Small Wars in the Age of Clausewitz: The Watershed between Partisan War and People's War," *Journal of Strategic Studies* 33, no. 1 (February 2010): 1444.

22. Robert A. Selig and David Curtis Skaggs, "Introductory Essay," in Johann Ewald, *Treatise on Partisan Warfare*, trans. Robert A. Selig and David Curtis Skaggs (Westport, CT: Greenwood, 1991), 12.

23. Peter E. Russell, "Redcoats in the Wilderness: British Officers and Irregular Warfare in Europe and America, 1740 to 1760," *William and Mary Quarterly*, 3rd ser., 35, no. 4 (October 1978): 631.

24. Quoted in Selig and Skaggs, "Introductory Essay," 13.

25. Capt. Thomas-Antoine le Roy de Grandmaison, *La Petite Guerre ou Traite de Service des Troupes Legeres en Campagne* [*Small War or the Employment of Light Troops on Campaign*] (1756), 1–2. https://archive.org/details/lapetiteguerreo00grangoog (accessed February 7, 2014).

26. Heuser, "Small Wars in the Age of Clausewitz," p. 137.

27. Capt. de Jeney, *Le Partisan ou de l'Art de Fair la Petite Guerre* [The partisan or the art of small war] (A la Haye/The Hague, 1759), 10. Translation is my own.

28. Roger Stevenson, *Instructions for Officers Detached in the Field: Containing a Scheme for Forming a Corps of a Partisan* [sic] (Philadelphia: R. Aikenm, 1775), 35.

29. Grandmaison, *La Petite Guerre*, 8. Translation is my own.

30. Max Boot, *Invisible Armies: An Epic History of Guerrilla Warfare from Ancient Times to the Present* (New York: W.W. Norton, 2013), 61.

31. Andres Emmerich, *The Partisan or the Use of a Corps of Light Troops to an Army* (London: H. Reynell, 1789), 1.

32. John Grenier, *The First Way of War: American War Making on the Frontier* (Cambridge, UK: Cambridge University Press, 2005). The title is a deliberate challenge to the notion that the "American way of war" has always involved mass and firepower.

33. Ibid., 10.

34. Ibid., 19.

35. Ibid., 43–52.

36. Robert Rogers, *Journals of Major Robert Rogers* (London: J. Millan, 1765); reprinted with an introduction by Howard Peckham (New York: Corinth Books, 1961), iv–v.

37. Grenier, *First Way of War*, 62.

38. Ibid., 113.

39. Russell, "Redcoats in the Wilderness," 642–644.

40. Rogers, *Journals of Major Robert Rogers*, 10–11.

41. Ibid., 11.

42. Ibid.

43. Hugo Grotius, *The Rights of War and Peace*, ed. Jean Barbeyrac, (Indianapolis: Liberty Fund, 2005), vol.1, ch. 2, II.3, from the 1738 English translation of Jean Barbeyrac's French edition by John Morrice, http://oll.libertyfund.org/?option=com_staticxt&staticfile=show.php%3Ftitle=1425&chapter=138595&layout=html&Itemid=27 (accessed February 7, 2014).

44. Ibid., vol. 2, ch. 1, II.2, http://oll.libertyfund.org/?option=com_staticxt&staticfile=show.php%3Ftitle=1947&chapter=121276&layout=html&Itemid=27 (accessed February 7, 2014).

45. Ibid., ch. 2.

46. Ibid., ch. 2, XI.

47. Ibid., vol. 3, ch. 12, VII.

48. Emmerich de Vattel, "On the Just Causes of War," in *The Law of Nations or the Principles of Natural Law*, book 3, ch. 3, §26, http://www.lonang.com/exlibris/vattel/vatt-303.htm (accessed February 21, 2014).

49. Ibid., §33.

50. Ibid., book 3, ch. 8, §158, http://www.lonang.com/exlibris/vattel/vatt-308.htm (accessed February 21, 2014).

51. Nadezhda Durova, *The Cavalry Maiden: Journals of a Russian Officer in the Napoleonic Wars*, trans. Mary Fleming Zirin (Bloomington: University of Indiana Press, 1989). Durova served during the Napoleonic Wars, but the Russian army of that era was still a dynastic one.

52. Ibid., 46.

53. Ibid., 42.

Chapter 3

1. Henry Wadsworth Longfellow, "Paul Revere's Ride," 1860, http://www.poets.org/viewmedia.php/prmMID/15640 (accessed March 8, 2014).

2. Paul H. Smith, "The American Loyalists: Notes on Their Organization and Numerical Strength," *William and Mary Quarterly*, 3rd ser., 25, no. 2 (April 1968): 269.

3. Michael Schellhammer, "John Adams's Rule of Thirds," *Journal of the American Revolution*, February 13, 2013, http://allthingsliberty.com/2013/02/john-adamss-rule-of-thirds/ (accessed March 8, 2014).

4. John Adams, "Letter to H. Niles," February 13, 1818, http://web.archive.org/web/20020602030340/http://www.cooperativeindividualism.org/adams_john_american_revolution.html (accessed March 8, 2014).

5. This estimate is based on figures in "Population of the British Isles," *Tacitus Historical Atlas*, http://www.tacitus.nu/historical-atlas/population/british.htm (accessed March 11, 2014).

6. Michael O. Logusz, *With Musket and Tomahawk: The Saratoga Campaign and the Wilderness War of 1777* (Philadelphia: Casemate, 2010), 39.

7. Christopher Hibbert, *Redcoats and Rebels: The American Revolution Through British Eyes* (New York: W.W. Norton, 1990), 81.

8. Anthony James Joes, *Guerrilla Conflict Before the Cold War* (Westport, CT: Praeger, 1996), 8.

9. Robert K. Wright, *The Continental Army* (Washington, DC: Center of Military History United States Army, 1989), 154.

10. South Carolina law is quoted in Lawrence Dilbert Cress, *Citizens in Arms: The Army and Militia in American Society to the War of 1812* (Chapel Hill: University of North Carolina Press, 1982), 59.

11. Mark V. Kwasny, *Washington's Partisan War, 1775–1783* (Kent, OH: Kent State University Press, 1996), 4.

12. Cress, *Citizens in Arms*, 53.

13. Robert A. Doughty et al., *Warfare in the Western World*, vol. II (Lexington, MA: DC Heath, 1996), 139.

14. Kwasny, *Washington's Partisan War*, 1–19.

15. General Sir Henry Clinton, quoted in Logusz, *With Musket and Tomahawk*, 152.

16. Ibid., 65, 237.

17. Ibid., 237.

18. Ibid., 305.

19. Bruce Chadwick, *The First American Army: The Untold Story of George Washington and the Men Behind America's First Fight for Freedom* (Naperville, IL: Sourcebooks, Inc., 2005), 264.

20. Ibid., 270.

21. Doughty et al., *Warfare in the Western World*, I:165.

22. Charles Royster, *A Revolutionary People at War: The Continental Army and American Character, 1775–1783* (Chapel Hill: University of North Carolina Press, 1979), 276.

23. John Grenier, *The First Way of War: American War Making on the Frontier* (Cambridge, UK: Cambridge University Press, 2005), 146–169.

24. Ibid., 166–168.

25. Joes, *Guerrilla Conflict Before the Cold War*, 16.

26. Kwasny, *Washington's Partisan War*, 113.

27. Ibid., 114.

28. Logusz, *With Musket and Tomahawk*, 156–157.

29. Ibid., 200.

30. Ibid., 137–139.

31. Ibid., 67.

32. Don Higginbotham, *Daniel Morgan, Revolutionary Rifleman* (Chapel Hill: University of North Carolina Press, 1961), 23.

33. Quoted in John W. Wright, "The Rifle in the American Revolution," *American Historical Review* 29, no. 2 (January 1924): 298.

34. The discussion of riflemen in the Revolution is from Neil L. York, "Pennsylvania Rifle: Revolutionary Weapon in a Conventional War?," *Pennsylvania Magazine of History and Biography* 103, no. 3 (July 1979), 302–324.

35. Joes, *Guerrilla Conflict Before the Cold War*, 26, 32.

36. J. Tracy Power, "'The Virtue of Humanity Was Totally Forgot': Buford's Massacre, May 29, 1780," *South Carolina Historical Magazine* 93, no. 1 (January 1992): pp. 5–6.

37. Ibid., 10–11.

38. David Ramsay, *The History of the Revolution of South-Carolina: From a British Province to an Independent State* (Trenton, NJ: Isaac Collins, 1785), II:110, quoted in Power, "'Virtue of Humanity Was Totally Forgot'," 11.

39. Peter N. More, "The Local Origins of Allegiance in Revolutionary South Carolina: The Waxhaws as a Case Study," *South Carolina Historical Magazine* 107, no. 1 (January 2006): 26–41.

40. Ibid., 33.

41. Quoted in Joes, *Guerrilla Conflict Before the Cold War*, 34.

42. John Buchanan, *The Road to Guilford Courthouse: The American Revolution in the Carolinas* (New York: John Wiley and Sons, Inc., 1997), 305.

43. Ibid., 288.

44. Wright, *Continental Army*, 166.

45. Ibid., 229.

46. Mark V. Kwasny, "Militia, Guerrilla Warfare, Tactics, and Weaponry," in *A Companion to the American Revolution*, ed. Jack P. Greene and J. R. Pole (Oxford, UK: Blackwell Publishers, 2000), 317.

47. Quoted in Buchanan, *Road to Guilford Courthouse*, 295.

48. Higginbotham, *Daniel Morgan, Revolutionary Rifleman*, 130.

49. Buchanan, *Road to Guilford Courthouse*, 296, 286.

50. Higginbotham, *Daniel Morgan, Revolutionary Rifleman*, 132.

51. Buchanan, *Road to Guilford Courthouse*, 301.

52. Ibid., 320.

53. The description of the battle is from Higginbotham, *Daniel Morgan, Revolutionary Rifleman*, 135–141.

54. Ibid., 142.

55. Henry Lee, *Memoirs of the War in the Southern Department of the United States* (Philadelphia: Bradford and Inskeep, 1812), 1: 302–303.

56. Buchanan, *Road to Guilford Courthouse*, 380.

57. Ibid., 380.

58. John Keown, "America's War for Independence: Just or Unjust?," *Journal of Catholic Social Thought* 6, no. 2 (2009): 282.

59. Royster, *Revolutionary People at War*, 81.

60. Jeremiah Greenman, *Diary of a Common Soldier in the American Revolution, 1775–1783*, ed. and annot. Robert C. Bray and Paul E. Bushnell (DeKalb: Northern Illinois University Press, 1978).

Chapter 4

1. Jeremy Black, *European Warfare, 1660–1815* (New Haven, CT: Yale University Press, 1994), 153.

2. Robert S. Quimby, *The Background of Napoleonic Warfare* (New York: Columbia University Press, 1957), 95.

3. Ibid.

4. Ibid.

5. Quoted in Jay Luvaas, *Napoleon on the Art of War* (New York: Free Press, 1999), 78. The work is a compilation of Napoleon's writings selected, edited, and translated by Luvaas.

6. Digby Smith, *The Greenhill Napoleonic Data Book* (London: Greenhill Books, 1998), 225–226.

7. Black, *European Warfare*, 61.

8. Ibid., 45.

9. Quimby, *Background of Napoleonic Warfare*, 123.

10. Theodore Ropp, *War in the Modern World* (New York: Collier Books, 1962, 1959), 100.

11. Marie-Cécile Thoral, *From Valmy to Waterloo: France at War 1792–1815*, trans. Godfrey Rogers (London: Palgrave Macmillan, 2011), 108.

12. Ibid., 108–109.

13. Quoted in ibid., 108.

14. Quoted in Robert A. Doughty et al., *Warfare in the Western World*, vol. I, *Military Operations from 1600–1871* (Lexington, MA: DC Heath, 1996), 184.

15. Rory Muir, *Tactics and the Experience of Battle in the Age of Napoleon* (New Haven, CT: Yale University Press, 1998), 6.

16. Jacques Antoine Hippolyte Comte de Guibert, *Essai general de Tactique* (London: chez les libraires associés, 1772), Chapter 2, in *The Strategy Makers: Thoughts on War and Society from Machiavelli to Clausewitz*, excerpted and translated by Beatrice Heuser (Santa Barbara, CA: Praeger/ABC-CLIO, 2010), 164.

17. Black, *European Warfare*, 168–169.

18. Doughty et al., *Warfare in the Western World*, I:187.

19. Muir, *Tactics and the Experience of Battle in the Age of Napoleon*, 51.

20. Paul Kennedy, *The Rise and Fall of the Great Powers* (New York: Vintage Books, 1989), 99.

21. Ibid., 98.

22. Ibid., 99.

23. Ibid.

24. David Gates, *The Napoleonic Wars, 1803–1815* (London: Arnold, 1997), 9.

25. Ibid., 9–10.
26. Ibid., 6.
27. Ibid.
28. Details on the 1792 campaign are from Gunther E. Rothenberg, *The Art of Warfare in the Age of Napoleon* (Bloomington: Indiana University Press, 1978), 32–33.
29. F. M. Anderson, ed., *The Constitutions and Other Select Documents Illustrative of the History of France, 1789–1907*, 2nd ed. (Minneapolis: H. W. Wilson, 1908), 184–185, http://www.fordham.edu/halsall/mod/1793levee.asp (accessed November 17, 2014).
30. Gates, *Napoleonic Wars*, 19.
31. Doughty et al., *Warfare in the Western World*, I:218.
32. Ibid., 221–222.
33. For an excellent account of the invasion see Eugene Tarle, *Napoleon's Invasion of Russia, 1812* (New York: Oxford University Press, 1942).
34. Smith, *Greenhill Napoleonic Data Book*, 391–392.
35. Doughty et al., *Warfare in the Western World*, I: 276.
36. Gunther E. Rothenberg, *The Art of Warfare in the Age of Napoleon* (Bloomington: University of Indiana Press, 1978), 170–171.
37. Ibid., 203.
38. Charles Esdaile, *The Peninsular War: A New History* (New York: Palgrave/Macmillan, 2003), 241.
39. Rothenberg, *Art of Warfare in the Age of Napoleon*, 191.
40. Ibid., 192.
41. Ibid., 192.
42. James W. Shoshenberg, "Austerlitz: Napoleon's Masterstroke," *Military History* (December 2005): 29.
43. Smith, *Greenhill Napoleonic Data Book*, 205.
44. Gates, *Napoleonic Wars*, 28.
45. Shoshenberg, "Austerlitz: Napoleon's Masterstroke," 31.
46. Ibid., 31.
47. J. Holland Rose, "The Ice Incident at the Battle of Austerlitz," *English Historical Review* 17, no. 67 (July 1902): 537–538.
48. Smith, *Greenhill Napoleonic Data Book*, 217.
49. Ibid., 216.
50. Charles Tilly, "The Analysis of a Counter-Revolution," *History and Theory* 3, no. 1 (1963): 31.
51. Charles Tilly, "State and Counterrevolution in France," in "The French Revolution and the Birth of Modernity" special issue, *Social Research* 56, no. 1 (Spring 1989): 82.
52. "Exterminer sans réserve tous les individus de tout age et de tout sexe, qui sera (sic) convaincu d'avoir participé à la guerre de la Vendée." Jean-Baptiste Huché, quoted in Claude Petitfrère, "La Vendée en Lan II: Défait et Répression," *Annales historiques de la Révolution française*, no. 300 (Avril–Juin 1995): 180.

53. Ibid., 179.
54. Quoted in Thoral, *From Valmy to Waterloo*, 40.
55. Quoted in Jonathan North, "General Hoche and Counterinsurgency," *Journal of Military History* 67, no. 2 (April 2003): 530.
56. Petitfrère, "La Vendée en Lan II: Défait et Répression," 182–183.
57. Quoted in North, "General Hoche and Counterinsurgency," 539.
58. "The Vendee Wars, 1793–99," http://www.inthevendee.com/vendee-wars/vendee-wars.html (accessed December 19, 2014).
59. Charles J. Esdaile, *Fighting Napoleon: Guerrillas, Bandits and Adventurers in Spain, 1808–1814* (New Haven, CT: Yale University Press, 2004), 37.
60. Smith, *Greenhill Napoleonic Data Book*, 263.
61. *Fighting Napoleon*.
62. Quoted in ibid, 117.
63. Quoted in ibid., 136.
64. Ibid., 43–44.
65. Ibid., 44.
66. Doughty et al., *Warfare in the Western World*, I: 251.
67. Muir, *Tactics and the Experience of Battle in the Age of Napoleon*, 9.
68. Quoted in Gates, *Napoleonic Wars*, 22.
69. Quoted in Thoral, *From Valmy to Waterloo*, 128.
70. John Harris, *Recollections of Rifleman Harris as Told to Henry Curling*, ed. Christopher Hibbert (Hamden, CT: Archon Books, 1970), 1.
71. John Green, *A Soldier's Life, 1806–1815* (London: EP Publishing Ltd., 1973), 11.
72. William Surtees, *Twenty-Five Years in the Rifle Brigade* (London: Frederick Muller Ltd., 1973), 1–2.
73. Jean-Baptiste Barrè, quoted in Muir, *Tactics and the Experience of Battle in the Age of Napoleon*, 4.
74. Harris, *Recollections of Rifleman Harris*, 27.
75. G. Crompton, quoted in Muir, *Tactics and the Experience of Battle in the Age of Napoleon*, 196.
76. Luvaas, *Napoleon on the Art of War*, 24.

Chapter 5

1. For a discussion of this process see David Landes, *The Unbound Prometheus: Technological Change and Industrial Development in Western Europe from 1750 to the Present*, 2nd ed. (London: Cambridge University Press, 2003).
2. For an examination of the birth of class see Harold Perkin, *The Origins of Modern English Society* (London: Routledge, 2002).
3. Benedict Anderson, *Imagined Communities: Reflections on the Origins and Spread of Nationalism* (New York: Verso, 1991).
4. Eugene Weber, *Peasants into Frenchmen: The Modernization of Rural France, 1870–1914* (Stanford, CA: Stanford University Press, 1976).

5. John Keegan, *A History of Warfare* (New York: Alfred Knopf, 1993), 306.

6. Max Boot, *War Made New: Technology, Warfare, and the Course of History, 1500 to Today* (New York: Gotham Books, 2006), 125.

7. *The Tribune Almanac and Political Register* (New York: The Tribune Association, 1863), 29, https://ia600407.us.archive.org/23/items/tribunealmanacpo1863newy/tribunealmanacpo1863newy.pdf (accessed December 29, 2014).

8. For discussion of the configuration and invention of the conical-cylindrical bullet, see Alan W. Howey, "Minié Ball," *Civil War Times* (October 1993), http://www.historynet.com/minie-ball (accessed December 29, 2014).

9. Marshal Brain, "How Flintlock Guns Work," http://science.howstuffworks.com/flintlock5.htm (accessed December 30, 2014).

10. Baron Antoine-Henri de Jomini, *The Art of War*, trans. G. H. Mendell and W. P. Craighill (West Point, NY: U.S. Military Academy, 1862), 70, http://www.gutenberg.org/files/13549/13549-h/13549-h.htm#CHAPTER_III (accessed December 31, 2014).

11. Theodore Ropp, *War in the Modern World* (New York: Collier, 1962, first published in 1959), 150–151.

12. Paul Kennedy, *The Rise and Fall of the Great Powers* (New York: Vintage Books, 1989), 180.

13. Economic statistics are from Robert A. Doughty et al., *Warfare in the Western World*, vol. I, *Military Operations from 1600–1871* (Lexington, MA: DC Heath, 1996), 337.

14. Ibid.

15. Larry H. Addington, *Patterns of War Since the Eighteenth Century*, 2nd ed. (Bloomington: Indiana University Press, 1994), 69.

16. Stanley Lebergott, "Why the South Lost: Commercial Purpose in the Confederacy, 1861–1865," *Journal of American History* 70, no. 1 (June 1983): 62–63.

17. Ibid., 70–71.

18. M. Brem Bonner and Peter McCordSource, "Reassessment of the Union Blockade's Effectiveness in the Civil War," *North Carolina Historical Review* 88, no. 4 (October 2011): 398.

19. David G. Surdam, "Northern Naval Superiority and the Economics of the American Civil War," in "Papers Presented at the Fifty-Fifth Annual Meeting of the Economic History Association," special issue, *Journal of Economic History* 56, no. 2 (June 1996): 478.

20. Ibid., 474.

21. Stephen Sears, *Gettysburg* (New York: Houghton Mifflin, 2003), 513.

22. Robert E. Lee, letter to Mary Lee, April 19, 1863, quoted in ibid., 15.

23. Sears, *Gettysburg*, 95.

24. For a discussion of Civil War signals see Pierre Wilhelm, "Telegraph: A Strategic Means of Communication during the American Civil War," *Revista de Historia de América*, no. 124 (enero–junio 1999): 81–98; and George Raynor Thompson, "Civil War Signals," *Military Affairs* 18, no. 4 (Winter 1954): 188–201.

25. James MacPherson, *Battle Cry of Freedom: The Civil War Era* (New York: Oxford University Press, 1988), 653.

26. For a discussion of Civil War infantry tactics see John K. Mahon, "Civil War Infantry Assault Tactics," Civil War special issue of *Military Affairs* 25, no. 2 (Summer 1961): 57–68.

27. Doughty et al., *Warfare in the Western World*, I: 417.

28. Mark Grimsley, *The Hard Hand of War: Union Military Policy Toward Southern Civilians, 1861–1865* (New York: Cambridge University Press, 1995), 112.

29. Daniel Sutherland, "Guerrilla Warfare, Democracy, and the Fate of the Confederacy," *Journal of Southern History* 68, no. 2 (May 2002): 270.

30. Quoted in Noel C. Fisher, "'Prepare Them for My Coming': General William T. Sherman, Total War, and Pacification in West Tennessee," *Tennessee Historical Quarterly* 51, no. 2 (Summer 1992): 78.

31. Quoted in ibid., 76.

32. Grimsley, *Hard Hand of War*, 166.

33. Ibid.

34. *General Orders No. 100: Instructions for the Government of Armies of the United States in the Field*, April 24, 1863, http://avalon.law.yale.edu/19th_century/lieber.asp#sec1 (accessed February 17, 2015).

35. Grimsley, *Hard Hand of War*, 151.

36. J. David Hacker, "A Census-based Count of the Civil War Dead," *Civil War History* 57, no. 4 (December 2011): 328.

37. Ibid., 348. Hacker rejects the traditional military death toll of 620,000 as too low.

38. Figures are extrapolated from those for 1870. "National Assessment of Adult Literacy," National Center for Educational Statistics, http://nces.ed.gov/naal/lit_history.asp (accessed February 24, 2015). Literacy figures, often determined by nothing more than the ability to sign one's name, are notoriously unreliable and difficult to interpret. There can be little doubt, however, that North and South fielded the most literate armies to that date.

39. James M. McPherson, *For Cause and Comrades: Why Men Fought in the Civil War* (New York: Oxford University Press, 1997), 19–20.

40. Ibid., 22–24.

41. Robert Hunt Rhodes, ed., *All for the Union: The Civil War Diaries of Elisha Hunt Rhodes* (New York: Vintage, 1991), 127–128.

Chapter 6

1. Guy Stanton Ford, "Boyen's Military Law," *American Historical Review* 20, no. 3 (April 1915): 537.

2. Ibid., 535.

3. Ibid., 537.

4. Details on the Prussian General Staff are from Theodore Ropp, *War in the Modern World* (New York: Macmillan, 1962, 1959), 155–157.

5. Quoted in T. N. Dupuy, *A Genius for War: The German Army and General Staff, 1807–1945* (London: MacDonald and Janes, 1977), 116.

6. Quoted in ibid., 116.

7. Karl von Clausewitz, *On War*, trans. J. J. Graham (London: N. Trübner, 1909), vol. 1, book I, ch. 24, http://www.gutenberg.org/files/1946/1946-h/1946-h.htm (accessed January 1, 2015).

8. John Hampden Jackson, *Clemenceau and the Third Republic* (London: Hodder and Stoughton Limited, 1946), 228.

9. For an excellent discussion of the relationship between railroads and the location of Prussian units see Dennis Showalter, "Mass Multiplied by Impulsion: The Influence of Railroads on Prussian Planning for the Seven Weeks' War," *Military Affairs* 38, no. 2 (April 1974): 62–67.

10. Geoffrey Wawro, *The Franco-Prussian War: The German Conquest of France in 1870–1871* (New York: Cambridge University Press, 2003), 47.

11. Robert A. Doughty et al., *Warfare in the Western World*, vol. I, *Military Operations from 1600–1871* (Lexington, MA: DC Heath, 1996), 475.

12. Dennis Showalter, "Soldiers into Postmasters? The Electric Telegraph as an Instrument of Command in the Prussian Army," *Military Affairs* 37, no. 2 (April 1973): 48–52.

13. Max Boot, *War Made New: Technology, Warfare, and the Course of History, 1500 to Today* (New York: Gotham Books, 2006), 132.

14. Ibid., 131.

15. Ibid., 139.

16. Wawro, *Franco-Prussian War*, 54.

17. Ibid., 57–59.

18. Dupuy, *Genius for War*, 102.

19. Wawro, *Franco-Prussian War*, 62.

20. Ibid., 73.

21. Ibid., 67.

22. Doughty et al., *Warfare in the Western World*, I: 486.

23. Wawro, *Franco-Prussian War*, 84.

24. Ibid., 213.

25. Ibid., 223.

26. Doughty et al., *Warfare in the Western World*, I: 486.

27. Larry H. Addington, *Patterns of War Since the Eighteenth Century*, 2nd ed. (Bloomington: Indiana University Press, 1994), 101.

28. Wawro, *Franco-Prussian War*, 288-289.

29. Quoted in Archer Jones, *Civil War Command and Strategy: The Process of Victory and Defeat* (New York: Free Press, 1992), 2.

30. Niccolo Machiavelli, *The Prince*, ch. VII, 1515; trans. by W. K. Marriott, 1908, http://www.constitution.org/mac/prince17.htm (accessed September 15, 2015).

Chapter 7

1. Peter Duckers, *British Military Rifles* (London: Shire Publications, 2008), 24.
2. Details on the Maxim gun are from Max Boot, *War Made New: Technology, Warfare, and the Course of History, 1500 to Today* (New York: Gotham Books, 2006), 151.
3. Statistics are for the 1911 Vickers M1 model, which came into use in 1911. World Guns, http://world.guns.ru/machine/brit/vickers-mk-e.html (accessed March 12, 2015).
4. "French 75 mm Gun," First Division Museum, http://www.firstdivisionmuseum.org/museum/exhibits/tankpark/75mm.aspx (accessed March 13, 2015).
5. Robert M. Ripperger, "The Development of the French Artillery for the Offensive, 1890–1914," *Journal of Military History* 59, no. 4 (October 1995): 599–618.
6. "The Barbed Wire Fence: 'A Classic Invention'," *Science News-Letter* 24, no. 642 (July 29, 1933): 74.
7. David Herman, *The Arming of Europe and the Making of the First World War* (Princeton, NJ: Princeton University Press, 1996), 75–75.
8. See Benedict Anderson, *Imagined Communities: Reflections on the Origins and Spread of Nationalism* (New York: Verso, 2006).
9. For discussion of the process of national consciousness formation see Eugene Weber, *Peasants into Frenchmen: The Modernization of Rural France, 1870–1914* (Stanford, CA: Stanford University Press, 1976).
10. John M. Gates, "The U.S. Army and Irregular Warfare" (unpublished manuscript, [1989]), 11.
11. Walter Bagehot, "Modern History Sourcebook: The Use of Conflict, 1872," http://www.iupui.edu/~histwhs/H374.dir/H374.webreader/darwin.bagehot.html (accessed March 19, 2015).
12. Rudyard Kipling, "The Whiteman's Burden," 1899, http://legacy.fordham.edu/halsall/mod/kipling.asp (accessed August 27, 2015).
13. See, e.g., Benjamin Madley, "California's Yuki Indians: Defining Genocide in Native American History," *Western Historical Quarterly* 39, no. 3 (Autumn 2008): 303–332.
14. Quoted in Gilbert King, "Where the Buffalo No Longer Roamed," *Smithsonian Online*, July 17, 2012, http://www.smithsonianmag.com/history/where-the-buffalo-no-longer-roamed-3067904/?no-ist (accessed March 23, 2015).
15. Interview with Alfred Terry, *Army and Navy Journal* 14, no. 14 (November 11, 1876), in Peter Cozzens, *Eyewitnesses to the Indian Wars, 1865–1890* (Mechanicsport, PA: Stackpole Books, 2005), 124–125.
16. Thomas Powers, "How the Little Big Horn Was Won," *Smithsonian Online*, November 2010, http://www.smithsonianmag.com/history/how-the-battle-of-little-bighorn-was-won-63880188/?no-ist (accessed March 23, 2015).
17. Alexandra Fuller, "In the Shadow of Wounded Knee," *National Geographic Online*, August 2012, http://ngm.nationalgeographic.com/2012/08/pine-ridge/fuller-text (accessed March 23, 2015).

Notes

18. Thomas T. Smith, "U.S. Army Combat Operations in the Indian Wars of Texas, 1849–1881," *The Southwestern Historical Quarterly* 99, no. 4 (April 1996): 516.

19. Ibid., 527.

20. Ibid., 506.

21. Ibid., 529.

22. Gilbert Kin, "Where the Buffalo No Longer Roam," *Smithsonian Online*, July 17, 2012, http://www.smithsonianmag.com/history/where-the-buffalo-no-longer-roamed-3067904/?no-ist (accessed March 25, 2015).

23. Smith, "U.S. Army Combat Operations in the Indian Wars of Texas," 529.

24. Max Boot, *The Savage Wars of Peace: Small Wars and the Rise of American Power* (New York: Basic Books, 2002), 113, 126–127.

25. Timothy K. Deady, "Lessons of a Successful Counterinsurgency Campaign: the Philippines, 1899–1902," *Parameters* 35, no. 1 (Spring 2005): 59.

26. Brian McAlister Linn, *The U.S. Army and Counterinsurgency in the Philippine War, 1899–1902* (Chapel Hill: University of North Carolina Press, 1989), 163–170.

27. David Shonfield, "Battle of Omdurman," *History Today* 48, no. 9 (September 1998), http://www.historytoday.com/david-shonfield/battle-omdurman (accessed March 27, 2015).

28. Ian Beckett, *The Victorians at War* (London: Hambeldon and London, 2003), 182.

29. Niccolo Machiavelli, *The Prince*, ch.VII (1515), trans. W. K. Marriott (1908), http://www.constitution.org/mac/prince17.htm (accessed March 27, 2015).

30. Isabel Hull, "The Military Campaign in Southwest Africa, 1904–1907," *German Historical Institute Bulletin*, no. 37 (Fall 2005): 39–40.

31. Tilman Diedering, "The German-Herero War of 1904: Revisionism of Genocide or Imaginary Historiography?," *Journal of Southern African Studies* 19, no. 1 (March 1993): 84.

32. Michael G. Hanchard, "Herero and Nama Rebellions, 1904–1907: A Prelude to the Modern Holocaust?," *Global Mappings*, n.d., http://diaspora.northwestern.edu/mbin/WebObjects/DiasporaX.woa/wa/displayArticle?atomid=619 (accessed March 29, 2015).

33. Hull, "Military Campaign in Southwest Africa," 40.

34. Volker Berghan, in *Germany in the Era of Two World Wars: From Militarism and Genocide to Civil Society* (Princeton, NJ: Princeton University Press, 2009), makes this point in reference to Germany, but it applies to the West in general.

35. The U.S. Marine Corps did produce a *Small Wars Manual* in 1940, but World War II eclipsed its experience, which had been all but forgotten by the time of Vietnam.

36. T. R. Moreman, "Sir Charles Edward Callwell," in *Oxford National Dictionary* (Oxford: Oxford University Press, 2004–2015), http://www.oxforddnb.com.ezproxy.depaul.edu/view/article/32251 (accessed March 31, 2015).

37. Ibid.

38. Sir Charles Edward Callwell, *Small Wars: Their Principles and Practice*, 3rd ed. (London: HMSO, 1906; first published in 1896), 23.

39. Ibid., 124–149.
40. Ibid., 149.
41. Michael Howard, "Men Against Fire: Expectations of War in 1914," in *Military Strategy and the Origins of the First World War*, ed. Steven Miller et al. (Princeton, NJ: Princeton University Press, 1991), 8.
42. Herman, *Arming of Europe*, 70.
43. Howard, "Men Against Fire," 8.
44. Ibid.
45. Barbara Tuchman, *The Guns of August* (New York: Macmillan, 1962).
46. For a detailed discussion of the Boer War see Thomas Packenham, *The Boer War* (New York: Random House, 1979).
47. Howard, "Men Against Fire," 14–15.
48. Ibid., 15.
49. Ibid., 16.
50. Ibid., 16.
51. Herman, *Arming of Europe*, 73.
52. George Alfred Henty, *With Kitchener in the Soudan: A Story of Atbara and Omdurman* (London: Blackie and Son, 1903), ch.14, http://en.wikipedia.org/wiki/With_Kitchener_in_the_Soudan (accessed April 1, 2015).
53. Winston Churchill, *A Roving Commission: My Early Life* (New York: Charles Scribner's Sons, 1930), 171.
54. Alfred Lord Tennyson, "The Charge of the Light Brigade," 1854, http://poetry.eserver.org/light-brigade.html (accessed April 2, 2015).
55. Rupert Brooks, "The Soldier," http://www.poets.org/poetsorg/poem/soldier (accessed April 2, 2015).
56. James Joll, *The Origins of the First World War* (New York: Routledge, 2007), 257.
57. Ibid., 265.
58. Ibid.
59. *Laws of War on Land* (Oxford: Institute of International Law, 1880), https://www1.umn.edu/humanrts/instree/1880a.htm (accessed April 3, 2015).
60. *Convention (I) for the Pacific Settlement of International Disputes*, Title 1, "On the Maintenance of the General Peace," art. 1, July 29, 1899, http://avalon.law.yale.edu/19th_century/hague01.asp (accessed April 3, 2015).
61. *Convention with Respect to the Laws and Customs of War on Land*, The Hague, July 29, 1899, http://avalon.law.yale.edu/19th_century/hague02.asp (accessed April 3, 2015).
62. "Declaration on the Launching of Projectiles and Explosives from Balloons," The Hague, July 29, 1899, http://avalon.law.yale.edu/19th_century/dec99-01.asp (accessed April 3, 2015).
63. "Declaration on the Use of Projectiles the Object of Which Is the Diffusion of Asphyxiating or Deleterious Gases," The Hague, July 29, 1899, http://avalon.law.yale.edu/19th_century/dec99-02.asp (accessed April 3, 2015).
64. "Declaration on the Use of Bullets Which Expand or Flatten Easily in the Human Body," July 29, 1899, http://avalon.law.yale.edu/19th_century/dec99-03.asp (accessed April 3, 2015).

Notes

65. *Convention for the Pacific Settlement of Disputes*, The Hague, October 18, 1907, http://avalon.law.yale.edu/20th_century/pacific.asp (accessed April 7, 2015).

66. *Convention Respecting the Rights and Duties of Neutral Powers and Persons in Case of War on Land*, The Hague, October 18, 1907, http://avalon.law.yale.edu/20th_century/hague05.asp (accessed April 7, 2015).

Chapter 8

1. "World War I Casualty and Death Tables," http://www.pbs.org/greatwar/resources/casdeath_pop.html (accessed April 7, 2015).

2. Figures on civilian deaths vary widely due to the difficulty in deciding which deaths can be truly attributed to the effects of war. For a compilation of various sources see "Source List and Detailed Death Tolls for the Primary Megadeaths of the Twentieth Century," which provides totals of 6.6–9 million, http://necrometrics.com/20c5m.htm#WW1 (accessed April 7, 2015).

3. "Counting the Cost," National Archives (UK) online exhibit, http://www.nationalarchives.gov.uk/pathways/firstworldwar/aftermath/counting_cost.htm (accessed April 7, 2015).

4. Ibid.

5. Alfred Schlieffen, "Great Memorandum," trans. with commentary by Gerhardt Ritter, in *The Schlieffen Plan: Critique of a Myth* (London: Oswald Wolff Limited, 1958), 134–147.

6. Ibid., 141.

7. The strength of the Western forces is from Larry H. Addington, *Patterns of War Since the Eighteenth Century*, 2nd ed. (Bloomington: Indiana University Press, 1994), 135; the strength of forces in East Prussia is from "The Battle of Gumbinen, 1914," http://www.firstworldwar.com/battles/gumbinen.htm (accessed April 11, 2015).

8. Quoted in Correlli Barnett, *The Swordbearers: Studies in Supreme Command in the First World War* (Bloomington: Indiana University Press, 1975), 35.

9. Barbara Tuchman, *The Guns of August* (New York: Macmillan, 1962).

10. Addington, *Patterns of Warfare Since the Eighteenth Century*, 135.

11. Ibid.

12. John Keegan, *The First World War* (New York: Vintage, 2000), 106.

13. Ibid., 36.

14. Addington, *Patterns of Warfare Since the Eighteenth Century*, 142.

15. For a detailed description of the trench system see John Ellis, *Eye Deep in Hell: Trench Warfare in World War I* (Baltimore, MD: Johns Hopkins University Press, 1976), 10–25.

16. Paul Kennedy, *The Rise and Fall of the Great Powers* (New York: Vintage Books, 1989), 265.

17. "Battle of Gorlice-Tarnow, 2–10 May 1915," http://www.historyofwar.org/articles/battles_gorlice_tarnow.html (accessed April 17, 2015).

18. Ibid.

19. Keegan, *First World War*, 248.

20. A. J. P. Taylor, *The First World War, an Illustrated History* (New York: Perigee Books, 1980), 101.

21. Ibid., 83.

22. Ibid., 99.

23. National Archive (UK), CAB 42/1/10, General Staff, War Office, "The War: A Comparison of the Belligerent Forces, 6 January 1915," quoted in David French, "The Meaning of Attrition, 1914–1916," *English Historical Review* 103, no. 407 (April 1988): 391.

24. Ibid., 392.

25. Robert A. Doughty et al., *Warfare in the Western World*, vol. II (Lexington, MA: DC Heath, 1996), 573.

26. Alistair Horne, *The Price of Glory: Verdun 1916* (New York: Penguin, 1994) provides the best account of the evolution of the battle.

27. Doughty et al., *Warfare in the Western World*, II: 573.

28. "Battle of the Somme, 1 July to 13 November 1916," http://www.bbc.co.uk/history/worldwars/wwone/battle_somme.shtml (accessed April 19, 2015).

29. Ibid.

30. Ibid.

31. David French, "The Meaning of Attrition, 1914–1916," *English Historical Review* 103, no. 407 (April 1988): 403.

32. Details from an account of the offensive are based on Graydon A. Tunstall, "Austria-Hungary and the Brusilov Offensive of 1916," *The Historian* 70, no. 1 (February 26, 2008): 30–53, http://onlinelibrary.wiley.com/doi/10.1111/j.1540-6563.2008.00202.x/pdf (accessed April 21, 2015).

33. "Weapons of War—Flamethrowers," http://www.firstworldwar.com/weaponry/flamethrowers.htm (accessed April 23, 2015).

34. "Bergman MP18 Gun," http://www.firstworldwar.com/atoz/mgun_mp18.htm (accessed April 23, 2015).

35. "Creeping Barrage," http://www.firstworldwar.com/atoz/creepingbarrage.htm (accessed April 23, 2015).

36. "Weapons of War: Mark 1 Tank," http://www.bbc.co.uk/history/worldwars/wwone/nonflash_tank.shtml (accessed April 24, 2015).

37. Addington, *Patterns of War Since the Eighteenth Century*, 157.

38. J. F. C. Fuller, *The Conduct of War* (New York: Funk and Wagnall's, 1961), 175–176.

39. Ibid., 177.

40. The description of new German tactics is from T. N. Dupuy, *A Genius for War: The German Army and General Staff, 1807–1945* (London: MacDonald and Janes, 1977), 170–171.

41. Addington, *Patterns of War Since the Eighteenth Century*, 164.

42. Ibid., 165.

43. Martin Kitchen, *The German Offensive of 1918* (Charleston, SC: Tempus, 2001), 24.

44. Taylor, *First World War*, p. 220.

45. Kitchen, *The German Offensive of 1918*, 35–36.
46. Kennedy, *Rise and Fall of the Great Powers*, 271.
47. Ibid., 274.
48. Ibid.
49. "WWI Casualties," http://ww1facts.net/quick-reference/ww1-casualties/ (accessed April 29, 2015).
50. Ibid.
51. James Lunt, "Lawrence and Arab Revolt," in *A History of World War I*, ed. A. J. P. Taylor (London: Octopus Books, 1974), 136.
52. Ibid., 136.
53. "Viewpoint: 10 Myths About World War 1 Debunked," *BBC Online Magazine*, February 25, 2014, http://www.bbc.com/news/magazine-25776836 (accessed April 30, 2015).
54. Ellis, *Eye Deep in Hell*, 28.
55. Ibid., 28.
56. The description of trench activities is based on ibid., 26–42, 72–79.
57. Erich Maria Remarque, *All Quiet on the Western Front*, trans. A. W. Wheen (New York: Fawcett Crest, 1945, 1929), 125.
58. Henri Barbusse, *Under Fire*, trans. W. Fitzwater Wray (New York: Dutton, 1969, 1916), 27.
59. Robert Graves, *Goodbye to All That* (New York: Doubleday, 1957, 1929), 228.
60. For a description of the truce see "What Really Happened in the Christmas Truce of 1914," http://www.bbc.co.uk/guides/zxsfyrd (accessed May 1, 2015).
61. Barbusse, *Under Fire*, 154.
62. Wilfred Owen, "Dulce et Decorum Este," 1917, http://www.warpoetry.co.uk/owen1.html (accessed May 1, 2015).
63. Vera Brittain, *Testament of Youth* (New York: Penguin, 2005, 1933).

Chapter 9

1. For a discussion of this topic see David Omissi, *Airpower and Colonial Control: The Royal Air Force, 1919–1939* (Manchester, UK: Manchester University Press, 1990).
2. See Amnon Sella, "Red Army Doctrine and Training on the Eve of the Second World War," *Soviet Studies* 27, no. 2 (April 1975): 245–264.
3. Ibid., 261.
4. *Field Service Regulations, United States Army 1923* (Washington, DC: Government Printing Office, 1924), 3, para. 57.
5. *FM 100-5: Tentative Field Service Regulations, Operations* (Washington, DC: Government Printing Office, 1939), 6–7, paras. 25, 28.
6. *FM 100-5: Field Service Regulations, Operations* (Washington, DC: Government Printing Office, 1941), 278, paras. 1146–1147.
7. See Lt. Col. Edward O'Shaughnessy Jr., "The Evolution of the Armored Force, 1920–1940," Individual Study Project (Carlisle Barracks, PA: U.S. Army War College, 1993).

8. The M2 Light tank details are from http://www.tanks-encyclopedia.com/ww2/US/M2_Light_Tank.php; the M2 Medium tank details are from http://www.tanks-encyclopedia.com/ww2/US/m2_medium_tank.php (accessed August 30, 2015).

9. J. F. C. Fuller, *The Conduct of War* (New York: Funk and Wagnall's, 1961), 244.

10. J. F. C. Fuller, *Lectures on Field Service Regulations III: Operations between Mechanized Forces* (London: Sifton Praed & Company, 1932).

11. Irving M. Gibson, "Maginot and Liddell Hart: The Doctrine of Defense," in *Makers of Modern Strategy*, ed. Edward Meade Earl (Princeton, NJ: Princeton University Press, 1971), 380.

12. Heinz Guderian, *Achtung Panzer! Die Entwicklung der Panzerwaffer, ihre Kampftaktik und ihre Operationa Möglichkeit* [Attention, panzer! The development of armored forces, their Battle tactics and their operational possibilities] (Stuttgart: Union Deutche Verlagsgesellschaft, 1937).

13. Fuller, *Lectures on F.S.R III*, 14.

14. Max Boot, *War Made New: Technology, Warfare, and the Course of History, 1500 to Today* (New York: Gotham Books, 2006), 223.

15. Heinz Guderian, *Panzer Leader*, trans. Constantine Fitzgibbon (Cambridge, MA: DaCapo Press, 2002), 24.

16. *Die Truppenführung* [*Troop Leading*], German Field Regulations, pt. I, 1933, II.28, trans. and pub. U.S. Army General Staff School, Fort Leavenworth, KS, 1936, Combined Arms Research Library Digital Library, http://cgsc.contentdm.oclc.org/cdm/ref/collection/p4013coll7/id/131 (accessed May 21, 2015).

17. Ibid., II.37.

18. For a discussion of the evolution of mechanized warfare see James S. Corum, *The Roots of Blitzkreig: Hans von Seeckt and the German Military Reform* (Lawrence: University of Kansas Press, 1992).

19. Julian Jackson, *The Fall of France: The Nazi Invasion of 1940* (Oxford: Oxford University Press, 2003), 17.

20. Giulio Douhet, *The Command of the Air*, trans. Dino Ferrari (Washington, DC: Air Force History and Museums Program, 1998, 1921), 20.

21. Ibid., 10.

22. Boot, *War Made New*, 248.

23. "Fleets 1939," WW2WEAPONS, http://ww2-weapons.com/fleets-1939/ (accessed May 20, 2015).

24. Details on Allied and Axis navies are from "Comparative Fleet Strengths: The United States and Japan, December 7, 1941," http://historicaltextarchive.com/sections.php?action=read&artid=194 (accessed May 20, 2015).

25. Army-Navy Game Day Program, November 30, 1941, http://historicaltextarchive.com/sections.php?action=read&artid=194 (accessed May 20, 2015).

26. Tom Barry, *Guerrilla Days in Ireland* (Cork, Ireland: Mercier Press, 1949), 83.

27. Letter of a British officer serving in Ireland to his mother, printed in *Hampshire Regimental Journal* 16, no. 8 (August 1922): 136–137.

Notes

28. For a discussion of the new tactics see Brevet Major T. A. Lowe, "Some Reflections of a Junior Officer in Ireland," *Army Quarterly and Defence Journal* 5 (October 1922): 50–58.

29. "Covenant of the League of Nations," https://en.wikipedia.org/wiki/Covenant_of_the_League_of_Nations (accessed August 31, 2015).

30. "Disarmament: Washington Naval Treaty," https://en.wikipedia.org/wiki/Covenant_of_the_League_of_Nations (accessed August 31, 2015).

31. "Kellog-Briand Pact, 1928," http://www.yale.edu/lawweb/avalon/imt/kbpact.htm (accessed August 31, 2015).

Chapter 10

1. Figures are from http://www.nationalww2museum.org/learn/education/for-students/ww2-history/ww2-by-the-numbers/world-wide-deaths.html (accessed August 31, 2015).

2. Casualty figures are from http://www.secondworldwarhistory.com/world-war-2-statistics.asp (accessed June 15, 2015).

3. "Blitzkrieger," *Time*, 34, no. 13 (September 25, 1939), 29.

4. Max Boot, *War Made New: Technology, Warfare, and the Course of History, 1500 to Today* (New York: Gotham Books, 2006), 225.

5. "Episode 2: Lightning War," *World War II in Colour* (World Media Rights, 2008–2009).

6. Williamson Murray and Allan R. Millett, *A War to Be Won: Fighting the Second World War* (Cambridge, MA: Belknap Press, 2000), 57.

7. "Battle of France," in *New World Encyclopedia*, http://www.newworldencyclopedia.org/entry/Battle_of_France (accessed May 22, 2015).

8. Larry H. Addington, *Patterns of War Since the Eighteenth Century*, 2nd ed. (Bloomington: Indiana University Press, 1994), 202.

9. Julian Jackson, *The Fall of France: The Nazi Invasion of 1940* (Oxford: Oxford University Press, 2003), 15.

10. Addington, *Patterns of War Since the Eighteenth Century*, 202.

11. Jackson, *Fall of France*, 38.

12. Ibid., 20.

13. *Life* 8, no. 11 (March 11, 1940), 21.

14. T. N. Dupuy, *A Genius for War: The German Army and General Staff, 1807–1945* (London: MacDonald and Janes, 1977), 4. Dupuy made this calculation based on the 1943 Salerno campaign, but a similar, perhaps even greater advantage probably existed in May 1940.

15. Jackson, *Fall of France*, 40.

16. Williamson Murray and Allan R. Millett, *A War to Be Won: Fighting the Second World War* (Cambridge, MA: Belknap Press, 2000), 73.

17. Jackson, *Fall of France*, 27.

18. Ibid., 24–25.

19. Ibid., 11.
20. Jackson, *Fall of France*, 225.
21. Robert Doughty, "The Myth of Blitzkrieg," in *Challenging the United States Symmetrically and Asymmetrically: Can America Be Defeated?*, ed. Lloyd Matthews (Carlisle Barracks, PA: Strategic Studies Institute, U.S. Army War College, 1998), 70–71.
22. Ibid., 71.
23. Ibid.
24. Ian Keershaw, *Fateful Choices: Ten Decisions that Changed the World, 1940–1941* (New York: Penguin, 2007), 85.
25. John Keegan, *The Second World War* (New York: Penguin, 2005), 135.
26. Ibid., 143.
27. Murray and Millet, *War to Be Won*, 119.
28. Ibid.
29. Richard Overy, *Russia's War* (New York: Penguin, 1998), 72.
30. Alan Taylor, "WWII: Operation Barbarossa," *The Atlantic*, July 24, 2011, http://www.theatlantic.com/photo/2011/07/world-war-ii-operation-barbarossa/100112/ (accessed May 28, 2015).
31. Overy, *Russia's War*, 94.
32. Ibid., 117.
33. Ibid., 113.
34. Paul Kennedy, *The Rise and Fall of the Great Powers* (New York: Vintage Books, 1989), 354.
35. Ibid., 355.
36. Keegan, *Second World War*, 211.
37. Ian Kershaw, *Fateful Choices*, 423–424.
38. John Keegan, *Six Armies in Normandy: From D-Day to the Liberation of Paris* (New York: Penguin, 1994), 31–34.
39. Ibid., 42.
40. Ibid., 223.
41. Overy, *Russia's War*, 185.
42. Ibid., 188.
43. The description of Soviet reorganization is from ibid., 190.
44. Murray and Millet, *War to Be Won*, 296.
45. Ibid.
46. Keegan, *Second World War*, 120.
47. "Timeline of the Air War, 1939–1945," http://www.pbs.org/wgbh/americanexperience/features/timeline/bombing/ (accessed June 2, 2015).
48. Statistics on the bombing campaign are from *United States Strategic Bombing Survey, Summary Report (European War)*, September 30, 1945, reprinted by Air University Press, October 1987, 4–5.
49. Kenneth P. Werrell, "The Strategic Bombing of Germany in World War II: Costs and Accomplishments," *Journal of American History* 73, no. 3 (December 1986): 709.

50. *United States Strategic Bombing Survey, Summary Report (European War)*, 5.

51. Kenneth P. Werrell, "The Strategic Bombing of Germany: Costs and Accomplishments," *Journal of American History* 73, no. 3 (December 1986): 711.

52. *United States Strategic Bombing Survey, Overall Report (Europe)*, quoted in Melden E. Smith Jr., "The Strategic Bombing Debate: The Second World War and Germany," *Journal of Contemporary History* 12, no. 1 (January 1977): 180.

53. Werrell, "Strategic Bombing of Germany," 711.

54. Ibid., 712.

55. Murray and Millet, *War to Be Won*, 332.

56. Werrell, "Strategic Bombing of Germany," 710.

57. Ibid., 710.

58. Murray and Millet, *War to Be Won*, 333.

59. The details on technology are from Robin Higham, "Technology and D-Day," in Eisenhower Foundation, *D-Day: the Normandy Invasion in Retrospect* (Lawrence: University of Kansas Press, 1971), 221–242.

60. Alfred Goldberg, "Air Campaign Overlord: To D-day," in Eisenhower Foundation, *D-Day*, 59.

61. Ibid., 62.

62. Ibid., 70.

63. Keegan, *Second World War*, 416.

64. Ibid., 416.

65. Quoted in ibid., 388.

66. Ibid.

67. Murray and Millet, *War to Be Won*, 424–425.

68. Overy, *Russia's War*, 287–288.

69. Ibid., 196.

70. Quoted in ibid., 195.

71. Keegan, *Second World War*, 218.

72. Ibid.

73. J. K. Zawodny, "Soviet Partisans," *Soviet Studies* 17, no. 3 (January 1966): 376.

74. For a detailed discussion of the intricacies of Yugoslav resistance see Simon Trew, *Britain, Mikhailović and the Chetniks, 1941–42* (London: Macmillan, 1998).

75. Zawodny, "Soviet Partisans," 369.

76. Ben Shepherd, "The Clean Wehrmacht, the War of Extermination and Beyond," *Historical Journal* 52, no. 2 (June 2009): 468.

77. For a discussion of the relationship between genocide and antipartisan operations see ibid., 455–473.

78. Keegan, *Second World War*, 495.

79. Shepherd, "Clean Wehrmacht," 459.

Chapter 11

1. http://www.rjgeib.com/heroes/tanimizu/yamamoto.html (accessed June 10, 2015).

2. Ian Keershaw, *Fateful Choices: Ten Decisions That Changed the World, 1940–1941* (New York: Penguin, 2007), 332.

3. Hideki Tojo, November 5, 1941, quoted in ibid., 331.

4. "Battle of Midway," http://militaryhistory.about.com/od/worldwari1/p/Midway.htm (accessed June 12, 2015).

5. John Keegan, *The Second World War* (New York: Penguin, 2005), 278.

6. Gerald Astor, *The Jungle War: Mavericks, Marauders, and Madmen in the China-Burma-India Theater of World War II* (Hoboken, NJ: John Wiley and Sons, 2004), 5.

7. Rana Mitter, *Forgotten Ally: China's World War II, 1937–1945* (New York: Houghton Mifflin Harcourt, 2013), 222.

8. "Central Burma," http://www.ibiblio.org/hyperwar/USA/USA-C-Burma45/ (accessed September 30, 2015).

9. "B29 Super Fortress," http://www.boeing.com/history/products/b-29-superfortress.page (accessed June 13, 2015).

10. Williamson Murray and Allan R. Millett, *A War to Be Won: Fighting the Second World War* (Cambridge, MA: Belknap Press, 2000), 505.

11. Ibid., 506.

12. *United States Strategic Bombing Survey, Summary Report (Pacific War)*, (Maxwell Airforce Base, AL: Air University Press, 1987), 84.

13. Ibid.

14. Ibid., 88.

15. Murray and Millet, *War to Be Won*, 507.

16. Keegan, *Second World War*, 576, 584.

17. Murray and Millet, *War to Be Won*, 520.

18. Astor, *Jungle War*, 138.

19. Quoted in Donovan Webster, *The Burma Road: The Epic Story of the China-Burma-India Theater in World War II* (New York: Farrar, Straus and Giroux, 2003), 164.

20. Ibid., 165.

21. Ibid., 166.

22. Paul Fussell, *Wartime: Understanding and Behavior in the Second World War* (New York: Oxford University Press, 1989), 129–143.

23. Quoted in ibid., 137.

24. "By the Numbers: The U.S. Military," National World War II Museum, http://www.nationalww2museum.org/learn/education/for-students/ww2-history/ww2-by-the-numbers/us-military.html (accessed June 20, 2015).

25. "Bushido Code: An Overview," http://www.pbs.org/wgbh/sugihara/readings/bushido.html (accessed June 20, 2015).

26. Lewis Jacobs, "World War II and the American Film," *Cinema Journal* 7 (Winter 1967–1968): 21.

27. Ibid., 10.

28. Ibid.

29. "By the Numbers: Worldwide Deaths," National WWII Museum, http://www.nationalww2museum.org/learn/education/for-students/ww2-history/ww2-by-the-numbers/world-wide-deaths.html (accessed June 21, 2015).

30. Ibid.

31. Details on Nanking are from "The Rape of Nanking," http://www.historyplace.com/worldhistory/genocide/nanking.htm (accessed June 21, 2015).

32. Quoted in Barrett Tillman, "William Bull Halsey: Legendary World War II Admiral," http://www.historynet.com/william-bull-halsey-legendary-world-war-ii-admiral.htm (accessed June 21, 2015).

33. Quoted in "General Curtis E. Lemay (1906–1990)," http://www.pbs.org/wgbh/amex/bomb/peopleevents/pandeAMEX61.html (accessed June 21, 2015).

34. Russell Weigley, *The American Way of War: A History of United States Military Strategy and Policy* (New York: Macmillan, 1973).

35. Ibid.

Chapter 12

1. Volker R. Berghahn, *Europe in the Era of the Two World Wars: From Militarism and Genocide to Civil Society, 1900–1950* (Princeton, NJ: Princeton University Press, 2006), 140. Figure for the two world wars represents battle deaths.

2. "The Development and Proliferation of Nuclear Weapons," http://www.nobelprize.org/educational/peace/nuclear_weapons/readmore.html (accessed June 25, 2015).

3. Winston Churchill, "The Sinews of Peace ('Iron Curtain Speech')," March 5, 1946, http://www.winstonchurchill.org/resources/speeches/1946-1963-elder-statesman/the-sinews-of-peace (accessed June 25, 2015).

4. Mr. James S. Lay Jr., Executive Secretary, National Security Council, *A Report to the National Security Council on United States Objectives and Programs for National Security*, NSC 68, April 14, 1950, 4.

5. Norman Friedman, *The Fifty-Year War: Conflict and Strategy in the Cold War* (Annapolis, MD: Naval, 2000), 36.

6. Article 5, North Atlantic Treaty, April 4, 1949, http://www.nato.int/cps/en/natolive/official_texts_17120.htm (accessed July 10, 2015).

7. Troop strengths in Europe in 1950 are from Friedman, *Fifty-Year War*, 139.

8. Allen R. Millet, "Introduction to the Korean War," *Journal of Military History* 65, no. 4 (October 2001): 931.

9. Ibid., 932.

10. Geoffrey Warner, "The Korean War," *International Affairs* 56, no. 1 (January 1980): 100.

11. T. R. Fehrenbach, *This Kind of War: The Classic Korean War History* (Washington, DC: Brassey's, 1963), 189.

12. Ibid., 185.

13. Quoted in ibid., 187.

14. Andrew Birtle, *US Army Counterinsurgency and Contingency Operations Doctrine, 1942–1976* (Washington, DC: United States Army Center for Military History, 2006), 31.

15. Ibid., 97.

16. Sun Tzu, *The Art of War*, trans. Thomas Clear (Boston: Shambhala Publishing, 1988), 54.

17. Mao Zedong, *On Protracted War*, May 1938, https://www.marxists.org/reference/archive/mao/selected-works/volume-2/mswv2_09.htm (accessed August 7, 2015).

18. Mao Tse-Tung [Mao Zedong], *On Guerrilla Warfare*, trans. Samuel B. Griffith II (Baltimore, MD: National and Aviation Publishing Company of America, 1992), 113.

19. Ibid., 112.

20. Thomas R. Mockaitis, *British Counterinsurgency, 1919–1960* (London: Macmillan, 1990), 1–6.

21. Robert Taber, *The War of the Flea: A Study of Guerrilla Warfare and Practice* (New York: Citadel Press, 1965), 26.

22. J. Bowyer Bell, *The Myth of the Guerrilla: Revolutionary Theory and Malpractice* (New York: Alfred A. Knopf, 1971).

23. Lt. Col. Philippe Francois, "Waging Counterinsurgency in Algeria: A French Perspective," *Military Review* (September–October 2008): 59.

24. Ibid., 60.

25. Colon Giles Martin, "War in Algeria: The French Experience," *Military Review* (July–August 2005): 53.

26. Ibid.

27. Keith Sutton, "Administration Tensions over Algeria's Centres de Regroupment," *British Journal of Middle East Studies* 26, no. 2 (November 1999): 243–270.

28. R. W. Komer, *The Malayan Emergency in Retrospect: Organization of a Successful Counterinsurgency Effort* (Santa Monica, CA: Rand, 1972), 2–3.

29. Ibid., 22–23.

30. For a detailed discussion of British COIN see Mockaitis, *British Counterinsurgency*.

31. See Thomas R. Mockaitis, *Resolving Insurgencies* (Carlisle Barracks, PA: Strategic Studies Institute, US Army War College, 2011), 52–56.

32. Millet, "Introduction to the Korean War," 923.

33. George Kennan, *Testimony Given Before the Committee on Foreign Relations of the U.S. Senate*, 89th Cong., February 10, 1966.

34. George Herring, *America's Longest War: The United States and Vietnam, 1950–1975* (New York: Alfred Knopf, 1986), 58.

35. Andrew Krepinevich, *The Army and the Vietnam War* (Baltimore, MD: Johns Hopkins University Press, 1986), 23–24.

36. Ibid., 197.

37. "Vietnam War: Battle of Ia Drang," http://militaryhistory.about.com/od/vietnamwar/p/Vietnam-War-Battle-Of-Ia-Drang.htm (accessed August 17, 2015).

38. [Harold Moore], "After Action Report, IA DRANG Valley Operation 1st Battalion, 7th Cavalry 14-16 November 1965," 18–19, http://www.au.af.mil/au/awc/awcgate/vietnam/ia_drang.pdf (accessed August 17, 2015).

39. Quoted in Mockaitis, *British Counterinsurgency*, 56.

40. Philip K. Davidson, *Vietnam at War: The History, 1946–1975* (New York: Oxford University Press, 1988), 353.

41. Ibid., 357.

42. Max Boot, *The Savage Wars of Peace: Small Wars and the Rise of American Power* (New York: Basic Books, 2002), 53.

43. Ibid., 304–308.

44. Davidson, *Vietnam at War*, 475.

45. Walter Cronkite, *CBS Evening News*, February 27, 1968, quoted in Mark Atwood Lawrence, *The Vietnam War: An International History in Documents* (New York: Oxford University Press, 2014), 124.

46. Harry G. Summers Jr., *On Strategy: A Critical Analysis of the Vietnam War* (Novato, CA: Presidio Press, 1982), 1.

47. Gary Hess, *Vietnam: Explaining America's Lost War* (Oxford: Blackwell, 2009), 4.

48. John F. Kennedy, "Inaugural Address," January 20, 1961, http://www.bartleby.com/124/pres56.html (accessed September 8, 2015).

49. Hess, *Vietnam*, 1.

50. David G. Fivecoat, "Leaving the Graveyard: The Soviet Union's Withdrawal from Afghanistan," *Parameters* 42, no. 2 (Summer 2012): 42–43.

51. Joseph J. Collins, "The Soviet-Afghan War," *Parameters* 14, no. 2 (Summer 1984): 51.

52. Ibid., 52.

53. Ibid., 51–52.

54. Fivecoat, "Leaving the Graveyard," 43.

55. Ibid.

56. Quoted in Serge Schemann, "Gorbachev Says U.S. Arms Note Is Not Adequate," *New York Times*, February 26, 1986, http://www.nytimes.com/1986/02/26/world/gorbachev-says-us-arms-note-is-not-adequate.html (accessed September 9, 2015).

57. Quoted in Fivecoat, "Leaving the Graveyard," 43.

58. Fred Halliday, "Soviet Foreign Policymaking and the Afghanistan War: From 'Second Mongolia' to 'Bleeding Wound'," *Review of International Studies* 25, no. 4 (October 1999): 684.

59. Fivecoat, "Leaving the Graveyard," 44.

60. Ibid., 45.

61. Halliday, "Soviet Foreign Policymaking and the Afghanistan War," 684.

62. Quoted in David Kilcullen, *The Accidental Guerrilla: Fighting Small Wars in the Midst of a Big One* (New York: Oxford, 2009), 88.

63. United Nations Charter, Chapter 7, Article 42, http://www.un.org/en/documents/charter/chapter7.shtml (accessed September 12, 2015).

64. Ibid. (accessed September 16, 2015).

65. Thomas R. Mockaitis, *Peace Operations in Intrastate Conflict: The Sword or the Olive Branch?* (Westport, CT: Praeger, 1999), 2.

66. "Facts and Figures," UNEF I, http://www.un.org/en/peacekeeping/missions/past/uneflfacts.html (accessed September 16, 2015).

67. Cable from the President of the Congo et al., to the Secretary-General of the United Nations, July 12, 1960, UN Document S/4382.

68. UN General Assembly Resolution, September 20, 1960, UN Document A/RES/1474/Rev.1 (ES-IV). This resolution augmented the Security Council Resolution of July 22, 1960, which authorized the mission on a more restrictive basis (UN Document S/4405).

69. Troop strength figures are from ONUC, "Facts and Figures," http://www.un.org/en/peacekeeping/missions/past/onucF.html (accessed September 19, 2015).

70. Richard Nixon, "Address to the Nation on the War in Vietnam," November 3, 1969, http://www.presidency.ucsb.edu/ws/index.php?pid=2303 (accessed September 18, 2015).

71. Major Paul P. Cale, "The United States Military Advisory Group in El Salvador, 1979-1992" (US Army Command and Staff College Paper, 1996), 8, smallwarsjournal.com/documents/cale.pdf (accessed September 18, 2015).

72. William Dean Stanley, "State Building Before and After Democratization: 1980–1995," *Third Quarterly* 27, no. 1 (2006): 102.

73. Thomas R. Mockaitis, *Resolving Insurgencies* (Carlisle Barracks, PA: Strategic Studies Institute, US Army War College, 2011), 54.

74. Tom Lehrer, "Who's Next?," 1965, http://www.metrolyrics.com/whos-next-lyrics-tom-lehrer.html (accessed September 19, 2015).

75. Tom Lehrer, "So Long Mom (A Song for World War III)," 1965, http://www.metrolyrics.com/so-long-mom-a-song-for-world-war-iii-lyrics-tom-lehrer.html (accessed September 19, 2015).

76. Michael Herr, *Dispatches* (New York: Vintage Books, 1991, 1977), 48–49.

77. Barry McGuire, "Eve of Destruction," 1965, http://www.azlyrics.com/lyrics/barrymcguire/eveofdestruction.html (accessed September 20, 2015).

78. Edwin Starr, "War," 1970, http://www.metrolyrics.com/war-lyrics-edwin-starr.html (accessed September 20, 2015).

Chapter 13

1. "Persian Gulf War," http://www.history.com/topics/persian-gulf-war (accessed August 19, 2015).

2. Ibid.

3. The discussion of stealth technology is based on "Stealth Technology: Theory and Practice," http://www.defense-aerospace.com/articles-view/feature/5/157481/aircraft-stealth%3A-the-view-from-russia.html (accessed September 21, 2015).

4. *An Agenda for Peace: Preventive Diplomacy, Peace Making and Peace-Keeping*, Report of the Secretary General, UN Document A/47/277-S/24111, June 17, 1992, para. 17, http://www.unrol.org/files/A_47_277.pdf (accessed September 24, 2015).

Notes   335

    5. UN Security Council Resolution 743, February 21, 1992, S/RES/743 (1992), para. 5, http://www.un.org/en/ga/search/view_doc.asp?symbol=S/RES/743%281992%29 (accessed September 24, 2015).
    6. Thomas R. Mockaitis, *Peace Operations and Intrastate Conflict: The Sword or the Olive Branch?* (Westport, CT: Praeger, 1999), 86.
    7. Susan Woodward, *Balkan Tragedy: Chaos and Dissolution After the Cold War* (Washington, DC: Brookings Institute, 1995), 33.
    8. Figures are from Sabrina Petra Ramet, *Balkan Babel: The Disintegration of Yugoslavia from the Death of Tito to the Ethnic War* (Boulder, CO: Westview Press, 1966), 265.
    9. UN Security Council Resolution, September 14, 1992, S/RES/776.
    10. James Gow, *Triumph of the Lack of Will: International Diplomacy and the Yugoslav War* (New York: Columbia University Press, 1997), 129–130.
    11. "Facts about Srebrenica," International Criminal Tribunal for Yugoslavia, http://www.icty.org/x/file/Outreach/view_from_hague/jit_srebrenica_en.pdf (accessed October 13, 2015).
    12. Government press releases were available within 10 minutes of the incident. See Mockaitis, *Peace Operations and Intrastate Conflict*, 114–115.
    13. Jan Zwierzchowski and Ewa Tabeau, "The 1992-95 War in Bosnia and Herzegovina: Census-Based Multiple System Estimation of Casualties's Undercount" (paper presented at the International Research Workshop on "The Global Costs of Conflict," The Households in Conflict Network [HiCN] and The German Institute for Economic Research [DIW Berlin], February 1, 2010), http://www.icty.org/x/file/About/OTP/War_Demographics/en/bih_casualty_undercount_conf_paper_100201.pdf (accessed October 13, 2015).
    14. "Bosnia," Women Under Siege, http://www.womenundersiegeproject.org/conflicts/profile/bosnia (accessed October 13, 2015).
    15. "United Nations Peacekeeping," UN Department of Public Relations, DPI/1306/Rev.3-June 1994-7M, 98.
    16. UN Security Council Resolution 751, S/RES/751, April 24, 1992, https://www.un.org/sc/suborg/en/s/res/751-(1992) (accessed October 13, 2015).
    17. UN Security Council Resolution 794, S/RES/794, December 3, 1992, http://www.un.org/en/ga/search/view_doc.asp?symbol=S/RES/794(1992) (accessed October 13, 2015).
    18. Kenneth Allard, *Somalia Operations: Lessons Learned* (Washington, DC: National Defense University Press, 1995), 24.
    19. UN Security Council Resolution 814, S/RES/814, March 26, 1993, http://www.securitycouncilreport.org/atf/cf/%7B65BFCF9B-6D27-4E9C-8CD3-CF6E4FF96FF9%7D/Chap%20VII%20SRES%20814.pdf (accessed October 13, 2015).
    20. "Further Report of the Secretary General Submitted in Pursuance of Paragraph 18 of Resolution 814 (1993), with Annex on the Re-establishment of Police, Judicial and Penal Systems," S/26317, August 17, 1993.

21. Report of the Secretary General on the Implementation of Security Council Resolution 837 (1993), S/26022, July 1, 1993, 3.

22. Details on the operation to capture Aidid are from Mockaitis, *Peace Operations and Intrastate Conflict*, 66–67.

23. Details on the Russian and Chechen rebel militaries and tactics are from Olga Oliker, *Russia's Chechen Wars: Lessons from Urban Warfare* (Santa Monica, CA: Rand, 2001), 5–22.

24. Ibid., 30.

25. Ibid., 33.

26. Ibid., 37.

27. "Putin's Way," *Frontline*, PBS, http://www.pbs.org/wgbh/pages/frontline/foreign-affairs-defense/putins-way/transcript-74/ (accessed October 20, 2015); and "September 1998 Russian Apartment Bombings," *The Fifth Estate*, Canadian Broadcasting Company, January 8, 2015, http://www.cbc.ca/fifth/blog/september-1999-russian-apartment-bombings-timeline (accessed October 20, 2015).

28. Jason Lyall, "Are Coethnics More Effective Counterinsurgents? Evidence from the Second Chechen War," *American Political Science Review* 104, no. 1 (February 2010): 1–20.

29. Ibid., 2.

30. Ibid.

31. Emil Pain, "The Second Chechen War, the Information Component," *Military Review* (July–August 2000), http://fmso.leavenworth.army.mil/documents/secchech/secchech.htm (accessed October 20, 2015).

32. Oliker, *Russia's Chechen Wars*, 75–76.

33. *War Crimes in Chechnya and the Response of the West*, Testimony before the U.S. Senate Committee on Foreign Relations, February 29, 2000, https://www.hrw.org/news/2000/02/29/war-crimes-chechnya-and-response-west (accessed October 20, 2015).

34. Helge Brumborg, "Report on the Size and Ethnic Composition of the Population of Kosovo," August 14, 2002, http://www.icty.org/x/file/About/OTP/War_Demographics/en/milosevic_kosovo_020814.pdf (accessed October 20, 2015).

35. Ivo Dalder and Michael O'Hanlon, *Winning Ugly: NATO's War to Save Kosovo* (Washington, DC: Brookings Institute Press, 2000), 27.

36. Miron Rezun, *Europe's Nightmare: The Struggle for Kosovo* (Westport, CT: Praeger, 2001), 45–46.

37. Dalder and O'Hanlon argue that this shift in objective is what ultimately led NATO to win "ugly." Dalder and O'Hanlon, *Winning Ugly*.

38. George W. Bush, *Address to a Joint Session of Congress and the American People*, September 20, 2001, http://georgewbush-whitehouse.archives.gov/news/releases/2001/09/20010920-8.html (accessed August 20, 2015).

39. Ibid.

40. Richard W. Stewart et al., *American Military History*, vol. II, *The United States Army in a Global Era, 1917–2008* (Washington, DC: Center for U.S. Army Military History, 2010), 469.

41. Ibid., 469–470.

42. Troop strengths are from Anthony Cordesman, *The Iraq War: Strategy, Tactics and Military Lessons* (Westport, CT: Praeger, 2003), 37–39.

43. Thomas E. Ricks, *Fiasco: The American Military Adventure in Iraq* (New York: Penguin, 2006), 106.

44. Information on the air campaign is from Gregory Fontenot et al., *On Point: the United States Army in Operation Iraqi Freedom, through 1 May 2003* (Fort Leavenworth, KS: Center for Army Lessons Learned, 2004), 86–87.

45. Global Security, http://www.globalsecurity.org/military/ops/iraq_casualties_march03.htm (accessed August 23, 2015).

46. *FM 3-24: Counterinsurgency* (Washington, DC: Department of the Army, 2006), 1.4.

47. Ibid., 141, 145.

48. Kimberly Kagan, "The Anbar Awakening: Displacing al-Qaeda from its Stronghold in Western Iraq," *Iraq Report* (Institute for the Study of War), August 21, 2006 to March 30, 2007.

49. UN Security Council Resolution, S/RES/1970, February 26, 2011, http://www.un.org/en/ga/search/view_doc.asp?symbol=S/RES/1970(2011) (accessed August 23, 2015).

50. UN Security Council Resolution, S/RES/1973, March 17, 2011, http://www.un.org/en/ga/search/view_doc.asp?symbol=S/RES/1973(2011) (accessed August 23, 2015).

51. "The World Is Actually Becoming Less Violent—Believe It or Not," *The World* (Public Radio International), broadcast September 29, 2014, http://www.pri.org/stories/2014-09-29/world-actually-becoming-more-peaceful-believe-it-or-not (accessed August 25, 2015).

Conclusion

1. Robert Thompson called this the "same element theory," using the cat analogy to make his point. *Make for the Hills: Memories of Far Eastern Wars* (London: Leo Cooper, 1989), 31.

2. For a discussion of these issues see Thomas R. Mockaits, *Soldiers of Misfortune?* (Carlisle Barracks, PA: Strategic Studies Institute, U.S. Army War College, 2014).

Bibliography

Primary Sources

Adams, John. "Letter to H. Niles," February 13, 1818. http://nationalhumanities center.org/ows/seminars/revolution/Adams-Niles.pdf.

An Agenda for Peace: Preventive Diplomacy, Peace Making and Peace-Keeping. Report of the Secretary General. June 17, 1992. UN Document A/47/277–S/24111.

Anderson, F. M., ed. *The Constitutions and Other Select Documents Illustrative of the History of France, 1789–1907.* 2nd ed. Minneapolis, MN: H. W. Wilson, 1908.

Army-Navy Game Day Program. November 30, 1941. https://collectableivy.word press.com/2009/02/22/army-navy-program-1941-uss-arizona/.

Bagehot, Walter. "Modern History Sourcebook: The Use of Conflict, 1872." http://www.iupui.edu/~histwhs/H374.dir/H374.webreader/darwin.bagehot .html.

Barbusse, Henri. *Under Fire.* Translated by W. Fitzwater Wray. New York: Dutton, 1969. First published 1916.

Barnett, Correlli. *The Swordbearers: Studies in Supreme Command in the First World War.* Bloomington: Indiana University Press, 1975.

Barry, Tom. *Guerrilla Days in Ireland.* Cork, Ireland: Mercier Press, 1949.

Brittain, Vera. *A Testament of Youth.* New York: Penguin, 2005. First published 1933.

Brooks, Rupert. "The Soldier." 1914. http://www.poets.org/poetsorg/poem /soldier.

Bush, George W. "Address to a Joint Session of Congress and the American People." September 20, 2001. http://georgewbush-whitehouse.archives.gov /news/releases/2001/09/20010920-8.html.

Cable from the President of the Congo, et al., to the Secretary General of the United Nations, July 12, 1960. UN Document S/4382.

Callwell, Sir Charles Edward. *Small Wars: Their Principles and Practice.* London: HMSO, 1906. First published 1896.

Churchill, Winston. *A Roving Commission: My Early Life*. New York: Charles Scribner's Sons, 1930.

Clausewitz, Karl von. *On War*. Translated by J. J. Graham. London: N. Trübner, 1909. First published 1873.

Convention for the Pacific Settlement of Disputes. The Hague, 1907. http://avalon.law.yale.edu/20th_century/pacific.asp.

Convention (I) for the Pacific Settlement of International Disputes. The Hague, 1899. at http://avalon.law.yale.edu/19th_century/hague01.asp.

Convention Respecting the Rights and Duties of Neutral Powers and Persons in Case of War on Land. The Hague, 1907. http://avalon.law.yale.edu/20th_century/hague05.asp.

Convention with Respect to the Laws and Customs of War on Land. The Hague, 1899. http://avalon.law.yale.edu/19th_century/hague02.asp.

Cronkite, Walter. *CBS Evening News*, February 27, 1968. In Mark Atwood Lawrence, *The Vietnam War: An International History in Documents*, 124. New York: Oxford University Press, 2014.

Declaration on the Launching of Projectiles and Explosives from Balloons. The Hague, July 29, 1899. http://avalon.law.yale.edu/19th_century/dec99-01.asp.

Declaration on the Use of Bullets Which Expand or Flatten Easily in the Human Body. The Hague, 1899. http://avalon.law.yale.edu/19th_century/dec99-03.asp.

Declaration on the Use of Projectiles the Object of Which Is the Diffusion of Asphyxiating or Deleterious Gases. The Hague, 1899. http://avalon.law.yale.edu/19th_century/dec99–02.asp.

Die Truppenführung [Troop Leading]. German Field Regulations, Part I, 1933, II.28. Translated and published by U.S. Army General Staff School, Fort Leavenworth, KS, 1936. Combined Arms Research Library Digital Library. http://cgsc.contentdm.oclc.org/cdm/ref/collection/p4013coll7/id/131.

"Disarmament: Washington Naval Treaty, Concluded 1922." https://en.wikipedia.org/wiki/Covenant_of_the_League_of_Nations.

Douhet, Giulio. *The Command of the Air*. Translated by Dino Ferrari. Washington, DC: Air Force History and Museums Program, 1998. First English edition 1942; first Italian edition 1921.

Durova, Nadezhda. *The Cavalry Maiden: Journals of a Russian Officer in the Napoleonic Wars*. Translated by Mary Fleming Zirin. Bloomington: University of Indiana Press, 1989.

Emmerich, Andres. *The Partisan or the Use of a Corps of Light Troops to an Army*. London: H. Reynell, 1789.

Ewald, Johann. *Treatise on Partisan Warfare*. Translated by Robert A. Selig and David Curtis Skaggs. Westport, CT: Greenwood, 1991. First published 1785.

Field Service Regulations, United States Army 1923. Washington, DC: Government Printing Office, 1924.

FM 3-24: Counterinsurgency. Washington, DC: Department of the Army, 2006.

FM 100-5: Field Service Regulations, Operations. Washington, DC: Government Printing Office, 1941.

FM 100-5: Tentative Field Service Regulations, Operations. Washington, DC: Government Printing Office, 1939.
Frederick the Great. "Les Principes Généraux de Guerre." In *Œvre de Frédéric le Grand*, 28:art. XXVI, 95. Berlin: Deckersche Geheime Ober-Hofbuch drucherei, 1846–1856. Digitale Ausgabe Universitätsbibliothek Trier, http://friedrich.uni-trier.de/de/oeuvres/28/toc.
Fuller, J. F. C. *Lectures on Field Service Regulations III: Operations between Mechanized Forces*. London: Sifton Praed & Company, 1932.
General Orders No. 100: Instructions for the Government of Armies of the United States in the Field. April 24, 1863. http://avalon.law.yale.edu/19th_century/lieber.asp#sec1.
Gerald of Wales. *Itinerary through Wales* (1191). http://www.archive.org/stream/itinerarythroug00girauoft/itinerarythroug00girauoft_djvu.txt.
Grandmaison, Thomas-Antoine le Roy de. *La Petite Guerre ou Traite de Service des Troupes Legeres en Campagne*. 1756.
Graves, Robert. *Goodbye to All That*. New York: Doubleday, 1957. First published 1929.
Green, John. *A Soldier's Life, 1806–1815*. London: EP Publishing Ltd., 1973. First published 1827.
Greenman, Jeremiah. *Diary of a Common Solider in the American Revolution, 1775–1783*. Edited by Robert C. Bray and Paul E. Bushnell. DeKalb: Northern Illinois University Press, 1978.
Grotius, Hugo. *The Rights of War and Peace*. Edited by Jean Barbeyrac. Vol. 1, ch. 2, II.3. Indianapolis, IN: Liberty Fund, 2005. From the 1738 English translation of Jean Barbeyrac's French edition by John Morrice.
Guderian, Heinz. *Achtung Panzer! Die Entwicklung der Panzerwaffer, ihre Kampftaktik und ihre Operationa Möglichkeit* [Attention, panzer! The development of armored forces, their battle tactics and their operational possibilities]. Stuttgart: Union Deutche Verlagsgesellschaft, 1937.
Guderian, Heinz. *Panzer Leader*. Translated by Constantine Fitzgibbon. Cambridge, MA: DaCapo Press, 2002. First published 1952.
Guibert, Jacques Antoine Hippolyte Comte de. *Essai general de Tactique*. London: chez les libraires associés, 1772. Chapter 2. Excerpted and translated by Beatrice Heuser, *The Strategy Makers: Thoughts on War and Society from Machiavelli to Clausewitz*. Santa Barbara, CA: Praeger/ABC-CLIO, 2010.
Harris, John. *Recollections of Rifleman Harris as Told to Henry Curling*. Edited by Christopher Hibbert. Hamden, CT: Archon Books, 1970. First published 1848.
Henty, George Alfred. *With Kitchener in the Soudan: A Story of Atbara and Omdurman*. London: Blackie and Son, 1903.
Herr, Michael. *Dispatches*. New York: Vintage Books, 1991. First published 1968.
Jeney, Captain de. *Le Partisan ou de l'Art de Fair la Petite Guerre*. A la Haye [The Hague], 1759.

Jomini, Antoine-Henri Baron de. *The Art of War*. Translated by G. H. Mendell and W. P. Craighill. West Point, NY: U.S. Military Academy, 1862

"Kellog-Briand Pact, 1928." http://www.yale.edu/lawweb/avalon/imt/kbpact.htm.

Kennan, George. *Testimony Given Before the Committee on Foreign Relations of the U.S. Senate*. 89th Cong. (February 10, 1966).

Kennedy, John F. "Inaugural Address." January 20, 1961. http://www.bartleby.com/124/pres56.html.

Lawrence, Mark Atwood. *The Vietnam War: An International History in Documents*. New York: Oxford University Press, 2014.

Laws of War on Land. Oxford: Institute of International Law, 1880. https://www1.umn.edu/humanrts/instree/1880a.htm.

Lee, Henry. *Memoirs of the War in the Southern Department of the United States*, vol. 1. Philadelphia: Bradford and Inskeep, 1812.

Lehrer, Tom. "So Long Mom (A Song for World War III)." 1965. http://www.metrolyrics.com/so-long-mom-a-song-for-world-war-iii-lyrics-tom-lehrer.html.

Lehrer, Tom. "Who's Next?" 1965. http://www.metrolyrics.com/whos-next-lyrics-tom-lehrer.html.

Letter of a British officer serving in Ireland to his mother. *Hampshire Regimental Journal* 16, no. 8 (August 1922): 136–137.

Lowe, Brevet Major T.A. "Some Reflections of a Junior Officer in Ireland." *Army Quarterly and Defence Journal* 5 (October 1922): 50–58.

Machiavelli, Niccolo. *The Prince*. W. K. Marriott, 1908. First published 1515.

Mao Zedong, *On Guerrilla Warfare*. Translated by Samuel B. Griffith II. Baltimore, MD: National and Aviation Publishing Company of America, 1992. First published 1937.

Mao Zedong. *On Protracted War*. May 1938. https://www.marxists.org/reference/archive/mao/selected-works/volume-2/mswv2_09.htm.

McGuire, Barry. "Eve of Destruction." 1965. http://www.azlyrics.com/lyrics/barrymcguire/eveofdestruction.html.

[Moore, Harold]. "After Action Report, IA DRANG Valley Operation 1st Battalion, 7th Cavalry 14–16 November 1965," 18–19. http://www.au.af.mil/au/awc/awcgate/vietnam/ia_drang.pdf.

"National Assessment of Adult Literacy." National Center for Educational Statistics. http://nces.ed.gov/naal/lit_history.asp.

Nixon, Richard. "Address to the Nation on the War in Vietnam." November 3, 1969. http://www.presidency.ucsb.edu/ws/index.php?pid=2303.

North Atlantic Treaty. April 4, 1949. http://www.nato.int/cps/en/natolive/official_texts_17120.htm.

Owen, Wilfred. "Dulce et Decorum Este." 1917. http://www.warpoetry.co.uk/owen1.html.

Remarque, Erich Maria. *All Quiet on the Western Front*. Translated by A. W. Wheen. New York: Fawcett Crest, 1945. First published 1929.

Bibliography

Rhodes, Robert Hunt, ed. *All for the Union: The Civil War Diaries of Elisha Hunt Rhodes*. New York: Vintage, 1991. First published 1985.

Rogers, Robert. *Journals of Major Robert Rogers*. London: J. Millan, 1765. Reprinted with an introduction by Howard Peckham. New York: Corinth Books, 1961.

Schlieffen, Alfred. "Great Memorandum." Translated with commentary by Gerhardt Ritter. In *The Schlieffen Plan: Critique of a Myth*. London: Oswald Wolff Limited, 1958.

Starr, Edwin. "War." 1970. http://www.metrolyrics.com/war-lyrics-edwin-starr.html.

Stevenson, Roger. *Instructions for Officers Detached in the Field: Containing a Scheme for Forming a Corps of a Partisan* [sic]. Philadelphia: R. Aikenm, 1775. First published in London 1770.

Sun Tzu, *The Art of War*. Translated by Thomas Clear. Boston: Shambhala Publishing, 1988.

Surtees, William. *Twenty-Five Years in the Rifle Brigade*. London: Frederick Muller, 1973. First published 1833.

Tennyson, Alfred Lord. "The Charge of the Light Brigade," 1854. http://poetry.eserver.org/light-brigade.html.

Terry, Alfred. Interview. *Army and Navy Journal* 14, no. 14 (November 11, 1876). In Peter Cozzens, *Eyewitnesses to the Indian Wars, 1865–1890*. Mechanicsport, PA: Stackpole Books, 2005.

The Tribune Almanac and Political Register. New York: Tribune Association, 1863.

United Nations Charter. Chapter 7, Article 42. http://www.un.org/en/documents/charter/chapter7.shtml.

United Nations General Assembly. Resolution on Expansion of Mission to the Congo. September 20, 1960. UN Document A/RES/1474/Rev.1 (ES-IV).

United Nations Security Council. Resolution for the Creation of the United Nations Protection Force (UNPROFOR) for Former Yugoslavia. February 21, 1992. UN Document S/RES/743.

United Nations Security Council. Resolution for the Enlargement for UNPROFOR. September 14, 1992. UN Document S/RES/776.

United Nations Security Council. Resolution on Authorization for Mission to the Congo. July 22, 1960. UN Document S/RES/4405.

United States Strategic Bombing Surveys. Washington, DC, 1945–1946. Reprinted, Maxwell Airforce Base, AL: Air University Press, 1987.

Vattel, Emmerich de. *The Law of Nations or the Principals of Natural Law*. Translated from the French by Joseph Chitty, Esq. Based on the 1797 edition, republished by T. & J. W. Johnson, law booksellers, Philadelphia, 1853.

Vauban, Sebastian LePestre de. *A Manual of Siegecraft and Fortification*. Translated with an introduction by George A. Rothrock. Ann Arbor: University of Michigan Press, 1968. First published posthumously in Leiden, 1740.

Secondary Sources

Addington, Larry H. *Patterns of War Since the Eighteenth Century*. 2nd ed. Bloomington: Indiana University Press, 1994. First published 1984.

Anderson, Benedict. *Imagined Communities: Reflections on the Origins and Spread of Nationalism*. New York: Verso, 1991.

Anderson, M.S., *War and Society in Europe of the Old Regime, 1618–1789*. New York: St. Martin's Press, 1988.

Asprey, Robert. *War in the Shadows: The Guerrilla in History*. New York: William Morrow & Company, 1994; 1st ed., 1975.

Astor, Gerald. *The Jungle War: Mavericks, Marauders, and Madmen in the China-Burma-India Theater of World War II*. Hoboken, NJ: John Wiley and Sons, 2004.

"The Barbed Wire Fence: 'A Classic Invention.'" *The Science News-Letter* 24, no. 642 (July 29, 1933): 74.

"The Battle of Agincourt." http://web.archive.org/web/20091027132428/http://geocities.com/beckster05/Agincourt/AgAftermath.html.

"The Battle of Gumbinen, 1914." http://www.firstworldwar.com/battles/gumbinnen.htm.

"Battle of France." In *New World Encyclopedia*. http://www.newworldencyclopedia.org/entry/Battle_of_France.

"Battle of Gorlice-Tarnow, 2–10 May 1915." http://www.historyofwar.org/articles/battles_gorlice_tarnow.html.

"Battle of Midway." http://militaryhistory.about.com/od/worldwari1/p/Midway.htm.

"Battle of the Somme, 1 July to 13 November 1916." http://www.bbc.co.uk/history/worldwars/wwone/battle_somme.shtml.

Beckett, Ian. *The Victorians at War*. London: Hambeldon and London, 2003.

Bell, J. Bowyer. *The Myth of the Guerrilla: Revolutionary Theory and Malpractice*. New York: Alfred A. Knopf, 1971.

Berghan, Volker. *Germany in the Era of Two World Wars: From Militarism and Genocide to Civil Society*. Princeton, NJ: Princeton University Press, 2009.

"Bergman MP18 Gun." http://www.firstworldwar.com/atoz/mgun_mp18.htm.

Birtle, Andrew. Andrew. *US Army Counterinsurgency and Contingency Operations Doctrine, 1942–1976*. Washington, DC: United States Army Center for Military History, 2006.

Black, Jeremy. *European Warfare, 1660–1815*. New Haven, CT: Yale University Press, 1994.

"Blitzkrieger." *Time* 34, no. 13 (September 25, 1939): 29.

Bonner, M. Brem, and Peter McCord. "Reassessment of the Union Blockade's Effectiveness in the Civil War." *North Carolina Historical Review* 88, no. 4 (October 2011): 375–398.

Boot, Max. *Invisible Armies: An Epic History of Guerrilla Warfare from Ancient Times to the Present*. New York: W.W. Norton, 2013.

Bibliography

Boot, Max. *The Savage Wars of Peace: Small Wars and the Rise of American Power.* New York: Basic Books, 2002.

Boot, Max. *War Made New: Technology, Warfare, and the Course of History, 1500 to Today.* New York: Gotham Books, 2006.

"B29 Super Fortress." http://www.boeing.com/history/products/b-29-superfortress.page.

Buchanan, John. *The Road to Guilford Courthouse: The American Revolution in the Carolinas.* New York: John Wiley and Sons, 1997.

"Bushido Code: An Overview." http://www.pbs.org/wgbh/sugihara/readings/bushido.html.

"By the Numbers: The U.S. Military," National World War II Museum. http://www.nationalww2museum.org/learn/education/for-students/ww2-history/ww2-by-the-numbers/us-military.html.

Cale, Major Paul P. "The United States Military Advisory Group in El Salvador, 1979–1992." U.S. Army Command and Staff College Paper, 1996. smallwarsjournal.com/documents/cale.pdf.

"Central Burma." http://www.ibiblio.org/hyperwar/USA/USA-C-Burma45/.

Chadwick, Bruce. *The First American Army: the Untold Story of George Washington and the Men Behind America's First Fight for Freedom.* Naperville, IL: Sourcebooks, Inc., 2005.

Chandler, David. *Marlborough as Military Commander.* London: Penguin, 1973.

Churchill, Winston. "The Sinews of Peace (Iron Curtain Speech)." March 5, 1946. http://www.winstonchurchill.org/resources/speeches/1946-1963-elder-statesman/the-sinews-of-peace.

Collins, Joseph J. "The Soviet-Afghan War: The First Four Years." *Parameters* 14, no. 2 (Summer 1984): 49–62.

"Comparative Fleet Strengths: The United States and Japan, December 7, 1941." http://historicaltextarchive.com/sections.php?action=read&artid=194.

Cordesman, Anthony. *The Iraq War: Strategy, Tactics and Military Lessons.* Westport, CT: Praeger, 2003.

Corum, James S. *The Roots of Blitzkreig: Hans von Seeckt and the German Military Reform.* Lawrence: University of Kansas Press, 1992.

"Covenant of the League of Nations." https://en.wikipedia.org/wiki/Covenant_of_the_League_of_Nations.

"Cover: Poilu." *Life* 8, no. 11 (March 11, 1940): 21.

"Creeping Barrage." http://www.firstworldwar.com/atoz/creepingbarrage.htm.

Cress, Dilbert. *Citizens in Arms: The Army and Militia in American Society to the War of 1812.* Chapel Hill: University of North Carolina Press, 1982.

Davidson, Philip K. *Vietnam at War. The History: 1946–1975.* New York: Oxford University Press, 1988.

Deady, Timothy K. "Lessons of a Successful Counterinsurgency Campaign: The Philippines, 1899–1902." *Parameters* 35, no. 1 (Spring 2005): 53–68.

"The Development and Proliferation of Nuclear Weapons." http://www.nobelprize.org/educational/peace/nuclear_weapons/readmore.html.

Diedering, Tilman. "The German-Herero War of 1904: Revisionism of Genocide or Imaginary Historiography?" *Journal of Southern African Studies* 19, no. 1 (March 1993): 80–88.

Doughty, Robert. "The Myth of Blitzkrieg." In *Challenging the United States Symmetrically and Asymmetrically: Can America Be Defeated?*, edited by Lloyd Matthews, 57–79. Carlisle Barracks, PA: Strategic Studies Institute, U.S. Army War College, 1998.

Doughty, Robert A., et al. *Warfare in the Western World.* vol. I, *Military Operations from 1600–1871*. Lexington, MA: DC Heath, 1996.

Duckers, Peter. *British Military Rifles*. London: Shire Publications, 2008.

Dull, John. *The Age of the Ship of the Line: The British and French Navies, 1650–1815*. Omaha: University of Nebraska Press, 2009.

Dupuy, T. N. *A Genius for War: The German Army and General Staff, 1807–1945*. London: MacDonald and Janes, 1977.

Ellis, John. *Eye Deep in Hell: Trench Warfare in World War I*. Baltimore, MD: Johns Hopkins University Press, 1976.

"Episode 2: Lightning War." *World War II in Colour*. World Media Rights, 2008–2009.

Esdalle, Charles. *Fighting Napoleon: Guerrillas, Bandits and Adventurers in Spain, 1808–1814*. New Haven, CT: Yale University Press, 2004.

Esdalle, Charles. *The Peninsular War: A New History*. New York: Palgrave, 2003.

Esper, Thomas. "The Replacement of the Longbow by Firearms in the English Army." *Technology and Culture* 6, no. 3 (Summer 1965): 382–393.

Fehrenbach, T. R. *This Kind of War: The Classic Korean War History*. Washington, DC: Brassey's, 1963.

Fisher, Noel C. "'Prepare Them for My Coming': General William T. Sherman, Total War, and Pacification in West Tennessee." *Tennessee Historical Quarterly* 51, no. 2 (Summer 1992): 75–86.

Fivecoat, David G. "Leaving the Graveyard: The Soviet Union's Withdrawal from Afghanistan." *Parameters* 42, no. 2 (Summer 2012): 42–55.

"Fleets 1939." WW2WEAPONS. http://ww2-weapons.com/fleets-1939/.

Fletcher, C. R. L. *Gustavus Adolphus and the Thirty-Years War*. New York: Caricorn Books, 1963.

Fontenot, Gregory, et al. *On Point: The United States Army in Operation Iraqi Freedom, through 1 May 2003*. Fort Leavenworth, KS: Center for Army Lessons Learned, 2004.

Ford, Guy Stanton. "Boyen's Military Law." *American Historical Review* 20, no. 3 (April 1915): 528–538.

Francois, Lt. Col. Philippe. "Waging Counterinsurgency in Algeria: A French Perspective." *Military Review* 88, no. 5 (September–October 2008): 56–67.

French, David. "The Meaning of Attrition, 1914–1916." *English Historical Review* 103, no. 407 (April 1988): 385–405.

Friedman, Norman. *The Fifty-Year War: Conflict and Strategy in the Cold War*. Annapolis, MD: Naval, 2000.

Bibliography

Fuller, Alexandra. "In the Shadow of Wounded Knee." *National Geographic Online*, August 2012. http://ngm.nationalgeographic.com/2012/08/pine-ridge/fuller-text.

Fuller, J. F. C. *The Conduct of War*. New York: Funk and Wagnall's, 1961.

Fussell, Paul. *Wartime: Understanding and Behavior in the Second World War*. New York: Oxford University Press, 1989.

Gates, David. *The Napoleonic Wars, 1803–1815*. London: Arnold, 1997.

Gates, John M. "The U.S. Army and Irregular Warfare." Unpublished manuscript, [1989].

"General Curtis E. Lemay (1906–1990)." http://www.pbs.org/wgbh/amex/bomb/peopleevents/pandeAMEX61.html.

Gibson, Irving M. "Maginot and Liddell Hart: The Doctrine of Defense." In *Makers of Modern Strategy*, edited by Edward Meade Earl, 365–387. Princeton, NJ: Princeton University Press, 1971. First published 1943.

Glanz, James. "Centuries after Henry V, Henry V's Greatest Victory Is Besieged by Academia." *New York Times*, October 25, 2009, sec. A, col. 0, Foreign Desk, 6.

"Global Security." http://www.globalsecurity.org/military/ops/iraq_casualties_march03.htm.

Goldberg, Alfred. "Air Campaign Overlord: To D-day." In Eisenhower Foundation, *D-Day: The Normandy Invasion in Retrospect*, 57–78. Lawrence: University of Kansas Press, 1971.

Gow, James. *Triumph of the Lack of Will: International Diplomacy and the Yugoslav War*. New York: Columbia University Press, 1997.

Graydon A. Tunstall. "Austria-Hungary and the Brusilov Offensive of 1916." *The Historian* 70, no. 1 (February 26, 2008): 30–53.

Grenier, John. *The First Way of War: American War Making on the Frontier*. Cambridge, UK: Cambridge University Press, 2005.

Grimsley, Mark. *The Hard Hand of War: Union Military Policy Toward Southern Civilians, 1861–1865*. New York: Cambridge University Press, 1995.

Hacker, J. David. "A Census-based Count of the Civil War Dead." *Civil War History* 57, no. 4 (December 2011): 307–348.

Halliday, Fred. "Soviet Foreign Policymaking and the Afghanistan War: From 'Second Mongolia' to 'Bleeding Wound'." *Review of International Studies* 25, no. 4 (October 1999): 675–691.

Hanchard, Michael G. "Herero and Nama Rebellions, 1904–1907: A Prelude to the Modern Holocaust?" Global Mappings, n.d. http://diaspora.northwestern.edu/mbin/WebObjects/DiasporaX.woa/wa/displayArticle?atomid=619.

Hedges, Chris. "What Every Person Should Know about War." *New York Times*, July 6, 2003. http://www.nytimes.com/2003/07/06/books/chapters/0713-1st-hedges.html?pagewanted=all.

Herman, David. *The Arming of Europe and the Making of the First World War*. Princeton, NJ: Princeton University Press, 1996.

Herring, George. *America's Longest War: the United States and Vietnam, 1950–1975*. New York: Alfred A. Knopf, 1986.

Hess, Gary. *Vietnam: Explaining America's Lost War*. Oxford, UK: Blackwell, 2009.

Heuser, Beatrice. "Small Wars in the Age of Clausewitz: The Watershed between Partisan War and People's War." *Journal of Strategic Studies* 33, no. 1 (February 2010): 139–162.

Hibbert, Christopher. *Redcoats and Rebels: The American Revolution Through British Eyes*. New York: W.W. Norton, 1990.

Higginbotham, Don. *Daniel Morgan, Revolutionary Rifleman*. Chapel Hill: University of North Carolina Press, 1961.

Higham, Robin. "Technology and D-Day." In Eisenhower Foundation, *D-Day: The Normandy Invasion in Retrospect*, 221–242. Lawrence: University of Kansas Press, 1971.

"HMS Victory." http://www.stvincent.ac.uk/Heritage/1797/Victory/index2.html.

Holland, Rose J. "The Ice Incident at the Battle of Austerlitz." *English Historical Review* 17, no. 67 (July 1902): 537–538.

Horne, Alistair. *The Price of Glory: Verdun 1916*. New York: Penguin, 1994. First published 1963.

Howard, Michael. "Men Against Fire: Expectations of War in 1914." In *Military Strategy and the Origins of the First World War*, edited by Steven Miller, 41–57. Princeton, NJ: Princeton University Press, 1991.

Howey, Alan W. "Minié Ball." *Civil War Times* (October 1993), http://www.historynet.com/minie-ball.

Hull, Isabel. "The Military Campaign in Southwest Africa, 1904–1907." *German Historical Institute Bulletin*, no. 37 (Fall 2005): 39–45.

"Isoroku Yamamotoa." http://www.rjgeib.com/heroes/tanimizu/yamamoto.html.

Jackson, John Hampden. *Clemenceau and the Third Republic*. London: Hodder and Stoughton Limited, 1946.

Jackson, Julian. *The Fall of France: The Nazi Invasion of 1940*. Oxford: Oxford University Press, 2003.

Jacobs, Lewis. "World War II and the American Film." *Cinema Journal* 7 (Winter, 1967–1968): 1–21.

Joes, Anthony James. *Guerrilla Conflict before the Cold War*. Westport, CT: Praeger, 1996.

Joll, James. *The Origins of the First World War*. New York: Routledge, 2007. First published 1984.

Jones, C. "Professionalization of the French Army under the Ancien Regime." In *The Military Revolution and the State, 1500–1800*, edited by Michael Duffy, 149–167. Exeter, UK: Studies in History, 1980.

Kagan, Kimberly. *Iraq Report: The Anbar Awakening; Displacing al-Qaeda from Its Stronghold in Western Iraq*. n.p.: Institute for the Study of War, 2007.

Keegan, John. *The First World War*. New York: Vintage, 2000. First published 1998.

Keegan, John. *A History of Warfare*. New York: Alfred Knopf, 1993.
Keegan, John. *The Second World War*. New York: Penguin, 2005. First published 1989.
Keegan, John. *Six Armies in Normandy: From D-Day to the Liberation of Paris*. New York: Penguin, 1994. First published 1982.
Keershaw, Ian. *Fateful Choices: Ten Decisions That Changed the World, 1940–1941*. New York: Penguin, 2007.
Kennedy, Paul. *The Rise and Fall of the Great Powers*. New York: Vintage Books, 1989. First published 1987.
Keown, John. "America's War for Independence: Just or Unjust?" *Journal of Catholic Social Thought* 6, no. 2 (2009): 277–304.
Kilcullen, David. *The Accidental Guerrilla; Fighting Small Wars in the Midst of a Big One*. New York: Oxford, 2009.
King, Gilbert. *The Savage Wars of Peace: Small Wars and the Rise of American Power* New York: Basic Books, 2002.
King, Gilbert. "Where the Buffalo No Longer Roam." *Smithsonian Online*, July 17, 2012. http://www.smithsonianmag.com/history/where-the-buffalo-no-longer-roamed-3067904/?no-ist.
Kipling, Rudyard. "The Whiteman's Burden," 1899. http://legacy.fordham.edu/halsall/mod/kipling.asp.
Kitchen, Martin. *The German Offensive of 1918*. Charleston, SC: Tempus, 2001.
Komer, R. W. *The Malayan Emergency in Retrospect: Organization of a Successful Counterinsurgency Effort*. Santa Monica, CA: Rand, 1972.
Krepinevich, Andrew. *The Army and the Vietnam War*. Baltimore, MD: Johns Hopkins University Press, 1986.
Kwasny, Mark V. "Militia, Guerrilla Warfare, Tactics, and Weaponry." In *A Companion to the American Revolution*, edited by Jack P. Greene and J. R. Pole, 314–319. Oxford: Blackwell Publishers, 2000.
Kwasny, Mark V. *Washington's Partisan War, 1775–1783*. Kent, OH: Kent State University Press, 1996.
Landes, David. *The Unbound Prometheus: Technological Change and Industrial Development in Western Europe from 1750 to the Present*. 2nd ed. London: Cambridge University Press, 2003.
Leakey, Richard. *The Making of Mankind*. New York: Dutton, 1981.
Lebergott, Stanley. "Why the South Lost: Commercial Purpose in the Confederacy, 1861–1865." *Journal of American History* 70, no. 1 (June 1983): 58–74.
Liddell Hart, Sir Basil. *Strategy*. Westport, CT: Praeger, 1967.
Linn, Brian McAlister. *The U.S. Army and Counterinsurgency in the Philippine War, 1899–1902*. Chapel Hill: University of North Carolina Press, 1989.
Logusz, Michael O. *With Musket and Tomahawk: The Saratoga Campaign and the Wilderness War of 1777*. Philadelphia: Casemate, 2010.
Lunt, James. "Lawrence and Arab Revolt." In *A History of World War I*, edited by A. J. P. Taylor, 133–137. London: Octopus Books, 1974.
Luvaas, Jay. *Napoleon on the Art of War*. New York: Free Press, 1999.

Lynn, John A. "Recalculating French Army Growth during the Grand Siecle." In *The Military Revolution Debate: Readings on the Military Transformation of Early Modern Europe*, edited by Cliff J. Rogers, 117–148. Boulder, CO: Westview Press, 1995.

MacPherson, James. *Battle Cry of Freedom: The Civil War Era*. New York: Oxford University Press, 1988.

MacPherson, James. *For Cause and Comrades: Why Men Fought in the Civil War*. New York: Oxford University Press, 1997.

Madley, Benjamin. "California's Yuki Indians: Defining Genocide in Native American History." *Western Historical Quarterly* 39, no. 3 (Autumn 2008): 303–332.

Mahon, John K. "Civil War Infantry Assault Tactics." Special issue on Civil War, *Military Affairs* 25, no. 2 (Summer 1961): 57–68.

Martin, Colon Giles. "War in Algeria: The French Experience." *Military Review* 85, no. 4 (July–August 2005): 51–57.

Mitter, Rana. *Forgotten Ally: China's World War II, 1937–1945*. New York: Houghton Mifflin Harcourt, 2013.

Mockaitis, Thomas R. *British Counterinsurgency, 1919–1960*. London: Macmillan, 1990.

Mockaitis, Thomas R. *The "New" Terrorism: Myths and Reality*. Stanford, CA: Stanford University Press, 2008. First published 2007.

Mockaitis, Thomas R. *Peace Operations and Intrastate Conflict: The Sword or the Olive Branch?* Westport, CT: Praeger, 1999.

Mockaitis, Thomas R. *Resolving Insurgencies*. Carlisle Barracks, PA: Strategic Studies Institute, U.S. Army War College, 2011.

Mockaits, Thomas R. *Soldiers of Misfortune?* Carlisle Barracks, PA: Strategic Studies Institute, U.S. Army War College, 2014.

More, Peter N. "The Local Origins of Allegiance in Revolutionary South Carolina: The Waxhaws as a Case Study." *South Carolina Historical Magazine* 107, no. 1 (January 2006): .

Moreman, T. R. "Sir Charles Edward Callwell." In *Oxford National Dictionary*. Oxford: Oxford University Press, 2004–2015. http://www.oxforddnb.com.ezproxy.depaul.edu/view/article/32251.

"M2 Light Tank." http://www.tanks-encyclopedia.com/ww2/US/M2_Light_Tank.php.

"M2 Medium Tank." http://www.tanks-encyclopedia.com/ww2/US/m2_medium_tank.php.

Muir, Rory. *Tactics and the Experience of Battle in the Age of Napoleon*. New Haven, CT: Yale University Press, 1998.

Murray, Williamson, and Allan R. Millett. *A War to Be Won: Fighting the Second World War*. Cambridge, MA: Belknap Press, 2000.

North, Jonathan. "General Hoche and Counterinsurgency." *Journal of Military History* 67, no. 2 (April 2003): 529–540.

Nosworth, Brent. *The Anatomy of Victory*. New York: Hippocrene Books, 1992.

Omissi, David. *Airpower and Colonial Control: The Royal Air Force, 1919–1939.* Manchester, UK: Manchester University Press, 1990.

Opération des Nations Unies au Congo (ONUC) [United Nations Mission in the Congo]. "Facts and Figures." http://www.un.org/en/peacekeeping/missions/past/onucF.html.

O'Shaughnessy, Lt. Col. Edward, Jr. "The Evolution of the Armored Force, 1920–1940." Individual Study Project. Carlisle Barracks, PA: U.S. Army War College, 1993.

Overy, Richard. *Russia's War.* New York: Penguin, 1998.

Packenham, Thomas. *The Boer War.* New York: Random House, 1979.

Parker, Geoffrey. *The Military Revolution: Military Innovation and the Rise of the West.* Cambridge, UK: Cambridge University Press, 1996. First published 1988.

Perkin, Harold. *The Origins of Modern English Society.* London: Routledge, 2002. First published 1969.

"Persian Gulf War." http://www.history.com/topics/persian-gulf-war.

Petitfrère, Claude. "La Vendée en Lan II: Défait et Répression." *Annales historiques de la Révolution française*, no. 300 (Avril–Juin 1995): 63–78.

Phillpotts, Christopher. "The French Plan of Battle during the Agincourt Campaign." *English Historical Review* 99, no. 390 (January 1984): 59–66.

Pointing, Clive. *Gunpowder.* London: Chatto & Windus, 2005.

"Population of the British Isles." In *Tacitus Historical Atlas.* http://www.tacitus.nu/historical-atlas/population/british.htm.

Power, J. Tracy. "'The Virtue of Humanity Was Totally Forgot': Buford's Massacre, May 29, 1780." *South Carolina Historical Magazine* 93, no. 1 (January 1992): 5–14.

Powers, Thomas. "How the Little Big Horn Was Won." *Smithsonian Online*, November 2010. http://www.smithsonianmag.com/history/how-the-battle-of-little-bighorn-was-won-63880188/?no-ist.

Quimby, Robert S. *The Background of Napoleonic Warfare.* New York: Columbia University Press, 1957.

Ramet, Sabrina Petra. *Balkan Babel: The Disintegration of Yugoslavia from the Death of Tito to the Ethnic War.* Boulder, CO: Westview Press, 1966.

Ramsay, David. *The History of the Revolution of South-Carolina, From a British Province to an Independent State.* Trenton, NJ: Isaac Collins, 1785.

"The Rape of Nanking." http://www.historyplace.com/worldhistory/genocide/nanking.htm.

Ricks, Thomas E. *Fiasco: The American Military Adventure in Iraq.* New York: Penguin, 2006.

Ripperger, Robert M. "The Development of the French Artillery for the Offensive, 1890–1914." *Journal of Military History* 59, no. 4 (October 1995): 599–618.

Roberts, Michael. "The Military Revolutions, 1560–1660." In *The Military Revolution Debate: Readings on the Military Transformation of Early Modern Europe*, edited by Cliff J. Rogers, 13–35. Boulder, CO: Westview Press, 1995.

Rogers, Cliff J. "The Military Revolutions of the Hundred Year's War." In *The Military Revolution Debate: Readings on the Military Transformation of Early Modern Europe*, edited by Cliff J. Rogers, 55–94. Boulder, CO: Westview Press, 1995.

Ropp, Theodore. *War in the Modern World*. New York: Macmillan, 1962. First published 1959.

Rothenberg, Gunther E. *The Art of Warfare in the Age of Napoleon*. Bloomington: Indiana University Press, 1978.

Rowlands, Guy. *The Dynastic State and the Army under Louis XIV: Royal Service and Private Interest*. Cambridge, UK: Cambridge University Press, 2002.

Royster, Charles. *A Revolutionary People at War: The Continental Army and American Character, 1775–1783*. Chapel Hill: University of North Carolina Press, 1979.

Russell, Peter E. "Redcoats in the Wilderness: British Officers and Irregular Warfare in Europe and America, 1740 to 1760." *William and Mary Quarterly*, 3rd ser., 35, no. 4 (October 1978): 629–652.

Santayana, George. Soliloquy no. 25, "Tipperary." In *Soliloquies in England*. New York: Scribner's, 1924.

Schellhammer, Michael. "John Adams's Rule of Thirds." *Journal of the American Revolution*, February 13, 2013, http://allthingsliberty.com/2013/02/john-adamss-rule-of-thirds/.

Schemann, Serge. "Gorbachev Says U.S. Arms Note Is Not Adequate." *New York Times* February 26, 1986. http://www.nytimes.com/1986/02/26/world/gorbachev-says-us-arms-note-is-not-adequate.html.

Sears, Stephen. *Gettysburg*. New York: Houghton Mifflin, 2003.

"Second World War History." http://www.secondworldwarhistory.com/world-war-2-statistics.asp.

Selig, Robert A., and David Curtis Skaggs. "Introductory Essay." In Johann Ewald, *Treatise on Partisan Warfare*, translated by Robert A. Selig and David Curtis Skaggs, 9–18. Westport, CT: Greenwood, 1991.

Sella, Amnon. "Red Army Doctrine and Training on the Eve of the Second World War." *Soviet Studies* 27, no. 2 (April 1975): 245–264.

Shepherd, Ben. "The Clean Wehrmacht, the War of Extermination and Beyond." *Historical Journal* 52, no. 2 (June 2009): 455–473.

Shonfield, David. "Battle of Omdurman." *History Today* 48, no. 9 (September 1998). http://www.historytoday.com/david-shonfield/battle-omdurman.

Shoshenberg, James W. "Austerlitz: Napoleon's Masterstroke." *Military History* (December 2005): 26–33.

Showalter, Dennis. "Mass Multiplied by Impulsion: The Influence of Railroads on Prussian Planning for the Seven Weeks' War." *Military Affairs* 38, no. 2 (April 1974): 62–67.

Showalter, Dennis. "Soldiers into Postmasters? The Electric Telegraph as an Instrument of Command in the Prussian Army." *Military Affairs* 37, no. 2 (April 1973): 48–52.

Smith, Digby. *The Greenhill Napoleonic Data Book*. London: Greenhill Books, 1998.

Bibliography

Smith, Melden E., Jr. "The Strategic Bombing Debate: The Second World War and Germany." *Journal of Contemporary History* 12, no. 1 (January 1977): 175–191.

Smith, Paul H. "The American Loyalists: Notes on Their Organization and Numerical Strength." *William and Mary Quarterly*, 3rd ser., 25, no. 2 (April 1968): 259–277.

Smith, Thomas T. "U.S. Army Combat Operations in the Indian Wars of Texas, 1849–1881." *Southwestern Historical Quarterly* 99, no. 4 (April 1996): 501–531.

"Source List and Detailed Death Tolls for the Primary Megadeaths of the Twentieth Century." http://necrometrics.com/20c5m.htm#WW1.

Spencer, Charles. *Blenheim, Battle for Europe*. London: Phoenix, 2004.

Stanley, William Dean. "El Salvador: State Building Before and After Democratization, 1980–1995." *Third Quarterly* 27, no. 1 (2006): 101–114.

"Stealth Technology: Theory and Practice." http://www.defense-aerospace.com/articles-view/feature/5/157481/aircraft-stealth%3A-the-view-from-russia.html.

Stewart, Richard W., et. al. *American Military History*. Vol. II, *The United States Army in a Global Era, 1917–2008*. Washington, DC: Center for U.S. Army Military History, 2010. First published 2005.

Summers, Harry G., Jr. *On Strategy: A Critical Analysis of the Vietnam War*. Novato, CA: Presidio Press, 1982.

Surdam, David G. " Northern Naval Superiority and the Economics of the American Civil War." *The Journal of Economic History* 56, no. 2 (June 1996): 473–475.

Sutherland, Daniel. "Guerrilla Warfare, Democracy, and the Fate of the Confederacy." *The Journal of Southern History* 68, no. 2 (May 2002): 259–292.

Sutton, Keith. "Administration Tensions over Algeria's Centres de Regroupment." *British Journal of Middle East Studies* 26, no. 2 (November 1999): 243–270.

Szabo, Franza J. *The Seven Years War in Europe, 1756–1763*. New York: Pearson/Longman, 2008.

Taber, Robert. *The War of the Flea: A Study of Guerrilla Warfare and Practice*. New York: Citadel Press, 1965.

Tarle, Eugene. *Napoleon's Invasion of Russia, 1812*. New York: Oxford University Press, 1942.

Taylor, A. J. P. *The First World War: An Illustrated History*. New York: Perigee Books, 1980. First published 1963.

Taylor, Alan. "WWII: Operation Barbarossa." *The Atlantic*, July 24, 2011. http://www.theatlantic.com/photo/2011/07/world-war-ii-operation-barbarossa/100112/.

Thompson, George Raynor. "Civil War Signals." *Military Affairs* 18, no. 4 (Winter 1954): 188–201.

Thoral, Marie-Cécile. *From Valmy to Waterloo: France at War 1792–1815*. Translated by Godfrey Rogers. London: Palgrave Macmillan, 2011.

Tillman, Barrett. "William Bull Halsey: Legendary World War II Admiral." http://www.historynet.com/william-bull-halsey-legendary-world-war-ii-admiral.htm.
Tilly, Charles. "The Analysis of a Counter-Revolution." *History and Theory* 3, no. 1 (1963): 30–58.
Tilly, Charles. "State and Counterrevolution in France." In "The French Revolution and the Birth of Modernity." Special issue, *Social Research* 56, no. 1. (Spring 1989): 71–97.
"Timeline of the Air War, 1939–1945." http://www.pbs.org/wgbh/americanexperience/features/timeline/bombing/.
Trew, Simon. *Britain, Mikhailović and the Chetniks, 1941–42*. London: Macmillan, 1998.
Tuchman, Barbara. *The Guns of August*. New York: Macmillan, 1962.
UNEF I. "Facts and Figures." http://www.un.org/en/peacekeeping/missions/past/unef1facts.html.
"The Vendee Wars, 1793–99." http://www.inthevendee.com/vendee-wars/vendee-wars.html.
"Vietnam War: Battle of I Drang Valley." http://militaryhistory.about.com/od/vietnamwar/p/Vietnam-War-Battle-Of-Ia-Drang.htm.
"Viewpoint: 10 Myths About World War I Debunked." *BBC Online Magazine*, 25 February 2014. http://www.bbc.com/news/magazine-25776836.
Warner, Geoffrey. "The Korean War." *International Affairs* 56, no. 1 (January 1980): 98–107.
Wawro, Geoffrey. *The Franco-Prussian War: The German Conquest of France in 1870–1871*. New York: Cambridge University Press, 2003.
"Weapons of War—Flamethrowers." http://www.firstworldwar.com/weaponry/flamethrowers.htm.
"Weapons of War: Mark 1 Tank." http://www.bbc.co.uk/history/worldwars/wwone/nonflash_tank.shtml.
Weber, Eugene. *Peasants into Frenchmen: The Modernization of Rural France, 1870–1914*. Stanford, CA: Stanford University Press, 1976.
Webster, Donovan. *The Burma Road: The Epic Story of the China-Burma-India Theater in World War II*. New York: Farrar, Straus and Giroux, 2003.
Weigley, Russell. *The American Way of War: A History of United States Military Strategy and Policy*. New York: Macmillan, 1973.
Werrell, Kenneth P. "The Strategic Bombing of Germany in World War II: Costs and Accomplishments." *Journal of American History* 73, no. 3 (December 1986): 702–713.
"What Really Happened in the Christmas Truce of 1914." http://www.bbc.co.uk/guides/zxsfyrd.
Wilhelm, Pierre. "Telegraph: A Strategic Means of Communication during the American Civil War." *Revista de Historia de América*, no. 124 (enero–junio 1999): 81–98.
Woodward, Susan. *Balkan Tragedy: Chaos and Dissolution After the Cold War*. Washington, DC: Brookings Institute, 1995.

"World Guns." http://world.guns.ru/machine/brit/vickers-mk-e.html.

"The World Is Actually Becoming Less Violent—Believe It or Not." *The World*. Public Radio International, broadcast September 29, 2014. http://www.pri.org/stories/2014-09-29/world-actually-becoming-more-peaceful-believe-it-or-not.

"World War I Casualty and Death Tables." http://www.pbs.org/greatwar/resources/casdeath_pop.html.

Wright, John W. "The Rifle in the American Revolution." *American Historical Review* 29, no. 2 (January 1924): 293–299.

Wright, Robert K. *The Continental Army*. Washington, DC: Center of Military History United States Army, 1989.

"WWI Casualties." http://ww1facts.net/quick-reference/ww1-casualties/.

"WWII." http://www.cordova.lib.il.us/wwii.htm.

York, Neil L. "Pennsylvania Rifle: Revolutionary Weapon in a Conventional War?" *Pennsylvania Magazine of History and Biography* 103, no. 3 (July 1979): 302–324.

Zawodny, J. K. "Soviet Partisans." *Soviet Studies* 17, no. 3 (January 1966): 368–377.

Index

Abenaki Indians, 48
Adams, John, 60
Adolphus, Gustavus, 25–28
Afghan-Soviet War, 258–261, 281
Afghanistan: Afghan-Soviet War, 258–261, 281; Cold War, 258–261; Global War on Terror, 286–287; insurgents, 11, 258–261
Africa Corps, 210
Agricultural revolution, 1
Aguinaldo, Emilio, 150
Aidid, Mohammed Farrah, 278–280
Aircraft, 144, 284; air cavalry, 240; antisubmarine, 214; helicopters, 240; rockets, 217, 240; stealth aircraft, 270–271; World War II, 191–194, 203, 213–217, 219, 226–227, 240
Al-Maliki, Nuri, 290
Al-Qaeda, 285–286, 289–290, 303
Alexander I, 92
Algerian Civil War, 250
All Quiet on the Western Front, 179
Allied forces, 10–11, 175, 202–205, 209–211, 214–220, 222–223, 228–229, 232, 234–235
American Civil War, 4, 127, 139, 142, 145, 148, 153, 238, 294–295; balance of power during, 110–111; collective punishment, 122; death toll, 123–124; experience of war, 124–125; food shortages during, 111, 122; guerilla warfare, 120–121; ideology, 122; industrialization and, 109–110; partisan units, 122; requisitioning, 122; strategy and the course of war, 111–114; trend toward total war, 122–124; unconventional warfare, 120–122
American War of Independence, 2, 47, 57–82, 294, 297; attitudes towards war during, 80–82; experience of war, 82; guerilla warfare, 72; hybrid warfare, 71–72; minutemen, 59, 63, 68; myth and reality, 59–61; opposing forces, 61–64; strategies and campaigns, 64–71; taxation and, 60; unconventional warfare, 71–76
Anaconda Plan, 113
Anglo-Irish War, 195–196
Antitank guns, 240
Arab Revolt, 233
Arizona, 193–194
Armies: dynastic, 26–30, 53–54; organization of, 5–7
Army of Northern Virginia, 114–115, 120
Army of the Potomac, 115–116, 120
Arnold, Benedict, 68–69

Asprey, Robert, 2
Atomic bomb, 4, 58, 89, 231–232, 236–237, 240
Auftragstaktik, 129–130, 134, 154
Augustine of Hippo, 50
Auschwitz, 58, 84, 237
Australia, 168, 228
Australian and New Zealand Army Corpse (ANZACS), 168
Austria: annexation, 197–198, 200; 18th century, 35–37, 39; Napoleonic Wars, 90–92, 94–95; population in 1812, 89–90
Austria-Hungary, 161, 163; Third Army, 168; World War I, 159, 165–167, 171

Bacon, Roger, 17–18
Bagehot, Walter, 147
Bagration, Pyotr, 97
Balzane, Achille, 136
Barbed wire, 144, 173
Barre, Siyadd, 277
Barrès, Jean-Baptiste, 103
Bataan Death March, 237
Batista, Fulgencio, 249
Battle of Agincourt, 15–17
Battle of Antietam, 113
Battle of Algiers, 251
Battle of Auerstädt, 93, 128
Battle of Austerlitz, 93, 102, 127
Battle of Blenheim, 39–44
Battle of Britain, 215, 271
Battle of Bull Run, 113
Battle of Bunker Hill, 60–62
Battle of Cambrai, 173–174
Battle of Concord, 62
Battle of Cowpens, 71, 78–80
Battle of Crecy, 15
Battle of France, 201–205, 207
Battle of Gettysburg, 113–120
Battle of Jena, 93, 128
Battle of Könniggratz, 134
Battle of Leipzig, 128

Battle of Lexington, 62
Battle of Little Bighorn, 148–149
Battle of Long Island, 66
Battle of Monmouth, 70
Battle of Omdurman, 150–151, 154–155, 157
Battle of Poitiers, 15
Battle of Princeton, 67, 72
Battle of San Privat, 135
Battle of Saratoga, 72–74
Battle of the Bulge, 220
Battle of the Coral Sea, 227
Battle of the Marne, 165
Battle of Trenton, 67, 70, 72
Battle of Vimerio, 103
Battle of Waterloo, 94, 105, 128
Battle of Wounded Knee, 149
Bavaria, 40, 42
Beckett, Samuel, 292
Belgium: neutrality, 163; World War I, 164, 166; World War II, 201–204, 219
Bell, J. Bowyer, 249
Bernadotte, Jean-Baptiste, 85
Bewegungskrieg, 200
Bin Laden, Osama, 8, 285–286
Bismark, 193
Black, Jeremy, 88
Bletchley Park, 222
Blitzkrieg, 199–201, 206, 288; origins of, 189–191
Blücher, 202
Boer Wars, 153, 158
Bolshevik Revolution, 175
Bonaparte, Napoleon, 31, 38, 57, 83, 86, 91–95, 100–101, 127, 206; history of warfare and, 104
Boot, Max, 2
Bosnian War, 272–277, 284; casualties, 277
Boston Tea Party, 64
Boutros-Ghali, Boutros, 272, 274, 278–279
Boyen's law, 128

Braddock, Edward, 48–49
Briand, Aristide, 197
British Expeditionary Force (BEF), 164, 202–203
British Parliament, 63–64
British Tank Corps, 174
Brittain, Vera, 180–181
Broglie, Victor F., 85
Brooke, Rupert, 155–156, 180
Brusilov, Alexei, 171, 174
Brussels Declaration of 1874, 156
Buford, John, 116
Burgoyne, John "Gentle Johnny," 67–68, 72–73
Burma, 233–234
Burnside, Ambrose, 118
Bush, George H. W., 264, 278
Bush, George W., 285, 287

Calwell, C. E., 152
Camouflage, 143
Canada, 37, 112; American Revolution, 67–69
Cannons: early, 6; grapeshot, 7; gunpowder, 18; siege, 7; "truck," 22
Canton system, 38
Capra, Frank, 236
Caracole, 34
Case Yellow, 201–202
Castro, Fidel, 249
Cavalry, 14, 32; definition of, 6
The Cavalry Maiden, 54
CBS Evening News, 257
Charles IV, 100
Charles of Austria, 94
Chechen War, 280–283, 295
Cheyenne, 149
Chiang Kai-Shek, 228, 248
China, 13–14, 269; gunpowder and, 17–18; Japanese invasion of, 194, 225, 228–229, 247; Korean Conflict, 246–247; Malaysian campaign, 251–252; Nationalists, 228, 247–248; nuclear weapons, 240; World War II, 194, 225, 228–229, 237; "X" force, 234
Chindits, 233–234
Churchill, Winston, 155, 218, 241
Clausewitz, Karl von, 52, 130–131, 134, 159
Clemenceau, Georges, 131, 238
Clinton, Bill, 278, 285
Clinton, Henry, 66, 69–70, 74
Cobra II, 288
Cold War, 222–223, 232, 239–267, 295, 301; changing attitudes toward war, 265–267; beginning, 241–244; post, 9, 269–292
Collins, Michael, 195
Colonial warfare: conventional wars, 152–154; European, 150–152; United States, 147–150
The Command of the Air, 191–192
Communism, 235, 239–267, 269, 285
Confederate Plan, 116
Conscription, 29, 154; Napoleonic Wars and, 103; Vietnam War and, 257
Continental Army, 59, 68, 71–79
Continental Congress, 62–63, 67, 69, 82
Contras, 263–264
Cornwallis, August, 70
Cornwallis, Charles Lord, 66, 70–71, 73, 76–77, 79–81
Counterinsurgency (COIN), 249–253, 256, 260–261, 263–264, 287, 289
Croatia: ethnic cleansing, 273–274, 283; irregulars, 45, 49–50
Cronkite, Walter, 257
Crossbows, 15
Cuba, 249
Cuban Missile Crisis, 244
Custer, George Armstrong, 149
Cyber-attacks, 272
Cyclopaedia, 22
Czechoslovakia, 198, 200

D'Azeglio, Massimo, 106
D-day, 217–222
Danish War, 134, 138
Davis, Jefferson, 112
Davout, Louis-Nicolas, 85
Dayton Peace Accords, 277
De Braose, William, 15
De Gaulle, Charles, 189, 251
De Grandmaison, M., 46–47
De Grasse, François, 71
De Gribeauval, Jean Baptiste Vaquette, 33, 86
De jure belli ac pacis (On the Laws of War and Peace), 50
De Marsin, Ferdinand Comte, 39
De Vattel, Emmerich, 51–52
Declaration of Independence, 81
Denmark, 37, 201
Dervishes, 150
Di Rita, 288
Dirigible, 144–145
Dönitz, Karl, 213–214
Doughty, Robert, 71
Douhet, Guilio, 191–192
Draft. *See* Conscription
Drones, 271
Duarter, José Napoleón, 264
Durova, Nadezhda, 54–55
Dynastic warfare, 44–47

Eighty Years' War, 21
Einsatzgruppen, 237
Einstein, Albert, 236
Elizabeth of Austria, 37
Emancipation Proclamation, 112
Emmerich, Andres, 47
England, 13; French and Indian War, 48–49, 60; military innovations, 24; naval warfare, 33; platoon firing, 34
Enlightenment, 13, 50, 81
Enterprise, 227
Essai général de Tactique (General Essay on Tactics), 86
Ethnic cleansing, 273–274, 283

Ethnocentrism, 235–238
Eugene of Savoy, 39–40, 42
Evert, Alexei, 171
Ewell, Richard, 116–117

Falaise Pocket, 220
Fall, Bernard, 261
The Fall of France, 206
Feudalism, 14
Ferguson, Patrick, 77
Field Service Regulations, 187–188
Field telephones, 107, 145, 154
Finland, 35
FLMN, 264
Foch, Ferdinand, 175
Foreign Legion, 154
Fort Oswego, 67
Fort Stanwix, 68
Fort Ticonderoga, 67
Fortifications, 20–23; dead zones, 21; star forts, 21
France, 13, 127, 161–162, 197; American Revolution, 67, 69; Battle of Agincourt, 15–17; colonial warfare, 146–147; expansion into the Low Country, 35–36; Fifth Army, 164; firearm innovations, 19–20; French and Indian War, 48–49, 60; naval warfare, 33, 193; Normandy, 219–223; nuclear weapons, 240; Pais de Calais, 218–220; population in 1812, 89; Resistance, 204; Seventh Army, 164; Sixth Army, 164; uniforms, 153; World War I, 159, 164, 168, 170–171; World War II, 201–206, 217–219, 226, 228
Franco, Francisco, 194–195
Franco-Prussian War, 135–137, 139, 141, 143, 158
Frederick I, 37
Frederick the Great, 36–38, 58, 127
French and Indian War, 48–49, 60, 294

French Revolution, 31–32, 45, 57, 83–104, 125, 160, 239, 297; changes in warfare, 84–86; citizen soldier and his impact on warfare, 86–89; course of, 90–94; experience of war, 101–104; guerilla warfare, 100–101; nature of, 95–97; naval warfare, 89; opposing forces, 89–90; patriotism, 87–88, 103; unconventional conflict, 98–101
Fuller, J. F. C., 174, 189
Fussell, Paul, 234

Gadhafi, Muammar, 290–292
Gage, Thomas, 64
Galahad Force, 234
Gallieni, Joseph, 165
Gates, Horatio, 68–69
Gatling gun, 142
General Order 100, 122–123
General Principals of War, 38
Geneva Conventions, 253, 260
Genocide, 125, 148, 151, 297
George, Lloyd, 169
George III, 57
Gerald of Wales, 15
German-Soviet Nonaggression Pact, 200
Germany, 161–162, 197–198; African campaigns, 151; American Revolution and, 62, 67, 72, 75; *Blitzkrieg*, origins of, 189–191; Eighth Army, 164; navies, 145, 193; Spanish Civil War, 195; Third Reich, 38, 205–206, 234; unification, 131, 133–137, 160; World War I, 38, 159, 165–168, 170–175; World War II, 199–224
Gideon Group, 233
Glidden, Joseph, 144
Global War on Terror (GWOT), 282–286
Goebbels, Josef, 235

Goering, Hermann, 212
Gorbachev, Mikhail, 259
Granger, Gordon, 121
Grant, Ulysses S., 114–115, 148, 238
Graves, Robert, 179–180
Great Britain, 39, 161, 197; African campaigns, 150, 153; American Civil War and, 111–112; American Revolution and, 59–71; Asian campaigns, 152; colonial warfare, 146–147; 18th century, 36, 42; Eighth Army, 210; Malaysian campaign, 251–252; Napoleonic Wars, 89–91, 95; navies, 145–146, 193; nuclear weapons, 240; population in 1781, 61; Propaganda Minister, 235; uniforms, 15; World War I, 164, 166, 168, 170–171, 173; World War II, 200–201, 213, 217, 233–234
Greece, 208
Greene, Nathaniel, 70, 76–77, 80
Greenman, Jeremiah, 82
Grenier, John, 48
Grey, Edward, 163
Grotius, Hugo, 50–52
Gruber, Ira, 71
Guatemala Civil War, 252
Guderian, Heinz, 189–190, 204
Guibert, Jacques Antoine Hippolyte de, 86
Gulf War, 270, 285, 295–296
Gunpowder, 17–20, 22, 296; corning, 17; smokeless, 143–144, 173

Hague Conventions, 157–158
Haig, Douglas, 170
Halsey, William, 237
Hammarskjold, Dag, 262
Hapsburg Empire, 22, 136, 140
Harquebus, 19
Harris, John, 103
Heath, Harry, 117
Henry V, 16

Henty, George Alfred, 154–155
Herero Revolt, 151, 154
Heydrich, Reinhardt, 10, 223–224
Hill, A. P., 116
Hitler, Adolph, 192, 197–198, 200, 202, 210–212, 214, 217, 222, 235; declaration of war on the U.S., 210–211, 236; invasion of the Soviet Union, 206–209; mistakes, 219–220
Hitler Youth, 206
HMS *Argus*, 193
HMS *Dreadnought*, 145–146
HMS *Victory*, 33
Ho Chi Minh, 253
Hoche, Louis Lazar, 99
Holocaust, 151
Holy Roman Empire, 36
Hooker, Joseph, 116
Hornet, 227
Howard, John Eager, 78–79
Howe, Jonathan, 279
Howe, Richard, 66–68
Howe, William, 66
Howitzers, 7; Krupp, 164; Skoda howitzers, 144
Huché, Jean-Baptiste, 98–99
Human Rights Watch, 283
Hundred Year's War, 14, 16; Second, 35, 84
Hungary, 207
Huntzinger, Charles, 204
Hussein, Saddam, 270, 285, 287–289
Hutier, Oskar von, 174
Hydrogen bomb, 240

Ideology, 11, 58, 122, 296–298; Nazi, 206
Imperial Japanese Army, 229
India, 14, 17, 233–234; nuclear weapons, 240
Indochina, 226
Industrial Revolution, 13, 58, 105–125; advances in military technology, 106–108, 128; revolution in military thought, 109
Infantry, 5–7, 20, 142; definition of, 5; massed, 34; revolution, 16
Insurgency, 10–11, 263–264; anticolonial, 249; definition, 248
International Law Institute, 156
International Security Assistance Force (ISAF), 287
"The Intolerable Acts," 64
Invisible Armies, 2
Iraq: Anbar Awakening, 290; Coalition Provisional Authority, 289; insurgents, 11, 287–290
Iraq War, 287–290
Ireland, 195–196
Irish Republican Army, 195–196
Islamic State in Syria and Iraq (ISIS), 290–291, 302–304
Italy, 197–198; unification, 160; World War I, 166; World War II, 213

Jackson, Julian, 2, 206
James II, 81
Japan, 153–154, 197–198; bombing of Pearl Harbor, 209–210, 213, 225–228, 234–237; naval aviation, 193–194; World War II, 4, 9, 58, 193, 211, 225–238
Jarell, Randall, 235
Jodl, Alfred, 206
Johnson, Lyndon B., 258
Johnston, Joseph E., 122
Jomini, Antoine-Henri, 109, 131
Just-war doctrine, 50–51, 81

Karmal, Babrak, 259–260
Kellogg, Frank, 197
Kellogg-Briand Pact, 197
Kennan, George, 253, 269
Kennedy, John F., 258
Kennedy, Paul, 30
Kesselschlachten, 134

Index 363

Khevenhüller-Metsch, Johann Joseph, 46
Khrushchev, Nikita, 223, 244
Kipling, Rudyard, 147
Knox, Henry, 69
Korea (united): nuclear weapons, 240; World War II, 238
Korean Conflict, 244–248
Kosovo, 283–284
Kosovo Liberation Army (KLA), 283
Kriegsakademie, 129
Krulak, Viktor, 257
Krupp 420 mm, 144
Kuomintang, 247–248

L'Hôpital des Invalides, 53
Land warfare doctrine, 185–189
Landsturm, 128
Landwehr, 128
Lawrence, Joshua, 117
Lawrence, T. E., 295
The Laws of War on Land, 156
Le Tellier, François-Michel, 28
League of Nations, 196–197, 200, 261–262
Lebensraum, 207
Lee, Charles, 69
Lee, Robert E., 113–117, 119, 127
Leher, Tom, 265
LeMay, Curtis "Bombs-Away," 230, 237
Lexington, 227
Liber Ignium ad Comburendos Hostes, 18
Libya, 290–291
Liddell Hart, Basil, 1–2, 189
Lieber, Francis, 122–123
Lieber Code, 122–123
Life magazine, 204
Lincoln, Abraham, 112, 115–116, 122
Lithuania, 37
Logistics, 8–9
Longbows, 14–17
Longfellow, Henry Wadsworth, 59–60
Longstreet, James, 116, 118

Louis XIV, 23, 27, 36, 39, 53, 94
Louis XVI, 57, 90
Louis XVIII, 57
Luftwaffe, 192, 212, 214, 217–219
Lumumba, Patrice, 262–263
Lundendorff, Erich, 165, 175
Lynn, John A., 21

MacArthur, Douglas, 230, 245–246
Machine gun, 5, 142–143, 173, 240; Bergman MP18, 172; light or "sub," 172
MacMahon, Patrice, 136
Maginot Line, 202–203, 205
Mahdi, 150
Malayan Emergency, 250
Manual of Siegecraft and Fortification, 26
Mao Zedong, 244, 247–248, 256
Marion, Francis "Swamp Fox," 75, 77
Marks, Erich, 220
Marlborough, John Churchill, Duke of, 39–44, 58
Marquis de Montcalm, 37
Marx, Karl, 106
Matchlocks, 19
Materialschlacht, 9
Maurice of Nassau, Prince of Orange, 25
Maxim, Hiram, 143
Maximilian, Elector, 39
McClellan, George, 113
McGuire, Barry, 266
Meade, George Gordon, 116–120
Mehmet II, 18
Merrill, Frank, 234
Merrill's Marauders, 233–234
Mikhailovic, Dragoljub, 224
Military Assistance Command Vietnam (MACV), 255
The Military Revolution Debate, 21
Milošević, Slobodan, 273–274, 283–284
Minié, Claude, 107

Minié ball, 107–108
Mirabeau, 38
Mitrailleuse, 142
Mladic, Radko, 276
Model, Walter, 220
Moltke, Helmuth von, the Elder, 130, 132–135, 137–139, 160, 163–164
Moltke, Helmuth von, the Younger, 162
Montgomery, Bernard Law, 211
Montgomery, Thomas, 279
Moore, Harold, 255
Moreau, Jean Victor Baptiste, 92
Morgan, Daniel, 68–71, 73, 76, 78–80, 120
Morgan's Rifles, 73–74
Morse Code, 145
Mubarak, Hosni, 285
Mughals, 17
Munich Accord, 198
Murat, Joachim, 100
Musket, 19; Brown Bess, 74; flintlock, 5, 32; rifled, 108; smoothbore, 5–6, 19–20, 32, 34, 108; socket bayonets, 32
Musketeers, 20, 24
Mussolini, Benito, 207–208
Mutually assured destruction (MAD), 242, 298
The Myth of the Guerilla: Revolutionary Theory and Malpractice, 249

Najibullah, Mohammad, 260
Nama, 151
Napoleon III, 136–137
Napoleonic Wars, 58, 83–104, 109; changes in warfare, 84–86; citizen soldier and his impact on warfare, 86–89; course of, 90–94; experience of war, 101–104; guerilla warfare, 100–101; nature of, 95–97; naval warfare, 89; opposing forces, 89–90; patriotism, 87–88, 103; unconventional conflict, 98–101

National Front. *See* Viet Cong
National Liberation Front (NLF), 250–251
National Security Council Paper 68, 241, 242
National Socialism, 235
Nationalism, 4, 83, 88, 125, 158, 196, 235, 238, 297
Natural law, 81
Naval warfare, 24, 33, 145–146; cannons and, 24; sonar, 214; U-boats, 213–214; Wolf Packs, 214; World War II, 192–194, 213–217
Nazis, 10, 58, 206–207, 212, 222, 235–251
Nelson, Horatio, 89, 92
The Netherlands, 39, 42; naval warfare, 33; platoon firing, 34; World War II, 201–204, 226
New Guinea, 227
New Zealand, 228
Newton, Isaac, 143
Nicholas II of Russia, 163
Nimitz, Chester, 230
9/11, 10, 285, 287
Nine Years' War, 36
Nixon, Richard, 257, 263–264
NKVD, 237
North Atlantic Treat Organization (NATO), 242–243, 275–277, 284, 287, 301
Northern Alliance, 286
Norway, 202
Nuclear weapons, 240, 266; arms race, 240, 296; intercontinental ballistic missiles (ICBMS), 240; multiple independently targetable reentry vehicle (MIRV), 240; submarine launched ballistic missiles (SLBMS), 240

Obama, Barack, 290
Omar, Mullah Mohammed, 286
Operation Barbarossa, 206–209

Operation Bargration, 220
Operation Blue, 211–212
Operation Citadel, 213
Operation Desert Storm, 270
Operation Enduring Freedom, 286
Operation Overlord, 218–219
Operation Storm, 277
Operations, 8
Order of Alexander Nevsky, 212
Ottoman Empire, 14, 17–18
Owen, Wilfred, 180

Pakistan, 240
Parker, Geoffrey, 26
Partisans, 10, 46, 223–224
Pashtun, 152
The Patriot, 59–60
Patriotism, 87–88, 103; compulsory education and, 125, 146, 160; World War II and, 212
Patton, George, 189
"Paul Revere's Ride," 59
Paulus, Friedrich, 211–212
Peace of Luneville, 92
Peace of Utrecht, 36
Peninsular War, 101, 120
People's Army of Vietnam (PAVN), 255–257
People's Republic of North Korea, 246, 247; Korean Conflict, 244–247
Persia, 35
Peter III, 37
Petite guerre, 45–46, 49
Pettigrew, J. Johnson, 119
Philippine, 152, 237
Pickens, Andrew, 75, 79
Picket's Charge, 118
Pickett, George, 118–119
Pike men, 32
Pinker, Steven, 292
Plan XVII, 161–162
Platoons, 33–34
Poison gas, 158, 172

Poland, 37, 194; resistance, 200; World War II, 199–201, 206–207, 213–214, 237
Pomerania, 199
Précis de l'Art de la Guerre:Des Principales Combinaisons de la Stratégie, de la Grande Tactique et de la Politique Militaire (Summary of the Art of War), 109
Prince of Wales, 194
Prussia, 36–39; American Revolution and, 69; military reforms, 128–130; Napoleonic Wars, 90–91, 93, 128, 160; population in 1812, 89; Seven Years' War, 37–39; World War II, 199
Prussian Railroad Department, 123–133
Public education, 125, 146, 160

Racism, 235–238
Radar, 219, 271
Railroads: European, 107, 128, 132–133, 220, 233; United States, 107, 148–149
Ramsay, David, 75
Rangers, 47–49, 67
Rape of Nanking, 237
Reagan, Ronald, 263
Red Army, 186, 209, 211–213, 218, 220, 222, 237–238, 241
Rees, Abraham, 22
Regimental flags, 104
Remarque, Erich Maria, 179
Republic of Korea (ROK): Army, 244, 246–247; insurgents, 247; Korean Conflict, 244–247
Repulse, 194
Resistance groups, 10
Reynolds, John, 117
Rhodes, Elisha Hunt, 125
Riefenstahl, Leni, 235
Rifles: breech-loading, 143–144; Chassepot, 135, 142; clip magazine, 142; Dreyse, 135; Howard repeating,

Rifles (*cont.*)
109; Kentucky long, 73–74; Lee-Metford, 142; Minié rifle, 19, 107–108, 117; short-barreled, 117; Spencer repeating, 109, 117

The Rise and Fall of the Great Powers, 30

Roberts, Michael, 26
Rogers, Cliff, 16
Rogers, Robert, 48–49
Romania, 207, 212
Romans, ancient, 1, 6
Rommel, Erwin, 210–211, 219
Roosevelt, Franklin, 210, 234
Rosecrans, William, 115
Royal Air Force (RAF), 203, 214–215, 217
Royal Irish Constabulary, 195
Royster, Charles, 82
Rumsfeld, Donald, 287
Russell, Robert, 48
Russia, 35, 153–154, 161–163; 18th century, 35, 37; Napoleonic Wars, 92–95, 101–102; population in 1812, 89; Third Army, 168; World War I, 159, 167–168
Russo-Japanese War, 145, 153–154, 158

Saint Just, Louis Antoine de, 87
Samsonov, Alexander, 166
Sandinistas, 263–264
Santayana, George, 1
Saxe, Maurice de, 32, 58
Schlieffen Plan, 163–164, 201
Schrecklichkeit, 10
Schutzstaffel, 237
Schuyler, Philip, 69, 73
Scientific racism, 4, 58, 89, 151
Scott, Winfield, 112
Second Indochina War. *See* Vietnam War
2nd Rhode Island Volunteers, 124–125
Seneca Indians, 72

Serbia, 163
Seven Week's War, 133, 137, 139
Seven Years' War, 37–39, 48–49, 84
Shakespeare, William, 16
Sheridan, Philip, 123, 149
Sherman, William T., 112, 121–122, 148, 238
Shirley, William, 49
Shrapnel, Henry, 7
Siberia, 209
Sickles, Daniel, 117
Siege guns, 6
Simcoe's Rangers, 75
Sinn Fein, 195–196
Sioux, 148, 149
Six-Day War, 262
Slavery, 112
Slim, William, 229
Small Wars: Their Principles and Practice, 152
Smith, Rupert, 276
Social contract theory of government, 81
Social Darwinism, 58, 147, 206–207, 297
Somalia, 277–280
Sonderweg thesis, 39
Soult, Nicolas-Jean de Dieu, 97
South African War, 153
Soviet Union, 186, 194, 197; Afghan-Soviet War, 258–261; Cold War, 241–244, 249–253, 258–261, 265–267; nuclear weapons, 240; Spanish Civil War, 195; World War II, 206–213, 217–218, 220, 222–224
Spain, 153; Eighty Years' War, 21; French Revolution and, 89, 101
Spanish-American War, 147, 150
Spanish Civil War, 3, 194
St. Leger, Barry, 67
St. Michael Offensive, 174–175, 190
Stalin, Joseph, 186–187, 200, 212, 217, 241, 244
Starr, Edwin, 266

Steevens, George Warrington, 151
Stevenson, Roger, 46
Stillwell, Joseph "Vinegar Joe," 229
Strategic bombing, 192, 216–217, 230–231, 234
Stuart, Jeb, 116–117
Summers, Harry, 258
Sumpter, Thomas, 74–77
Supreme Headquarters Allied Powers Europe (SHAPE), 243
Surfdom, 13
Sweden: 18th century, 35; Napoleonic Wars, 95; neutrality, 207
Switzerland, 166

Taber, Robert, 249
Tactics, 8, 24–26; creeping barrage, 172–173; hurricane barrage, 172
Taliban, 286–287, 303
Tallard, Camille de, 39–42
Tanks, 186–189; Mark series, 173, 202, 203, 213; Matilda series, 202; Tiger heavy, 213
Tarleton, Banastra "Bloody Tarleton," 75, 77–79
Telegraph, 107, 145
Tennyson, Alfred Lord, 155
Teresa, Maria, 36
Terrorism, 11
Terry, Alfred, 148
A Testament of Youth, 180–181
Teutonic Knights, 212
Thirty Years' War, 4, 27, 31, 39, 46, 50, 102, 125, 297; casualties, 31
Three Emperor's League, 161
Time magazine, 200
Timoshenko, Semyon, 212
Tito, Josef Broz, 224, 273
TNT, 144
Tory Legion, 75, 77, 79
Total war, 122–124, 151, 176, 236–238
Treaty of Aixe la Chappelle, 37
Treaty of Paris, 37
Treaty of Westphalia, 239

Trenches, 166–167, 173, 246; fire, 167; frontline system, 167
Trimble, Isaac, 119
Tripitz, 193
Triumph of the Will, 235
Truman, Harry, 240, 246
Tudman, Franjo, 276
Tukhachevsky, Mikhail, 186–187
Turkey, 166–168
Turreau, Louis Maire, 99

United Kingdom, 161, 159
United Nations: Charter, 261, 292; Emergency Force (UNEF), 262; Mission in Kosovo (UNMIK), 284; mission in Somalia (UNSOM), 278–280; Mission in the Congo (ONUC), 262–263, 277; peacekeeping missions, 261–263, 272–277; Protection Force (UNPROFOR), 274–277, 284; Security Council, 261, 272, 274, 278, 284; Truce Supervision Organization (UNTSO), 262; *Universal Declaration of Human Rights*, 292
United Provinces: fort design in, 21–22; independence from Spain, 22
United States, 153, 196, 198; bombing of Pearl Harbor, 209–210, 213, 225–228, 234–237; Cold War, 241–244, 253–258, 262–267; nuclear weapons, 240; resettlement of indigenous populations, 147–150; tactics, 238; territorial expansion, 58, 147–150; Vietnam War, 253–259; War Department, 236; World War I, 238; World War II, 209–211, 213, 217, 225–228, 233–236, 238
U.S. Army Air Force (USAAF), 215, 217, 230
U.S. Strategic Bombing Survey, 230

USS *Cole*, 285
USS *Enterprise*, 194, 237

Vauban, Sebastian le Pestre de, 21, 24, 26
Versailles Treaty, 187, 190, 196–197, 200
Viet Cong, 255–257
Vietnam War, 138, 232, 238, 253–258, 295; American intervention, 253–259; films about, 267
Vom Krieg (On War), 130
Von Benedek, Ludwig, 134
Von Bülow, Karl, 165
Von Falkenhayn, Erich, 170
Von Hindenberg, Paul, 165
Von Kluck, Alexander, 164–165
Von Mack, Karl Freiherr von Leiberich, 92, 96
Von Mackensen, August, 168
Von Manstein, Erich, 202, 212
Von Rennenkampf, 166
Von Runstadt, Gerd, 219
Von Scharnhorst, Gerhardt, 94
Von Schlieffen, Alfred, 162
Von Seeckt, Hans, 190
Von Steuben, Wilhelm, 69, 74
Von Trotha, Lothar, 151
Von Wrangel, Friedrich, 133

War: abhorrence of, 305; asymmetric, 9–11; changing attitudes towards, 299–301; conventional, definition of, 9–11; current trends and future prospects, 301–306; evolution of, 294–301; frontier, 47–49; future of, 293–306; guerilla, 10, 72, 93, 100–101, 120–121, 150, 247, 249–253; human society and, 298–299; hybrid, 294–296; privatization of, 304; special forces, 304; technology and, 305; unconventional, definition of, 9–11; unknowns, 306

War in the Shadows, 2
War of 1812, 112
War of the Austrian Succession, 36–37, 49
War of the Fifth Coalition, 90
War of the First Coalition, 90–92
War of the Fourth Coalition, 90, 93
War of the League of Augsburg, 36, 39
War of the Second Coalition, 90
War of the Sixth Coalition, 90
War of the Spanish Succession, 36, 39, 84
War of the Third Coalition, 90, 93, 95
War Office, 185
Wars of German Unification, 127–140, 296; modern warfare, 138–140; unconventional warfare, 137–138
Warsaw Pact, 243, 269
Washington, George, 62, 66, 69, 72, 80
Washington, William, 78
Washington Naval Conference, 197
Washington Treaty, 242
Watt, James, 105
Wavell, Archibald, 233
Weber, Eugene, 106
Wehrmacht, 201, 209, 217, 220, 222
Weigley, Russell, 238
Wellesley, Arthur, 93–94, 101
Westermann, Francois Joseph, 99
Westmoreland, William, 256
Wilderness War of 1777, 73
Wilhelm II of Germany, 163
Wingate, Orde, 233
Wireless communication, 107
With Kitchener to Khartoum, 154–155
Wolf, James, 37
World War I, 3, 35, 159–181, 238, 297; aftermath, 181; attitudes towards war, 178–181; attrition, 169–172; casualties, 53, 159, 239; deadlock and trench warfare, 166–167; Eastern Front, 171; experience

of war, 177–178; Gallipoli campaign, 168; innovation, 107, 172–174; military plans and the outbreak of war, 160–163; opening campaigns, 163–166; St. Michael Offensive, 174–175, 190; striving for breakthrough, 167–169; technological advances after, 184–185; technological advances before, 144–145; total war, 176; unconventional war, 177; Western Front, 162, 166, 169–170, 172, 174

World War II, 3–4, 37, 53, 58, 84, 102, 144, 196, 241, 249, 260, 297; Asia and, 225–238; attitudes towards war, 234–236; casualties, 124, 199, 222, 230–231, 237, 239; decolonization following, 11; Eastern Front, 211–213, 222, 237; Europe and, 199–224; films about, 236; Germany, 10, 38; interwar conflicts, 194–196; island hopping during, 230–232; land war in Asia, 228–229; Nazi retaliation during, 10, 224; resistance movements, 10, 223–224; technological advances during, 240–241; total war, 236–238; unconventional operations, 223–224, 232–234; victory in Europe, 217–222

Yamamoto, Isoroku, 9, 225–227
Yom Kippur War, 262
Yorktown, 227
Yugoslavia, 272–277, 283; World War II, 208, 224

Zhou Enlai, 246
Zhukov, Georgi, 209, 212–213, 220, 222–223
Zulu, 151–152

About the Author

Thomas R. Mockaitis, PhD, is professor of history at DePaul University, Chicago, IL, where he teaches courses on conventional and unconventional conflict. His published works include numerous books and articles on counterinsurgency and terrorism, among them ABC-CLIO's *The Iraq War: A Documentary and Reference Guide*; *Osama bin Laden: A Biography*; *Iraq and the Challenge of Counterinsurgency*; *The "New" Terrorism: Myths and Reality*; and *Peacekeeping and Intrastate Conflict: The Sword or the Olive Branch?* Other books include *British Counterinsurgency: 1919–1960* and *British Counterinsurgency in the Post-Imperial Era*. Mockaitis conducts counterterrorism programs internationally with other experts through the Center for Civil-Military Relations at the Naval Post-Graduate School. A frequent media commentator on terrorism and security matters, he has provided commentary on Public Television, National Public Radio, BBC World News, all major Chicago television stations, and various local radio programs. He appears regularly as a terrorism expert for WGN TV News. Mockaitis earned his bachelor's degree in European history from Allegheny College and his master's degree and doctorate in modern British and Irish history from the University of Wisconsin-Madison. He maintains a blog on contemporary security issues: tmockait.wordpress.com

Printed in the USA
CPSIA information can be obtained
at www.ICGtesting.com
LVHW011748100224
771437LV00001B/49